THE TYRANNY
OF DISTANCE

THE TYRANNY OF DISTANCE

How Distance Shaped Australia's History

GEOFFREY BLAINEY

M

Sun Books

Sun Books
THE MACMILLAN COMPANY OF AUSTRALIA PTY LTD
107 Moray Street, South Melbourne 3205
6 Clarke Street, Crows Nest 2065

Associated companies and representatives
throughout the world

Copyright © Geoffrey Blainey 1966, 1982

First published by Sun Books 1966
Reprinted 1967, 1969, 1970, 1971, 1974, 1976, 1977, 1980
Revised edition 1983
Reprinted 1985, 1987

National Library of Australia
cataloguing in publication data

Blainey, Geoffrey Norman, 1930 —
The tyranny of distance: how distance
shaped Australia's history/[by] Geoffrey
Blainey. — South Melbourne, Vic.: Sun
Books, 1966.
ISBN 0 7251 0019 2

1. Communication and traffic —
Australia. 2. Australia — History.
3. Transportation — Australia. I. Title

380.30994

Printed in Hong Kong

Contents

The Illustrations   *vi*
The Maps   *vii*
Preface   *viii*
Acknowledgements   *xi*

PART ONE: DESTINY AND DISTANCE
1. Search   3
2. Exile   18
3. Isolation   40
4. Limpet Ports   71
5. Whalemen   99
6. Land Barrier   118
7. The Art of Abduction   147

PART TWO: THE TAMING OF DISTANCE
8. Gold Clippers   175
9. Black Cloud   206
10. A Magician's Act   227
11. Railway Boom   243
12. A Hollow Triumph   265
13. The Horseless Age   288
14. Antipodes Adrift   314
15. The Shrinking Seas   338

Notes   344
Index   360

The Illustrations

between pages 68–9

Wild Seas, 'roaring forties' Dismasted ship
Red Jacket in ice *Pamir*, windjammer
Spray of *Nella Dan*

between pages 132–3

Tahiti, 1769 Fort Dundas, aerial view
Sydney and harbour Macquarie Island seal
Norfolk Island coast Antarctic whale
Norfolk Island pines

between pages 196–7

Port Adelaide, 1840s Hobart Mail coaches
Geelong, 1850s Tasmanian punt, *c.* 1890
Queensland teamster Sailing ship at wool store
Melbourne bullock drays

between pages 228–9

Between decks, *c.* 1850 Ballarat, *c.* 1890
Port Melbourne, 1870s Broken Hill donkey team
Gulgong goldfield, 1870s Kalgoorlie doss house
More men of Gulgong

between page 260–1

Heard Island coast Steamship *Rome*, 1881
Rev. Dr. W. Scoresby Albany, old coaling port
Rose, iron steamer, 1840s Port Adelaide's masts

between pages 292–3

Building a railway, 1890s Telegraph station, *c.* 1890
Passenger train, narrow gauge Murray wool boats, *c.* 1905
Night train, Mount Isa Melbourne cab rank, 1870s

between pages 324–5

Royal Tar, 1893 *Southern Cross* over Canberra
W. A. timber fleet Arthur Butler's plane
Camel cart Boer War celebration, 1902
Leonora mail car, 1911

Maps

1. Sea Routes to and from Australia, *c.* 1800.   24–5
2. The Strategy of Bass Strait.   79
3. Australia.   134–5
4. The 'Great Circle' Route, 1850s.   181
5. Inland Transport in south-east Australia,
   1880.   229

Preface

Distance is as characteristic of Australia as mountains are of Switzerland. By sealanes or airlanes most parts of Australia are at least 12,000 miles from western Europe, the source of most of their people, equipment, institutions and ideas. The coastline of Australia also stretches for 12,000 miles and the coast encloses as much land as the U.S.A., excluding Alaska. The distance of one part of the Australian coast from another, or the distance of the dry interior from the coast, was a problem as obstinate as Australia's isolation from Europe.

Australians have always recognized that distance or isolation was one of the moulds which shaped their history, but it is fair to suggest the factor of distance has been surprisingly unsuccessful as an explanation of important Australian events or situations or characteristics. I had that belief when I began this book. Originally I intended to write on the coming of mechanical transport to Australia — steamships, railways, aircraft, automobiles — with some attention to their effects. The section entitled 'The Taming of Distance', is a shorter version of the book I originally wrote. When that planned book was nearly completed, it became clear that another section was needed to explain the effect of isolation on Australia in the long era when sailing ships and bullocks were the main means of transport. The first section of this book, entitled 'Destiny and Distance', was the result.

When I ceased to see the book upside down, I found I had ended up with a kind of history of Australia: not a comprehensive history, but then every history of every country is a mirror of the author's own interests and therefore selective rather than comprehensive. It seemed that distance was a central factor in Australia's history. At the same time it was not the only one, and if this book gives the impression that climate and resources and European ideas and wars and markets and money and other moulding influences were unimportant then it is unintentionally distorting history.

In understanding Australia's history, the idea of distance may be as revealing as say Frederick Jackson Turner's 'frontier theory' is in probing the history of the United States. Distance — or its enemy, efficient transport — is not simply an explanation for much that happened in Australia's history. Once the problem of distance is understood it also becomes difficult to accept many of the prevailing interpretations of other events in Australia's history. Distance itself may not explain why they happened, but it forces a search for new explanations. As a two-handed weapon, distance offers new explanations of why Britain in 1788 decided to send settlers to Australia, why the first colony nearly collapsed and why it eventually survived, and why new military camps were placed at scattered points on the Australian coast — camps that gave Britain virtual possession of the entire continent. The idea of distance throws new light on the rise of and importance of whaling, wool, gold and the dynamic export industries of the nineteenth century, on the immigration of Chinese in the 1850s and Italians a few decades later, and on immigration from the British Isles throughout Australian history. It illuminates the reasons why Australia was for long such a masculine society, why it became a more equalitarian society than North America, and why it was a relatively peaceful society. It seems to offer new insight into the flow of investment and technology, the rise of cities and regions, changes in social life, and some of the fascinating episodes of Australian transport such as the break of railway gauges and the feats of sailing ships. Nor do the themes traced in this book exhaust the likely effects of distance on Australia's history.

It may be that distance and transport are revealing mirrors through which to see the rise of every satellite land in the new world, because they keep that land's vital relationship with the old world in the forefront.

1965   • GEOFFREY BLAINEY

Preface to Revised Edition

In preparing this edition I have made small alterations here and there — occasionally in a phrase, sometimes in a sentence. The chapters which I have greatly revised are the second and the final two. The second chapter, discussing the reasons for the British decision to send convicts to Australia, aroused intense controversy long after the book was published. The last chapters described the reign of distance in the early 1960s, but that world has shrunk; and the new ending to the book shows, I hope, that change.

Perhaps I could offer one other comment. The phrase 'tyranny of distance' has become one of the busiest in Australian political and economic debate. Sometimes I think people take the phrase further than it should be taken and certainly further than the book intended. My book is essentially about people and commodities, and for them the cost of distance has usually been high. But for ideas the freight has often been cheap. In the history of this land, ideas have usually leaped with relative ease across the ocean and even across the inland.

1982   GEOFFREY BLAINEY

Acknowledgements

While writing this book I was helped by many people and institutions. In particular I was helped by the staff of libraries and archives in which I worked: the Public Record Office in London, the State Library of Victoria, the J. S. Battye Library of West Australian History, the Archives Dept. of the Public Library of South Australia, and the University of Melbourne's Baillieu Library, Giblin Library, and Archives. In addition two libraries which I was unable to visit, the Mitchell Library and the Archives of the State Library of Tasmania, kindly supplied some of the illustrations in this book.

I gained a lot from discussing some of my theories and interpretations with D. J. Mulvaney of the Australian National University, with E. A. Beever, K. Trace, J. A. C. Mackie and E. A. Huck, of the University of Melbourne, and with some of my students in Australian economic history in 1964 and 1965. I am also grateful to L. L. Robson, F. Strahan, J. W. T. Merewether, S. Murray-Smith and F. H. Drummond of the University of Melbourne who guided me to valuable sources of information which I would otherwise have missed; to Miss Joyce Wood who drew the maps; to Mrs J. Edgar who typed the manuscript; to Mrs Margot Beever who at short notice compiled the index; and to Brian Stonier of Sun Books whose advice has been valuable from the time when the book was only a vague idea.

PART ONE
DESTINY AND DISTANCE

1 Search

In the eighteenth century the world was becoming one world but Australia was still a world of its own. It was untouched by Europe's customs and commerce. It was more isolated than the Himalayas or the heart of Siberia.

The only European and Asian navigators who visited Australia came each season in flocks through the skies. Arctic tern flew in thousands from north-west Russia to spend the southern summer in the Antarctic, and many followed the route which ships would later use down the Atlantic and along the roaring forties past southern Australia. Spine-tailed swifts flew across the world from Japan to Tasmania, their arrival and departure times more regular than any sailing ship of that era. Sooty shearwater migrated from Norway and Greenland to the cold cliffs of New Zealand; and short-tailed shearwater bred in burrows near the surf of the southern Australian coast, flying north each April or May to the Bering Sea at the far end of the world. In Australia the seasons, conveniently, were upside down.

Each year hundreds of ships, like birds, glided from Europe to hotter lands to fill themselves with food and materials which Europe could not produce. As late as the eighteenth century, however, they shunned Australia. That land seemed to grow no bush or flower or grain which Europe wanted. It seemed to yield no precious metal or mineral. It produced no animal or fish for which European merchants· were willing to risk their ships in long voyages. Its Aboriginals were not ocean seafarers,

3

nor were they traders or collectors of precious stones, and they could show visiting seamen no commodity of value. Even if navigators from every European nation had explored every bay and inlet of the long coastline of Australia by the year 1750, they would probably have found nothing to induce them to promote trading posts. So far as we know, Australia had only one commodity which was valued beyond its shores in the eighteenth century — the trepang or sea slug which was collected by Indonesians who sailed in small craft across the Arafura Sea to northern Australian beaches. More than two centuries after European traders had invaded the Indies, Australia's one contribution to international commerce was the sea slug.

In those years since Spanish and Portuguese seamen had found a sea route to Asia, a long string of trading posts was opened. In the vast area stretching across the Indian and Pacific Oceans from Africa to America, there were Dutch, British, Spanish, Portuguese, French, and Danish warehouses and castles and forts and ports. Their interest was not in settling Europeans on the land to farm or mine, because millions of natives could grow all the goods they required. Their interest was solely in exchanging precious metals, lead, woollen cloth, glass, wines, silks and European toys for tropical products. Almost every year convoys of their ships made the slow journey home to Europe past the Cape of Good Hope. They carried home pepper, nutmeg, mace and rare spices, tea, indigo, calicoes, silks and saltpetre.

They carried home only those commodities which earned a high price for each hundredweight. The distance of the Indies from Europe and the risk and expense of the sea voyage confined the trade to luxuries. Any exotic commodity which could be sent in ships to Europe more cheaply from nearer countries such as West Africa or the West Indies was bought there rather than from the distant lands beyond the Cape of Good Hope or Cape Horn. It did not matter how diverse and rich were the resources of some countries bordering the Indian or Pacific oceans; all that mattered was whether they could produce goods that were rare and therefore valuable in Amsterdam or Madrid or London. And Australia gave no sign to those who had landed from passing ships that it could supply Europe with even one valuable commodity.

Portuguese sailors probably saw parts of the tropical north-west coast of Australia. Since about 1516 Portugal had held a colony in Timor, only three hundred miles from Australia. As the north-west monsoon blew for three months of the year, occasional Portuguese ships must have been driven within sight of our coast; but they would have seen nothing to excite them. That coast was settled sparsely. Its Aboriginals had no trade goods which could match the sandalwood and beeswax of Timor, and the great daily ebb of the coastal tides was a menace to careless sea-captains.

Dutchmen also sailed along much of Australia's coast, alert merchants and piercing-eyed navigators who saw nothing which pleased them. Ever since 1616 Dutch convoys had followed the route charted crudely and devised brilliantly by Hendrick Brouwer of the United East India Company of The Netherlands, who discovered that the quickest route on the outward voyage from Holland to Java was to sail east from the Cape of Good Hope for about 3000 miles and then steer north to Java. In sailing east from the tip of South Africa the ships harnessed the strength of the westerly winds on the fringes of the Roaring Forties and usually made swift passages to the vicinity of the western coast of Australia, where they changed course and sailed north towards Java. They thus opened what was to become, in the first era of Australian history, a speedway for sailing ships.

The Roaring Forties held hazards. A master of a ship sailing from the Cape of Good Hope across the Indian Ocean towards Australia could steer east with his compass; and he could also study the position of the sun at midday and so check his latitude or distance from the equator and thereby the accuracy of the course he had followed. Unfortunately this was an age in which the chronometer was unknown, and it was virtually impossi-

ble for a navigator to determine with accuracy his longitude at sea. He could not tell his exact position each day
along that watery line from South Africa to the Australian
coast. If the westerlies howled for days and he underestimated the speed of the ship, or if the ship was blown far off
course and dark clouds shielded the midday sun and
prevented him from ascertaining his latitude, he was at
the mercy of the gods.

Some ships bound for Java strayed too far south and
east and when they changed course for the run up to Java
found a long barren coast blocking their passage; in 1627
a Dutch ship sailed a thousand miles along the southern
coast of Australia and was 500 sea miles from the site of
what is now the city of Adelaide before she retreated.
Other Dutchmen crossing the Indian Ocean in warmer
latitudes were blown too far to the east and saw the
western coast of Australia. In the winter of 1629, the
winds of the Roaring Forties being strongest in winter, the
large Dutch ship *Batavia* of perhaps 600 tons eluded her
convoy and ran on to the Abrolhos Islands near the
western coast of Australia. She carried about 316 people,
and some were drowned, and some died in the sand, and
125 were murdered by their own countrymen in a savage
mutiny ashore. A few survivors reached Java in an open
boat, and a ship was sent to rescue the remaining survivors, salvage treasure and cargo, and to punish the
murderers. Two of the murderers, an 18 year old cabin
servant and a 24 year old soldier, were reprieved from
death on condition that they allowed themselves to be
exiled on Australia's mainland some thirty miles away.
The first of an army of criminals which would be exiled in
Australia, they went ashore near the present town of
Geraldton with beads, bells, knives, small mirrors and
Nuremberg toys as gifts or items of barter for the blacks.
'Man's luck,' they were assured, 'is found in strange
places.' They had found a strange place but what luck
they found was dubious; they were not seen again.

As Australia's west coast flanked one of the world's
richest trade routes, it was seen and visited at countless

points by Dutch ships passing on their way from Europe or by a few Dutch ships which were sent from Djakarta in search of new lands and riches. The first Dutch commercial fleet had reached the East Indies in 1596 — eight years after the year of the great Armada — and in the following half century Abel Tasman and Dutchmen had traced nearly two-thirds of Australia's coastline. They had seen the flat hot coast near the Gulf of Carpentaria, the forbidding land that fringed the Arafura Sea, Timor Sea, Indian Ocean and Southern Ocean, and the timbered hills overlooking the Tasman Sea. They had passed close to hills of treasure, fragments of which were centuries later to find their way to Antwerp smelters and Amsterdam banks. They had probably seen the red cliffs of bauxite in north Queensland, had passed close to the uranium of northern Australia and the mountains of iron ore in the north-west, close to the gold of numberless places not far from the coast, and had seen the mountains that concealed gold and silver and lead and copper and tin in western Tasmania. They had seen more than half the coastline of Australia and Tasmania and New Zealand, and even if they had seen the kindlier eastern and south-eastern coast of Australia their judgement would have been as pessimistic. They were neither miners nor manufacturers. They were traders searching for marketable goods. The Aboriginals along the coast had no marketable goods; the coast itself grew nothing that was valuable in European markets; and nearly all those pockets of mineral were unpayable in the seventeenth century. The Dutchmen wisely concluded that Australia was valueless.

As Australia was unworthy to be a European trading post, there remained only the hope that it could be a useful port of call for Dutch ships voyaging out to trading posts in the East Indies. But the Dutch already used Table Bay near the Cape of Good Hope as a port of call. There they could get fresh water and greens and meat and firewood and, if necessary, scrape the bottoms of their ships; and from 1652 a small band of Dutchmen was permanently

7

settled at Cape Town. A similar refreshment port on
Australia's western coast would have been an extrava-
gance, for that leg of the voyage from Cape Town to
Djakarta was usually too quick to require another port of
call.

The same globe-circling westerly winds which had
blown Dutchmen on to Australia's western coast and part
of its southern coast affected Spanish ships which approached the East Indies and the Philippines from the
opposite direction. Three Spanish expeditions crossed the
South Seas from Peru in the forty years 1567–1607, but
they sailed too close to the equator in their westbound
passage to have more than a slight chance of finding the
eastern coast of Australia. The strong westerlies in the
high latitudes deterred them from following a course
which would have reached the favoured south-eastern
part of Australia. The Spanish ship which probably
passed closest to Australia was commanded by Luis Vaez
de Torres, who passed through the wide strait between
New Guinea and northern Australia in 1606.

Most Australians patriotically like to think that the
Portuguese, Spaniards and Dutch would have prized the
continent if they had chanced to see a more favourable
line of coast. But Torres, in missing Australia, missed
nothing of value to the Europe of his day.

2

Perhaps two centuries and a half passed from the day
when the first European sailors saw Australia's west or
north-west coast to the day when the first European
sailors saw the east coast or the hidden face of Australia.
That period witnessed the slow decline of Spain, the rise
and decline of The Netherlands, the rising power of England and her North American colonies. It saw a rapid increase in international commerce, the growth of science,
the beginning of an industrial revolution and the birth of
Watt's steam engine. It was a new Europe which the navigator James Cook left in August 1768 on the voyage which

would discover the east coast of Australia.

Cook's voyage itself had been spurred by the rising interest in practical and theoretical science, for his first destination was the new-found island of Tahiti in the South Pacific, where he was to study the planet Venus as it crossed the face of the sun on 3 June 1769. To cross the world to take part in an inverted rite of sun worship does not seem to be a mission of scientific importance; but in 1769 it certainly was. By observing the transit of Venus, the distance of the sun from the earth could be computed; and that computation was fundamental to astronomy in an era when astronomy was the sister science of navigation. It was not enough to rely on observing the transit from European observatories. If the day was cloudy or unfavourable and the observation from England or France or North America was dulled, the astronomers had to wait 105 years for another chance. Hence Cook's voyage in the converted collier *Endeavour* around Cape Horn to Tahiti, which he reached seven weeks before the day of the eclipse.

Cook was then aged forty, a tall man, with long brown hair tied behind, and brown eyes arched by bushy brows. He was a cool, brave navigator, a dexterous map maker, and also a mathematician and astronomer. On Tahiti the sun was not masked by cloud during the six hours when Venus made its transit, but a dusky haze around Venus itself impaired the accuracy of the observations; the subsequent calculating of the distance of the earth from the sun was several million miles astray. The remainder of Cook's voyage, however, succeeded in a way which he had scarcely predicted.

The first aim of Cook's voyage had reflected England's rising interest in science and navigation, and the second aim reflected England's rising interest in new lands and new sources of trade. Between 1748 and 1775 the volume of shipping engaged in England's three long-distance routes — to North America, the West Indies, and Asia — was doubled. England understandably was more and more attracted to new lands as a source of commercial gain, and that attraction tinted the instructions given to Captain Cook. His instructions were to search the South Pacific for the mysterious south land, for at that time it was valid to speculate that the unexplored area between New Zealand and South America could not simply be ocean and nothing but ocean. The area was vast enough to conceal another Asia, and that new Asia might be as valuable for trade as the old.

The main reason why that area had never been explored lay in the winds. The logical approach to the South Pacific was around Cape Horn, but the prevailing westerlies and the drifting icebergs deterred or deflected ships which tried to struggle due west across the Pacific from the Horn. Once they had rounded Cape Horn they sailed more to the north or north-west, and moreover the sources of trade drew them in those directions. Even when Captain Samuel Wallis, a Cornishman, was sent in the *Dolphin* from England in 1766 with specific instructions to round the tip of South America and sail west in search of the missing continent, he was unable to fight his way against the westerlies in high latitudes. He veered north-west to warmer seas and milder winds, and in latitude 17° south he found Tahiti. He reached England in May 1768, just in time to provide Cook with news of a base from which he could observe the transit of Venus. Above all he reported seeing high land on the skyline to the south of Tahiti.

The astronomical work done, Cook sailed south from Tahiti in search of the south land. Finding only the swell of a mighty ocean, he went west to New Zealand and spent the summer in a running survey of its coasts. He then sailed west to search for the coast of eastern Australia, the coast the Dutchmen had missed.

At daylight on 20 April 1770, after running before a southerly gale, he saw sloping, timbered hills in the distance. For nine days he followed the coast and its blue spine of mountains, hoping that the line of surf on the beaches would suddenly give way to a safe anchorage. Eventually he found the anchorage at Botany Bay, a few miles south of where the city of Sydney now stands, and for a week Cook's men explored the shore, observed the native fishermen, gathered a pile of botanical specimens, and chattered about the strangeness of the land they had found.

The land was more than strange: it was incomprehensible to people from the other side of the world. In the *Endeavour* was Joseph Banks, one of Europe's most gifted natural scientists, but in his eight days ashore he had little hope of understanding even the seasons of this distant land. He and Cook saw freshwater creeks running into Botany Bay — creeks swift enough to turn the large waterwheel of a flour mill. They saw sweeping vistas of coarse grass and sent men to cut hay in what they thought were English meadows. They happened to be visiting Botany Bay at what is normally the wettest time of the year, and were seeing dry land at its kindest; but they later came to the mistaken conclusion that they had seen the land at its drabbest and dryest. This optimism was crucial in Australian history. If they had really understood the infertile soil and the extreme summer heat, their report would have rejected Botany Bay. And no British settlement of the Australian continent would have been founded in 1788.

Cook sailed along almost the entire east coast of Australia and, though unable to tell if it was part of the same land the Dutchmen had seen to the west, he annexed it for Britain under the name of New South Wales. He completed his exploration by passing through Torres Strait to Djakarta, then home by way of Cape Town and St Helena. In England after a voyage of nearly three years he confided to a Whitby friend: 'I have made no great discoveries, yet I have explored more of the South Sea than all that have gone before me.' His statement seems humble today but was true. He had found no commodity that could enrich England. He had admittedly seen, in Tahiti and New Zealand and Australia, bays at which small colonies of Europeans could probably support themselves in reasonable comfort by farming and fishing.

But he did not need to add, because it was too obvious to be worth adding, that vast unpeopled areas of North America had all those advantages and, in addition, exportable commodities and the incalculable asset of proximity to Europe.

After exactly a year in England James Cook sailed again with two ships to search for the mythical Southern Continent which had infatuated explorers and geographers for centuries. From the Cape of Good Hope he sailed east in the high latitudes, the first seafarer to crisscross that Great Circle route which would become the swiftest route to Australia in that unforeseeable time when Cook's own New South Wales was to be the mecca for gold seekers. He sailed into cold seas where the westerlies roared and the silent islands of ice were adrift. And in the second of his three summers in that region he crossed the Antarctic Circle and was bold enough to remark that no man would ever go farther south than he had gone.

When summer faded away Cook cruised in warmer seas, and in one sweeping voyage far to the east of Australia in 1774 he found many islands. One of the most insignificant was Norfolk Island, walled by rocky cliffs, far out in the ocean, nearly one thousand miles from Australia. On Tuesday 11 October 1774, two boats were hoisted out and Cook and a small party went ashore. William Wales, the astronomer, noted in his journal that the flax plant grew luxuriously in the island's warm moist climate and was even better than the New Zealand flax, being so thick on the shores that it was 'scarce possible to get through it'. Cook himself marvelled at the shapely spruce pine that cloaked the island. His men chopped down one of the smallest trees in order to shape a spare topgallant mast or yard, and Cook judged the pine to be finer naval timber than the impressive species of pine he had seen in New Zealand and New Caledonia. 'My carpenter,' he confided, 'tells me that the wood is exactly of the same nature as the Quebeck Pines. Here then is another Isle where Masts for the largest Ships may be had.' Those few hours spent on a balmy spring day on that uninhabited island far out to sea were, unknown to him, perhaps more important than the weeks he had spent on Australian soil and coast in his previous voyage. Those few hours probably had deep effects on subsequent British enterprises in the South Seas.

When Cook finally reached England again in July 1775 he had been at sea for six of the previous seven years and had probably found more new lands and sailed in a wider expanse of unexplored sea than any navigator before or after. But it seemed at the time that the main value of his voyages was perhaps less in the land he had found than in the aids to navigation which he had proved. He had tamed two of the traditional foes of long voyages. He had had surprising success in alleviating scurvy — the deficiency in vitamin C which had been fatal to thousands of sailors and passengers on long voyages. And he had showed for the first time the value of a momentous idea in the art of navigation — a quick way of finding a ship's longitude and therefore her exact position at sea.

The inability of seamen to find their longitude at sea caused countless wrecks, forced ships in many overseas trades to follow an indirect and wasteful course, and was the bane of map makers. A way of finding longitude at sea was one of the most arduous quests of practical science in the seventeenth and eighteenth centuries and was almost the philosopher's stone of navigation. Longitude at sea was determined by comparing local time with Greenwich or standard time; it was possible to determine local time by observing the position of the sun but it was only possible to determine Greenwich time by measuring the angular distance of the moon from the sun and by doing a long series of mathematical equations which few navigators had the skill or the time to carry through. The publication of the *Nautical Almanac* in 1767 enabled a skilled navigator to compute Greenwich time in about a quarter of an hour instead of three to four hours. A year later the *Endeavour* sailed with a copy of the almanac in the cabin and a navigator capable of using the almanac. Cook's was the first exploring ship that could find out her exact position at sea and the exact position of the coasts and reefs and harbours she found.

On his second voyage into the South Seas Cook carried a simpler device. He had an intensely accurate watch, set and corrected at Greenwich before he left, and he carried Greenwich time wherever he wandered. Hitherto no known timepiece could keep the precise time during a long passage in which a ship passed through intense cold and heat. An inaccuracy of only a few seconds in a watch was enough to produce a grave error in longitude. The chronometer which Cook carried had been invented by John Harrison and faithfully copied by the watchmaker Larcum Kendall, and after nearly three years at sea Cook observed, at Cape Town on 22 March 1775, that the error in the watch was astonishingly small, 'Mr Kendals Watch has exceeded the expectations of its most Zealous advocate and by being now and then corrected by lunar observations has been our faithfull guide through all the vicissitudes of climates.' The watch had enabled Cook to make in the South Seas more accurate charts than any navigator had ever made.

In the 1770s a few visionaries must have realized the value of Cook's voyages in shrinking the waste of ocean that isolated the South Seas from Europe. He had proved that a ship could carry Greenwich time on the most arduous and prolonged voyage, and that led not only to more accurate charts but also enabled merchant ships, as we shall see later, to follow shorter courses between distant ports. He had also shown that lemon juice, sauerkraut, malt, carrot marmalade and other concoctions, were a preventive of scurvy on long voyages. A chronometer and barrels of sauerkraut would transform distant voyages, but Cook was far ahead of his time. Most ships that sailed to the South Seas even half a century later carried neither the answer to longitude nor to scurvy.

By the canons of science and navigation Cook's voyages were astonishingly successful, but by the normal canons of eighteenth century commerce they were disappointing. In the twentieth century, when so many of the coasts he had found and charted are prosperous European settlements, Cook's discoveries seem magnificent. But in the 1770s Cook was not seeking new lands in the South Seas where migrating Europeans could settle and, by their own energy rather than the forced labour of coloured slaves, reap crops and tend cattle and build towns and live the same life they had lived in Yorkshire and Galway. In that era the only such European colonies across the seas were on the colder Atlantic coast of North America. Those seaboard colonies supplied most of their own needs. They were close enough to Europe to ship across their timber and fur, and to import manufactured goods from Europe at prices which the cost of shipment did not make prohibitive. Similarly, European migrants were willing to make the sea journey across the north Atlantic to settle near the New England coast or the St Lawrence, because the voyage was not unduly long, not unduly dangerous, not unduly dear, and not seriously menaced by scurvy or fevers. In contrast neither natural resources nor distance had fitted Australia or New Zealand to become European 'colonies of settlement' in the 1770s.

The typical European overseas colony in the latter part of the eighteenth century depended on foreign trade. It existed because the soil or climate was able to produce a commodity which Europe itself was unable to produce. It flourished because that commodity commanded a sufficient price in Europe to afford the high cost of shipment. Nearly all such colonies were in hot parts of the globe. Native labourers or coloured slaves recruited from abroad produced the commodity, so the demand for Europeans in the colony was small; they came not as unskilled labourers but as merchants, plantation managers or owners, soldiers and administrators. The common

European colony was a ghetto of Europeans on the fringes of a land populated by coloured peoples. In one group of colonies such as the sugar-fields of the West Indies or the tobacco plantations of Virginia or the silver-fields of Mexico, the Europeans supervised and organized the coloured labourers who produced the commodity for foreign trade. In another group of colonies such as the Dutch East Indies or India the small colony of Europeans was simply a trading post which exchanged European goods for spices or indigo or tropical products produced independently by natives of the land. It is obvious that not one of the lands which Cook found in the South Seas seemed likely to serve as a colony of trade; they produced no new commodity fit for European commerce. On the other hand some could be converted into plantations and grow perhaps cotton or sugar for export to Europe, but the defect of this alternative was that these lands were so far from Europe that high costs of transport would probably preclude them from competing with other tropical lands.

A final type of European outpost in the eighteenth century was the small base on the coast that served the needs of Europe's trading colonies. These tiny bases sold no commodity to Europe. They simply served the commerce that flowed to Europe. The little island of St Helena in the south Atlantic or the Dutch base at Cape Town which served as halfway houses and restaurants for the commerce to Asia were typical of the small restaurant colonies. It was barely conceivable, at the time when Cook's discoveries were first spoken of by European merchants and scientists, that harbours in eastern Australia or New Zealand might become restaurant ports for passing ships. They were too far away from trade routes.

Thus, in 1775, at the conclusion of Cook's second voyage in the South Seas, his discoveries led more to mental speculation than to action. The South Seas were not fit to become colonies of European settlement like Massachusetts. They were not fit for tropical plantations like Jamaica. They were not fit for a colony of trade like

Calcutta. And they were not fit for a restaurant colony like St Helena.

But certain events on the western side of the Atlantic were, in the most unpredictable way, about to transform the value of Cook's new lands. The older North American colonies had revolted against Britain and, as Cook sailed home up the English channel in July 1775, George Washington was leading the colonists' army in the siege of the English-held city of Boston. The colonists' ultimate victory and the creation of the independent United States of America had no conceivable meaning to the natives in Australia and the warm islands of the South Seas, but it was to disturb their isolation and re-shape their lives.

2 Exile

In all the years before 1787 only one European ship had been known to call at Australia's eastern coast, but in 1787 a fleet of eleven English ships was preparing to visit that coast. On the Mother Bank near Portsmouth lay two armed naval vessels, three storeships or cargo ships, and six transports. The transports, however, could hardly be called orthodox passenger ships. Anyone who visited them would have seen iron bars bolted over the hatchways, loopholes through which muskets could be fired into the passengers' quarters, and a barricade fitted with pointed iron prongs on the upper decks near the mainmast. Most of the passengers in the fleet that sailed from England on Sunday 13 May 1787 were convicted criminals. Few larger fleets had ever left Europe to settle a new land. Few pirate fleets had ever carried such a band of malefactors.

The sailing of the first fleet to Botany Bay in Australia seems at first sight to need no more explanation than the listing of the following procession of events. Britain for long had exiled many of its criminals to colonies across the Atlantic. By 1776, however, the revolt of the American colonies had deprived Britain of the outlet for convicts, and soon English gaols and prison hulks began to bulge with criminals. Finally, Britain decided to exile to the eastern coast of Australia many of those convicts whom it would once have shipped to North America. Australia, it seems then, was colonized simply as a British gaol; and nearly every Australian accepts that verdict.

It is puzzling, however, that Britain should have selected Australia as her overseas prison. Australia was too far
away. Lord Howe, First Lord of the Admiralty, writing
on Boxing Day 1784, had disparaged the idea of any civil
or convict settlement in eastern Australia on the grounds
of 'the length of the navigation, subject to all the retard-
ments of an India voyage'. The cost of sending convicts to
Australia was much larger than the cost of sending convicts to an isolated British possession in the northern
hemisphere. Sheer distance, even without adding the
dangers of a voyage in unknown waters, demanded a
price. The two Admiralty ships which escorted the first
fleet were thereby virtually removed from the active naval
list and the nine chartered ships were costly not only because their owners had to feed the convicts on the long
voyage out but also because many of the ships, on reaching Australia, had little prospect of finding a return cargo
in the Indian or Pacific oceans. Even if the new settlement managed to grow much of its food, the convicts still
had to be clothed and equipped and the big contingent
of officials and their families still had to be provided with
many luxuries and necessities sent at high expense from
Europe. Captain Arthur Phillip, Australia's first governor, giving his opinion on the new settlement in July 1788,
thought no other country 'could be more disadvantage-
ously placed with respect to support from the mother
country, on which for a few years we must entirely
depend'.

The settling of eastern Australia was a startlingly costly
solution to the crowded British prisons. It was also a very
slow solution to what is often said to have been an urgent
problem. For Australia was far away; and a long time
elapsed before England heard the news of the safe arrival
of its vanguard, and nearly two and a half years passed
from the sailing of the first fleet of convict ships to the
sailing of the second fleet. An awareness of these problems
of distance provokes the question why Britain did not
adopt a cheaper, quicker outlet for its overflowing prisons, either by building new prisons at home or by finding

a nearer land of exile on the coast or islands of the Atlantic. The question appears to yield unexpected answers.

2

In the eighteenth century the British practice of transporting many of its convicts rested on the idea that they should be useful servants of, rather than an encumbrance on, the State which they had sinned against. Transportation was not only a method of punishment but also a sound economic policy. Shortly before the North American colonies rebelled, Britain was literally giving convicts to contractors who in turn shipped them to Maryland, Georgia, and southern colonies and sold them to planters and employers at a profit. Britain therefore gained by the emigration of criminals. It did not have to pay for their deportation. It no longer had to feed and clothe and guard them during the term of their sentence, and their labour strengthened the colonial economy.

These advantages were not forgotten after 1776 when Britain, unable to ship convicts to the rebellious American colonies, looked for other cheap places of exile. Rather than transport convicts to British possessions where they could not be usefully employed, Britain kept in its own prisons and river hulks those whom the courts had sentenced to transportation in the decade after 1776. A few were shipped abroad but only to places where their labour met a demand. Several hundred convicts went to the Gold Coast as soldiers to fight the Dutch in 1781, a pardon their reward. Two years later a London merchant, George Moore, purchased some English convicts, failed in his attempts to land them in the United States and failed in his attempts to land them near the logwood camps in the British Honduras. There the settlers preferred unconvicted black slaves to convicted white slaves. They argued that English convicts would damage the character and credit of the colony.

These mishaps did not exhaust the list of convenient lands to which convicts could possibly be sold. They could be sold to the sugar plantations of the West Indies but the planters already had a sure supply of coloured slaves who worked well in a tropical climate; moreover an influx of British convicts could undermine discipline and incite slaves to revolt. Any suggestion to ship convicts to plantation islands in the West Indies would probably also be resented by the powerful slave-trading interests in England. The big fleet of English ships that carried slaves from West Africa to the West Indies and the American mainland lost their monopoly of supplying slaves to tobacco plantations in the deep south of the newly independent United States of America, and naturally they did not want their profitable slave market in the West Indies weakened by competition from English gaols. Britain's share of the Atlantic slave traffic was falling in the 1780s, and the beneficiaries of that traffic could argue in the English parliament that a strong slave trade was a tough school of seamanship and one source of Britain's maritime power. In the hundred years to 1786 it was estimated that perhaps 2 million slaves had been shipped across the Atlantic to British colonies in the Americas and the West Indies. As virtually all those slaves had been carried in British ships, the slave traffic must have been an immense stimulus to shipping. But now that traffic was declining; it would decline more if English convicts were sent to the West Indies.

Perhaps it was the slave traders' friends who emphasized the advantages of shipping convicts from England to West Africa rather than to the West Indies. Gambia and the Gulf of Guinea were relatively close to England, so the cost of shipping out convicts would not be high. Furthermore, slave ships could carry out the convicts to West Africa, gather a cargo of slaves and carry them to Jamaica, and then maybe carry sugar back to England, thus making a profitable round voyage. Many English politicians stressed the virtues of sending convicts to West Africa but the defects of that land of exile were also obvious. It had plenty of cheap labour and therefore English convicts could not serve England — except by their absence. It was not certain whether the convicts could grow enough food to sustain themselves and their guards. It was certain that the tropical climate would turn banishment into death for many convicts and their military guards.

The search for a place of exile turned from tropical to temperate Africa, and in July 1785 a parliamentary committee recommended Das Voltas Bay in South West Africa, near the mouth of the Orange River. It lay on the unoccupied coast between the Portuguese colony of Angola and the Dutch colony of Cape of Good Hope, astride the great trade route between Europe and India and the Orient. That was its glowing attraction, for it could be a refreshment base and port of call for British ships which hitherto had to depend on the East India Company's small volcanic island of St Helena or the Dutch harbour of the Cape. The British convicts moreover could be carried out cheaply and miserably in slave ships. In the temperate climate a small band of free settlers could usefully employ the convicts to grow food for the market provided by passing ships, thus saving the State from the expense of maintaining the convicts. It could be a base for whaling ships and for merchant ships trading to South America or West Africa. The whole ingenious scheme was married to thrift, convenience, and the national interest. In fact the parliamentary committee was careful to recommend that Das Voltas Bay should only be settled if the 'commercial and political benefits' justified the inevitable expense.

The naval sloop *Nautilus* sailed to inspect Das Voltas Bay. With a botanist to assist in the inspection, the commander of *Nautilus* had no doubts that the site was too dry and sandy and barren. As soon as the *Nautilus* returned with the report, the English government dropped Das Voltas Bay and announced, suddenly and unexpectedly, that it would send as expedition of convicts to Botany Bay in eastern Australia.

Why did Britain decide suddenly to send convicts to Australia? Some historians say that England chose Australia because it had no alternative overseas gaol after the rejection of Das Voltas Bay. But there were prompter and cheaper solutions than sending convicts to Australia. They could be sent to Canada or to islands in the West Indies. Admittedly those colonies had complained in the past at proposals that they should accept British criminals, but they had complained primarily because the old method of exiling convicts was to sell them to residents of the colonies. They had not complained at the novel idea of setting up a *guarded* prison settlement say in a remote corner of Nova Scotia or Jamaica, and that after all was the essence of the new convict system proposed for Australia. Alternatively if Britain did not wish to risk offending its own overseas colonists, it could make a prison settlement in one of the uninhabited islands of Bermuda or the West Indies, where the convicts could grow most of their own grain and meat. Finally, Britain could solve the crisis of its crowded gaols, as other European countries solved the same problem, by building more gaols at home. If British cabinet ministers, in full knowledge of these alternatives, selected Australia solely as a dumping ground for convicts, then they must have been temporarily deranged. That explanation is feasible rather than convincing.

The mystery of why England decided to send many of its convicts to the opposite side of the world was brilliantly probed by Mr K. M. Dallas in a lecture to a small, sceptical audience in Hobart in 1952. He suggested that England needed a new sea base and refitting port in order to strengthen her commercial empire in the East. Botany Bay, he argued, was to be that maritime base. It was to be a port of call and supply for ships in four promising trades. One trade was the China tea trade, a vital source of British commerce and comfort. The China tea trade soared after 1784, when England lowered import duties on tea in order to check the smuggling of duty-free tea. Moreover, the proportion of tea carried away from China in English ships increased drastically in little more than a decade from about one quarter to three quarters, making

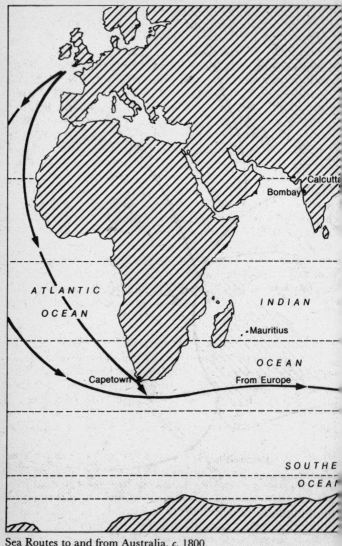

Sea Routes to and from Australia, *c.* 1800.

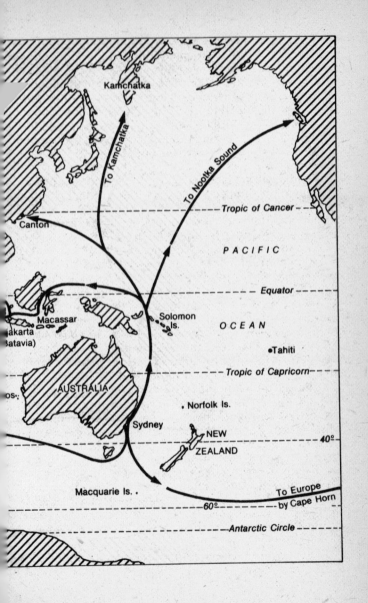

Kamchatka

To Kamchatka

To Nootka Sound

Canton

Tropic of Cancer

PACIFIC

Equator

Macassar

Solomon
Is.

OCEAN

akarta
Batavia)

•Tahiti

Tropic of Capricorn

AUSTRALIA

os·,

• Norfolk Is.

Sydney

NEW
ZEALAND

40°

Macquarie Is. ·

To Europe
by Cape Horn

60°

Antarctic Circle

the long tea route a vital artery of English shipping and
wealth. Tea ships traditionally used the narrow straits
near Sumatra, which were often menaced by pirates and
in years of war could be menaced by Dutch ships. An
alternative way of reaching China was to sail east from
the Cape of Good Hope, sail around Tasmania and up the
east coast of Australia, calling at Botany Bay and then
weaving a course through the islands to the east of New
Guinea and so north-west to China. That was a safe, alternative route between England and China, assuming that
England first established a half-way house at Botany Bay.

Around the same route and into the same half-way port
in Australia could come English ships bound for the
Pacific coast of north-west America where commerce in
sea otter skins was booming in the 1780s; and indeed
George Vancouver tried that route in 1791 when he sailed
from Falmouth, England, to Vancouver Island in order to
take formal possession of the territory from Spain. Botany
Bay could also become a base for whaling ships; American whalers were venturing from the south Atlantic
ocean into the Indian and South Pacific oceans, and
English whalers were about to follow in their wake.
Finally the convict settlement at Botany Bay could be a
base from which British ships quietly emerged to dabble
in smuggling and privateering in the rich Spanish trade
that linked the Philippines, Mexico and South America.
Whales, Spanish loot, North American fur, and China
tea, were four prizes which a sea base in eastern Australia
could possibly help capture for England. A fifth potential
prize may also be added. In 1784 the British, by the Treaty of Paris, had been granted the precious right to take
their ships freely through the East Indies. Eager to break
further into the Dutch monopoly of trade in the islands,
they founded the port of Penang in the Malay Peninsula
in 1786, and it is conceivable that a port in Australia
would offer a base for excursions to the opposite end of the
Dutch trading realm.

English ships trading in all these seas could, if necessary, call at Botany Bay for fresh water and food and fuel

and supplies in an age when scurvy still plagued the high seas and the duration of every sea voyage was unpredictable. Merchant ships could call for repairs, whaling ships could call for supplies or unload their catch for transhipment to England, and in time of war naval or merchant ships could shelter in Botany Bay.

Most of these commercial hopes had been expressed early in the 1780s by English adventurers or rocking-chair colonizers. Dallas saw their significance. The late-eighteenth century was still a time when the sealanes were a high road to wealth, a time when valuable new products were found more often in new lands than in laboratories and pilot plants. Those vast seas and coastlines stretching between South Africa and South America and between Alaska and the 'roaring forties' were a prize for which European merchants were increasingly striving. The interest in harbours, especially as half-way houses on potential trade routes, reflected this faith that a glittering oceanic realm of commerce was about to open up. The nation hoping to command that commerce would need new ports. Above all it had to be careful that the potential seabases of importance did not fall into the hands of rivals. Botany Bay was such a base. Like a vacant allotment at an intersection in a busy city, it would not always remain vacant.

The rivalry in these Twin Oceans on the other side of the Capes become intense. England held the richest prize, India. But England did not even command the sea route to India. The Dutch held the Cape of Good Hope and therefore the main entrance to this realm. The Spanish held the approaches to Cape Horn and therefore the other sea entrance to the realm. Even the French were placed favourably, for they held the islands of Mauritius and Réunion which they could use in time of war to plunder English merchantmen sailing between South Africa and India. The Dutch were favourably placed because they could control the narrow straits of the Indonesian archipelago through which English ships sailed on their way to and from the Chinese tea ports. The Dutch also held one of the noblest and most strategic harbours in the Twin Oceans — the Ceylon part of Trincomalee, which English naval officers not merely wanted but positively craved.

All that England possessed on the route to India and China was the island of Saint Helena in the south Atlantic, and that small island was neither well placed nor well equipped as a port of call in peace or a port of refuge in war. It is easy then to understand why England had placed such hopes on finding a North West Passage through the cold seas to the north of North America, thereby linking the north Atlantic and the north Pacific. Even in the 1780s, after Cook's last voyage had failed to find that passage, England did not abandon hope that someday a hidden waterway might be found through the maze of frozen islands. Such a waterway would provide a new route from England to China and over to India.

In the mid 1780s England and France increased their rivalry in the Indian Ocean and its approaches. They had fought less than three years ago, in the War of American Independence. Now they jostled again for strategic sites and spheres of influence. The French created a base in the south-east of Madagascar and signed a treaty with the king of Cochin China — the beginnings of their formal relations with a territory that was to end nearly two centuries later in the Vietnam War. The English toyed with Das Voltas Bay and opened a port at Penang in the Malayan peninsula. In 1786 they also sent an expedition of four vessels to occupy briefly the coral atoll of Diego Garcia, which nearly two centuries later — when England and France had given way as naval rivals to Russia and the United States — was to become an important United States base.

This jostling and jockeying was a vital background to the decision of the English government to send a fleet to occupy Botany Bay. In some ways the decision was made for the far future. For the short term it was simply vital that France should not be allowed to occupy such a strategic site. France was already too active, and in 1786 the prime minister, Pitt, feared that France might already be assembling naval forces in Mauritius and planning to deprive Britain of her jewel, India.

3

There was another vital, but often-ignored, reason for the decision to send the convicts to Australia. When Lord Sydney in August 1786 revealed the decision he argued that such a settlement would ease the dangerous pressure on English gaols and prison hulks. He also explained that Australia had several enticing articles of commerce. One was the flax plant which grew luxuriantly. British manufacturers judged it superior to Baltic flax for the making of canvas and sailcloth and superior to Baltic hemp for the making of ships' cables, and Lord Sydney noted that a rope cable made of South Seas flax would be stronger than one made of European hemp; indeed a cable of the one with a circumference of ten inches would be stronger than a cable of the other with a circumference of eighteen inches. A sure supply of flax, wrote Lord Sydney, 'would be of great consequence to us as a naval power'. At the same time the tall trees which grew to the water's edge in New Zealand and in islands near Australia would yield masts of unparalleled size and quality for the British fleets in India. Australia would thus be 'reciprocally beneficial' both to English gaols and to English seapower. Thus Lord Sydney affirmed the traditional principle that England expected more gains than the simple pleasure of ridding her soil of criminals. Australia then was not designed simply as a remote gaol, cut off from the world's commerce. It was to supply strategic materials.

Historians often observed that England hoped to win valuable raw materials in Australia, but they discounted these hopes as quaint displays of window dressing or eighteenth century optimism. And yet those reasons can only be discarded by ignoring the facts of economic life. In that era Britain's military strength and an increasing part of her commerce relied on seapower, and flax and ships' timber were as vital to seapower as steel and oil are today. In letters in which British politicians explained their reasons for selecting Botany Bay they did not have to emphasize that flax and timber were vital to their country; it was too obvious to be spelled out. The men to whom they addressed their letters knew the importance of a secure supply of naval stores and the dangers facing Britain's sources of naval stores.

In the eighteenth century a fleet of ships carried flax from the Baltic ports to England. It was a costly trade and in the 1780s England spent about £500,000 a year on imported flax, mostly from St Petersburg in Russia. Tens of thousands of acres on the southern shores of the Baltic and in northern Russia grew the slender weed-like plant, and when the flax was about knee-high and the seeds were ripening and the lower leaves were falling, the plant was pulled from the ground, tied in stooks, and then treated in a long cycle of manual operations. The bark which coated the thin stem of the plant was fibrous, and from the fibres came the threads that made sailcloth and linen. The long fibre of Russian flax was ideal for making sailcloth; and the safety and speed of English ships in war and peace depended on a continuous and certain supply of flax from the Baltic.

England relied on the Baltic for ships' spars, and for the hemp and flax from which were manufactured ships' ropes and sailcloth. Any blockade of the Baltic was thus a blockade against English seapower. From the year 1780 England's ability to carry on war against France and rebelling American colonies was endangered by the north European powers which formed the Armed Neutrality and harried merchant ships in the Baltic Sea. England's lifeline of flax and hemp was frayed; stockpiles dwindled. In 1781 the English parliament relaxed its strict Navigation Acts and allowed foreign ships to carry flax and hemp to England for the duration of war. At the same time England hurriedly encouraged the cultivation of flax and hemp in its own soil. High bounties were offered on home-grown flax. Acres of flax were planted in Yorkshire and Lincolnshire but the local crop was inferior to the Russian.

When peace came in 1783, England's concern for flax did not cease. The prime minister, William Pitt, maintained a strong navy with more seamen than ever before in time of peace and spent heavily on new ships of war. But England's navy could not be entirely secure if it still relied on naval stores from the Baltic. Supplies of flax and hemp and naval timber could perhaps be relied upon even less in any future European war. Russia, for long an ally of England, was beginning to drift away at the very time when its rising military strength was worrying many Englishmen. And yet Russia was at least as indispensable to England in the age of sail as was the Middle East in the age of oil. If England in 1936 had found the main oilfields of the world in the control of a potential enemy it would have been in the same insecure position which it had held in 1786.

England applied compulsion and persuasion in an effort to create a strong flax industry. In 1785 the governor of Quebec was ordered, when granting any land with soil fit for growing flax and hemp, to insert a clause in the deed compelling the owner to sow seeds of flax and hemp in part of his land each year. A year later the English parliament agreed to pay bounties on flax and hemp imported from Canada or grown in England. In August 1786, less than a week after Lord Sydney announced the decision to send convicts to Australia, the Privy Council committee on Trade and Plantations was meeting at the Court of St James to hear evidence on England's continued reliance on Russian flax and hemp. In the same month the comptroller of the navy, Sir Charles Middleton, was informing the prime minister that England relied on hemp shipped from the Baltic, and reminding him of the scarcity of hemp which had worried England's cabinet in 1781, a war year. It is perhaps not a coincidence that at a time when England was reviewing its sources of naval stores, it should decide to send its unwanted convicts to a land that seemed rich in these strategic materials.

Flax grew on Norfolk Island, about a thousand miles east of Botany Bay. It grew prolifically by European standards; whereas flax which grew more than three feet high in northern Europe was considered tall, much of the flax on Norfolk Island grew to a height of more than eight feet. Above all, its fibre was nearly three times as long as the fibre of Baltic flax; and it was believed that the longer the fibre, the stronger the sail canvas which could be produced. Flax not only was a source of sailcloth but also a substitute for hemp in the making of ropes for ships' rigging; and the samples of New Zealand and Norfolk Island flax which Cook's *Endeavour* took to England impressed the experienced men who examined or tested them. Their opinion was echoed by Sir George Young, who predicted that the flax from the Pacific would out-strip all other fibres in the making of canvas and cordage.

The flax which Captain Cook had observed in the islands of the South Pacific in 1774 attracted France as well as England. French seapower also depended on Baltic flax and hemp, and one mission of the exploring expedition which sailed from France under the command of Jean de la Perouse in August 1785 was to carry home specimens of the flax plants from the South Pacific. The French Academy of Sciences gave him precise instructions, assuring him that if he carried plants safely home they 'would probably be one of the most valuable presents the navigator could bestow on our soil'. De la Perouse anchored off Norfolk Island in the third year of a voyage which had zigzagged far across the Pacific, but strong surf prevented his boats from reaching the island. A month or so later his ships sank off the Santa Cruz Islands, at the very time when the first English flax-seekers were occupying Norfolk Island.

Norfolk Island had another prop for English naval power. The island was capped with a forest of tall green Norfolk Island pines, whose trunks were so straight and tall and springy that any alert sailor could see their potential value as a source of ships' mainmasts and spars. The forest was another prize for a convict settlement in

32

Australia, because England relied heavily on foreign timbers for the building and repairing of ships. Most British ships of the line had Baltic planking and spars, North American mainmasts, Ukrainian topmasts, and a hull framework of Sussex oak. When the American colonies rebelled against England, the white pine forests of Maine and New Hampshire ceased to send their mainmasts to England, and the English ships of war had no adequate substitute. As masts had to keep their resin in order to remain springy and stormproof and as the resin vanished after ten or twelve years, the masts had to be replaced regularly. England, however, lacked spare masts. The naval historian Robert G. Albion has produced strong evidence that scarcity of new mainmasts was one reason why England lost the war and her American colonies. After the war Canadian forests supplied more naval timber, but England still depended on many kinds of timber from many foreign ports. Though Australia was too far away to supply England with cheap timber for shipbuilding, Australia's position in a remote part of the southern hemisphere was in a sense an advantage. Scores of English merchant ships traded in the Indian Ocean and the Pacific, and an occasional naval fleet was engaged in those seas, and when ships lost masts or spars in storm or battle they had to replace them with timber shipped at heavy expense from north Atlantic or Baltic ports. As the trunk of the stately Norfolk Island pine seemed ideal for masts and spars, it could be shipped cheaply and rapidly to any port in the East India Company's domain.

Norfolk Island seems to be a key to the plan to send convicts to Australia. In a decade when British commerce was advancing strenuously in the Pacific and the Far East this island was the most promising source of naval stores in that vast region. In a decade when England was more conscious than ever of the need for a sure supply of naval stores — a supply that did not have to come from hostile nations — the island was even more valuable. The governor of the new settlement in Australia had firm orders to occupy the island.

It may be argued that no sane statesman would place such hopes on a small, secluded island with steep cliffs towering above the surf and no sheltered port and only thirteen square miles of land. As Captain Cook had seen the same flax and fine forests growing in New Zealand — large islands with safer harbours and infinitely more land on which to grow food — why didn't England select New Zealand as the gaol and the provider of raw materials? The answer was that the flax and forests of New Zealand seemed inferior to those of Norfolk Island; moreover New Zealand had fighting inhabitants, whereas Norfolk Island was uninhabited.

If Norfolk Island was so important, why then was the Australian mainland also settled? The island itself was so small that, even if denuded of timber, it could not be expected to produce enough grain and meat to feed a large population. Its acreage was too cramped to produce a large supply of flax. Its coast was rocky and lacked a safe harbour. But if the flax plants or seed could be transplanted to Botany Bay, similar climate, limitless land, and forced labour might aid its cultivation on any scale that seemed necessary. Norfolk Island was the plant nursery; Botany Bay was to be the market garden and flax farm. It was also to be the sea base.

4

The eleven ships sailed down the English Channel on a near-summer day in May 1787, and soon after they lost sight of land the convicts were allowed daily on deck, unencumbered by irons. The fleet called for fresh water at Tenerife in the Canary Islands, staying a week. It anchored at Rio de Janeiro for nearly a month, making repairs and buying rum, wine, fresh provisions, and ten thousand musket balls. It spend another month at Cape Town, taking on fresh provisions and filling a menagerie on deck with poultry, rabbits, 4 goats, 7 horses, 8 cattle, 28 pigs, and 46 sheep.

So far the leisurely world cruise had been in convoy with H.M.S. *Sirius* hustling the laggards; but after sailing from Cape Town the tight convoy was broken. Nevertheless all ships entered Botany Bay in eastern Australia within two days of one another in January 1788. The course they had followed from England amounted to some 14,000 miles and had taken eight months and a week, of which actual sailing time was six months. Some convicts had been penned aboard for more than a year when they finally went ashore.

Botany Bay seemed another Das Voltas Bay, barren in the glare of summer. A few miles to the north was Port Jackson, a landlocked harbour with a safe entrance, and after a few days the fleet abandoned its first bay and moved to Port Jackson. There, in a small inlet named Sydney Cove, the fleet slowly discharged its cargo and just over one thousand people, three quarters of them convicts and the remainder officers and marines, wives and children. From the confinement of the ships they moved to the biggest penitentiary on earth.

Less than a month after the fleet reached Australia the Lieutenant Governor and Commander in Chief, Captain Arthur Phillip, obeyed his orders to place a small party on Norfolk Island and so 'prevent it being occupied by the subjects of any other European power'. The *Supply* sailed from Sydney with six months' provisions and a landing party of sailors, convicts, and two men who understood the cultivation of flax. They saw Norfolk Island rising out of the ocean on the fifteenth day, and they spent another five days in search of a gap in the coral rocks encircling the island before they safely landed.

No European outpost in the world in 1788 was so far from the smell of gunpowder and the noise of naval battle as this island which had been primarily settled to serve the supply lines of war. A cluster of huts in a clearing on the shores of a warm blue sea, it appeared more like a beachcombers' camp than a convict camp; but the appearance was contradicted by the armed marines, forced labour, daily food rations, and the church parade each

Sunday. The convicts cleared a few acres of forest, hoeing the deep mulchy soil and planting wheat and barley and vegetables. They carried fresh water from a stream and fished from the rocks and hunted pigeons, mutton birds, turtles, and the rats that swarmed in the green paradise. Their first task was to grow enough food for their own needs, and hard work and rich soil had some success. More convicts were sent from the mainland to clear forest and plant crops. For a time Norfolk Island had nearly as many people as the town of Sydney.

Survival soon became the aim of the convict colonies. The original plan that surplus men and land could grow flax was not followed; every surplus man and every cleared acre had to grow grain. But even if the first crops of grain had been prolific, the flax industry would have faltered. The men who landed at Norfolk Island in the original party were said to understand the art of dressing flax, but through the acute problems created by fibre of phenomenal length they were unable satisfactorily to separate fibre from stalk. Samples of flax were sent to Sydney, where the governor placed them in his despatch box for transmission to England in the ship *Golden Grove*. On 17 November 1788 he wrote a covering note to Under Secretary Nepean:

Sir,

The flax contained in this box is from Norfolk Island.

I have mentioned in my former letters the want of a person that understands the preparing and manufacture of flax. If properly dressed, I think it would be superior to any that grows in Europe.

It was so rare for a ship to sail between England and Australia that nearly two years passed before his request was answered. Five farming superintendents came in the *Lady Juliana* in 1790 to train convicts in farming methods, and one said that he knew how to cultivate and dress flax. He was sent at once to Norfolk Island, and allotted as many male and female convicts as he needed. Almost three years after the island had been settled, the flax master produced a piece of coarse cloth woven from flax fibre. It was probably one of the costliest pieces of canvas ever made.

As natives of New Zealand were known to weave the fibres of this distinctive flax, the simplest solution was to kidnap or cajole a few New Zealanders. The colony itself could spare no ship to make a recruiting voyage. An offer of £100 to the captain of a whaler to pick up two New Zealanders was ignored. Eventually in April 1793 one of Vancouver's ships, the *Daedalus*, returning from the north-west coast of America, reached Sydney with two native men who had been enticed aboard in New Zealand. One was a priest and the other a warrior, and on Norfolk Island they proved themselves inexperienced in the art of dressing and weaving flax. They explained that in New Zealand the women worked the flax. Even so, before they were repatriated, they taught the convicts to improve the quality and output of the cloth. Soon thirty yards of coarse canvas was being woven each week, and the commander of the island believed that the industry was so capable of expansion that if necessary it could employ 500 convicts.

Flax did not become the central industry of Norfolk Island, and though the industry was also transplanted to Sydney it did not flourish there. The length of the fibre did not produce the superior sailcloth which had been expected; instead it produced a weak canvas at high cost. Moreover, the threat to the supply lines across the Baltic Sea did not erupt, and even after France and England went to war in 1793 the Baltic remained an open if troubled sea and Russia still loaded its bundles of flax and hemp into a procession of English ships. One epitaph on Australian flax was written as early as 1797. The land that was intended to produce strong rope and flax in abundance was so short of canvas and rope that Sydney's largest boat was idle because it could obtain no sail cloth. A second, ironic epitaph was written in 1824 when £900 of Riga linseed was landed at Sydney to promote the growth of Baltic flax on Australian soil.

The green forests of tapering Norfolk Island pines still stood at attention, awaiting naval orders and emergencies. The experienced carpenter on the *Supply* swore in 1788 that the timber was nearly as light as the best Norwegian masts. Some of the trees rose 180 feet, and for nearly half the way up the trunk there were no branches — an asset in timber intended for masts. The master of the same ship assured Governor Phillip that a ship could load masts and spars at the island with more safety than at Riga Bay on the Baltic, where many English ships called annually for timber. Both carpenter and master were wrong. It was hazardous to load ships in the swell off the beach, but a few top-gallant masts and lower spars were loaded into two ships leaving for England, where they were to be examined at the naval dockyard at Deptford on the Thames. When several years later George Vancouver was preparing to leave England on his long expedition to north-west America, the timber fellers at Norfolk Island were dragging logs to the beach to equip him with spare spars. Then the optimism ceased. Timber fellers found that many pines were outwardly sound but rotten behind the bark. Norfolk Island pine was too risky for the spars of large ships. The dream of equipping the fleets in the East Indies faded, and much of the forest was split into firewood.

The decision of the English to settle eastern Australia had proved to be a fiasco. They had sent the first fleet to Botany Bay in the hope of giving England the naval supplies they might someday need and ridding England of the people they didn't need. But the naval supplies — the flax and the pine — were not forthcoming. And the cost of keeping the convicts in a far-off land exceeded the benefits hoped for. The first settlements had been based on the hope that convicts would soon grow all their own food, and that hope had rested on the days which Cook and Banks had spent at Botany Bay in 1770. Their discoveries in those eight days proved to be a delusion. If England had been much closer to eastern Australia, detailed investigation would probably have preceded the decision to colonise; but distance precluded such knowledge.

All the short-term hopes had failed. There remained

the long-term hope that an Australian port — a port of call and refuge — would ultimately strengthen England's strategic and commercial interests in those wide oceans now opening out to European ships. Even this hope, in the first lonely years, seemed forlorn. Sydney could not serve passing ships if it could hardly feed itself. It was like a wounded seabird, stranded on a lonely rock.

3 Isolation

The convict settlement stood on the slopes of a blue harbour, just out of sight of the ocean. The prison had no walls and those who wished to escape had a whole continent in which to vanish. But New South Wales was in fact a tighter prison than any Devil's Island or any fortress on land. The ocean was the wall of the prison, imprisoning not only the convicts but also the governor and officials and marines.

The first fleet had safely crossed the seas, but her sailors did not then fully realize the might of the seas at the southern end of the globe. Any ship passing between Europe and Australia had to spend much of her time in the vast ocean that stretched east from the Cape of Good Hope to Cape Horn. In that ocean the trade routes to and from Australia ran in the zone of latitude extending from 40 to 60 degrees south. That zone, if the whole globe is divided into parallel zones of latitude, stands out because ocean so predominates over land; about 97 per cent of the surface of that zone is covered by sea, whereas less than half of the corresponding zone in the northern hemisphere is covered by sea. The absence of big masses of land in that part of the southern hemisphere give the winds a consistency which they lack in other parts of the world. The winds blow from the west in every season of the year. Marines called the winds 'the brave west winds', and they came to call the seas beyond the parallel of 40 degrees south 'the Roaring Forties'.

Sailors who had spent a life at sea in the Baltic and

Mediterranean and North Sea or in the north Atlantic Ocean did not appreciate the strength and staying power of the westerlies in the chill waters of the southern hemisphere. They had no idea of the speeds which a ship could sustain for days in the Roaring Forties, and no idea of the fierceness of the waves which the wind whipped by its friction. When an Australian-bound ship passed the Cape of Good Hope she was followed for weeks by long ridges of water running high and fast, the crests of the waves white with froth, or a clear brilliant green, or gloomy grey. Matthew Maury, the American scholar of the oceans, likened the waves to the 'green hills of a rolling prairie capped with snow'. They were often majestic and beautiful, often terrifying. At times, if two ships were close together in these seas, they could be momentarily hidden from each other's sight when both were in the trough of the sea and a towering wave intervened. At times a ship running in a gale under a reefed foresail found herself in a hollow so deep that the wave running behind snatched away the wind and almost becalmed her; there was then a danger that the following wave would break right over her. If tidal waves are excluded, the waves in that ocean are probably the highest in the world.

The winds were not always strong and the waves were not always high on the route to Australia. The sea could be smooth, the wind quiet. The captain of the sailing ship *Otago*, in the Roaring Forties to the south of the Cape of Good Hope, noted on 13 November 1870, as no doubt other masters had recorded before him: 'Sea very smooth. Ship going 11–12 knots at Midnight and scarcely swinging the cabin lamps.' Or the wind could suddenly drop, as he recorded when he was hundreds of miles south of Australia on the same voyage: 'Soon after noon the wind died away suddenly and we had some tremendous seas break over us, one filling the main deck and the saloon', and even flooding the drawers where he kept his books. In his previous years at sea he had never seen such big unbroken waves. Many sailors on convict ships making for Australia got the same shock.

Icebergs drifted north from Antarctica across the Australian sea route. They were dazzling in the sun but dangerously hidden by mist or night. The icebergs in the southern hemisphere are said to be bigger and more numerous than in the northern, and some near Cape Horn were estimated to be a thousand feet high by sober, reputable masters of ships on the Australian run. On some days sailing ships passed more than a hundred icebergs in a day, white or opaque, dark green or brown, islands of ice on which the waves dashed. In the southern summer of 1854–5 an enormous island of ice was afloat in the relatively warm latitude of 40° south, just south-west of the island of Tristan da Cunha. Lying near the sea route to Australia it was observed by a score of ships. Some of those ships saw nothing but ice for days, because the mass of ice was about 60 miles long and shaped like a horse-shoe, and some emigrant ships sailed unknowingly into the icy bay, and one, the *Guiding Star*, did not sail out again. An iceberg did not have to be a towering mountain to sink a ship. Many ships were only saved from disaster by an alert sailor on look-out who saw waves breaking suspiciously in the same place or heard the strange noise of the sea washing over submerged ice.

For more than eighty years every ship that sailed to an Australian port from Europe had to cross that ocean and suffer its strong winds and mountainous waves and gliding icebergs. As most ships came to Australia by way of the Cape of Good Hope and returned by way of Cape Horn, at least 12,000 miles of their round voyage was in the Roaring Forties or Fifties. In that mighty sweep of ocean virtually no port of refuge existed between South Africa and Australia or between New Zealand and Chile. If a ship foundered in mid ocean and the crew took to the boats they had small chance of reaching land.

2

The convicts and their guards on the shores of Sydney Harbour in the first year soon became more conscious of their isolation. The argument sometimes heard in England — that the convict settlement should be as far as possible from England in order that few of the convicts should be able to return home when their sentences had expired — became a mockery. Distance not only prevented convicts from returning; it also threatened to starve them. The colony depended on food ships from England until the time should come when it could grow most of its own food. The months passed, and no sail was seen from the headlands guarding the harbour. All eyes turned to the earth, watching for the first shoots of wheat that had been hastily planted near the harbour. But the task of clearing rocks and trees from the soil was like digging out a mountain to catch a rabbit. The soil was light and sandy. Most of the grain which convicts had sown in the first season did not germinate, partly because of the poor soil and partly because much seed had been overheated or injured by weevils during its long stay in the holds of ships. Optimistically the governor ordered that ground be sown again with seed he had saved for the following years.

Livestock and poultry shipped to Sydney with the first fleet did not flourish, even though they were guarded as sacred. When five ewes and a lamb were killed by dogs, the loss was considered a public calamity. The colony's herdsman allowed the colony's only two bulls to stray away with four cows, and search parties failed to find them. Convicts fishing in the harbour invariably returned with miserly catches. As the settlement grew no fresh fruit and only a few baskets of vegetables, many men and women fell sick with scurvy. In June 1788 the *Supply* was sent four hundred miles across the Pacific to isolated Lord Howe Island in the hope of catching turtles to feed the invalids, and she reported that the turtles had disappeared. Everybody in the settlement got a weekly ration of food, but many had eaten it by the third or fourth day; being experienced thieves they then stole food or killed livestock. A few thieves were dropped from the gallows, but violent deaths, though common, did not sufficiently diminish the population to allow the food to go farther.

No ship from England arrived. Governor Phillip realized that his provision stores still held enough flour and pork to feed the colony for at least a year, but he could not be certain that a supply ship would arrive from England within a year. He still commanded two ships, of which the 20-gun *Sirius* was the larger, being more than 500 tons burden. He decided in September 1788 that the *Sirius* would have to sail to some distant port and buy supplies; and to increase her carrying capacity he removed eight of her twenty guns. These sailing preparations were nervously made, for Phillip knew that if the *Sirius* should be wrecked on her voyage and if English supply ships should not arrive, the colony would own only one small ship.

On 2 October 1788 the *Sirius*, commanded by a 50 year old Scot named John Hunter, sailed from Sydney. Twelve days after Hunter had begun a voyage that was to symbolize Australia's isolation, a few of his fellow Scots first tried an invention which was eventually to do more than anything to ease Australia's isolation. On 14 October the first British steam boat made its maiden voyage on a lake near Dumfries. Using Symington's patent engine and thrashing the water with two paddle wheels, it delighted spectators on the shores of the lake and a correspondent of the *Glasgow Mercury*: 'Its utility on canals, and all other navigations, points it out to be of the greatest advantage, not only to this island, but to many other nations of the world,' he prophesied. More than sixty years were to pass before a steam engine first challenged canvas on the ocean route to Australia, and even then that challenge was at first faint. It was faint because in the trade route between Australia and Europe the westerly wind was an uncanny ally of sailing ships, blowing them both to and from Australia. It was an odd coincidence that in the very month that the Scotsmen first harnessed steam to shipping in the northern hemisphere, Captain John Hunter began to prove how effectively winds could be harnessed on his side of the world.

Hunter's destination in 1788 was the Dutch port and garrison town of Cape Town, and he had been advised by

Governor Phillip, himself a mariner, to sail the *Sirius* around the southern tip of Tasmania and then west to the Cape of Good Hope, a passage of some 5000 miles. Hunter, however, had other ideas. He suspected the prevailing westerlies would make that course slow and arduous. He thought that if he sailed east instead of west he would have favourable winds the whole way, and though by sailing past Cape Horn he would add perhaps 4000 miles to his passage he would still save time. And of course time was precious. Moreover, he had only four months' provisions for his crew, and if he sailed the course the governor had suggested he might take so long in battling against adverse winds that his provisions would run out. Above all his crew was physically not strong, for not one man in the last year had tasted fresh meat and vegetables; Hunter believed that to sail with the wind behind him would be less demanding on his crew.

The *Sirius* sailed to the south of New Zealand and then east towards Cape Horn. In the high latitudes late in November her men saw icebergs, and the ship frequently had to change course to avoid collision. At one stage she 'passed through a lane or street, if it may be so called, of ice-islands', wrote Hunter, and several days passed before she reached the end of that dangerous street. In all she spent 28 days amongst the icebergs, and but for the shortness of the summer nights in those high latitudes Hunter thought the ship would have almost certainly been crushed by an iceberg gliding invisibly at night. Before they had passed beyond the ice the crew began to suffer from scurvy; one seaman died and many were sick. Nevertheless, despite ice and scurvy, the *Sirius* sailed quickly from Cape Horn to Cape of Good Hope, anchoring beneath Table Mountain on the first day of the new year or just three months after leaving Sydney.

Hunter bought wheat and barley to replace the seed that had been planted in Australia. He bought medical supplies because the first fleet had reached Australia with virtually no medicine except wine, and he filled all his remaining space with flour. After seven weeks in Cape

Town the *Sirius* continued her journey to the east, was nearly driven ashore by a gale of wind while rounding the south of Tasmania, and was lucky to reach Sydney. She had been away barely seven months, and in that time she had sailed around the world. She had been so battered in her last storm, however, that she had to spend months in the shallows of a quiet cove, lying on her side for repairs.

The provisions in *Sirius* were enough to feed the thousand people for four months. Nevertheless, the jubilation at her safe return was half-hearted. She had sailed in the Roaring Forties at the most favourable seasons of the year but had several times on the voyage been in much danger. And the news her captain heard in Cape Town suggested that no relief ships had left England. The *Sirius*'s remarkable voyage had merely sharpened the sense of isolation in the small colony.

A flagstaff was erected at the South Head of the harbour so that the arrival of the English supply ships could be signalled at once to the governor at Sydney. It was as vital as the radio masts of a modern country, but throughout 1789 it signalled no news. The colony celebrated its second anniversary with a ration of the Cape Town flour brought by the *Sirius*, the original English supply being exhausted. Voyages to Lord Howe Island produced only a few turtles for the soup pots. Farms and gardens near Sydney and inland at Parramatta were not fertile enough to satisfy the eye or stomach.

Norfolk Island, a thousand miles across the Pacific, had richer gardens and more fish and edible birds than Sydney, and it seemed that the chance of survival was stronger if one third of the people on the mainland were shipped to the sub-tropical island. In March 1790 the colony's only two ocean-going vessels were risked together in carrying 281 persons to the island and its dangerous bays. Their sailing was delayed in the hope of good news from the flagstaff overlooking the ocean, but they eventually had to sail.

The weekly ration of uncooked food allowed to adults who remained at Sydney was reduced to a diet of slow starvation. In the first year they had been given, once a week, seven pounds of flour, seven pounds of beef or four pounds of pork, three pints of pease, six ounces of butter, and half pound of rice. By the end of April 1790 the weekly ration no longer included pease or butter; the ration of flour and rice had almost been halved; and the halved ration of pork was so shrivelled that it was barely worth eating. Many convicts were no longer strong enough to hoe the soil vigorously, and the governor humanely accepted the fact. He also placed his own private supply of flour in the common store and lived on the same weekly ration of meat and flour as the convicts and marines.

The governor had decided to send the *Sirius* on another long voyage to buy supplies. With winter drawing near he realized that it would be unsafe to send the ship again around the stormy capes of South Africa, and so he ordered Captain Hunter to take her to China and buy salted provisions. Hunter first had to disembark the convicts and marines at Norfolk Island, return to Sydney to learn whether any supply ship had arrived from England in his absence, and then, if no ship had arrived, take the *Sirius* through the smoother tropical seas to Canton. The plan dissolved. At Norfolk Island on 19 March 1790, a fine day, *Sirius* was wrecked on a reef close to the shore.

There remained only one ship, the small brig *Supply*, and though she was too small to carry many tons of food she was sent to the Dutch port of Djakarta to buy food and also to charter a ship which would carry a larger tonnage of food. The two settlements of Sydney and Norfolk Island, separated by almost a thousand miles of ocean, now had no ship, very little food in the locked and guarded storehouses, and a few acres of planted seed which would not be fit for harvesting for half a year.

The Englishmen who had planned the convict colony in Australia had assumed that the soil was fertile. They had assumed that the fall of rain was reliable enough to grow crops, though the assumption was careless since no Englishmen had spent more than a few days in the neighbourhood of Botany Bay and Sydney. They had assumed

that a motley gang of convicts, many of whom had never
done hard physical work and all of whom had been confined on cramped ships for most of the previous year,
could be turned into skilled, energetic farmhands and
gardeners with a flick of the lash. But perhaps the most
serious error in the official blueprint for Australia was the
misjudging of distance. The deterioration of seed on the
long outward passage had been a major cause of the mean
harvests. And once harvests had failed, the colony was far
from any Dutch or English outpost which sold food and
livestock and European goods. That distance from a relief
port was much increased by ignorance of the prevailing
winds and adjacent coasts, and by the dearth of ships
under Governor Phillip's command.

It is impossible to tell how closely the colony in Australia approached the point of rebellion or retreat. As the
food stores were emptied and the daily ration shrank, the
chance of rebellion and riot must have increased. Discipline of the marines was possibly endangered even more
than that of the convicts, and one does not need a vivid
imagination to sense that the rebellion and murder that
took place off the western coast of Australia when the
Dutch ship *Batavia* ran aground in 1629 could have been
repeated at Sydney or Norfolk Island in 1790, so ending
the first chapter in Australian history.

3

While convicts in Australia crouched over iron pots on
wood fires and boiled their salted pork and rice, a few
heavily-laden supply ships were tossing on the long sealane from England. The first relief ship did not sail from
Plymouth until July 1789, two years and two months after
the first fleet had sailed. *Lady Juliana*, old and leaking, carried only a small stock of provisions, and twenty casks of
her precious flour were destroyed by sea water during the
passage. Her main freight was mouths to feed, for she
carried more than two hundred convicts, all women, and
many weak through old age. If they reached Australia,

they would eat more grain than they could grow.

A fast naval vessel of 44 guns, the *Guardian*, left England with more than a year's provisions for Australia and chests of medicine, casks of wine, blankets and clothes and tools, and a miniature fruit orchard. Although she had given two months start to *Lady Juliana* and her wild women, she passed them somewhere in the Atlantic, called briefly at Cape Town for a farmyard of livestock, and set out to cross the Indian Ocean. Two days before Christmas 1789, she was sailing the cold seas not far from Prince Edward Island when she hit an iceberg. To save the ship the master threw overboard most of her cargo and all her livestock. Five boats were launched and some were lost; but the ship herself was nursed back to Cape Town where she lay, a virtual wreck, when the *Lady Juliana* dawdled into port.

Slowly the *Lady Juliana* crossed the Indian Ocean to Australia, and reached Sydney Heads on the cold wintry afternoon of 3 June 1790. News of her arrival was signalled from the long-idle flagstaff, and passed from mouth to mouth until it reached the hungry men hoeing hungry ground at the most distant clearing. Within a few days her letters and newspapers from England and, above all, a little of her flour were ashore. The famine was over.

Famine was quickly followed by glut, and by the end of the same month four more English ships had entered the harbour. All the convict transports which arrived in June 1790 had lost, through scurvy or dysentery or fever, some 281 lives, of whom twenty were women and children. Nevertheless, the British population in Australia was doubled that month. For the following twelve months not one ship from England or any European country sailed into Sydney, and then a dozen came in what seemed quick succession, virtually doubling the population again. Utter isolation and sudden invasion was a continuing cycle in Sydney's early life.

The famine of 1790 was not repeated again, though the colony was on meagre rations many times during its first quarter of a century. Convicts' scythes cut a larger

acreage of maize and wheat and barley each year and
herds of sheep and cattle increased slowly, but the population was soaring. On 8 March 1794 the very last provisions were emptied from the stores, and six hours later an
English storeship was seen from the headland. The governor commented a trifle cynically that if the ship had not
arrived the settlers' only distress would have been to live
on bread alone, for a plentiful harvest was ready for reap-
ing. Eighteen months later Sydney nervously awaited
news of two provision ships because the government
stores held scarcely a pound of salted meat, and were
forced to hand out sugar and molasses instead of meat;
the colony admittedly had growing flocks and herds but if
they were decimated in the abattoirs, the expense of
importing new animals would be high. Late in 1796 the
governor complained again that he was short of every
kind of implement and tool. Carpenters barely had
enough nails to finish the buildings they were working on.
'We are nearly destitute of cloathing, either for old or
young,' he wrote, and even convicts seemed likely to be
scarce through the liberation of men whose sentences had
now expired. The chant of woe was sung for years, rising
and falling with the cycles of poor and rich harvests. Even
when the colony was just over a quarter century old,
drought so pushed up the local price of wheat in 1814 that
two shiploads of grain from Calcutta were hungrily awaited. Failure of crops seems to have shadowed the careers of
successive governors, but the cost and risk and delay in
importing alternative foodstuffs made every drought and
flood in Australian farmlands a double crisis.

The fragile lifeline across the ocean from Europe was
weakened when France and England went to war in 1793.
English merchant ships were fair prey for French men of
war and privateers, and moreover those ships sailing to
Australia depended almost entirely on foreign ports of call
— on Spain's Canary Islands, on Portugal's Madeira and
Rio de Janeiro, and on Holland's Cape of Good Hope —
for fresh water, meat, and repairs. Of the four ports only
Rio seems to have been a safe anchorage throughout the

long war. To Australia, however, the most vital of the four ports was Cape Town, for it was a half-way house and a valuable source of seed and flour and livestock for Sydney. Cape Town was captured by the British in September 1795 — 'a circumstance which is of particular consequence to this distant part of his Majesty's dominions', observed the governor at Sydney when he heard the news.

War increased the cost of insuring ships and cargoes bound for Australia in an age when marine insurance was always high. The practice of sending ships in armed convoys for the first part of the passage to distant ports probably delayed the sailing of some ships for Australia during the war, for they had to wait until the convoy was ready to sail. In the mid 1790s, as an effect of war, the British government sent few convicts to Australia, and so fewer ships were available to carry urgently wanted supplies and equipment to Sydney. But even if there had been no war in most of the era 1793–1815 Australia would have still had irregular shipping links with England. The annual consignments of convicts and cargoes for Australia were not large. As large ships were usually chartered for the long voyage to Australia, few ships were needed each year, and so the shipping link was irregular.

Ships sailing from Australia to England were even more irregular. Despatches and news from Australia were often twelve or eighteen months old before they reached England. Most ships that carried convicts and stores to Australia unloaded them as quickly as possible and then sailed to China or India under charter to the East India Company. The governor might hand a despatch to the master of the ship the day she sailed from Port Jackson — a despatch politely complaining to the home government of shortages of food or materials — and the despatch would go slowly to Canton in the master's cabin, maybe taking four months in the adverse monsoon. In Canton the ship might wait several months for the new season's teas to reach port, spend several more waiting her turn to be loaded, then sail sluggishly in the face of an unfavourable monsoon to the Indian Ocean and so home around the Cape of Good Hope. When the Secretary of State for the Home Department read the requests from Sydney, and if he agreed to fulfil them, he might wait months before a ship was ready to sail to Australia, and that ship might be a slow sailer. Thus more than two years could easily elapse from the time the governor at Sydney wrote his request until the day the cargo arrived.

If convict transports and storeships in the 1790s had frequently sailed direct from Sydney to Cape Horn and so home to London or Plymouth, they would have indirectly eased the sufferings of the new colony. But ships rarely sailed direct from Sydney to England because Sydney had no export cargoes to offer; the long homeward passage was thus profitless. Hence the common detour from Sydney to Asia in search of a cargo. Hence the complaint of Governor Hunter in April 1796 that Sydney officers (or emancipated convicts) who wished to return to England must endure the tedious and dangerous journey by way of Calcutta or Canton, paying in passage money more than they had earned during their entire stay in the colony and, if they were sick, possibly dying on the voyage. He suggested that every two or so years a ship should sail directly from Sydney to England. And long before his suggestion could receive a reply (for it was carried in a ship bound for England via India) he chartered the store ship *Britannia* and sent her direct to England with invalids and returning gentlemen.

Australia was so far from England, and communication between the two was so irregular, that Sydney slowly drifted into Asia's net of commerce. The English government, perturbed in the early 1790s at the enormous cost of supporting a convict colony that had been planned as a venture in frugality, decided that many items of food could be supplied more cheaply from Calcutta than from London. Australian governors, counting the dwindling barrels of flour and preserved meat in their stores, also realized the value of Asian ports. They had several advantages over Cape Town as supply bases. The wild weather on the route from Sydney to Cape Town deterred creaking ships from that route in winter, and instead they went in the smoother tropical seas to India or the East Indies. The practice of convict ships to sail from Australia to Asia on their homeward passage opened a newsline between Sydney and Asian ports, and news that Sydney lacked flour or spirits or meat spurred Indian shipowners to send cargoes to Australia on speculation. In contrast Cape Town had a slower and a less regular newsline from Australia. Being only a small town it had few merchants and shipowners who could ship a cargo to Sydney on speculation. Possessing few farms near the bay, it could not even supply grain and greens for the crews of visiting ships in the dry seasons of the late 1790s, and was forced to import Indian rice and English flour.

4

The busiest sea route from Sydney to the outside world in the first years went north towards New Guinea and the Solomon Islands; this fact has been so long forgotten that one's first impression, on realizing it, is incredulity. It was the main route from Australia to the Dutch East Indies and India and China, and for a time even a popular route for ships seeking the shortest passage back to England. But the northern route had its dangers and its obstacles.

'I must observe, once for all,' wrote Lieutenant Richard Bowen in London in June 1793, 'that nothing can be done in those seas without understanding and attending to the monsoons.' Any ship which sailed from Sydney to Asia at the start of the southern summer was butting her bow against a wall soon after reaching tropical seas. She met the scudding steamy clouds of the north-west monsoon and that adverse wind ruled from about December to March. On the other hand if the ship made for Java during the remainder of the year she was usually favoured by the south-east monsoon. That milder, dryer wind did not necessarily grant a speedy passage but it was a more favourable wind than the summer monsoon and certainly more favourable than the strong westerlies which held back ships that decided to make for Asia by sailing along the southern coast of Australia.

The first navigators who left Sydney for Asia were virtually blindfold. They had the charts of Carteret and Cook, but those charts covered only a small part of the route and advised them where not to go rather than where to go. Masters still had to find the best passages through uncharted islands. They had to avoid submerged rocks, face unknown winds and currents, and be alert for raiders or pirates near the narrow straits.

The tracks of the first ships sailing from Sydney to Java reveal their captains' gropings for a safe path. Their shortest path would have been through the narrow strait separating Australia and New Guinea, but they were frightened to use Torres Strait. Nor did they sail along the northern coast of New Guinea, the second shortest route. Instead they usually used some of the narrow straits between the Solomon Islands, went past the most northerly point of the Bismarck Archipelago, then went in a westerly direction roughly parallel to the coast of Dutch New Guinea, and finally made south along the Strait of Macassar, between Borneo and the Celebes. It was there that the convict transport *Friendship* was scuttled while on her circuitous way back to England in October 1788.

In 1790, when the colony had seen no new ship from England for more than two years, the small brig *Supply* was sent along the tedious route to Djakarta to buy meat and rice and flour for the starving colony. Meeting contrary winds, she was away six months and two days, and by the time she reached Sydney the second fleet had arrived from England and the colony's larder was full. Australia's first cargo of merchandise from its near north was followed a few months later by another cargo in the heavily laden Dutch ship *Waaksamheyd*, and on her return passage to Djakarta she took a short cut through the Bismarck Archipelago, using the narrow St George's Channel which the Englishman Philip Carteret had discovered between New Britain and New Ireland nearly a quarter of a century before. Despite the short cut she took 25 weeks — or almost half a year — between Port Jackson in Australia and her anchorage in Batavia Road, Java.

Each year a few more ships slowly followed the wide loop of a course from Sydney around the north of New Guinea to Java. It was a wasteful and costly course because both the start and end lay south of the equator, and yet the course actually crossed the equator. It not only went too far north, but in rounding the Solomon Islands also went too far east. If ships could only sail through Torres Strait, to the south of New Guinea, they would save 1500 to 2000 miles on a voyage to Java or, the more popular destination, Bengal. To every shipowner and mariner those miles could clip a month or more from the passage, and in seas ruled by the monsoons a month in time could save nine.

The gap between the most northerly point of Australia, Cape York, and the nearest point on the coast of New Guinea was nearly one hundred miles, and in theory the strait was wide enough for a drunken navigator to pass safely through. Unfortunately the longest reef in the world guarded the eastern approach to Torres Strait and thereby guarded Australia's short cut to the Indies. The Great Barrier Reef started near the southern coast of New Guinea and stretched in roughly a south-easterly direction across Torres Strait and down the eastern coast of Australia almost to the Tropic of Capricorn. An uneven rock wall, with calm water on one side and surf on the other, it ran some 1100 miles through tropical seas. Formed by the skeletons of tiny coral animals, beautiful in its colouring when exposed at low tide or when viewed through still water, it was exotic but treacherous. Navigators who wished to use Torres Strait had to find gaps in the Great Barrier Reef. While there were narrow gaps in the reef, some gaps concealed submerged rocks or were liable to swift tides and sudden gusts of monsoonal winds Even if a ship passed safely through one of the openings in the reef, she still had to make her way through a long stretch of Torres Strait where parts of the sea bed of sharp coral were dangerously close to the surface or visible in shoals and islands. In passing through Torres Strait a ship had to snake through a maze of submerged coral for about 150 miles, always with a look-out on the masthead, and always with a man sounding the depth of the water.

Torres, the Spaniard, had sailed through the strait that takes his name in 1606, a charmed passage which was seemingly forgotten by all but a few Spaniards for a century and a half. Captain James Cook, following the east coast of Australia in 1770, had sailed unknowingly for a thousand miles up the calm narrow inner passage that separated the Great Barrier Reef from the eastern coast of Australia. He almost lost his ship on a shoal inside the reef. After repairing her he sailed through a crack in the reef into the deep Pacific Ocean, followed the reef to the north, and then — in order to reach Torres Strait to the west — he had to find a gap in the reef again. The surf pummelled the reef, the waves rising like white mountains to mark its course, and the *Endeavour* made for a narrow opening only to find an ebb tide running against her; she would almost certainly have been smashed apart but for her men manning the boats and towing her back to deeper, smoother water. Cook tried another opening only a quarter of a mile wide, and quickly a flood tide swept the ship through the gap into the quieter waters near Torres Strait. He sailed west, a boat always out in front to signal the depth of the water, and safely passed through the strait. He had resolved the long disputed point on whether New Guinea and Australia were parted by sea. His voyage gave other navigators hope that a safer channel through Torres Strait could be found if ever ships wanted to go that way.

Ships wanted to go that way, once the British settlement was clinging to the eastern Australian coast and trade in the South Pacific was blossoming. Torres Strait seemed the ideal passage from Australia and the South Pacific to England in that short era before sailors realized that the everlasting westerlies in high latitudes made the Cape Horn route the swiftest. When Lieutenant

William Bligh was sent in 1787 in the *Bounty* to gather breadfruit trees in Tahiti, and to carry them to the West Indies sugar plantations as a potential food supply for the slaves, he lost his ship through mutiny early on the return voyage. He and eighteen of his crew were set adrift in an open boat, and they sailed the boat through Torres Strait to the European outpost in Timor.

It was not easy to sail a small boat across the Barrier Reef and through the strait; it was exceedingly hard to sail a large ship. His Majesty's frigate *Pandora*, sent from England to Tahiti in search of the mutineers, captured a band of them in 1791 and set sail for home by way of Torres Strait, but was wrecked near a gap in the Great Barrier Reef near the tip of north Queensland. With the loss of the ship which had been sent to capture the mutineers who had captured the breadfruit ship, the pursuit had to begin again. Bligh, with two more ships, gathered the breadfruit plant at Tahiti and steered for Torres Strait. Twenty days after his ships had entered the coral strait they reached open sea at the opposite end. It had been a nightmare passage through the short strait and had failed to yield a safe course for other ships to follow. And ironically the breadfruit, which had been obtained only after the loss of two ships and many men, was shunned by Negro slaves in Jamaica.

The attempt to transplant a fruit tree from the South Pacific to the Caribbean — from one island where food was plentiful to another island where food was plentiful — may have seemed odd to the settlers in eastern Australia who were so short of food. But if Torres Strait could be used for transhipping plants across the world, it could perhaps be used for shipping foodstuffs and cattle from India to Australia.

Nothing more clearly illustrated the importance of finding a quick route from Australia to India than the adventures of an Indian shipowner and master named William Bampton. Encouraged by the English government's suggestion that it might be cheaper for India rather than England to supply the convict settlement with many essential stores, he took supplies and livestock to Sydney purely as a speculation. In February 1793 his large Bombay ship *Shah Hormuzear* anchored in Sydney Cove, and he went ashore and haggled with the New South Wales Commissary or quartermaster. Eventually he sold his valuable cargo of barrels of beef, casks of flour, bags of wheat and rice, paddy, pollard, pease, sugar, a cask of cognac brandy, 3 pipes of Madeira wine, and a variety of useful oddments ranging from reams of Portuguese paper to copper sheets and twenty pairs of grindstones.

The colony was then so short of livestock that the governor persuaded Bampton to return to India for another cargo. He was to fit up stalls between decks and take on board a hundred large Indian horned cattle and three asses. He was also to carry — but he was firmly told not to carry them on the same deck as the cattle — 100 tonnes of pork or Irish-cured beef and 300 tons of rice or dhal. On his way to India he was to take supplies to the small settlement at Norfolk Island. Within ten months of leaving the island he was to complete the round voyage to India and Sydney Cove, wind and weather and dangers of the sea permitting.

Bampton had the highest incentive to make a fast passage to India, and he decided to find a way through Torres Strait. The London whaling ship *Chesterfield*, sailing for home, accompanied Bampton's ship much of the way, and from Norfolk Island the two ships sailed north-west in the winter sun towards the Great Barrier Reef, which straddled the entrance to Torres Strait. The monsoon was in their favour and the master of the *Shah Hormuzear* and many of the coloured seamen were experienced in the art of sailing in uncharted tropical seas. They were troubled, however, as all who had been before them, to find a passage through the deceptive shallows and the islands of the strait. They were 72 days in crossing the Great Barrier Reef and negotiating the strait, and being merchant ships, they resented lost time more than the government ships which had tested that route. They were four and a half months out from Sydney before they reached Timor, where Bampton lost more days by gathering a valuable cargo of sandalwood. By the time he reached Djakarta the adverse monsoon was blowing. Moreover he learned that war had recently broken out in Europe and that French privateers infested the straits of Sunda and Banca, through which he had to pass in order to reach any English colony. After a long delay in Djakarta the *Shah Hormuzear* was escorted through Sunda Strait by a Dutch frigate, and when eventually she crossed the Indian Ocean to Bombay only two months of the ten in her contract remained.

Captain Bampton was still keen to fulfil his valuable contract with the governor of the colony. As a sign of good faith or as an insurance against forfeiting the contract he sent an instalment of the promised rice and grain from Bombay in the *Fancy*. The little vessel rode the rollers of the Indian Ocean in the winter of 1794, and ran into Sydney harbour in the fourteenth month of the ten-month contract. Bampton meanwhile pottered about Bombay, waiting a chance to hire a large ship that could carry cattle safely through the boisterous seas to the south of Australia. Eventually he bought the *Endeavour*, of some 800 tons, a big ship by the standards of that age. She needed docking to prepare her for rough seas (so he said) and more months passed. He had to buy cattle for the stalls which were fitted between decks, and after buying some in Surat he decided (so he said) that he had to fatten them with hay and grain for another two months or they might die on the voyage. At last he sailed from Bombay on 19 March 1795 with 500 tons of grain in the hold and 132 cows, bullocks, and asses bellowing and braying between decks. Fortunately the passage from India to Australia was sometimes three times as fast as the passage in the opposite direction, and he reached Sydney on about the seventy-third day — almost the same number of days which he had spent in passing through the short Torres Strait. His ten-month contract was now entering its twenty-fifth month. Sydney had waited two years for the cattle and provisions it had urgently ordered from India, but it was accustomed to waiting.

The story should end here, but trade in Australian seas was always risky. Soon after the cattle had been landed in Sydney about twenty died. Nevertheless Bampton collected his bill of payment, probably the biggest hitherto drawn in Australia, and sailed away to New Zealand, where he lost his ship in Dusky Bay.

Most traffic from Sydney to India continued to flow in that slow, wide circle around New Guinea and its pendants of islands, while the traffic from India to Sydney completed the wide sweep rather more rapidly by crossing the Indian Ocean and catching the favourable westerlies that blew to the south of Australia and Tasmania. The circular course was prescribed by the prevailing winds, but the radius of the circular course was exasperatingly enlarged by the eastern coastline of Australia, which in effect was half as long again as it is today. The strait between the north of Australia and New Guinea, as Bampton had observed, was a very crooked strait, too slow and tricky for ships to attempt. And the equally short strait between the south of Australia and the island of Tasmania was still undiscovered. Thus a mass of land stretched like a long wall from the north-west point of Dutch New Guinea down to the spray of the southern capes of Tasmania, in latitude 44° south. It stretched from the equator half-way to the south pole. It had only two narrow breaks, one untamed and the other unknown.

After Bampton and his *Shah Hormuzear* in 1793 had averaged little more than two miles a day in passing through the strait, the route and its hidden shoals was avoided for nearly a decade. At last a quicker and safer passage through Torres Strait was sought by Matthew Flinders, a young English naval captain who had sailed with Bligh for breadfruit. In 1802, Flinders approached Torres Strait from the Pacific, crossing the Great Barrier Reef. Though his ship *Investigator* was rotten and though he anchored every night and sailed cautiously each day, he went through the strait in five days.

In the following year Flinders planned to return to England, and on his way he decided to try the northern strait again in the hope of popularizing it as a corridor between the Pacific and Indian oceans. He left Sydney in H.M.S. *Porpoise*, accompanied by the London ships *Cato* and *Bridgewater*, and the three ships sailed together up the eastern coast of Australia. On the night of 17 August 1803, just when they were entering tropical waters, *Porpoise* and *Cato* saw breakers ahead. The waves were breaking on a coral reef far from land, and the two ships were onto the reef before they had time to veer around. Ninety-four men managed to reach a sandbank in mid-ocean. Whether it was a permanent or shifting bar of sand they did not know, but as the other ship had avoided the reef and was still visible they expected to be rescued at any hour. To their anger, however, the *Bridgewater*, instead of rescuing them, resumed her voyage. Flinders and thirteen other men bravely launched a little cutter saved from the wrecks and sailed 700 miles south to Sydney to break the news.

In Sydney, where ships were so often scarce, the only available vessel on which Flinders could return to England was the fragile home-made schooner *Cumberland* of 29 tons. Flinders sailed her through Torres Strait in just over three days, and half of his time in the strait was spent either at anchor, or in trips ashore or detours to survey other parts of the strait. In Australia's early history the finding of a navigable stretch of water was often more important than the finding of an immense area of cultivable land; and Flinders' charts of Torres Strait were of immense value to the colony. Unfortunately the voyage which did so much to ease Australia's isolation ended in isolation and misery for the voyager. Flinders called at Dutch Timor, then sailed for the Cape of Good Hope, but the schooner was leaking and the pumps were badly worn so he called at the sweating French colony of Mauritius, east of Madagascar. He did not realize that, six months before he sailed from Sydney, Britain and France had renewed their war. In Mauritius he was clapped into gaol.

The Great Barrier Reef and the strait which it guarded ceased to be a wall blocking Australian commerce. The charts of Flinders guided scores of ships through the dangerous strait, and other navigators found alternative courses. Captain Cripps, of the brig *Cyclops*, sailing from Sydney to Calcutta in 1812, opened a completely new route through sheltered water that ran north for a thousand miles between the Queensland coast and the Great Barrier Reef; ships on that Inner Passage did not have to cross the great reef, were in calm water the entire distance, but could not sail at night. Phillip Parker King, native of Norfolk Island, charted that passage with wonderful accuracy, but most sailing ships bound for India avoided it. They carried only small crews and therefore lacked the manpower to haul up the anchors every morning from very deep water. Only in the last third of the nineteenth century, when gold and sugar ports flourished on the Queensland coast and steamships were replacing sailing ships, did the Inner Passage become the most popular approach to Torres Strait.

Fuzzy-haired natives paddling canoes in Torres Straits would have noticed that nearly all ships passing through in the first decades were westward-bound. Most made for Calcutta or Madras or Bombay, often calling at Djakarta on the way except during some stages of the Napoleonic Wars. There were some years early in the nineteenth century when Australia seemed to be a satellite of India as well as a colony of England. In 1817, for example, probably two of every three ships which left Sydney for foreign ports went to Java or India; those ships were usually in ballast and usually passed through Torres Strait. In the same year three of every ten ships that reached Sydney from overseas ports came from Calcutta, though that was an exceptionally busy year for Indian cargoes.

Cargoes from Bengal fed and equipped the colony and also gave it a hangover. Bengal livestock multiplied on scores of farms near Sydney and Bengal oxen pulled carts of colonial produce to port. Bengal clothes and cottons were widely worn. In many months Bengal rice and flour and salted meat was the staple diet of convicts and marines and free settlers in Australia. Bengal rum, said to be stronger than Jamaican rum and not so sweet, was Australia's first national drink and at times a form of national currency. Out of the depths of every ship from India was carried a procession of rum casks. 'And though every possible measure was adopted to prevent all that arrived from being landed, yet, such was the avidity with which it was sought after, that, if not permitted, it was generally got on shore clandestinely; and very few ships carried back any of what they had brought,' wrote David Collins, the judge-advocate of the colony until 1796. 'To this source,' he added, 'might be traced all the crimes that disgraced, and all the diseases that injured the colony.'

Some London merchants complained of India's luck in Australian ports. William Wilson, a merchant in Fenchurch Street, told the home government that perhaps not five merchants in Britain had been made the richer by Australian trade, whereas many Englishmen living in India were growing rich by sending to Sydney ships 'laden half with Rice and half bad Spirits'. India's success might have been annoying but was not surprising. India was much closer to Australia than was England or any vigorous British possession. The passage from India to Australia was usually wind-blessed and fast. As so many ships leaving Australia went first to India in search of a cargo, Indian ports received early news of Australia's famines. On the other hand English merchants were penalized by distance and by the mesh of English commercial laws. English shipowners trading to Australia before 1813 had to apply for a licence from the East India Company, whereas Calcutta shipowners could in practice trade freely; moreover an English ship sailing to Australia before 1820 had to be of more than 350 tons burden, whereas most Indian ships trading with Australia were much smaller.

While many ships sailed from Sydney through Torres Strait to India, others sailed by a different route to China to take on cargoes of tea for the English market. In Sydney's first twenty years many big ships that carried out the convicts and stores from England were under charter to the East India Company, and as soon as they had discharged their freight they sailed for Canton. In many years more ships left Sydney for Canton than for London. Some commercial prophets of the 1780s had argued that an English sea base in eastern Australia would be valuable because it would lie near an alternative route from England to China; and to later writers of history these prophets seem deranged. Australia, they argue, was too remote to be on any trade route to China. There is evidence, however, that some English ships with no cargo for Sydney preferred to round Australia on their way to China. For in the years 1803–5, when a French squadron based on Mauritius was cruising in the Indian Ocean and menacing the traditional route from Europe to China, the new route past eastern Australia to China was safer though three or four thousand miles longer.

On a summer's evening late in 1804 the people on Norfolk Island were alarmed to see the sails of nine large ships appear in the south-west and, favoured by a heavy gale, come closer to the island. They were so isolated and starved for news that the sight of a sail was exciting but the sight of nine sails must have been bewildering. The commandant, knowing that France and England were again at war, concluded that an enemy fleet was approaching. He gave orders that a large group of Irishmen, the troublemakers on the island, should be locked in the gaol so that they could not aid the enemy. Darkness fell, and during the night the commandant prepared his feeble defences. Next morning the fleet could be seen near Cascade Bay, so troops and a big gun were hurried to that side of the island. At seven in the morning the fleet hoisted English colours and fired a gun. The island's commandant, possessing no boat in that remote bay, signalled for the fleet to hoist a boat and send it ashore. For five hours no boat was hoisted, and the commandant became suspicious that the English colours were a decoy. Eventually about midday a boat was seen to be lowered, an officer from the fleet was rowed ashore, and he ended the suspense by reporting that the fleet was English, consisting of eight East Indiamen under convoy of the ship *L'Atheniene* of 64 guns. They were bound for China; and since leaving England had touched only at Rio de Janeiro, had passed far to the south of the Cape of Good Hope, and had cut through Bass Strait. They reported that the other ship in the convoy had disappeared from sight somewhere in the southern Indian Ocean. However, she was merely lagging, and reached Norfolk Island three days after the China convoy had sailed away.

Ships sailing from Sydney or Norfolk Island to China had to weave through the string of islands that were strewn across the Pacific to the east of New Guinea; and the prevailing winds favoured a different course for each season of the year. The shortest course in distance passed close to New Guinea and slipped between New Ireland and the Solomons; the longest course passed to the east of New Caledonia and the New Hebrides, a thousand miles to the east of the short course; and there were passages between those two extremes. Once clear of the barrier of tropical islands ships veered to the north-west, crossed the equator, and sailed in open sea to the north of the Philippines and so to Canton.

Some United States ships making for Canton also favoured that route when they found they could make high profits by filling the needs of the remote settlement at Sydney. The American brigantine *Philadelphia*, hearing at Cape Town that Sydney could be a profitable market, called at Port Jackson on her way to China on 1 November 1792. To the commissariat she sold 569 barrels of American-cured beef and 27 barrels of pitch and tar, and to thirsty officers at the settlement she sold much of her cargo of rum, gin, wine and tobacco. In the same hot summer, soon after the brigantine had sailed, another Yankee ship emerged from the haze blanketing the ocean outside Sydney Heads. She was the *Hope*, of Rhode Island, one of the first half-dozen American ships ever to trade with China. In Sydney she wanted wood and fresh water — wood for the galley fires and water for drinking. It was understandable that she wanted supplies, as she appears to have come west in the face of adverse winds from the lonely Falkland Islands and Cape Horn. At the same time there was a whiff of suspicion that she really had called on Christmas Eve to sell the season's greetings, and so make money on an otherwise profitless voyage to China. Her Yankee master produced a storehouse of provisions — American beef and pork and flour and of course alcohol, much of which he sold to the commissariat.

In bays and inlets on the New England coast were many Yankee skippers who would carry cargo to any port in the world, and carry it cheaply because their American-built ships were strong but cheap. They knew that it was illegal to sell certain cargoes in Sydney and that the governor might therefore refuse to admit their provisions, in which event they had no other market within thousands of miles. They gambled that Sydney would be thirsty or hungry and therefore ignore the law. Thus Yankee enterprise won a good share of that Australian market which a tangled mesh of British laws had tried to preserve for British shipping.

In that long U-shaped run from New England around the Cape of Good Hope and Tasmania to China, the Australian coast became an attractive stopover for some American ships. On the outward run to China ships were lightly laden but if they could sell a cargo in Sydney the voyage was far more lucrative. Moreover once the colonies of fur seals on the rocky islands of Bass Strait were found, American ships could send a crew ashore to club and skin seals and then carry the seal skins to China where they at first drew attractive prices. The fast ship *Semiramis* was probably the first to combine the lucrative trades by selling a cargo in Sydney, hunting seals in Bass Strait, carrying sealskins to China and carrying home a cargo of China tea; and she commenced that voyage by making her run from Rhode Island to Sydney in the astonishing time of 101 days — or only about one-half of the time which some ships took for the voyage from a north Atlantic port. At least 22 American ships bound for China called at Sydney on their way in the thirteen years 1792 to 1805; and other ships probably followed the same route to China without coming close to the Australian coast. In the wake of Yankee ships bound for China came the Boston and Nantucket whalers which sometimes called at Sydney or Hobart to fetch wood and water or to sell provisions and often spent months hunting whales or seals in Australian waters in the course of meandering, scurvy voyages in the South Seas.

The huddle of buildings near the waterfront at Sydney was visited from the early 1790s by occasional ships using an even longer and lonelier route. The fur trade on the Pacific coast of North America was attracting adventurers, and ships from England and New England called at Sydney on their long diagonal course across the Pacific to Nootka Sound and the coast near the mouth of the Columbia River. A few Russian ships also called at Sydney on their passage from the Baltic Sea to the Bering Sea and the cold peninsula of Kamchatka which jutted south from Asia towards Japan. In Sydney one winter's day in 1807, when no ship had arrived from Europe for ten weeks, the Russian armed storeship *Neva* quietly appeared. She was carrying stores from Kronstadt, near St Petersburg, to the Russian colony on Kodiak Island, off the coast of Alaska. It may seem strange that a ship passing from one part of Russia to another should sail far south of the equator and call at Sydney on her way. But the alternative route from Europe to the north Pacific went even farther south, around Cape Horn, and moreover missed the westerlies that favoured the *Neva's* chosen route.

Tropical islands astride the new trade route from Sydney to China or the cold north Pacific carried scattered groves of sandalwood, and ships on those routes may have discovered some of the sandalwood. The scented timber was as precious to China as Chinese tea was to Europe, and growing close to a trade route to China it soon be-

came a useful item of trade. Sydney was the nearest port
to the sandalwood islands and in the first decade of the
1800s became a base for the trade. The Fiji Islands, two
thousand miles north-east of Sydney, were the early mecca of American, British, and a few Sydney sandalwood
traders. They sailed their vessels through treacherous
gaps in coral reefs, risked shipwreck in sudden cyclones,
and made fortunes if they were lucky and shrewd. Natives
were persuaded to cut sandalwood in shaded ravines between the mountains, carry it to the blue sea, and barter it
to sea captains in return for hardware, iron, trinkets, and
whales' teeth. The crooked sticks of sandalwood could
adequately reward the risks of the shippers and the expensive freight to market, for they were often worth more
than £50 a ton in Sydney and perhaps twice as much in
China where the fragrant wood was carved ornamentally
or burned ritually in temples and joss houses. The rents of
a few church pews in Boston and Providence and north
Atlantic ports were probably paid by sandalwood traders
and shippers, who had grown wealthy by supplying in-
cense to the heathen for whom they prayed.

Sydney was not only a port of call on side routes from
Europe to Asia and the Pacific but a base for many trades
in the islands of the South Pacific. Ships came in with
sticks of sandalwood from many islands stretching from
New Caledonia to Fiji, with barrels of salt pork from
Tahiti, with bêche-de-mer and pearl shell bartered on
lazy beaches, ships' spars cut in forests on the water's
edge in New Zealand, sealskins from the Bass Strait
islands, and whalebone and sperm oil from a vast stretch
of the South Pacific and Southern Ocean. All except the
pork, which was apportioned out in the weekly rations to
convicts and garrison, were transhipped from Sydney to
foreign markets.

So Sydney was becoming the seabase which some of the
pamphleteers of the 1780s prophesied. At the same time it
could no longer be envisaged as a gaol which was half-
way to Hades, a limbo from which no convict could return. Sydney was becoming a busy port at the entrance to

(ANARE photo: R. J. H. Thompson)

Wild seas in the Roaring Forties, for long Australia's only sealane to Europe.

The clipper *Red Jacket* meets ice near Cape Horn, 1854.

(ANARE photo: A. Campbell-Drury)

Antarctic supply ships, such as *Nella Dan*, are amongst the few ships now braving seas once favoured by clippers.

(*Australasian Sketcher*, 1881)

Gloomy sketches in the weeklies were common in the era when most
Australians had experienced the Southern Ocean's fury.

Pamir, one of the last windjammers on the Australian route.

an unwalled gaol. It was in effect no more remote than Newgate prison because many convicts were able to steal, or stow away in, some of the ships that called.

Hobart was Australia's second largest port by 1820 and, like Sydney, the gate of an open gaol. Its harbourmaster could recall four vessels which had been captured by convicts and sailed away in the previous dozen years. Convicts boarded the *Argo* and *Unity* and sailed them out of Hobart, and were not heard of again. the schooner *Young Lachlan* was captured by convicts and wrecked near Java, and a stolen schooner-rigged boat was recaptured in Bass Strait. Many other convicts who tried to seize ships were either stalled by informers or overpowered. Sydney, a larger port, had had much more experience of convicts who satisfied their love of tall ships and the open sea.

Small ships were moored in an isolated part of the estuary at Hobart, and to prevent seizure by convicts their sails were unbent and their rudders removed. Larger vessels in the harbour, especially Indian brigs manned by Lascars, were given a military guard at night if the harbourmaster thought their officers were not alert. Ships could not sail from port in the hours of darkness, except with official permission.

Convicts who were not ambitious to become shipowners could still stow away in outgoing ships. Masters of visiting ships therefore had to give five days' notice before they sailed from Hobart, and the merchant of the town who acted as agent for the ship forfeited the large sum of £800 if the ship sailed away with convicts or unauthorized passengers. When a ship was about to sail, all government-employed convicts in the port were mustered to ensure that no convicts had boarded the ship; as a double precaution, constables searched the ship two or three times and then boarded her for part of the passage down the estuary. And yet all the vigilance of a pocket Police State could not prevent some convicts from sailing to England or Asia. In 1818 officials in Hobart heard a whisper that men planned to stow away in the ship *Frederick*, which had loaded cattle for Mauritius and was busy loading hay as stockfeed for the voyage. Officials went to the ship, searched her, and found no stowaways. Still suspicious, they spent six days examining and prodding every bundle of hay that was rowed to the anchored ship. They finally allowed her to sail — with two convicts and a civilian debtor hidden somewhere aboard.

And yet Australia contrived to fulfil its dual role of gaol and port of call; in fact its place on the trade routes aided rather than weakened the penal settlement. At first Australia had been so cut off from its source of supply in England that its role as a convict settlement was probably imperilled. The cost of maintaining the convict settlement was unexpectedly high. Instead of the envisaged garden of Eden that was to supply all its own needs and flax for sailcloth as well, Australia cost Britain the huge sum of £1,000,000 in the first twelve years, and at the end of that time its population was only 5000. But this cost would have been far higher if Australia had not been on a deviation route to China for American as well as English ships, and if it had not been succoured from India. Without these aids the supplies from England to Australia would have been so erratic and expensive that the colony could have been stunted or have even ceased to be a receptacle for new convicts.

Australia's place on new trade routes was decisive in its early history. It aided the convict settlement. It prompted the rise of a free group of Australian traders who did not depend heavily on the favours of governors, who were alert for new ways of making money, and who were eventually to hasten Australia's transition from a gaol to a series of free colonies. One other effect of the passing trade routes was the rise of a ring of new outposts at scattered points of the Australian coast; and those outposts were to give Britain possession of nearly all areas of Australia that were worth possessing.

4　Limpet Ports

In 1800 Britain had occupied only two patches of Australian soil. One patch stretched about thirty miles from Sydney towards the near mountains that were blue in the west; the other settled patch was Norfolk Island, far out in the Pacific. The coast was so lonely in 1800 that anyone circumnavigating the continent would have seen, after sailing from Sydney, only smoke rising from Aboriginals' fires in remote places, smoke rising from cauldrons on the north coast where visiting fishermen from the Celebes preserved trepang in summer, and perhaps the huts or tents of a temporary camp of sealers on rocky headlands in the south-east. But anyone who made the same long voyage thirty years later would have come across isolated ports, flourishing or gasping or dead. The coast by then resembled a necklace with much lace and a few beads haphazardly arranged. Some ports were only one or two hundred miles apart but others were some 1500 miles apart.

New British camps were not placed on the shores of Australian harbours unless there was a strong incentive. One incentive came from the needs of the convict system. Just as Britain had found it convenient to exile criminals to Sydney, so Sydney eventually needed places to which it could exile criminals who had committed a second crime while serving their original sentence. Such places had to be on the coast, so that they could easily receive supplies and soldiers and criminals from Sydney; such places had to be isolated from Sydney by wide rivers and rugged country so that convicts could not escape overland back to Sydney; and yet the places could not be so isolated that the cost of sea communication with Sydney was too high. Thus the new penitentiary ports, opened between 1803 and 1824, were all on the coast, and not too far from Sydney.

The first of these new ports was at Newcastle, at the mouth of the Hunter River, a hundred miles north of Sydney. Today a haze of smoke veils a city of nearly a quarter million people and one of the largest steelworks in any British country, but early in the nineteenth century Newcastle was a hated camp where some of the most intractable convicts hewed coal, burned lime, cut cedar trees and continually plotted escape. Further north, where a wide, brown river emptied into the ocean at Port Macquarie, another small band of convicts hoed fertile soil on the fringe of a forest that served as sentry. Farther north, in sub-tropical heat, another convict camp was pitched in 1824 on the banks of a wide river; and that convict camp was the genesis of Brisbane, a city of a million people. Eventually the imaginary walls of these prisons toppled, and free settlers moved in with flocks or farm implements.

Norfolk Island superseded these outlying gaols. It had already failed as a nursery for naval stores and as a granary, and its failure was aggravated by its lack of a safe harbour. In Sydney successive governors had to pay exorbitant sums to induce shipowners to carry supplies to and from the island. It was as far from Sydney as the border of Soviet Russia is from London, and that distance was lengthened by the difficulty of sea communication. From 1813 to 1825 the island was deserted except for the abandoned pigs and goats which foraged amongst waving stretches of flax and stately island pines. But its isolation was at last recognized as its asset and it was re-settled as 'a great Hulk or Penitentiary': an antidote for a transportation system which, England feared, was losing its terrors.

The new settlements on Norfolk Island and on a relatively short strip of the adjacent but distant Australian mainland were the result of the increasing flow of convicts to Sydney. They were mere outliers of Sydney, sinks that drained its overflow. They were settled because Sydney needed its own remote gaols. They did not reflect a deliberate attempt to occupy and colonise as much of the Australian coastline as possible. It was the official policy to restrict the Australian colony to the fringe of a narrow strip of east coast, and though that policy was ignored in the 1820s by settlers who wandered from Sydney far inland with their sheep and cattle, the area of eastern Australia which was occupied at the end of the 1820s was relatively small.

It was not only the main convict zone on the east coast which extended its shadow. A new line of more isolated settlements were made on the north, south, and west coasts. Their creation is usually ascribed to fear of the French, for most of these outposts were hurriedly formed at times when France showed some interest in Australia. But why did Britain fear rumours that France had designs on parts of Australia? Why did it jump nervously when a French tricolour appeared on the horizon in times of European peace? The common assumption is that Britain wanted to possess the whole continent and especially the favoured regions and their natural resources. The new outposts were supposedly designed to guard the land and proclaim British possession.

One may suggest that Britain was more interested in controlling Australian seas than Australian land. It was more interested in maritime strategy than in the unknown, inaccessible wealth of the Australian interior. All the new outposts made away from the east coast in the first forty years were at strategic points of important sea routes. These military outposts were designed as springboards for guarding or promoting a trade route, not beachheads for guarding or settling the interior. Australia was like a huge barren rock in an ocean. Its most valuable territory were those projecting headlands where passing whales could rub off the barnacles.

The *Sydney Cove* sailed from Calcutta in 1796, one of the fleet of Indian ships which served as Asian and South Sea hawkers. She was carrying provisions and livestock and thousands of gallons of Bengal rum in the hope of earning a quick fortune in Sydney. Sailing to Australia by the customary southern route she met heavy seas south of Tasmania in February 1797 and began to leak. Hauling up to the north on the final leg of the passage she took in more water than her Lascars could pump. Her master made for land and succeeded in beaching her on Preservation Isand, to the north-east of Tasmania. The ship was a wreck. The survivors were 400 sea miles from Sydney and out of sight of a sea route on which few ships sailed.

Some of the ship's company set out in a longboat for Sydney. They crossed rough water to the Australian coast, followed it north, and were wrecked. A remnant straggled on foot up the coast, and some were picked up by a fishing boat and taken to Sydney. Ships and boats sent south to rescue the survivors and salvage cargo found that Preservation Island did not belie its name. There, for probably the first time, was observed a strange small animal that shuffled from its burrow like a bear: a marsupial wombat, which was promptly preserved in spirits and sent to the Literary and Philosophical Society of Newcastle-upon-Tyne for scientists to marvel at. On the island's beaches were also seen colonies of seals with thick fur, and soon traders were shipping tens of thousands of sealskins to Canton and London. But the island gave hint of a more valuable discovery. The island in fact lay on the eastern fringe of the strait separating Australia from Van Diemen's Land (Tasmania), and when the master of the wrecked ship reached Sydney he apparently reported that the strong south westerly swell and the tides and currents suggested that the island was in a channel linking the Pacific and the southern Indian Ocean. On 1 August 1797 John Hunter, governor of New South Wales, wrote to the English man of science, Joseph Banks, that it seemed certain that the strait existed. The vital observation had eluded Tasman the Dutchman, Cook the Englishman, and Bruny D'Entrecasteaux the Frenchman. It had eluded dozens of sea captains who had sailed close to the narrow strait on their way to Sydney in the previous decade. And it has since eluded dozens of historians who attribute the finding of the strait to two later explorers, Bass and Flinders.

Sydney lacked small coastal vessels — not surprisingly since they could so easily be captured, manned, and sailed away by convicts — and so there was some delay before the new strait could be explored. At the end of 1797 a young surgeon, George Bass, went south from Sydney in a 28 feet whaleboat with six strong oarsmen and ventured into the strait. It was a rough stretch of water, and Bass could not get more than half way through. A stouter vessel was provided in the following summer, a 25-ton sloop, built at Norfolk Island of the pine which at one time promised to equip the Indian fleet with masts. With a fixed bowsprit and one mast she was superior to the six-oared whaleboat. Her commander, Matthew Flinders, the 24-year-old naval lieutenant who was soon to conquer Torres Strait, was a sharp navigator, and he safely sailed through Bass Strait. He proved irrefutably that it was a strait, was navigable to the largest ships, and was some 140 miles in length from Cape Otway in the west to Wilson's Promontory in the east.

A long line of writers have praised his contribution to geographical knowledge. What is often overlooked is the practical value of the discovery. He and Bass had found a new seaway at a crucial point of the route from Europe and India to Sydney. It was not only safer and less boisterous for ships but saved up to 700 miles. The strategic value of that strait at the start of the nineteenth century was so obvious that it did not need stressing in contemporary records. Hence those who read the records more than a century later perhaps underestimated the role of maritime strategy in explaining vital events that soon followed the opening of the strait.

Bass Strait was still only sketchily charted. The islands that straddled the strait at both entrances waited for ships indiscreetly sailing in darkness or fog. A few ships, however, were using the strait, sailing-ships which landed parties on the rocks to catch and skin seals and sea elephants, or ships from India and England and the Cape of Good Hope cutting through to Sydney. The new governor of New South Wales, Philip Gidley King, noted in 1803 that overseas ships had 'saved much time, bad weather, and most probably lives by that Passage in preference to going to the Southward of Van Dieman's Land'. Late in 1804 at least ten ships passed through the strait on their passage from London to Canton for tea, the grandest fleet yet seen on the Australian coast.

As a naval officer, King was aware that Bass Strait could easily become the lifeline of the colony and that, in foreign possession, the lifeline could be endangered. The only narrow strait on the entire route from Europe to Australia, it would be an ideal base for enemy raiders and privateers in war, or it could provide a European colonial power with a useful refreshment port and trading base in peace. To the British settlement in Australia that southern strait was strategically much more important than the northern or Torres Strait, because ships using the Torres Strait would be sailing away from Australia in ballast whereas most of the ships that used Bass Strait would be heavily laden with cargoes for Sydney. The only escape from the trap, if France should by chance establish a port in or near Bass Strait, was the alternative route around the south of Tasmania. But even that route could be attacked from a base in Bass Strait. To experienced naval officers, the strait must have seemed the most vulnerable position in the South Pacific.

These fears were aroused in 1802 when two French ships lazily explored Tasmanian waters and Bass Strait. Although Britain and France were at war when Commodore Baudin's ships had sailed from Havre in October 1800, the British Admiralty had given the Frenchmen a passport of immunity because their main aim was scientific discovery. Officials in Sydney then had no cause to fear armed attack from the Frenchmen but they could still be nervous when they heard how minutely the French-men were studying Tasmanian bays and estuaries. Gov-ernor King would have probably worried little if the Frenchmen had charted a less strategic stretch of Aus-tralian coast. And after June 1802, when he heard belated news that France and England had signed a truce, he might not have been nervous if the French had actually planted a colony on some remote part of the long Aus-tralian coastline. But Bass Strait was different; while the Frenchmen were there it was almost as if they were chart-ing the entrance to Sydney; moreover the strait had valuable sealing grounds.

The crew and scientists on the French ships *Géographe* and *Naturaliste* were suffering from scurvy and decided to return to Sydney. When the 30-gun corvette *Géographe* reached the Sydney heads she had so few men capable of working on deck that she only reached the harbour with the help of some English sailors who had rowed out to aid her. In Sydney the Frenchmen were generously fed and the sick were nursed and the officers entertained, but Governor King was quietly suspicious of their intentions. Soon after their departure from Sydney on 18 November 1802, he was told that some French officers during their stay had mentioned that they would fix a site for a French settlement in south-eastern Tasmania. King decided to forestall them. Five days after the two French ships had left Sydney the tiny schooner *Cumberland* followed their route and eventually found them anchored in a bay of King Island, at the western end of Bass Strait. The *Cumberland* had only seventeen men, but they marched along the shore, hoisted the English flag on a tree near the beach, and waited on the island until the French com-pleted their scientific observations and sailed away.

Governor King understood that the place most likely to be selected as a French seabase and port of refreshment was in the south-east corner of Tasmania. He sent an expedition there in June 1803 but winter storms drove it back. Three months later the first Tasmanian settlement was planted on the Derwent estuary, a safe and charming stretch of water banked by wooded hills and towered over by a table mountain that was spread with snow in winter. The commandant and his horse, and 49 soldiers, convicts, and free settlers, camped near what is now the city of Hobart.

Meanwhile two ships from England were approaching Bass Strait, where they had orders to form two bases. Coming in answer to worried despatches which Governor King had written to London when the French ships were surveying the coast, they entered the narrow throat of Port Phillip Bay just one month after the settlement had been made at Hobart. Three hundred convicts, their military guards, and eighteen free settlers and their families landed at Sorrento, eight miles inside the harbour. It was a sterile, sandy neck of land, ideal for a holiday resort, but they were not on holiday.

Port Phillip Bay was the safest and most capacious harbour on the shores of Bass Strait. However, the commander of the new outpost, Lieutenant Colonel David Collins, grumbled continually. The puzzle is why he did not move from the dry sandy entrance of the bay to that more attractive site thirty miles up the bay, where Melbourne now stands and where a small town could have easily fed itself with grain and meat. The likely answer to this riddle is suggested by the map. The northern or Australian shore of Bass Strait was shaped like an arc, and Port Phillip Bay was the point of that arc most distant from the routes through the strait. Collins therefore may have argued that if he placed his convict camp 'thirty miles to the north of the mouth of the bay, he would be taking up a position that was too far from the sealane to be strategic. He also implied that the entrance to Port Phillip Bay was too temperamental to justify a colony anywhere inside; he saw fast tides rippling through the narrow entrance and he knew that, when the wind blew from the wrong quarter, ships might wait days before they could safely sail through the jaws of the bay.

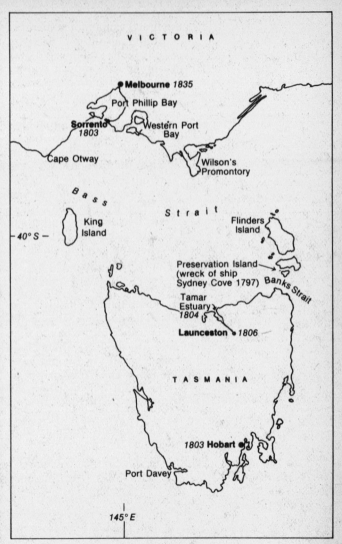

The Strategy of Bass Strait.

His conclusion that a small convict settlement and seabase could not flourish on a site which was later to prove adequate for one of the large cities of the world can probably only be explained by probing Collins the man and his mind. He had spent more than eight years in Sydney before returning to England in 1796, and he remembered its isolation and famines; hence his inflated concern that those experiences might be repeated if he placed his settlement on a coast where the soil was not rich and the port did not entice passing ships. It is reasonable to surmise that if Collins had been a different kind of man, or if another officer had led the expedition, a site would have been chosen on Port Phillip Bay. It happened that one of the richest alluvial gold regions in the world extended to within forty miles of that bay; and that gold, which was not mined vigorously until 1851, might have been exploited a decade or two earlier if a permanent settlement had existed on the bay from the year 1804.

In the summer of 1803–4 Collins was restless to leave his sandy beach and the hidden gold that lay beyond. The problem was where to go. Letters discussing the problem passed six hundred miles around the coast between Collins in Port Phillip and Governor King in Sydney. King, a naval officer, knew that the final decision had to be made by Collins but he used subtle persuasion in advocating a settlement on the southern shores of Bass Strait at the mouth of the Tamar River. A port there could shelter and repair ships that hunted seals in Bass Strait. From such a port Collins could supervise the sealing islands and expel the Yankee vessels who were dominating the catch; the seals, ignorant of the law, did not realize that once they swam onto British rocks they could only legally be clubbed and skinned by men from British ships. Above all, argued King spuriously, most ships passing through the strait hugged the southern shore in order to escape the full force of the ruling south-westerlies. And the mouth of the Tamar was on the southern shore.

A few vessels, however, inspected the Tamar and found the entrance was tortuous. The harbour just inside the heads was cramped. The soil and grass were uninviting. Collins therefore was faced with the very impediments which made him so anxious to leave Port Phillip.

In 1804 Collins moved his convicts to the young settlement at Hobart in south-eastern Tasmania. He justified his move by explaining that when Hobart's existence became known abroad, merchant ships from Europe, America, and India would make it a 'Port of Shelter' on their way to Sydney or China or the Pacific. But those ships would not call at Hobart unless they sailed the old route around the south of Tasmania rather than the new short cut through Bass Strait. Collins had shut his eyes to the advantages of Bass Strait and therefore to the very reasons which had made the English government send him there.

He also ignored his orders to place a small guard and a few convicts on King Island, a windblown sealing resort which guarded the western entrance to Bass Strait. When he was warned by Governor King that a convict camp on the island would frighten away the sea elephants — the mainstay of a small industry — Collins half disbelieved him but half accepted the pretext for inertia. Two years after he had left England to create the bases in Bass Strait he still had qualms about his neglect of the strategic island.

The strategic value of Bass Strait seemed to be recognized more in Westminster than in Australia. The English government had sent Collins to the north shore of the strait in April 1803; in the following month its war with France was resumed and a month later it resolved to place a settlement on the southern shore of the strait. Almost a year elapsed before this decision reached Sydney in a whaling ship. Governor King then promptly sent two small vessels to Bass Strait, and just as promptly winter storms drove them back. At last in November 1804 a new colony stood by the mudflats at the mouth of the Tamar River in northern Tasmania. The site was strategic but the grass and soil were mean, and at the close of the second summer the colony was shifted nearly forty miles up the winding river to Launceston. Thus even that port ceased to be useful for ships using Bass Strait.

The home government in 1803 thought the strait was so vital that they had ordered three bases to be made — on the north shore, the south shore, and on King Island. When they made those plans the entire South Seas held, to their knowledge, only the two original British settlements — Sydney and Norfolk Island. Bass Strait seemed so important that it justified an increase in Australian settlements from two to five. Not one of those settlements on the shores of Bass Strait had been a success, and in November 1812 Governor Macquarie, making his first visit to the strait, observed the urgent need for a port where ships passing through the strait could call for repairs and refreshments. Curiously, it was not the home government which had reversed its orders to place three settlements on the strait. It was the men who had been entrusted with the making of the bases who had withdrawn from the strait. One can sympathize with their retreat. They were soldiers, not sailors. Their experiences at Port Jackson had warned them of the weakness of a base which, through poor soil, could not feed its own people, let alone visiting ships. They knew too that ships would not willingly call at a port of refreshment which had a dangerous entrance. If they were too rigid in their definition of fertile soil they had at least learned Sydney's lesson, and if they were too rigid in defining a safe harbour they had at least learned Norfolk Island's lesson.

3

The strategic seaway at the south of Australia had inspired the settling of Tasmania but the strategic seaway at the north of Australia remained unoccupied. London and Sydney could see the value of Torres Strait. They also knew the dangers of a port on its shores. They knew the heat oppressed, they knew of no harbour, and the supply lines from Sydney to a port in Torres Strait would cost much in money and wrecked ships. Nevertheless if the visiting Frenchmen of 1802 had decided to return home through Torres Strait instead of through Bass Strait, the governor in Sydney would possibly have created an outlying British port in northern Australia.

The long northern coast lay entirely in the tropics and in the path of the monsoons, and even today is deserted except at a few favoured points. One is accustomed to think that the coast lacked strategic value until the rise of Asian military powers in the twentieth century, but in the previous century the same coast still faced the Indonesian Archipelago, which even then was an arena of international rivalries. Australia's northern coast was less than four hundred miles from the nearest Dutch islands, and many warm Australian bays and beaches paid their annual tribute to the Dutch trading empire.

Each December the start of the moist north-west monsoon in the Java Sea was a signal for Indonesian seamen, the celebrated Buginese, to prepare for their annual visit to the northern Australian coast. At the Dutch port of Macassar, at the south end of the Celebes, their small fleet of proas took on rice and water and firewood at the deep waterfront. Wooden vessels with high square stern and low blunt bow, usually of 30 to 50 tons burden, their bamboo cabins were so arranged on the high poop that the vessels resembled floating pigeon houses. But when they sailed before the favourable monsoon and the great matting sail was bloated by the wind, they were formidable and fast.

The fleet visited bays in Arnhem Land and the Gulf of Carpentaria in north Australia, and at low tide their crews waded with spears into the water or fished from long canoes. The goal of their annual pilgrimages was the long sea slug, known as sea cucumber or trepang or bêche-de-mer. Indonesians speared the slugs in shallow water and carried them ashore to nests of stone furnaces. There they boiled them in cauldrons, dried them in the hot sun, and cured them in flimsy smoke houses made of bamboo matting and palm leaves. In the first months of each year, on sweltering beaches, smoke rose from their furnaces along a strip of coast where more than a thousand men were fishing or preserving trepang. When the cooler south-east monsoon came, the cargoes of trepang were carried back to the Celebes and traded with Chinese or Dutchmen, usually in return for manufactured goods. Most of the trepang went on to China where it flavoured the soups of the rich. What the annual trepang harvest from Australia was worth is not clear, but it was certainly a rich harvest for the merchants of the Celebes and an envious one for British traders. More important, in the eyes of some British traders, was the idea that the trepang fleet resembled a Trojan Horse that might admit their products into the Dutch trading empire in the east.

After the Napoleonic Wars, rivalries of Dutch and British traders for the commerce of the Indonesian archipelago had become intense. Britain competed more successfully than ever before. For much of the war Holland had been cut off from its Indonesian trading posts and for part of the war it had actually lost Java and the Moluccas to the British, and therefore English merchandise flowed freely into ports where previously it could only enter illicitly. Britain thus created a strong market for the cheap products of its own industrial revolution, the gaudy cotton and woollen apparel and the cheap metalware. In 1814 Britain exported only £104,000 of cotton goods to Mauritius, the Indonesian archipelago, the Philippines, and Canton, but by 1821 these cotton exports were eleven times as valuable. Much of the increase came from native buyers in Indonesia. Thousands of Javanese paraded in cheap red cloth from Manchester's mechanized mills.

Britain made more cheaply than any other nation the textiles which Indonesians prized. From the year 1819 it also possessed Singapore, an ideal trading base for its commercial invasion of the Indonesian islands. The cold mills of north England and the hot island of Singapore formed an alliance which the Dutch struggled to break. Holland's only weapon was its control of the Indonesian Islands, and in the early 1820s it harried British ships and taxed their cargoes heavily. At the western end of the islands it could not quench the fleets of small vessels trading with Singapore but at the eastern end of the islands it retained most of the commerce.

In the west the Dutch tried by diplomacy to move the British from their foothold in Singapore, and in the east the British tried to weaken Dutch commerce by creating a second Singapore on Australian soil. From a base in northern Australia the products of England's industrial revolution could infiltrate the eastern islands in the holds of the trepang fleet. Buginese fishermen could sell their trepang to British merchants in northern Australia in return for the cloth and metalware. As the Buginese were traders and seafarers they could distribute British manufactures throughout the eastern end of the archipelago and probably return with spices, coffee, and tropical goods. The same type of trading system was making Singapore a rich port; and several deserted harbours in northern Australia seemed as well placed as Singapore. Similarly, just as Singapore was a strategic point on the normal trade route and opium passage from India to China, a port in northern Australia could offer some similar advantages to British naval and merchant ships. It would be close to Dutch fortified ports and barely a thousand miles east of a popular sealane from Britain to China which passed the island of Bali.

This bold, sensible plan was first put to the British government in September 1823 by William Barns, a trading buccaneer who had just returned to London from the east. Within three months his plan had wide support. The governments of Britain and Holland were starting to negotiate a new treaty defining their respective spheres of influence in the Indonesian Archipelago, and many British traders feared that their government in the parleying might concede the Dutch demand that Singapore be abandoned. On 13 December 1823, two days before the first conference, a lobby of London merchants* engaged

---

* It is curious to see side by side, on the list of nineteen English mercantile houses which backed the plan, the firms Macaulay & Babington, and Buckle, Bagster & Buckle. Two sons of principals

in the East Indian trade urged their government to create an Australian Singapore. A sheltered bay on the north Australian coast could be ideal for a trading base. Six weeks later, while Anglo-Dutch conferences were still dragging, the secretary to the Admiralty argued that Britain should not 'hesitate a moment' in sending an expedition to northern Australia. Britain hesitated a few more moments and then despatched an expedition to Sydney to take on supplies and convicts for the creation of its new port. Many historians suggest the north Australian base was a martello tower guarding Australia's soil from the French or Dutch, but it was not even on the Australian mainland. It was essentially an armed trading post.

A log fort was built late in 1824 on a narrow strait separating Melville Island from Bathurst Island, just north of where the north Australian port of Darwin now stands. Known as Fort Dundas, it was only about 300 miles from Timor and seemed to be close to the path of the Macassar fleet that sailed to and fro with the monsoons. The strait approaching the fort, however, was tortuous, and marred by racing tides and shifting shoals. Moreover, unknown to the commander of the fort, the Treaty of London of March 1824 had granted Britain secure control of Singapore and granted the Dutch a trade monopoly of most islands at the Australian end of the archipelago. Melville Island therefore relied solely on the visits of the Buginese fleet, but it was too far from their trepang bays. Not one Indonesian sail was seen during the five years a watch was manned at the fort.

London merchants who had pleaded for their new Singapore seemed now to rely on their old, once it had been made secure for Britain. Some, however, tried Melville Island, sending out the brig *Stedcomb* under William Barns. It presumably carried all those British manufactures which Barns knew would attract the In-

---

of those firms became England's famous historians in the mid-nineteenth century, Macaulay and Buckle.

donesian fleets: the chintz cloth printed with flowers in bright colours, white cloth, blue cloth, and coarse red cloth; cutlery, anchors, brass wire, and nails; muskets, six-pounders, birdshot, and gunpowder; looking glasses and lavender water and 'in short every Article of European manufacture'. The *Stedcomb*, however, was capture-by pirates, and of her crew only two boys were saved. Freemen and convicts at the fort stayed on in their loneliness, suffering from the summer humidity, scurvy, and shortages of food, for the supply line through Torres Strait from Sydney was long and irregular.

London sent out Captain James Stirling in H.M.S. *Success* to Sydney with orders to take on convicts and supplies and sail north to found a second settlement on one of the Australian bays which the Indonesian fleet annually visited. The presence of a British warship on the coast, it was hoped, would scare pirates and reassure the Buginese fleet that Britain meant to protect its commerce. In June 1827 Captain Stirling chose Raffles Bay, on one of the most northerly peninsulas of the Australian mainland, nearly 200 miles east of Fort Dundas. The sight of stone trepang furnaces and wooden curing frames was proof that Indonesians visited the bay. Moreover Stirling thought the bay was so close to the Torres Strait route from Sydney to India that it could become a port of refreshment for passing ships.

So a trading fort named Fort Wellington was built — a hexagonal stockade which enclosed a square log tower, twenty feet high, and fitted with loopholes for soldiers to fire through. An outer paling fence protected the thatched barracks and stores and huts near the walls of the stockade. But within four months Raffles Bay was a prison of gloom. The pale blue sky above the fort and the exotic scrub around it were sinister to European eyes. It was not yet summer but the heat seemed intense, and in the surrounding scrub the Aboriginals were suspicious of the intruders. One soldier had been speared, another had vanished into the scrub, and the surgeon had died of fever. In October 1827 the scurvy was so severe that 49 of the 77 men, women, and children were ill. Soldiers who were supposed to be defending the fort were hobbling about on crutches, their legs black and swollen from scurvy. Though the bay was close to the Torres Strait trade route, no ship called at the macabre port of refreshment. Perhaps the port was too concealed from the open sea by jutting headlands, so a painted signboard was fixed to a 45 feet pole on a headland. Aboriginals tore it down.

In the following February, on a humid Sunday afternoon shortly before sunset, the big sail of a proa was seen near Raffles Bay: the first proa sighted by a British trading post in northern Australia. The proa was towed into the bay and captain and crew were treated with courtesy and invited to return by the fort's Malay interpreter, O'Dean. At the end of March more proas arrived and fished for trepang in front of the fort on moonlit nights, and when they sailed back to Macassar with the new monsoon their crew, presumably, were wearing their gifts of cotton cloth and printed calico. In the following trepang season 34 proas, manned by more than one thousand men, entered Raffles Bay. Regular contact with the Indonesian fleet had at last been made, but understandably there were no merchants at the trading post to barter textiles and metals for their trepang. By the time the fleet made its next annual visit both trading forts had been abandoned.

It is hard to accept the common verdict that the trading forts in north Australia were airy ventures which should never have been suggested and which had no hope of success. In design they were realistic, and Raffles Bay was possibly on the verge of success when it was suddenly closed on orders from London.

The two pinpoints on the north coast had been settled to solve a problem of distance; they were close to that end of the Indonesian archipelago which was remote from Singapore and other British trading ports, and they were close to the routes of the trepang traders. Likewise the trading forts had been foiled primarily by problems of distance. The first fort had survived for five trepang seasons but was so far from the trepang fisheries that it was not visited by one proa. Both forts were impeded by distance from Sydney; it was their source of provisions and a possible source of merchandise for trade, and the two thousand mile passage from Sydney made their upkeep abnormally high. The British government's premature decision to abandon Raffles Bay reflected the delays in communicating with such a remote place. For it was on the basis of a report written at Raffles Bay in October 1827 that Britain decided to withdraw, and the order to withdraw did not reach Raffles Bay until August 1829; and in those twenty-two months the prospect of success had drastically increased. The trading fort was abandoned because London believed not one Indonesian had visited it. In fact, for the two summers preceding its closure a large fleet of proas had made visits.

4

When the first fort was built on the north Australian coast, it was as marooned as a beetle in a bottle. If its men needed help they would have had to sail, depending on the time of the year and the winds, either around Australia in an anti-clockwise direction to Hobart in Tasmania or in a clockwise direction through Torres Strait to Brisbane. There was then not one British outpost on the west or south coasts of Australia. Britain thought so little of the prospects of any harbour on the west coast that it had not bothered to claim formal possession of the coast. Similarly, about one third of the south coastline was not even formally claimed, and the only attempt to establish an outpost on the remainder of the south coastline had been on Port Phillip Bay, abandoned twenty years previously.

The spur to create outposts in the forgotten south came from the French. In 1826, a year of European peace, they sent an expedition under the command of J. Dumont D'Urville to reconnoitre Australian and New Zealand seas. The British reaction was nervous and quick; they suspected that France might make a colony on the untouched west coast. On 1 March 1826 the British secretary for colonies, Earl Bathurst, wrote three letters to Governor Darling in Sydney, ordering him to forestall the French.

One would imagine that one of three letters written to the same man on the same subject on the same day would clearly explain the writer's reasoning, but the fact that he wrote three letters suggests that he was excited and confused. He gave no motive except suspicion of France. His letters simply ordered Governor Darling to send soldiers and convicts from Sydney on a passage of some 2000 sea miles to Shark Bay on the opposite side of Australia. As the west coast always appeared dry and barren to passing Dutch, French, and English navigators, one can only suggest that its strategic position — not any potential wealth in its soil — was the asset that interested Earl Bathurst in March 1826. The coast was close to popular sea routes from Europe to India or China, for ships scudded east of the Cape of Good Hope with the prevailing winds towards Australia, the India-bound ships sailing two thirds of the way and the China-bound ships nearly the entire way to the western Australian coast, before they hauled to the north. The same strip of Australian coast was close to the Dutch East Indies, just a month's sailing from India, and so placed that in time of war it could send out ships to prey on the prized merchant fleets crossing the Indian Ocean. While Britain by the 1820s had ample bases on the fringes of the Indian Ocean, France was then — through its loss of Mauritius in the recent wars — weak on the shores of that vital ocean. And the simplest way for Britain to retain its mastery of that ocean and to retard any French ambitions was to occupy the only known harbour of any promise on Australia's west coast.

Ten days after writing his treble order to occupy Shark Bay, Earl Bathurst had second thoughts. Shark Bay was reputed to be a desolate hell, almost on the tropic. It had a magnificent position athwart Asian trade routes but nothing else. Without water and fertile soil it was incapable of becoming a satisfactory house of correction for criminals or a half-way house for either French or British ships. That line of of reasoning probably made him suggest, on 11 March 1826, that the landing party should first try King George Sound, a fine harbour with a milder climate and a more fertile coast. It was 700 miles to the south of Shark Bay, near the south-west corner of the continent, and as it faced the Southern rather than the Indian Ocean it could not command trade routes from Europe to India and China and the Indonesian Archipelago. Whether Earl Bathurst had sufficient knowledge of Australian geography and wind directions to understand that fact is uncertain. On the other hand he may have argued that there were only two known bays in strategic positions on the vast coastline of what is now the State of Western Australia, one being Shark Bay and the other King George Sound, and that Britain should occupy the one which had a fringe of watered, fertile soil necessary to sustain a seabase or port of refreshment.

The commanding position of King George Sound (now Albany) stood out on an atlas. It was on a craned neck of the continent, not unlike the Cape of Good Hope and Cape Horn. The advantages of its site were probably so obvious to even a naïve map-gazer in the great era of sea strategy that British or colonial administrators did not need to mention them in their correspondence; they took them for granted. That type of advantage becomes hard for a historian to document or easy to overlook. Fortunately, such an appreciation of King George Sound does exist. It is not in the letters flowing between Sydney and London and discussing the assets and defects of the proposed outpost. It is tucked away — as an afterthought, a point almost too elementary to make — in the twentieth paragraph of a letter from Major Lockyer, the first commandant of the lonely outpost. 'The importance of King George's Sound as a place necessary to occupy must strike every person acquainted with this Country,' he wrote on 18 April 1827. 'An Enemy holding it would with its Cruizers completely intercept and greatly annoy the Trade [except by Convoys]* to Van Dieman's Land and Port Jackson from Europe the Cape of Good Hope, Isle of France and India.' In other and clearer words it was almost as important as Bass Strait, because it guarded the main route to Australia and the south-west Pacific.

Britain's reaction to reported French designs on Australia in 1826 came more from a sense of sea strategy rather than from a belief that Australian soil was valuable. This interpretation gains support by noticing the position of the other Australian harbour settled in 1826 in order to forestall the French. The harbour was Western Port, on the shores of Bass Strait, in the south-east corner of Australia. When Earl Bathurst ordered that soldiers and convicts from Sydney should form a camp on Western Port, he possibly recalled that the French expedition of 1802 had inspected it, and he certainly implied that he knew the strategic value of the strait which the harbour flanked. There a French port, in the event of war, might disrupt British shipping making for Sydney and many Pacific ports, and in peacetime it could be a springboard for French trading or colonising excursions to Pacific islands, or nearby whaling or sealing grounds.

The feared French corvette called at both King George Sound and Western Port in the spring of 1826, without hoisting a flag or landing caretakers. Sealing gangs near both lonely harbours were no doubt surprised to see the Frenchmen come and go, followed shortly by parties of Sydney convicts and soldiers who built huts and dug fortifications and gardens.

The military camp at Western Port was abandoned in its second year. The camp at Albany on King George Sound survived five years, being supplied at heavy cost from Sydney by ships which beat up against boisterous westerlies along the south coast or used the circuitous route through Torres Strait. A generation later Albany

---

* My brackets.

was a sleepy coaling port for steamships crossing the Indian Ocean from Suez, and two generations later a port for the West Australian gold rushes. The few Parisian investors who landed at Albany's long jetty on their way to the goldfields in the 1890s possibly regretted that their countrymen so long ago had missed their chance to annex the port and the treasure that lay behind it. But in the 1820s Australia's main merit in European eyes was not its vast interior but a line of coast which was so long that one part faced the Indonesian archipelago, another part faced the Pacific, another part the Indian Ocean and its trade routes, and another part the normal trade route from Europe to Sydney. Its main merit was that it lay on the route to somewhere else.

Australia was about to become a land of some importance in its own right, a terminus instead of a wayside station, and the transition was visible in another settlement which was made on the west coast at what is now the city of Perth. The discovery of the site was an indirect effect of fear of Indonesian pirates on the north coast and fear of French ambitions on the west coast. Captain James Stirling had sailed H.M.S. *Success* from England with instructions to intimidate pirates in the Timor Sea and to open a new trading fort; he was the man who was to select Raffles Bay. Calling at Sydney late in 1826, he realized that if he promptly went north he would have to fight the north-west monsoon in Torres Strait and open the new fort in the rainy season. He decided to spend summer in the south. It was the time of the French scare, D'Urville's corvette was refitting in Sydney harbour, and a brig had just left for King George Sound with a party of occupation. Captain Stirling therefore thought he should spend the summer investigating a stretch of the west coast, between Shark Bay and King George Sound, which no British ship had yet surveyed. He thought the Swan River, discovered by a Dutchman at the end of the seventeenth century, should be inspected quickly or it might be snapped up by France.

Early in 1827 Stirling found safe anchorages — their

safety proved deceptive — near the mouth of the Swan River. He explored the river, marvelling at the stately black swans from which it had been named, and vowing that it would give cheap water carriage to products from an immense and attractive terrain. The land near the river seemed as fine as the Plain of Lombardy, and almost as well placed. Stirling noted that it was on the eastern route to China, close to India and Mauritius and the Indonesian archipelago, and blessed by favourable winds. It could trade its own products of the temperate zone for the products of tropical countries, thus repeating the marriage of economies which the West Indies and British North America had consummated with such success in the eighteenth century. Its climate and position could make it a convalescent colony for jaded Europeans from India. As a naval and military station it could command much of the Indian Ocean. All that Stirling's design for a colony lacked was a name, and he even thought of that; he suggested *Hesperia*, because it faced the setting sun.

A colony near the Swan River might have been alluring to a European power which lacked ports in eastern seas; but Britain did not lack such ports, and France seemed to have diverted its interest from Australia to New Zealand. It could of course become a prison, but Britain had ample prisons in eastern Australia, and the governor in Sydney was already complaining that one reason for the rising cost of the convict settlements in Australia was that so many were now scattered around the long coast. He explained that it would be foolish to govern and supply a convict colony on the Swan River from Sydney. So adverse were the winds that a ship from Sydney would probably be slower in reaching Swan River than a ship from South Africa or India.

The British government was willing to create a colony on the Swan River if capitalists rather than taxpayers shouldered the main financial risks. The East India Company rejected a plan to occupy the river but a few private investors were tempted. Thomas Peel, for one, was willing to pay the cost of shipping 400 emigrants to

Swan River in return for a quarter of a million acres of land, and others were eager to invest capital and carry out labourers in return for grants of free land. So in 1829 a ship of war from Cape Town sailed to Swan River to take possession of the land and was followed by a small fleet carrying free settlers from England. Fremantle became the port near the river mouth, and Perth village, twelve miles up the river, became the capital of the new colony of Western Australia.

The flocks of black swans which floated on the wide river were decimated by settlers' guns and dogs, but black swans still multiplied at a faster rate than white men. The soil, the scope for trade with tropical lands, had both been exaggerated. The new colony was more a symbol than a success. Like the earlier settlements strung along Australia's coast, it was chosen because of its strategic position, but it also reflected a new form of colonisation. It was the first Australian colony or coastal outpost to be founded largely by private settlers rather than by a government. It was the first — since the original settlements of 1788 — which hoped to grow not only its own foodstuffs but raw materials (tobacco, cotton, and flax) for export to Europe. Its founders were more interested in the promise of Australian soil than any previous colonisers. They heralded a swing of interest from Australian seas to Australian land.

Western Australia was the first new colony to fight the problem of distance from Europe without the generous aid of the British government, for the expensive ship fares of most newcomers to eastern Australia had been gladly paid by the British government, and moreover much of the demand for agricultural products in eastern Australia had been financed by the British treasury in order to feed its establishment of officials, soldiers, and convicts. Western Australia failed to master that problem of distance, and became through its own choice a gaol for British convicts in 1850.

In pegging military camps and trading forts on the Australian coast in the 1820s Britain formally laid its claim to all Australia. Originally Britain had claimed less than half of the land surface of Australia and its offshore islands, and for one generation after the coming of the first fleet it was satisfied with its share. Its western boundary was the 135th meridian of longitude, a line which passed just east of the present town of Alice Springs, and that boundary seems to have been chosen arbitrarily. During the years in which it was the western boundary of British Australia, probably not one Briton ever walked across that boundary.

When the trading fort was built on Melville Island in 1824, Britain annexed the northern coast of Australia as far west as the 129th meridian. With a stroke of the pen, and more in the interests of uniformity than acquisitiveness, Britain claimed the corresponding coast on the south a year later when it commissioned Sir Ralph Darling as governor of New South Wales. Thus a strip of land equal to one sixth of Australia or nearly as large as Saudi Arabia was added to British territory. The remaining third of Australian soil, an area nearly as big a Argentina, was formally annexed in 1829 when the colony was placed on the Swan River.

Ironically Britain claimed the whole continent simply in order to claim a few isolated harbours astride trade routes. It was like a speculator who, buying a huge wasteland flanking a highway because it had a few fine sites for road-cafes and filling stations, found later that much of the land was fertile and productive. It seems fair to suggest that Britain did not particularly want the continent. Moreover, even when it had formally claimed possession of all Australian soil in 1829, one may suggest that its claim to *all* Australian territory was shaky. Formal annexation did not automatically grant secure possession of a new country. Captain Samuel Wallis had found and annexed Tahiti for Britain in 1767 but the

Spanish later also annexed it peacefully and the French finally settled it. St Allouarn claimed western Australia for France in 1772 but Britain later annexed it and occupied it. Britain realized that its only real claim to any part of the Australian coast came from actual occupation, and when in 1826 Britain feared that the French might occupy Western Port near Bass Strait, it did not simply argue that the port had been formally claimed by Britain since 1770 or that it was close to areas which the British had long held and colonised. The only way to prevent a French port from peacefully springing up was to occupy the harbour ahead of France; and in 1826 Britain did.

If the French had coveted a share in Australia, there were still inviting strips of coast which, as late as 1829, were far from any harbour where a British outpost existed or had existed. The most attractive strip of neglected coast was in the south, running east from Port Lincoln to the beginning of Bass Strait. It contained the mouth of the only long river system in the continent. It included some of the richest and most attractive coastal country on the continent — the finest parts of what are now South Australia and western Victoria. And much of it had been seen and praised by earlier French navigators.

Why that coast was so long neglected has puzzled historians, and it must continue to be puzzling so long as one accepts the belief that Britain was basically interested in occupying coasts that washed rich Australian regions. On the other hand, if one accepts the idea that sea strategy dictated the sites of early outposts, and that sea was more important than land, then it becomes clear why that charming strip of coast was neglected. It mostly lay in a bight, an indented arc of the coastline, and was thus too far north of the popular sea route which passed from Europe and India to Sydney and the west Pacific. That bight not only lacked any value as a defensive post but it also lacked value as a springboard for trade. Whereas the north coast faced the Indonesian archipelago, and the west coast faced the lands flanking the Indian Ocean, and the east coast faced Pacific islands, this favoured strip of coast faced the ice of Antarctica. In strategic terms it was of scant value, and for that reason it was probably ignored.

That coast was suddenly invaded by free British settlers in the mid-1830s, and the towns of Melbourne and Adelaide were born. The peaceful invasion snatched away France's last chance of occupying peacefully a part of Australia whose climate and soil, measured by the standards of nineteenth century Europe, were attractive.

There remains the enigma of why New Zealand was so slow to be annexed by Britain. The islands of New Zealand had a kind climate in the eyes of Englishmen, finer natural resources than most parts of Australia, and rich whaling grounds offshore. New Zealand was only 1200 miles from the main Australian ports of Sydney and Hobart and therefore less isolated than the outposts on the western and northern coasts of Australia. Missionaries and whalemen and timbermen settled on the coast of New Zealand long before the British government firmly proclaimed its sovereignty in 1840. The enigma of the delay in occupying New Zealand, it would seem, can be simply explained by glancing at the islands' position. While the continent of Australia flanked routes to many trading points, New Zealand was too far to the east and south to be prized as a potential port of call. Understandably it was long ignored by Britain.

Much of Australia's early history was influenced by its proximity to trade routes and to promising spheres of trade. Much of its later history was influenced by the fact that it was on a limb, far from the trunk routes of world trade. By the 1830s that change was visible. Australia was becoming more a terminus and goal for shipping and less a port of call. Its shipping links with Europe were now much more important than its shipping links with Asia and the Pacific. Australia was becoming useful, not so much as a dead-end house for English criminals and a half-way house for English ships, than as a source of Britain's raw materials — wool from the land and whale oil from the sea.

5 Whalemen

The biggest whales in Australian waters weighed as much as 25 elephants or nearly as much as some of the smaller ships that went whaling. Chasing whales was therefore the most dangerous and masculine of all seafaring trades. The insidious enemies of whales, however, were not the crews with harpoons and lances but rather women and their households in Europe and North America. They kept the world's whaling fleets at sea in the first half of the nineteenth century. Their corsets and umbrella frames and the hoops beneath their dresses came from the slender, flexible mouth-bones in the bay whales. The superior candles they placed on their dinner tables were made from spermaceti, a solid wax taken from cavities in a whale's head. A whale's outer coating of blubber yielded a fatty oil which was the familiar oil of the domestic lamp, or an ingredient of soap. The rarest product of a sperm whale was ambergris, a grey opaque substance which came from an uncommon disease in a whale's intestines and was sometimes found floating on the sea. One of the most precious items in commerce, sold by the ounce and occasionally sold at a higher price than gold, it heightened the smell of perfume or flavoured dishes of Cordon Bleu cooks.

The species called the sperm whale — of which Moby Dick was a legendary member — was the most sought in the oceans around Australia and New Zealand. It was a toothed whale, and as it fed on cuttlefish and the giant squid in deep waters it was usually hunted far from land in some of the roughest seas on the globe. Sperm whaling therefore called for strong, well-equipped ships that could remain at sea for several years.

A whaling ship could wander the ocean for months without even seeing a sperm whale, but failure could be followed by sudden success; sperm whales were polygamous and swam slowly in large herds. The monotony on a whaling ship that had not seen a whale in months of searching swung to jubilation when a sailor on the masthead saw, on the horizon, the rising spouts of spray from a herd of whales; but by the end of the day there was perhaps a bunk in the forecastle that would not be used again on that voyage. For the bull sperm whale could grow 65 feet long, and he was then twice as long and perhaps ten times as heavy as the long rowing boats that chased him. He could smash a boat in two or overturn it with a lash of his tail or drag it under the water. He and his herds were hunted incessantly in the oceans lapping Australia. They unwillingly enriched Australian commerce.

The first recorded British whaler to hunt in the South Pacific was the *Emilia*, owned by Samuel Enderby & Sons of London. She fought her way round Cape Horn one year after Australia was first settled, and captured many sperm whales and filled her hold with barrels of sperm oil and spermaceti. When in 1790 she returned safely to the river at Gravesend, Samuel Enderby eagerly heard her news and inspected her cargo. 'From her account,' he wrote, 'the whales of the South Pacific Ocean are likely to be most profitable; the crew are all returned in good health, only one man was killed by a whale.'

If more British whaling ships were to be enticed from the familiar Atlantic whaling grounds that were closer to their home ports, they needed more incentive than the *Emilia's* cargo and low mortality rate seemed to offer. The convict settlement and the safe harbour at Sydney provided an incentive. Whaling ships that had spent a year or more wandering the South Pacific could call at Sydney for fresh water, meat, and essential repairs. Moreover, if

British whaling ships were permitted to carry cargoes and convicts from London to Sydney, they would earn rather than lose money in the long voyage out to the whaling grounds. In essence the problem of British whaling ships in Australian seas was not to find a homeward cargo — for they had their heavy barrels of oil — but to find a profitable cargo for the outward voyage.

Britain fostered whaling because a strong whaling fleet was a magnificent school for seamen and a source of vital raw materials. It was also convenient for the British Government to encourage some ships to sail from England to Australia, thereby gaining cheaper fares and freights for convicts and supplies sent to the new settlement. So in the convict fleet that reached Sydney in 1791 five of the six convict transports were whalers, which, on landing their convicts, went to sea to chase whales. The whaling ships *Britannia* and *Will* and *Ann* sailed from Sydney on 24 October 1791, and at sunrise next morning saw sperm whales around the entire horizon. The wind was strong and a high sea was running, and not until afternoon did the captains dare lower their whale boats. Quickly the crews rowed to the nearest whales, their harpoons hit them, and at close quarters they killed seven whales with thrusts of their long lances.

A strong gale setting in from the south-west, the boats succeeded in towing only two whales back to the ships. Next morning in quieter seas the wooden stagings were lowered from each ship and the crew rapidly hacked the useful parts from the whale and let the mutilated carcass drift away. Hatches were lifted from the try-works on deck, furnaces lit and iron-pots filled with blubber, and the putrid steam from the cauldrons began to cake the white sails with the grime that distinguished successful whalers at sea.

Those whales were probably the first of tens of thousands captured off the Australian coast. An irregular line of whaling ships came to Australia in the 1790s, many carrying convicts, and most returning home from the South Seas with rows of barrels arranged in the hold. The value of their catch is not known, but between 1800 and 1806 eighteen British whalers called at Sydney with seal oil, sealskins, and 2800 *tuns* of sperm oil. A *tun*, the common whaling measure, equalled about 210 imperial gallons, and at the current London oil prices those whaling cargoes were worth perhaps £200,000, a huge sum.

The convict settlement at Hobart Town, on the beautiful cold-water estuary in southern Tasmania, gave whalers a new supply base alongside the breeding grounds of another commercial whale, the black whalebone or bay whale. A cask of oil from its blubber was usually worth only half as much as a cask of sperm oil, but there was compensation in the rows of hundreds of thin horny plates that framed the sides of its upper jaw. When the whale swam through the water the whalebone sprang down to form a hairy grid or gigantic strainer across the mouth. The whale allowed the seawater to pass into its jaws and push through the strainer until it formed a reservoir at the back of the mouth. The krill and other tiny crustaceans flowing in with the water were meanwhile trapped against the strainer or wall of whalebone; and the whale simply pushed out the reservoir of water with its tongue and swallowed the trapped sealife.

Unlike the toothed sperm whale which fed on squid in deep waters, the bay whale usually found more of his feed in shallow waters close to land. Likewise the cow whales preferred to breed in sheltered water near land, and that was a crucial fact for the whalemen. At the breeding season cow whales swam into estuaries and bays to give birth to a whale calf, and the calves were suckled until they were strong enough to swim out to the exposed ocean. As a calf put on a ton about every eight days, it did not have to wait long in the coastal bays. Even so, as the generations bred in the same southern Australian bays at the same time each year, they were vulnerable to any whalers who camped on the shores in the breeding season. The bay whalers required no ocean-going ship, merely a try-works on the beach and a few whale boats which they pushed into the water once they saw the spout of a whale.

It was simple suicide for a pregnant whale, bloated with blubber, to swim up the estuary of the Derwent and spout within sight of the cluster of huts at Hobart. And yet every winter they began to appear in the Derwent estuary towards the end of May, and for the following three months they dominated the river, brushing past the small rowing boats. Reverend Robert Knopwood, Anglican clergyman at Hobart, went up the estuary in a small boat on 1 July 1804 to preach at Risdon, and that night he jotted in his diary: 'We passed so many whales that it was dangerous for the boat to go up the river, unless you kept near the shore.' Soon it was dangerous for whales to go up the river. Seamen rowed out to capture them and haul them ashore to improvised boiling works. British or American whaling ships wintered in sheltered bays along the Tasmanian coast, and in 1818 the English ship *Ann* caught thirty whales in the Derwent and one whale that year was harpooned and lanced within sight of Hobart.

2

For at least a generation England's and New England's ships ruled the whaling grounds near Australia and New Zealand and in fact that vast whaling area stretching from Kerguelen Island in the Indian Ocean to the Pacific coast of Chile. Their provisions and most of their crew came from the northern hemisphere, and they usually sold their own oil barrels in Salem or London at the close of their whaling voyage. If they called briefly at Hobart or Sydney for fresh water or wood, they rarely spent much money on salted meat or supplies. In port their whale oil remained below their own decks and could not be classed as an Australian export. Whaling's influence on Australia's own stripling economy was small until a fleet of Australian ships joined the chase.

For some decades the Australian ports had few rich men who could buy a whaling ship and finance a risky, costly voyage to the nearby whaling grounds. T.W. Birch of Hobart Town was rich enough, and enterprising too. After reaching Hobart in May 1808 as medical officer on the whaling ship *Dubuc* he settled as a merchant, bought his own ships, and often sent them whaling. His best known vessel was the brig *Sophia*, of a mere 120 tons register, and though she was barely one third as big as the average whaler from New Bedford or London she could enter remote uncharted bays in winter to catch the whalebone whale or follow the sperm whale on the high seas in summer.

Birch's most celebrated captain was James Kelly, one of the first Australian-born sea captains and a bold navigator and whaleman. With a crew of 26 Kelly took the brig to a remote Tasmanian Bay, camped on the shore by the boiling-down works, and his men raced out to sea in thirty-foot whaleboats when they saw a black whale spouting. 'The early part of the morning is the time in which the whales are chiefly caught, and then the cold is severe,' Kelly told the Bigge commission in 1820. When icy winds ceased to blow from snow-topped mountains and the oceans were warmer, sperm whales migrated down from tropical seas, and Kelly sometimes hunted them on the banks off Tasmania's South West Cape or between Tasmania and New Zealand. If he wanted to spend almost the whole year whaling he could then trail the migrating sperm whales to the north east coast of New South Wales or Norfolk Island, finally returning to port just before the pregnant whales heralded winter in Tasmania's bays. This became a common time-table for Australian-owned whaling ships when ultimately the colonial industry grew strong.

Birch found that a Hobart ship had an advantage over a foreign whaling ship. His ship did not have to make the long voyage from the homeport to whaling grounds on the far side of the world, and moreover he could supervise his own ship more efficiently. He soon knew, however, the troubles in operating a whaling ship from an Australian port. He was not allowed to employ any convict or emancipated convict in deep-sea voyages, and Australia at that time had few free men who were experienced sailors. From the year 1809 any oil fished by colonial ships had to pay such a heavy import duty on entering Britain that Birch was forced to trade most of his oil with Calcutta merchants in exchange for goods. After July 1813 he had to pay an import duty on sperm and whale oil that his ship landed at Hobart and Sydney, even though that oil was re-shipped for export to Calcutta or London. On the other hand any English-owned whaling ship escaped the Australian duty by taking her own catch of oil back to England, and moreover she paid no import duty in England. It was not surprising that in 1820 the *Sophia* was the only Tasmanian whaling vessel in seas that often seemed full of whales.

Australian merchants who ran whaling ships, unlike American and British whalers in these waters, were not simply whaling specialists. They had a beachcomber's eye for any new commodity which promised profit. Thus T.W. Birch built a schooner of 60 tons in Hobart, the *Henrietta Packet*, and sailed round the southern coast of Tasmania at the end of 1815 and discovered the beautiful harbour of Port Davey which his men later visited to catch whales in winter. Leaving the *Henrietta Packet* at Port Davey, the master James Kelly went north with a few men in a small whaleboat and discovered Macquarie Harbour, the only safe harbour on the west coast of Tasmania. On its stony beaches he saw hundreds of logs of the beautiful, sweet-scented Huon Pine, ideal for building boats and houses, and his employer Birch was quick to harvest the timber. Six times the schooner sailed the 200 miles from Hobart to Macquarie Harbour and cut or gathered logs of Huon Pine. The harbour the whalemen found became a convict settlement from 1821 to 1833, and late in the century the port for Tasmania's richest mineral region. Similarly the mouth of Australia's one great river system, the Murray, was discovered by sealers and whalers.

Some Australian merchants dabbled in sealing as well as whaling, and their sloops and schooners spent summer at the bleak islands in Bass Strait. Their men landed on the islands, clubbed the seals, and stripped the sleek black skin from the carcass. In February 1804, there were only 22 private sloops and schooners based on Australian ports, and half of them were engaged constantly or occasionally in the sealing trade in Bass strait. More than 100,000 sealskins were landed at Sydney from colonial vessels between 1800 and 1806, and some were sewn into colonial shoes and most went to China or to fur-hat factories in England.

Tasmania was nearer the sealing islands, and Tasmanian ships of 40 to 90 tons sailed to King Island or the Furneaux Islands and increased the slaughter until the summer invasion of seals on many sandy beaches dwindled from thousands to tens. By 1820 the islands had a resident population of escaped convicts who had half rowed and half sailed from Tasmania in cockleshells or who had been landed from visiting schooners. They enslaved black women as their mistresses and huntresses, ate kangaroos and wombats or mutton birds, and sold sealskins and kangaroo hides in exchange for spirits and slop clothing to Birch and other merchants whose ships called once a year. By 1830 the Bass Strait islands had lost their importance as ports of call for colonial trading vessels and had won a reputation as the Barbary Coast of the South Seas, the home of Long Tom and Abyssinia Jack and other villains who, having slaughtered most of the seals, now had more leisure to slaughter or mutilate native women and fellow sealers.

The seal trade flourished on Kangaroo Island, opposite the coast of South Australia, years before that opposite coast was settled, and Birch's brig and other ships called to buy sealskins or the salt which preserved Hobart's and Sydney's meat. From about 1811 some Sydney ships went each season to Macquarie Island, far out in the ocean between Tasmania and the Antarctic Circle, and they quickly decimated the fur seals and boiled the carcasses of floundering elephant seals for oil. The sealers must have known that in their total war on seals they were killing a lucrative trade for Australian ships, but if some sealing parties had curbed the slaughter at the breeding grounds in order to prolong the trade they would have been merely turning over seals to rival parties on the same shores.

The shrinking piles of sealskins in waterfront warehouses in Sydney and Hobart ceased to worry shipowners. In their place were more barrels of whale oil and bundles of whalebone than colonial ships had ever caught before. Australia's whaling industry became vigorous in the late 1820s. The London price of sperm oil and whale oil was rising, and the shackling duties on colonial oil imported into England were cut. Australian ports now had enough rich merchants to buy or finance whaling ships and enough free sailors to man the ships. Whereas the Sydney merchants William Walker and Richard Jones (president of the Bank of New South Wales) owned the colony's only five whaling vessels in 1827, three years later there were 17 Sydney ships hunting whales. The mania for whaling grew. In 1835 at least 76 Australian ships were engaged in deep-sea whaling, and the Australian fleet was much larger than the once-strong British whaling fleet in the South Seas.

Emigrant ships near the Australian coast saw the signs of the whaling revival. On a thousand nights in those waters a sailor keeping watch on the masthead heard only the dark procession of waves slapping the ship and saw only the sleeping decks below. But in the 1830s there were nights when for an instant he saw a faint flame lick the sea, then fade. If he was an experienced sailor he knew that not far away the furnaces on the deck of a whaling ship were boiling the blubber of a captured whale. If in the first daylight his ship chanced to be closer to the whaler, he perhaps saw its grimy sails. If the wind was blowing his way, he sniffed the blood and blubber.

The life of the crew in an Australian whaling ship was possibly more endurable than in an American whaling ship which, because of the long distance from home port to whaling grounds, might be at sea two or three years. The average Australian whaling voyage lasted less than a year, but the conditions on board were still cramped and the daily work exhausting if sperm whales were blowing. The crew lived, slept, and usually ate in the poky forecastle, the part where the ship began to curve and narrow towards the bow. To reach their quarters they lowered themselves through a small hole in the deck, climbed down a short ladder, and groped their way to one of the wooden bunks arranged in two tiers around the wall. The only natural light came through the narrow manhole — and the light was blocked by a hatch in rough seas — and the ceilings of most forecastles were so low that a tall man bumped his head if he unbent. On some ships twenty or more men — Englishmen, Sydney lads, Australian Aboriginals, and maybe the odd Nantucket man or Maori — lived in the forecastle with their seachests crowding floorboards that might be scrubbed clean or might be slippery with food scraps or quids of chewing tobacco.

Farther aft, towards the middle of the ship, was a small compartment with six or eight bunks that held the harpooners, boat-steerer, the steward who waited on the mates, and the cooper who made and sealed the barrels of sperm oil and spermaceti. And farther along the deck, away from the try-works that boiled the blubber, was the cabin occupied by the mates and the relatively spacious stateroom used by the master and on some voyages, his wife.

Although sailors in a whaling ship had cramped quarters and ate monotonous food and bowed to strict discipline, they may well have been the elect of Australian working men in the 1830s. Theirs was a free man's calling in a country where most occupations had the taint of the broad arrow. Whalemen were also the only Australian workmen to share in the profits of their employers' ventures. When they signed on with a whaling ship at Hobart or Sydney, they were advanced money to buy clothes and tobacco and seakit, were promised a ration of food and spirits throughout the voyage, but were usually given no fixed wage. Instead they received a share of the value of the oil and whalebone which his ship caught at sea. This proportion varied from ship to ship and voyage to voyage, but a harpooner often got one sixtieth share and the ordinary seaman one eightieth share of the voyage's catch, the catch being valued at rather less than prevailing market prices. The crew were thus shareholders in the voyage, and if their ship returned heavily laden to Hobart or Sydney, the bar receipts of the 'Mariners Compass' and the 'Whalers Return' and other waterfront hotels usually soared. On the other hand, if the ship arrived with only a few score barrels of oil after a year at sea, the crew and mates and captain received virtually nothing for lending their labour and risking their life. As some of the colonial whaling ships were valued at only £1000, and as one year's pay for a ship's company of 26 men at normal rates of a coastal ship would have almost amounted to another £1000, the owners of whaling ships cut their losses whenever the voyage failed.

Sailors, knowing that every whale they caught increased their own pay, were more willing to take risks in the riskiest of all professions. When returned whalemen gathered to swap yarns in the quayside hotels they did not need to exaggerate their reminiscences; many of their most restrained and truthful stories swayed on the edge of incredulity. When the Tasmanian whaler *Offley* went far west to Kerguelen Island about 1859 in search of whales, one sailor's hand was so bitten by frost that gangrene set in and the captain had to amputate the fingers with a blow of an axe. The same ship in 1863 launched four whaleboats in squally weather to fight a bull whale, and all four boats were crushed by the whale. In the same season the whaler *Maid of Erin* put out a whaleboat to overtake a whale; as the five oarsmen rowed rapidly towards the rear of the whale, the whale suddenly turned and charged the boat. One of the men jumped from the boat into the mouth of the whale and was not seen again.

Even timid whales could overturn the slender whaleboats. The *Fortitude* was a regular Hobart whaling ship of the 1840s, and late one afternoon her master Captain Bayley went out in one of the whaleboats with five of the crew to catch a whale. The man in the bow hit the side of the whale with the harpoon, and as the whale raced away it pulled taut the long rope linking the harpoon with the whaleboat, and began to drag the whaleboat through the water at high speed. That often happened during a whaling voyage and usually the whale became exhausted and the boat crew then moved in and killed it with a long lance. On this evening, however, the plan somehow went astray. The men on the deck of the *Fortitude* watched the whale and the towed whaleboat disappear into the fading light, and when darkness fell and the whaleboat had not returned they lit flares to guide the boat back. Morning came and the boat had still not returned. From the masthead sailors saw nothing unusual on the horizon until late morning when they saw seabirds hovering to leeward. On approaching the site they saw an overturned boat and a man clinging to it. The man was Captain Bayley, he was quite unconscious, and his weight was supported by the water and by the swollen forefinger he had pushed into the boat's plughole. He was saved but the other boatmen were not found.

3

The fast increase of Australian ships that hunted the sperm whale was matched by strenuous whaling in those quiet bays of southern Australia to which the whalebone whales came each winter. American and French and British whaling ships in Australian waters had often set up shore parties on the Australian coast in winter for the bay whaling season, and now they had to compete with Australian whaling ships or small gangs of men who hugged the coast in 30-foot whaleboats until they found a promising bay. A small shore base needed only two cedar or Huon pine boats, a boiling-down plant, and 16 or 20 men. For a mere £300 a merchant could buy his boats, provisions for three months, a generous ration of rum (such spirits were freed of customs duty as an encouragement to whaling) and build the rough huts and cooperage and boilers by some lonely bay.

Around the Tasmanian coast in the 1830s when cold winds whipped the waves and the first light broke, whalemen on lookout or high ground would signal the arrival of a whale. Men would promptly push the boat into the water and row out. If they threw the harpoon accurately, and the harpoon did not later tear loose from the blubber, and the connecting rope did not snap, and if the whale did not overturn the boat, and if they finally succeeded in lancing the whale until the sea was streaked with blood, they still had the hardest task before them — the towing of a dead whale weighing thirty or fifty tons to the beach.

Bay whaling in Tasmania was so profitable in the 1830s that soon each of the favoured bays had several rival parties, alert to launch their narrow boats as soon as they saw a whale. At Recherche Bay, in southern Tasmania, 21 boats were said to have chased one whale. In some Tasmanian bays the boats that first reached the whale and successfully harpooned it had their connecting lines cut by rival boat crews. Others found that a whale they had harpooned and cornered was suddenly killed and captured by a rival boat. At the peak, Tasmania possibly had 35 whaling stations in its secluded bays, and the competition for the diminishing schools of whales was so intense that the Government was forced to make laws to settle the disputes that shook the whaling camps.

If a small schooner hugged the southern coast of Australia from Sydney to Perth in the 1830s the men on watch might have seen the flames and flares from whaling stations at many scattered points along three thousand miles of coastline that was otherwise deserted. South of Sydney, at the bay that is now Eden, Tasmanian adventurers arrived about 1828 and stored their catch of oil and whalebone on the beaches. They were followed by the Imlays and by the famous buccaneer Benjamin Boyd, who built his Boyd Town of stone that has slowly crumbled away, and who used Aboriginal and Australian boat crews and the unpaid labours of packs of 'Killer' whales who helped kill the whalebone whales and, after tearing out the tongue, left the carcass for the boats to haul ashore. Here, in Twofold Bay, the last whale was captured in 1928, exactly a century after the first whale was lanced to death.

Tracing the coast for another five hundred miles towards the west one came across the whaling camps of Port Fairy and Portland Bay — the first permanent settlements in what became the rich colony of Victoria. Scratched on the map by bold Tasmanians who had crossed the choppy straits in search of wintering whales, they employed one hundred expert whalemen in the season of 1836. Long after Port Fairy and Portland had been captured by the sheep kings who held the inland plains, the skeletons of whales littered the beaches. The skeletons lay like a sequence of fossils uncovered in layers of old rock — positive proof that whalemen came before woolmen on a coast where whaleman came to be forgotten.

A few hundred miles farther west were the whaling camps on Kangaroo Island and on Encounter Bay, where now the South Australian holiday towns of Victor Harbor and Port Elliot stand. Whaling was the first profitable export industry in this colony of South Australia. Another thousand miles around barren coast, near the present port of Esperance (W.A.), was another string of whaling stations in the south-west corner of the continent. It was one of these whaling stations that the overland explorer Edward Eyre stumbled upon after his epic walk westward along the shores of the Great Australian Bight in 1841. His life was saved by French whalemen wintering in an inlet where whalebone whales were spouting.

The 1830s was the great decade of colonial whaling, whether in the bays or the deep sea. The Tasmanian industry hit its summit in 1837 and New South Wales in 1840. In the ten years 1832–41 New South Wales exported whale products worth £1,700,000, and as far as one can ascertain all that oil and whalebone was caught by colonial ships. In that era Europe's demand for whale products was unusually high and the price of sperm oil in 1840 was probably higher than in any of the previous thirty years.

But then came the slump. The price of sperm oil halved in less than two years, and was slow to recover.

At the same time laws of nature united with laws of economics to humble the bay whalemen. At many bays in eastern Tasmania in the early 1840s rival shore parties waited in puzzlement for weeks before even one cow whale came to breed. They should not have been puzzled; in former seasons they had killed so many whalebone whales in their breedings bays that the whale population was falling. A whale usually gave birth to only one whale calf in each two years and in most Australian bays it was the pregnant whale that was most prized for her heavy coating of blubber. Even if whalemen failed to capture the pregnant whale they could do the same damage later by capturing her when her new-born calf was still being suckled. Bays were a kind of maternity hospital which suddenly became a slaughter house.

'The practice of Australian whalers of killing the calves in order to secure the capture of the mothers, was the chief cause of the ruin of the fishery,' wrote Timothy Coghlan. However, this folly of the whalemen had devastating effects only in the coastal bays. Sperm whales, the mainstay of whaling, bred in deep water and so were less vulnerable. And in the 1840s the packs of sperm whales had been perhaps reduced but not obliterated by the ceaseless hunting. There were still thousands of sperm whales migrating each year between cold and tropical seas, and in the late 1840s Hobart whaling promoters were inspired by rising oil prices to send into the oceans the largest whaling fleet that had ever left the island.

Hobart even surpassed Sydney as a whaling port. On Good Friday 1847, when one can imagine pious whaling masters from Salem and New Bedford seated in Hobart churches, there were said to be 47 whaling ships anchored in the Derwent. Most of the whalers were American, but Hobart's own fleet was expanding with new ships from Tasmanian shipyards. In 1848 the value of Hobart's ships' catch was over £100,000 — the second best on record. In the following year Hobart owned 37 whaling ships with more than a thousand men on board, and the combined tonnage of these ships exceeded that of the 135 other coastal vessels belonging to Hobart.

The whaling revival was cut short in its most promising year. Australians began to hurry to the new Californian goldfields and many men or cargoes went in slow, converted whaling ships. Other whalers dismantled the try-works on deck and joined in the reviving coastal trade between Sydney and Adelaide and Hobart. Once Australia's own gold rushes began, whaling lost its last vestige of importance. The few whalers that continued for decades to sail from Hobart and Port Jackson were now in a heroic backwater.

The United States had the largest whaling fleet on the globe. Within a few thousand miles of the Australian coast, whalers from New England came to outnumber those from England. England's whaling industry had been so pampered by bounties and protected by duties on imports of foreign oil that when it ceased to be coddled it ceased to compete effectively; in 1848 only one British whaling ship sailed into Sydney. In contrast American whaling ships, mostly from Boston and Salem, infested the South Seas and their crews skylarked in Australian ports. An owner of a British whaling ship suggested to a House of Lords committee in 1848 that one reason for America's success was that most of her ships 'go out on the Temperance Principles', whereas British crews would not sail without a grog allowance. It may be that sober Yankee harpooners threw more accurately, and that Yankee boat crews were less foolhardy, and that on the masthead an Australian seaman half filled with rum was not as sharp-eyed for the spout of the whale. But it was only in the 1840s that most American whalers sailed without intoxicants, and by the end of that decade their fleet in the South Seas was waning. Moreover, the value of Australia as a port of refreshment ceased when it became a gold port, and a Salem captain who took his ship into Sydney in 1851 could go ashore on business and not notice that all his crew followed him — never to return.

Gaslight was already challenging the sperm candle and oil lamp in the cities of Europe. In 1859 the world's first successful oil well was drilled in Pennsylvania and soon kerosene was burning in lamps that had once burned whale oil. The United States' first large venture in Australian commerce was inspired by oil from whales; its largest venture today is inspired by oil from rocks.

4

The value of whaling in early Australia seems to have been almost forgotten. From the year 1813, when the exploring of the Blue Mountains pointed to rich pastoral plains beyond, or from the early 1820s when wool exports began to soar, wool dominates history books and shrouds our eyes. But if eventually a reliable series of Australian export figures for the years 1788–1828 is compiled, it will be suprising if Australian-owned whaling and sealing vessels — with their early start — are found to be less productive than sheep in those first forty years. In the following six years export figures do exist, and in all Australia whaling narrowly exceeds wool in that period; as late as 1833 whaling is New South Wales' main export industry. Then wool races away, yielding in the last three years of the 1830s almost double the export value of Australia's whale products.

One suspects that our reluctance to see the importance of whaling stems from an apathy towards maritime history. In Australia, except for shiplovers, the sea and ships are still virtually banished from written history. Perhaps our justification for this attitude is that Australia for more than a century has paid huge sums to the overseas ship-owners who have always manned its sea routes to the outside world. We do not readily believe that an industry carried on at sea could benefit us as much as an industry of comparable size operating on Australian soil.

Whaling not only provided a valuable export. It also was a stimulus to the rise of a free economy in which men could invest or trade or work (and so have independent political attitudes) without depending on the favours of the government for cheap convict labour, or the crucial government market for foodstuffs and wares. It perhaps was a sharper stimulus than wool, because whaling ships and nearly all bay stations hired only free men whereas wool growers at first depended much on the labour of convict shepherds and shearers and teamsters assigned them by the government. Whaling enriched — and sometimes impoverished — free merchants and ship-owners in Australian ports. Whaling taught young Australian seamen their trade; it opened uncharted bays along the coast. There were years in which two thirds of the tonnage of Australian shipping was engaged in whaling; but whaling seems to have dovetailed with rather than dislocated coastal shipping. Merchants built ships to go whaling, and later diverted them to profitable coastal runs; merchants built ships to carry timber or coal along the coast, and if those cargoes were unrewarding they sent their ships to the whaling grounds. Without a colonial whaling industry the coastal fleet would have been smaller and less efficient.

One of the reasons why the ports of Sydney and Hobart held such a puzzlingly high part of the population of Australia in the 1830s was the strength of whaling. American and French and English whalers called increasingly for repairs and provisions, and it was estimated in Hobart in the early 1840s that each foreign vessel in port spent an average of £300, not counting the sovereigns their crews slapped onto counters in waterfront inns. So attractive were the profits from visiting whaling ships that Benjamin Boyd tried to entice them to Boyd Town in the 1840s by frequent advertisements in the Hobart press, announcing that foreign whalers visiting his port could get wood and fresh water, salted or fresh meat, vegetables, slops, ships's stores, and the skills of shipwrights and boat-builders.

Sydney and Hobart, however, gained far more from their own fleet than from the foreign whalers. These ports housed the families of more than a thousand absent whalemen in some years, they took the spending money of returning whalemen, they stored and then exported the oil barrels and whalebone, supplied a mountain of provisions to whaling ships leaving on long voyages, built their barrels and stitched their sails and made their whaleboats, and above all they built their whaling ships. Shipbuilding was probably the largest and certainly the most dynamic colonial manufacture in the first half of the nineteenth century, and Tasmania alone in the 1840s built 400 vessels ranging from small cutters to ships of 500 tons that joined the England-Australia run. Whaling was a mainstay of the shipyards, and scores of large whaling ships were launched in Hobart or Sydney, with popular ceremonies and quaint toasts. 'Sudden death to our best friends, success to their killers, long life to our sailors' wives and greasy luck to the whales' — that was one toast drunk when the whaler *Lady Emma* was launched at Battery Point in Hobart in December 1848. It was a toast not only to whaling but to an industry on which many ports fattened.

For once the long distance from the old world had profited Australia. The clear advantage Australian whaling and sealing ships had over foreign competitors was closeness to the fishing grounds. That proximity was, for more than half a century, one of the nation's few assets.

6   Land Barrier

Most early Australian towns faced the sea and won most of their wealth and gained their importance from the sea and its trades. The sea was more a line of communication than a barrier. Distance was more easily conquered on sea than on land. Water carriage was the cheapest of all forms of transport, and a Sydney merchant in 1820 could send a barrel of whale oil more cheaply to London than to a point only one hundred miles inland from Sydney. He could send goods more cheaply across the world than across the mountains he saw from his warehouse door.

Australia has a spine of low mountains which runs roughly parallel to the east coast for virtually the entire two thousand miles. Near Sydney the spine or plateau is known as the Blue Mountains, and no way across them was discovered until 1813. Later generations of Australians came to accept the idea that the mountains were a wall which for a quarter of a century confined settlement to the coastal plain near Sydney, a physical barrier which was so formidable that it dispirited those who thought of climbing it or frustrated those who tried. Recently, however, a geographer, Dr Tom Perry, convincingly argued that the Blue Mountains were not crossed for a quarter of a century primarily because the early settlers had adequate land on the coastal plain near Sydney and therefore did not need to explore the mountains in search of new land beyond. Even if that area occupied by mountains had in fact been a grassy plain sloping gently inland, settlement in the first quarter century would not have penetrated far into that area. The cost of inland transport was too high to make crop-farming profitable far from the coast.

The most serious effect of the spine of high land was that the watershed of the rivers was close to the east coast. The rivers flowing across the narrow coastal plain to the Pacific were therefore short, and in the upper reaches were too swift to be navigable. This was the real barrier to the spread of settlement towards the interior. In every country in the world, before the invention of railways, the only cheap avenue of inland transport was a river or canal. Inland waterways were vital in opening much of the interior of the United States of America — the Mississippi river boat was as important for commerce as it later was for film makers — but long rivers opened few valuable areas of inland Australia. Similarly, man-made canals gave many regions near the Atlantic coast of the U.S.A. the benefits of cheap carriage on barges early in the nineteenth century, but the terrain of eastern Australia was unfit for the digging of long canals.

The lack of long inland waterways in Australia is often ignored, but it explains much of Australia's early history. The absence of long inland waterways partly explains why Australia was so slow in growing enough to feed itself: its settlers had no access to those interior lands on the east side of the continent which were most suited for growing grain, and until the 1840s — when the fine coastal wheatlands near Adelaide were opened — the years in which Australians grew all the grain they ate were exceptional. Lack of inland waterways also explains why Britain seems to have been more interested in annexing strategic harbours than annexing the whole continent. Lack of waterways explains why exploration of the inland was so slow. It suggests one strong reason for the slow discovery and development of the rich mineral fields in the inland. And, as we'll see, it partly explains the importance of sheep in Australian history.

Without long rivers or canals the first Australian settlements had to hug the coast. Most convict ploughmen and herdsmen worked within a day's walk of the sea. Farmers had to plough and sow land lying near the coast. Even the pastoral men preferred the coastal grasslands, and in 1821 more than seven of every ten sheep and eight of every ten head of cattle on the Australian continent grazed within a radius of forty miles from Sydney. The continent then had nearly 30,000 Europeans, of whom all but 2000 lived in Sydney or on the undulating plain nearby. The first impression of migrants reaching Sydney was the sight of the sails of the high windmills flaying the horizon, and virtually all the grain they ground was grown near Sydney.

Even in that area so close to the sea, agriculture would have been less flourishing without short navigable rivers which enabled small vessels to carry the harvest from farms clustered along river flats. The granary of the colony was on the fertile river flats of the Hawkesbury, about 35 miles from Sydney, and though vessels had to sail more than a hundred miles from the wheatlands down the winding river to the sea and follow the coast southwards to Sydney Heads, that tedious and tortuous passage provided cheaper freights for wheat than the direct overland route to Sydney. Lachlan Macquarie, governor from 1810 to 1821, employed convict gangs, and the funds raised from a tax on rum, to build a fine grid of turnpike roads from Sydney to the outer farmlands; but even straight allweather roads did not enable bullock carts to carry grain as cheaply as the river boats.

The small island of Tasmania had nearly half as many people as the entire Australian continent held in the late 1820s, mainly because Tasmania had rich soil close to estuaries that indented the coastline. On an arm of the Derwent estuary, at Pittwater, was a narrow plain, and in summer sunsets the miles of ripe grain seemed like a golden lake with hardly a fence to ruin the illusion. There perhaps a thousand people, freemen and convicts, lived in what one envious merchant called 'the largest and wealthiest settlement in the island', and the pillar of their wealth was as much the arm of shallow sea as the rich stiff loam. Farmers only had to pay owners of small vessels a mere one tenth of their grain in order to ship their crop forty miles to Hobart, though if blustery southerlies were blowing up Pittwater the voyage could take a fortnight. Similarly, farms near the estuaries at Hobart or Launceston could ship their wheat to Sydney, a distance of about 700 miles, nearly as cheaply as the farmers who lived near the trunk roads only thirty or forty miles from Sydney. In the era of bullocks and unformed roads, carriage on land (for each mile) was often twenty times as dear as carriage on sea, and that was one item of arithmetic that many Tasmanians knew by heart.

The short rivers which were navigable in their lower reaches were vital to farming but they could also be obstacles. Many Tasmanian farmers on the north side of the Derwent River had to carry produce across the river to the main market at Hobart, paying Austin the Ferryman dearly to carry their bullock carts. The ferry was the portal to a large area of farmland and 'sufficient to blast the hopes and mar the future fortunes of the Island', the land commissioners told the governor in 1826. 'Your Excellency may suppose the delay that a Traveller has to encounter, when we inform your Excellency that altho' there are two Punts, the owners employ but four Men altogether, a number barely sufficient to work one over, so that it not unfrequently happens, (as it did with us) that the Passenger has to endure the misery of delay for perhaps three or four hours before he can cross, and obliged to listen to the insolence of a set of ruffianly Boatmen if he attempts to remonstrate, and who knock about and abuse his Horse with impunity . . .' The farmer paid heavily for every bullock, cart, and bushel of wheat which was rowed across the river, often paying one seventh of the market value of his load if he carried the customary wheat. It was not only the vexatious delays at the ferry, the abuse of the boatmen, and the greed of the ferry owner which angered the commissioners but also those other impediments to crossing and recrossing the river. A public house stood on each river bank to waylay the farmer; 'if he steers clear of

Scylla, Charybdis in all probability engulphs him', wrote the commissioners.

2

Possibly no country in the world worshipped the horse with the same fierce veneration as Australia in the nineteenth century. In many cities and towns the day of an important horse race meeting was declared a public holiday. Vast crowds assembled at racecourses and racing results had a news value which often exceeded that of national calamities or international wars. While the most popular object of display in the British Museum is the Elgin Marbles and the most popular object in many American museums of natural history are the skeletons of dinosaurs, the most popular exhibit in Melbourne's museum is the stuffed skin of a champion racehorse named Phar Lap. Horses in Australia received some of the veneration that cows received in India. Whereas India's sacred cows were economically useless and still venerated, Australia's horses do not seem to have been venerated until the era when they were most useful to the country's economic life; and that era came later.

While the Australian pastoral industry was small, the demand for horses was small. Cattle owners often used horses to round up their cattle in rough, unfenced country, but sheep owners employed shepherds who went on foot. The demand for horses as riding animals was small and above all the demand for horses as draught animals was smaller. The main disadvantage of a horse harnessed to a vehicle was that it demanded too much expensive fodder. Even a riding horse needed a larger daily ration of expensive fodder than a draught bullock, if it was to remain fit for hard work. In the middle of the nineteenth century, when the government of New South Wales had to supply forage for the animals its policemen and officials used in the outlying districts, the daily ration of fodder for each horse was usually ten pounds of oats, four pounds of bran, four pounds of wheat straw, and twelve pounds of cultivated hay; and the cost of buying that fodder from farmers and carting it to the various government stables was high. On the other hand working bullocks were given only half of that daily ration; and if necessary they could remain in harness for long periods and eat nothing but the grasses growing near the road. Bullocks — or often convicts — were thus the main carriers in inland Australia for at least two generations.

The economics of a dray and three pairs of bullocks dictated how far farmers could move from the seaports or coastal rivers. By modern criteria the economic of bullock haulage seem astonishingly simple, and to city dwellers they seem at first glance to be favourable. But in the 1820s a team of three pairs of working bullocks usually cost from £90 to £120; and it was nearly as hard for a manual labourer to save that sum as it is for a modern wage-earner to save the price of a medium-sized motor truck. A bullock team was also expensive to maintain. A farmer had to allot part of his land to growing hay or oats to feed the team. As most farms were unfenced, the bullocks could wander and ruin young crops. Moreover, the typical working bullock was a lightweight by modern standards, usually being a cross between a Bengal cow and a Cape of Good Hope bull, and its strength in pulling a dray was not impressive. The load it could haul was restricted because a two-wheeled dray rather than a four-wheeled wagon was the usual vehicle. The dray was preferred because if it stuck in a boggy patch of road, it could be dragged sideways, or swivelled about the face the other direction and then pulled out; a dray was also more manoeuvrable than a wagon on a dry track, and could dodge tree stumps or the chasms which rain had scoured. Six bullocks were working well if they hauled a dray containing 40 bushels of wheat or just over one ton of cargo.

Not much has been written about bullock drays, and yet in one sense their strength and weakness was the key to the early development of inland Australia. A bullock team charged a high rate for each ten miles it travelled, and that money had to come from the value of the produce it carried. If it carried a load of hay, and the hay was worth only £5 a load at market, it could only profitably carry hay a distance of a few miles. If it carried the most valuable farm crop, wheat, and a load of wheat was worth £18 at market, the cost of bullock transport to towns only thirty miles away left the farmer with only small profit. Except where navigable rivers flowed, the bullock dray limited the radius of intensive settlement. In essence only a commodity which was extremely valuable, on a ton basis, could afford transport from regions lying more than forty miles from deep water. Australia had no such agricultural commodities. The only known plants which could be grown in a temperate climate and command a sufficient price for each ton to afford the freight from the inland to port were flax and hemp, and their cultivation in Australia had failed.

What, then, could the vast inland produce? If it could not profitably grow any crops for a distant market, perhaps it could raise animals. Rich pastures across the mountain range could fatten cattle in thousands, and the cattle did not need to be carried in bullock carts to the nearest port; they could walk, though they might lose fat on the road. There was limit, however, to how much fried steak and roast beef Australia's small population could eat, and a limit to the salted beef which could be sold to passing ships. A few barrels of salted beef could be exported occasionally to the Orient, but the sea freight was dear. *Fresh* beef could not be exported — there was no refrigeration. The hides of cattle could be shipped to England, and were by the thousands, but it did not pay to graze cattle for their coats rather than their meat.

There was only one rural commodity which the soils and pastures of inland Australia could produce in large quantities in the era of dear inland transport. The commodity was wool. The climate and limitless grasslands were ideal for woolly sheep; Aboriginals or carnivorous animals who lived on the grasslands were not numerous enough to check the invasion of sheep. Above all, the price

124

of wool in England was normally so high that Australian sheep graziers could afford not only the high cost of sending their wool far overland to the nearest port but also the cost of sending wool from an Australian port to Europe. Wool was valuable enough to pay its own way across the world. This simple point has always been obscured by the practice of pricing wool at so much a pound and grain at so much a bushel. But if the price of these commodities is measured in long tons, the superior value of wool stands out. In the decade 1811–20, for example, the price of wheat did not often exceed £20 a ton in Australia and was much less in England; in contrast, in that decade, the price of average-quality wool in England was rarely less than 2s. a pound or £224 a ton and was often more. In early Australia a ton of wool was usually at least ten times as valuable as a ton of wheat, and sometimes twenty or more times as valuable. Whereas a settler who grew wheat 150 miles inland from Sydney would have paid more than the wheat was worth to transport it merely to Sydney, let alone London, his wool was usually valuable enough to afford the freight across the world.

Wool's ability to overcome the problem of distance would open huge stretches of the interior; it would also make the faraway interior more dynamic and vital than the cramped coastal river flats and plains. Coastal soil grew wheat, maize, pork, mutton and vegetables cheaply for the majority of Australians who lived on the coast, but those commodities were not valuable enough to pay the freight to overseas markets. Rural output in the old districts near Sydney and Hobart was therefore limited by the smallness of Australia's market and the rate at which human stomachs multiplied. The wool from the interior, however, went to the newly mechanized woollen mills of Europe where it was manufactured into apparel for a market that was world-wide and growing rapidly. The scope for the expansion of Australia's wool industry was therefore much greater than for any of its food-growing industries.

Australia still had to compete with European farmers

who grew wool for European markets. Spanish or Silesian flockowners had the advantage that their sheep grazed closer to navigable water and closer to the cities where wool was sold. They also had the advantage, as the century advanced and Europe's population increased and the demand for foodstuffs increased, that they could make more money from many of their acres by turning from wool to meat or by ploughing sheep pastures into croplands. Therefore Europe grew a declining proportion of the wool which its mills demanded, and the part was open for Australia to produce more and more wool. Australia's inland plains were fit for wool, and, until the coming of railways, scarcely fit for anything else. Thus the scene was laid early in the nineteenth century for the forced march of sheep.

The first flocks of sheep huddled on the plain near Sydney. Prized for their mutton rather than their fleece, they were slow to disturb the world's wool markets. Before much wool could be profitably exported, hundreds of thousands of sheep were necessary. The importing of any sheep from Europe was expensive because of the space they occupied in a ship and the fodder they ate on the long voyage, though not all the fodder was eaten since many of the sheep died at sea. The Riley family spent £3600 on the first 200 Saxon sheep they landed in Sydney, and such a big expense harassed them for several years. As Australia had no sheep in 1787, and as the nearest ports at which sheep could be procured were Cape Town and Calcutta and the nearest ports at which superior merinos could be procured were in Europe, the basis of the Australian flocks was created slowly. Only the government or wealthy settlers could afford to import fine-woolled sheep from overseas, and the government was not interested. Only a few thousand sheep were imported from Europe in Australia's first thirty-five years, and as sheep did not breed like rabbits and as they died in drought or were slaughtered for their mutton, the sheep population was slow in reaching its first million. The Australian yearly wool clip did not exceed £100,000 until the end of the 1820s — long after the first large parcel of Australian wool was sold abroad.

Flockowners needed much capital to buy sheep, or much cunning to steal them. Moreover they needed capital to tide them over the long time during which the wool was growing or travelling to market. A migrant who started out by buying a flock of new-shorn sheep had to wait a year before he could shear them again; if his sheep were far inland and the roads were too parched or too muddy, four more months might elapse before the wool reached port; as most ships sailing from Sydney went to the Orient for cargoes he might wait for months before a ship sailing direct to London was willing to carry his wool; the voyage might last five months the wool might lie in an English warehouse for months before being sold; and the sheepowner might have to wait another five or six months before an English ship reached Sydney with the full proceeds of his first sale of wool or the news of the price it had earned. These delays, in all, could total nearly three years. And during these years of waiting for an income the sheepowner had to pay his shepherds, shearers, the men who carted his wool to port and carried back his supplies, the shipowner who arranged the freight of the wool to England, and an endless variety of agents, storekeepers, contractors, merchants and employees of one sort or another. A sheepowner had to be a small capitalist even if only to borrow the money he needed.

While the charm of wool was its ability to master the problems of distance — both over land and over water — the same problems of distance appear to be part of the explanation of two puzzling facets of the industry: why it was slow in becoming important and why it was primarily for men of capital. One may suggest that if Australia occupied the position which the U.S.A. occupied on the globe, and thereby had the asset of proximity to Europe, its wool industry would have risen dramatically and would not have been so markedly an industry for wealthy men, an industry which funnelled much wealth into few hands.

The plain near Sydney had enough grass and water to sustain the colony's flocks in the first thirty years. But as flocks multiplied each lambing season, a few men who were hungry for land drove their flocks across the Blue Mountains to the beautiful undulating plains on the other side. Altready by 1819 there were 24 flocks of sheep and 1400 cattle on the other side of the mountain and the beginnings of a village of turf and timber huts at Bathurst, 150 miles west of Sydney. The exodus over the Blue Mountains swiftened, and six years later one third of Australia's sheep were there.

The road over the low mountains to Bathurst was the main gateway to the interior, the longest and soon the most important road in the continent. A road was completed in 1815, soon after explorers had found a way over the plateau, and was steadily improved by gangs of convicts, some working in chains, and all distinctive in their striped costumes of yellow and black. They were convicts whose continued misconduct in the service of private settlers had led them to the road gangs by way of the courts; in the phrase used by Governor Darling in 1828, they were 'Double distilled Villains'. Nevertheless, while the governor could despise the moral character of the 1300 men on his roads, he could not malign their physical strength and their skill with pick and shovel and wheelbarrow. Without their cheap labour the colony could not have afforded a network of three fine roads — Great Northern, Great Southern, and Great Western — radiating far inland from the sea; and without those roads the problem of the flockowners on the other side of the plateau would have been acute.

'The power which the Government possesses, by means of forced labour, of at once opening good roads throughout the country, has been, I believe, one main cause of the early prosperity of this colony,' wrote Charles Darwin, the biologist, and his comment was sound. As a young man with his personal fame still far in the future, he had called at Sydney while cruising the world in the *Beagle*, and in January 1836 he hired a man and two horses to follow the long road over the Blue Mountains to Bathurst. In the heat they rode along the macadamised road from Sydney to Parramatta, saw the gangs of convicts working in chains on the road, and thought the fenced countryside was rather English in appearance though the inns were rather more frequent. Spending the first night at the Emu Ferry on the banks of the Nepean, they were ferried across the next morning and began the ascent into the sandstone plateau. The roadside fences vanished and the farms were left behind, and the road was a solitary ribbon through the lonely scrub, 'the most frequent object being a bullock-waggon, piled up with bales of wool'. The deep cutting at the pass through Mount Victoria seemed to Charles Darwin to be equal in design and construction to any road in England, but he ceased to be reminded of England when he descended from the plateau and crossed on the fourth day the bare brown downs of Bathurst, the famous sheep country, veiled in the dust of a burning north wind.

Even after the main roads crossed the mountains to the inland plains, they could still be dangerous if the country was dry. In the autumn of 1839, three years after Charles Darwin rode west, a young Scottish migrant named James Graham took the main road running south-west from Sydney, It was the time when the annual wool clip was being carted by bullock drays to Sydney and 'I daresay you are aware,' he told his father in Fifeshire, 'that the greatest part of the work in this country is performed by bullocks.' As Graham rode inland he saw slow clouds of dust approaching him, the dust churned by bullock drays, for the road was so pounded and powdered that in places he could sink his walking stick eighteen inches into the dust. As he continued inland he saw how drought could hobble the wool industry. The sun had dried the grass and evaporated the water from the roadside waterholes, and every two or three miles he passed dead bullocks on the side of the road or bullocks which were dying or which soon would die unless they reached water. Sometimes weak bullocks, released from the dray at a drying waterhole, had rushed into the shallow water, become stuck in the thick mud, and being too weak to lift their legs, had died in the water. Often Graham came across a dray of wool camped beside the road and the bullock driver would explain that the team had died and that he himself had run out of food.

The improved roads were worth a fortune to the wool men. The cost of carting a ton of goods between Sydney and Bathurst was about £20 a ton in the mid 1820s; within a few years it was almost halved, and in the following decades continued to fall. In years of low wool prices, cheap cartage saved many sheepowners from financial ruin. Even when the price of wool was good, that saving in cartage made the difference between a pleasant profit and a jubilant profit.

How intimately the prosperity of the flockowners depended on the efficiency of inland roads and bullock drays has largely been forgotten; and it is easy to assume that, once firm roads had been carved across the mountains to the inland plains, the cost of carting the annual bales of wool to port was not a high proportion of a sheepowners' spending. In 1841, for example, one intelligent flockowner totted up the running costs for all the sheep runs in New South Wales and estimated that the cost of carting the wool to Sydney was only 5 per cent of the wool growers' working expenses. What was more telling, however, was that perhaps £90 of every £100 spent by a wool grower went into the wages and rations of his overseers, shepherds, watchmen, and shearers; and the more distant his sheep run lay from a seaport the more it cost him to carry up the flour and tea and foodstuffs which he rationed out to his employees each week, and the higher the wages he had to pay in order to attract workmen to such a remote area where a tot of rum or a plug of tobacco was exorbitantly dear. The cost of transport was a large part of nearly every sovereign which a wool grower spent. Accordingly there were areas near the end of the long inland roads where the mounting cost of transport rather than the dryness of the interior slowed the wanderings of shepherds and flocks.

The invasion of inland pastures was swift. It encompassed big areas of land because most land seekers were not just content to find sufficient grassland on which to pasture their existing flocks. As a flock of sheep doubled every few years, its owner wanted a kingdom large enough to hold the number of sheep he thought he would own in five or ten or fifteen years' time. Men who needed only 5000 acres of land·claimed 100,000 or more acres, their claims consisting not of buying the land but of erecting shepherds' huts and sheepyards at scattered parts of their sheep runs. As more and more sheepmasters crossed the mountains and pastured or 'squatted' their flocks on the fringes of existing sheep runs, many of the old owners were hemmed in; and some would abandon their existing runs in order to move out to new pastures or would send half of their flocks out to form new sheep stations in the dried country far from port. This was not an orderly, neat invasion of new country. It was more like a gold rush.

Whereas in North America so many of the settlers who pushed into new land travelled in wagon trains to defend themselves against the Indians, the typical pioneers who pushed inland in Australia in the pastoral age went in small parties with only as many men as the size of their flocks required. (John Hepburn, a sea captain who had become sheepowner, set out from the coast south of Sydney in 1838 with 1650 sheep, 18 bullocks and two drays, four horses and a cart; but with him went only eleven men and two children. His party was larger than the typical sheepman's caravan.) Whereas the typical settlement on the frontier of North America was probably a huddle or a community, the typical settlement on Australia's pastoral frontier before 1850 was dispersed. The sheepowner, so long as new land was plentiful, drove their sheep far from the nearest neighbour. The relatively mild threat of attack from Aboriginals (who unlike North American Indians rarely acquired firearms) made dispersal possible. The speed at which flocks of sheep multiplied made it essential to disperse the sheep estates far from one another.

Sheepmasters opened long stretches of coastline where earlier convict settlements had failed. The northern shore of Bass Strait, twice briefly occupied and abandoned, was invaded by sheep in the mid 1830s, one line of flocks straggling overland from the plains beyond Sydney, the other line of flocks crossing the choppy strait in cramped ketches and schooners from Tasmania's crowded grasslands. The village of Melbourne became landing place or supply base for flocks that swarmed across the lightly-timbered grasslands in much of the area that became the colony of Victoria.

The march of shepherds slowed in the 1840s but at the end of that decade the sheep had spread across an enormous belt of land. Sheep were dotted over all grasslands on the islands of Tasmania, and were even on the poorer grasses around the cold lakes in the central mountains. On the south-eastern part of the Australian continent there were sheep scattered nearly all the way from the moist country at the back of Bundaberg in Queensland to the dry hills near Port Augusta in South Australia. Shaped like an arc the sheep country occupied nearly one quarter of the Australian coastline, with gaps only where desert or tumbled mountains or forest intervened. One side of the arc was the ocean and the other side was the vast dry core of the interior. The arc was widest in New South Wales, being 250 miles wide from coast to plain in most places, and along the lower reaches of the Darling River stood huts and bough yards which were more than 400 miles from the sea by the shortest sheep route. If a traveller of superhuman strength and patience had decided to see the full spread of sheep country in 1850 and had travelled through the centre of the pastoral arc from one end to the other he would have gone, by the shortest route, about 1400 miles without once having to dismount and open a gate; and on very few evenings would his camp

Venus Fort, Tahiti, built by Captain Cook in 1769 to observe the transit of Venus.

Modern Sydney, an indirect but more tangible effect of Captain Cook's first voyage.

Norfolk Island and pine trees, envisaged as a prop of English seapower.

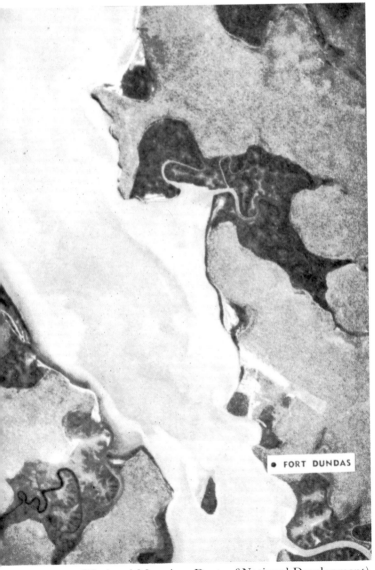

FORT DUNDAS

(National Mapping: Dept. of National Development)
Fort Dundas on Melville Island, founded in 1824 as a new Singapore.
The aerial photo shows the weaknesses of the site: the tortuous strait
far from sealanes, the sand shoals, and the dark mangrove swamps.

Macquarie Island fur seals, and the whales migrating from Antarctica, were early sources of Australia's wealth.

fire have been out of earshot of the bleat of sheep. This arc or crescent of sheep land, if transposed onto a map of the United States of America, would have curved from Boston to New Orleans.

Wool enabled settlement to push profitably far from the Australian coast. Without the incentive of wool Australia in 1850 would have consisted of a few ports surrounded by a narrow belt of farmland. Wool not only opened much of the inland but also tied Australia to Europe. Australia's commercial life had been linked strongly to Asia and the Pacific in the first thirty years, but with the mounting strength of the Australian-owned flocks and whaling fleets, Australia produced its main exports for the European markets. Its growth came to depend less on the big sums which the British Government spent on maintaining its convicts and their keepers in Australia, and more on the price of wool and whale oils on the British markets. Australia's economic life was no longer so insulated from the outside world. A fall in the price of wool in England was reflected months later in the tempo and mood of commerce in Sydney; a strong rise in the price of wool spurred financial booms in Australia. Australia's inland plains were married to Europe's expanding textile mills, and the marriage had many offspring.

Curiously, the exodus of sheep to faraway grasslands did not lead to a strong swing of population from seaports to the inland. No great towns arose at those inland points where many wool tracks converged. Even inland towns with a thousand people were rare. While shepherds and shearers and dray drivers were dispersed in the inland, the main seaports continued to grow so swiftly that in 1850 Australia was one of the most urbanised countries in the world. About four of every ten Australians lived in the six main ports of Sydney, Melbourne, Geelong, Adelaide, Hobart and Launceston, and more than half of Australia's population lived in towns and villages. It is easy to see how in the early years the convict system and whaling and sealing and the varieties of deep-sea commerce gathered a high proportion of the people into the main

133

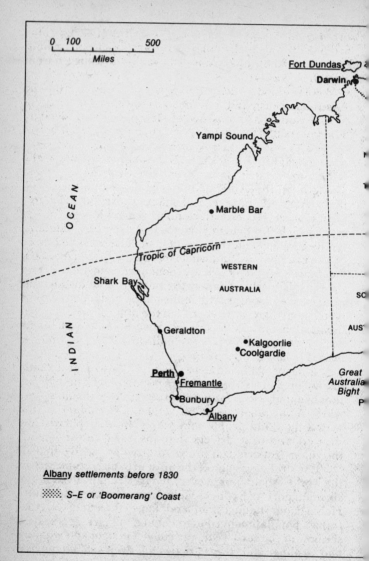

seaports; but one would expect the relative decline of these early trades and the rise of a rich wool industry far inland to have checked the tendency for such a large proportion of Australians to huddle together in the main coastal towns.

Again it is distance which seems to explain why wool so fostered the centralisation of population. The sheep runs were scattered over a vast domain, most being far inland and many pastoral homesteads being a half or full day's ride from the nearest neighbour. If the sheep districts had been as closely populated as farming districts they would have given birth to many inland commercial towns, but their population was sparse and few inland towns arose. Moreover, the sheep districts suffered through a curious leakage of population. To a married migrant arriving at an Australian seaport from Britain with his wife and children, a sheep run offered few social amenities, rarely a school or a church service, small hope of a job for any of his daughters who were old enough to work, and a wage that did not buy much because the prices of all goods except mutton and sheepskin rugs were heavily inflated by the expense of inland transport. Therefore married men tended to seek work in the main seaports; and the sheep owners largely employed the single men who were always plentiful in early Australia. As women and children were relatively scarce in the pastoral regions, the inland population was surprisingly small. Each breadwinner in the pastoral regions of Victoria in 1851, for example, supported only half as many dependent women and children as each breadwinner supported in the main seaports of Melbourne and Geelong. The population of seaports was thus relatively inflated. Moreover their high quota of women and children needed houses, schools, churches, roads, foodstuffs and manufactured goods, thus creating more work in the seaports and thereby increasing their population. In that way the isolation of the sheep runs swelled the existing towns on the coast.

The few big towns fattened not only on the isolation of the wool districts but on Australia's isolation from

Europe. The cost of bringing many manufactured goods from Britain was so high that Australian townsmen were encouraged to make them. A visitor wandering through Sydney or Hobart in the 1840s would have seen breweries, distilleries, soap and candle factories, foundries, dray and coach builders, and a variety of poky factories and repair shops. Many of these industries no doubt would have flourished even if Australia was no further from England than the Scilly Isles. But some of these goods were only made in Australian towns because, if they had been ordered from England, they would have taken too long to arrive, or been too expensive, or deteriorated on the long sea passage. The ocean was Australia's first tariff wall.

4

In narrating why new countries grew and flourished it is customary to assign the cause to their poverty or richness in natural resources. But it is not simply the abundance of resources — whether fine soils or grasslands or minerals or forests — that creates development. The exact position of each resource, the points on the map which they occupy, is decisive. Resources lying side by side are usually far more valuable than if they are parted by long distances. This was particularly true in inland Australia where distance was such an obstacle.

The plains and foothills where sheep grazed held part of their wealth in the grasses and part in the ground. In south-eastern Australia sheep pads crossed some of the world's richest goldfields and lodes of copper and silver as well. One of the first effects of the proximity of pastoral and mineral resources was the way in which the wool industry hastened the opening of the mining industry. This is so obvious that it is usually overlooked.

The taming of distance is essential before minerals can be found and mined. Mineral deposits lying near the coast are likely to be discovered before mineral deposits lying far from the coast. Alternatively, mineral deposits lying near human settlement are likely to be discovered long before minerals that lie far from a hut or road. The first Australian metal fields to be opened were, understandably, in regions already occupied by sheep. Shepherds and sheepowners walking over the ground in the course of their daily work were the great mineral discoverers in early Australia.

Rich mines were opened close to the coast of South Australia less than a decade after that colony had been founded. In 1841 silver-lead mines were opened on the brown hills only four miles from the main town of Adelaide. Fifty miles to the north, a sheepowner's son found copper at Kapunda while picking wildflowers and a man found copper while riding through the rain in search of lost sheep. Farther north, at Burra, a shepherd found richer copper while walking with his sheep. Burra in the late 1840s became one of the world's major copper producers, at times employing more than a thousand bullock drays on the first leg of the long journey to Welsh smelters. Fortunately, the ore was rich enough and close enough to the coast to afford the heavy expense of crossing the world.

The sheeplands of south-eastern Australia were immeasurably richer in gold than copper. The gold, however, was at first not so easy to find. Whereas the larger copper lodes were visible from afar by the brilliant blue and green colours of the rocks on the ground, the gold was rarely visible except to the sharp-eyed man. A rich reef of gold usually held less than one part of gold to every thousand parts of barren rock, and most of the loose alluvial gold was sprinkled sparsely amongst earth and gravel. Those shepherds who did find gold were often secretive, knowing that if they told others of their discovery they themselves would have less chance of finding other specks or nuggets of gold in the vicinity. The English common law decreed that gold in the ground belonged to the Crown, thereby deterring men with capital or mineral knowledge from searching for gold with the same vigour with which they sought copper. Nevertheless, despite all these impediments, many shepherds found gold in New South Wales in the 1840s. Some of the discoveries were widely known, for gold was sold to jewellers in the seaports and occasionally put on display in shop windows. In the late 1840s those isolated discoveries became more frequent. It only required one rich find, the publicising of its whereabouts, and a sudden rush of gold seekers to dig energetically in the vicinity; and then the spasmodic, surreptitious treasure hunt would become a systematic, expanding industry. One such rush occurred to a sheep run twenty miles from Ballarat in 1849, but through an unusual combination of events the men narrowly failed to locate the layers of gold hidden just below the grass.

Australia was probably on the eve of its own gold rushes at the very time when rich gold was found on the other side of the Pacific, in the timbered foothills of California. In January 1848 a few men digging a tailrace for a water-powered sawmill chanced to excavate down into a buried layer of gold and gravel. Gold had been discovered a few years previously in exactly the same circumstances in what became the Australian goldfield at Beechworth, but the discoverers there had not realized that the yellow grains were gold; in that California water race, in contrast, the mineral was identified as gold. Digging revealed more gold. Searchers found gold in other valleys. A rush set in from the small town of San Francisco and, as the news blew across the world, from hundreds of distant ports.

California was closer to Sydney than to New York in the era when there was no Panama Canal and no railways spanning North America. In the year of the Forty Niners the fastest vessels sailed from Sydney across the Pacific to San Francisco in ten weeks. That was three weeks shorter than the swiftest passage ever made by a sailing ship on the long route from New York to San Francisco by way of Cape Horn. Sydney therefore became one of the supply bases for the California goldfields, exporting everything from pickles to prefabricated houses. Australia also exported people to California, losing in two years one in every fifty of her population.

Edward Hargraves, the man who triggered off Australia's gold rushes in 1851, had visited California, where he lazily observed the gold quest. Without that experience he would not have found gold in Australia. Nor would he have found gold in Australia if other men had not already discovered gold before him. He rode on their shoulders, if one may use such a metaphor for a man who was cunning, persuasive, easy-going, and weighed some eighteen stone. Early in 1851, on his return from California, he rode from Sydney across the Blue Mountains to the sheep country to search for payable gold in places where shepherds had already found gold. Though he himself did not find payable gold, he taught others how to search. When they found extensive deposits of gold near the site of a shepherd's earlier find, Hargraves smoothly claimed the credit as well as the rewards. He deserved those rewards — the £16,000 from Australian governments and the gold cups, gold spurs, gold whip, gold nuggets, and gilt-edged testimonials bestowed on him by a grateful public. A gold-lined sheepskin would have completed his outfit, for the first gold rush came as much from the sheepskin as from the wolf it symbolically clothed.

In May 1851 the rush set in to the new goldfield 160 miles west of Sydney. A wave of gold discoveries followed quickly to the south, not far inland from Melbourne, which had just been made the capital of the new colony of Victoria. That too was sheep country and the inhabitants were alert for gold as they went about their daily work. Rich gold was found in white quartz rock only a stone's throw from a sheepowner's homestead at Clunes, and a rush began. Gold was found by the village blacksmith only a mile or two from his forge at the pastoral village of Buninyong, and another rush began. The first gold of Ballarat was found by an upcountry wool road, the first gold of Bendigo was found near a shepherd's hut, the first gold of Mount Alexander was picked up near a rough yard where sheep were penned at night. By the close of the first gold year, 1851, Victoria was outstripping New

South Wales in richness, and together they were about to challenge California as the most productive gold region on the globe. When news of the richness of the goldfields finally reached Britain, the common vision of Australia as a land of punishment was replaced by a vision of a land of reward. While wool was an industry for men who had capital, gold was for a long time an industry for poor men. To thousands of British emigrants the attractions of gold were sufficient to compensate for the expense and tedium of the sea voyage to Australia.

Gold, even more than wool, was able to pay with ease the cost of being carried from inland Australia to the banks of Europe. One ton of gold was worth over £100,000; the cost of carrying it from the gold mine to Europe was therefore only a trifling fraction of the value of the gold. Nevertheless, the main hindrance to the mining of gold was the cost of inland transport.

Many goldfields were almost choked by the yokes of the slow-moving bullock teams. Crowds of men quickly assembled on the early goldfields, and almost all their food except mutton and lamb's fry had to be carried up from the seaports. Diggers entering a typical general store on the goldfields could buy Barrett's best twist tobacco, ten pound tins of confectionery, or a tin of Epsom salts. They could buy doeskin cloth trousers, and pilot-cloth monkey jacket and a red nightcap, or they could carry away nails, shovel, pick, and crosscut saw; but nearly everything thay bought was expensive because it came from Europe. The cost of carrying those goods across the globe, however, was much less than the cost of carrying them from the nearest Australian seaport to the goldfield.

A Victorian parliamentary commission reckoned in September 1854 that consumers on their goldfields were paying £2 million to £3 million a year for the carting of supplies from the coast. That was an immense freight bill; Victorian gold diggers in that year probably received not much more than £7 million for the gold they sold. The size of that freight bill is more remarkable when it is remembered that the average dray-load had to be carted no more than a hundred miles from port to gold camp.

The bush tracks to the goldfields had steep hills and unbridged creeks and in winter they were boggy or impassable. The cost of carrying supplies was inflated by the scarcity of labour, for teamsters demanded high wages, and farriers and wheelwrights and blacksmiths earned as much as many gentlemen-farmers earned in England. Carting provisions to the goldfields was additionally expensive, since nearly all drays had to return empty to Melbourne or Sydney. The leather bags of gold, the only back loading, were not entrusted to bullock drays, which were cumbersome and easy to rob.

On any given day several thousand drays were possibly travelling or camped along the roads between ports and goldfields, but after winter rains more drays were probably idle than active. During the winter of 1854 so few drays could get through the mud to the Victorian goldfields that Melbourne merchants had to pay the colossal sum of £100 a ton to send their goods 100 miles into the interior. At the height of summer, however, the same cargo might be carted for £10 a ton.

The main carriers were bullocks, each team carrying up to three tons of goods in summer. They dawdled along the roads, the driver walking beside the dray with a heavy blue veil on his face to fend off flies and dust. As the roads to the main goldfields were improved with bridges and cuttings and embankments and roadmetal, bullock teams lost their clear supremacy as inland carriers. The sheer strength which had enabled them to master boggy patches or steep hills was no longer so necessary on improved roads. Bullocks, not usually being fitted with shoes, hurt their hooves on the sharp stones on the new macadamised roads. New farms near the main roads to the goldfields now cheaply provided the hay and fodder so essential for horse teams, and by the mid-1850s a pair of draught horses pulling a light dray with one ton of cargo was a common sight. On firm roads horses were much faster than bullock teams and their only disadvantage was their high purchase price. On some roads one could count

400 plodding dray horses in a day, and those horses together were probably worth as much as the largest sailing ship in the world.

The human traffic to the goldfields was mostly on foot. Wealthier travellers might ride horses or drive carts, but the cost of a horse and daily horsefeed was too high for most itinerant diggers. Similarly, passenger coaches were too expensive for the man on the road, charging him the equivalent of one or two weeks' wages for a ride of a hundred or so miles.

Horse-drawn coaches were the fastest means of travel to the goldfields and the fastest coaches were owned by Cobb & Co., which in time became as famous in Australia as Wells Fargo was famous in western America. Freeman Cobb, himself an American, used light American-style coaches with leather springs to carry passengers and mails quickly to the Victorian goldfields from 1854. On the firmer roads in summer he used larger coaches carrying 15 or 16 passengers and drawn by six horses; 'they are horses that stand pretty high, with a good action', he noted proudly. As drivers he usually engaged Americans, paying them well but insisting that they drink no alcohol while holding the reins. By changing the horses at hotels or staging places every ten miles or so along the road, his coaches often averaged nine miles an hour on roads to the goldfields. In summer, for example, his coaches left Melbourne daily at six in the morning and often reached the gold town of Castlemaine, in high ranges 77 miles away, by 2.30 in the afternoon. Rival lines of coaches, which crammed in the passengers and changed horses infrequently and charged lower fares, usually took twice as long on the same journey. When eventually railways drove the horse-drawn coaches from the busiest roads, Cobb & Co. moved to the back country of eastern Australia. They were said in 1870 to be harnessing 6000 horses a day, and were then perhaps one of the largest coaching firms in the world.

Throughout the 1850s and 1860s gold was Australia's main export. Not until 1870 did wool again surpass gold. Both wool and gold had the same peculiar advantage to a new, distant country. Each ton was so valuable that it could easily withstand the heavy expense of cartage from the interior of Australia to ports of Europe. Whereas most other commodities grown or gathered in Australia were only produced in limited quantities because they could only be sold in the small Australian market, wool and gold could be produced in immense quantities because they could reach a world market. Gold and wool thus created far more employment and wealth than any other commodities in Australia. They provided more incentive for money and men to cross the world to Australia. The booming gold and wool industries enormously increased the demand for Australian manufactures and farm products; they stimulated commerce, trades, and professions; they increased the demands for houses, shops, offices and schools, for roads and wharves and reservoirs. In short, they multiplied the jobs which the country could provide. If Australia had been unable to produce wool or minerals — commodities which could be sold on the distant world markets — its population might have been less than one million instead of three million at the end of the first century of European colonisation.

Many of these multiplying effects of the early gold rushes came from the physical location of the Victorian and New South Wales' gold deposits. They lay near fine sheep lands, forests, fertile land for farming, and were relatively near the continent's main ports, Melbourne and Sydney. Much of the gold would not have been mined if miners had lacked these other natural advantages. Because ports were near, the cost of European goods was cheaper. Because forests were so near, the goldfields got cheap timber for their underground workings and cheap firewood for their steam boilers. Because fertile soil was so near they ultimately got cheap grain and meat. Thus the cost of living for miners was lower. They could work many gold deposits which would have been profitless if they had lain in a less accessible and favoured region. A larger and more prosperous population on the goldfields in turn led to a larger working population on the adjacent farmlands and forests and in the coastal cities which served the inland. The concentration of people in the inland ultimately led more quickly to the building of railways, and those railways were cheaper to operate because they served a busier area generating more traffic. All these assets spurred the coastal ports, giving their factories a larger market and some of the economies of large-scale production. Just as the coal of the Ruhr and the iron of Lorraine created together a rich industrial area along the changing borders of France and Germany, so the varied natural resources in the south-east corner of Australia strengthened one another in a visible but subtle way. The resources and industries being side by side, distance was shortened and the cost of transport was less of a burden.

Although in time the gold rushes moved around the rim of the continent, the south-east became more and more the hub. Sydney and Melbourne — nearly 600 miles apart — alternated as largest cities, and New South Wales and Victoria alternated as the most populous colonies. They were freely endowed with potential resources; more important, their plentiful resources were compact and could thus be exploited more cheaply and fully. When the twentieth century dawned, and manufacturing became a dynamo of Australia's growth, the south-east already had the largest cities and the largest market. It was the cheapest area in which to manufacture, and the growth of factories further increased its dominance.

Today two of every three Australians live in New South Wales and Victoria, mostly in coastal cities. Alternatively, if the south-eastern rim of the continent is defined as the coast stretching from Port Pirie to Adelaide to Melbourne to Sydney and Brisbane and all the interior within 200 miles of that coast, then the result is a coastal tract shaped like a boomerang. 'The Boomerang Coast' holds less than one tenth of the country's area and much less than half of the country's natural resources, but it holds eight of every ten people.

Some critics argue that it is unrealistic that most Australians should live on the Boomerang Coast when vast areas elsewhere are sparsely settled or deserted. The density of population along the Boomerang Coast, however, is realistic, economically and socially. As most people and economic activities are concentrated into one relatively compact region, the cost of transporting raw materials, foodstuffs, manufactured goods, and power is cheaper. Within that region distance is still a problem but a manageable problem. Through the concentration of population on the Boomerang Coast, Australia spends much less of its energy in carrying goods and supplying services over vast distance. Its standard of living and its ability to support a larger population are much higher than if its main economic activities and its population had been scattered around the rim of the continent. The Boomerang Coast, and the dominant cities on that coast, were the simplest solution to the problems of distance.

7   The Art of Abduction

The wide ocean parting Australia and Europe impeded the export of Australian commodities. The same wide ocean was also a barrier to the migration of people from Europe. Whereas one powerful cause of the United States' rapid growth of population in the nineteenth century was its closeness to Europe, the most powerful brake on Australia's growth of population was its distance from Europe. Historians of the United States often overlook this obvious fact, preferring to concentrate on the natural resources of their land and the enterprise of their people as the dynamos of national growth. In Australia we also overlook this obvious fact, concentrating on Australia's deficiency of natural resources as the only reason why Australia was not a serious rival to the United States.

In the first half of the nineteenth century a working family in Britain who thought of starting a new life in a new land was not easily attracted to Australia. If a mill worker in Manchester or a farmer on a rented farm in Norfolk discussed the prospects of emigrating, the plans they made around kitchen tables were usually fixed on North America. They probably knew people who had migrated there. The sea voyage was much shorter and decisively cheaper to New York than to Sydney, and if they eventually disliked living in North America they had some hope of returning to England but if they eventually disliked their life in Australia they had only faint prospect of being able to pay the passage back to England. The ocean and all the disadvantages of isolation eliminated

Australia as a goal for most emigrants who had to pay their own fares.

In Australia's first half century most migrants came unwillingly. Australia's increase of population was geared to the increase of crime in the British Isles and to the punitive measures prescribed by parliament and courts. In islands which were disturbed by swift social and economic change, sufficient convicts were available for deportation to give Australia a steady flow of migrants. There were even times in the first forty years of Australia's history when it received too many migrants; the new convicts had to be fed and clothed, and that strained the supply stores.

The convict system was vital to Australia. If Australia had received no British convicts and instead had had to rely on free migrants from Britain, it would have probably attracted very few people in the first half century 1788–1838. Clearly, Australia's main economic activities were suckled by the convict system. The strength of agriculture was a simple reflection of the size of the local population and the number of mouths which needed food, and that in turn depended closely on the inflow of convicts. The strength of local manufactures and commerce was tied to the convict system; importers and shopkeepers and tradesmen and professional men depended for their living on the sums of money which Britain annually spent on the upkeep of convicts and guards. In 1830 Australia's population (not counting the Aboriginals) had risen to 70,000; but if His Majesty's Government had not been so generous in paying the fares of its selected migrants, it is difficult to imagine that the population even under the most favourable conditions could otherwise have exceeded 10,000.

The convict system hastened the rise of a dynamic export economy, producing goods for an expanding world market. If Australia had not been a gaol, a strong Australian-owned whaling fleet might not have arisen before 1850. Convicts cheaply built the whaling ships and emancipated convicts and their free-born sons manned them. The rich men who financed the whaling voyages probably financed them with profits made from farming or commerce within a convict economy.

Australia ultimately straddled the sheep's back, but the sheep in the first era of the pastoral industry were often carried on convicts' backs. The government assigned convicts to the sheepowners, who fed and clothed them and used them as dray drivers and shepherds. In the era before plains were crossed with fences, each pastoralist had to employ a shepherd for each of his many flocks, and the shepherd kept the sheep from straying, defended them from attack by Aboriginals or wild dogs, and his presence at lambing time cut the mortality of ewes and lambs. As the English wool market became more attractive, and the Australian flocks were multiplied with each lambing season, the demand for shepherds and hutkeepers and pastoral workers increased at such a pace that the arrival of convict ships was eagerly awaited. Without convicts, liberated convicts, and their native-born sons, the flocks of sheep and the wool industry could not have grown swiftly. The convict system in essence was a form of compulsory, assisted migration. It eased the problems created by Australia's distance from Britain. Without it, relatively few people from the British Isles would have made the costly journey across the world in Australia's first half century.

But the walls of the gaol would not stand indefinitely. Like the walls of Jericho, they could be flattened by the loud shouts and trumpets of organised pressure groups. By the 1830s trumpets were blowing inside and outside the walls. In Australian seaports were groups — free immigrants or men who had served their sentences — who argued that the convicts' cheap labour kept down the wages of free men and contaminated society. In Britain influential critics denounced the convict system. It was expensive to Britain; as a punishment it was a lottery; as a means of reforming criminals it was probably ineffective; and the prospect of deportation no longer seemed such a stark deterrent to criminals.

The exact causes of the decline of the convict system are still a topic of debate amongst writers of history. Whether Britain was guided more by economy, or by humanity and changing views of criminal punishment, or by a changing concept of colonisation and empire, is not clear. Whatever the cause, Britain decided in 1840 to send no more convicts to the mainland of Australia. For another twelve years, however, convicts were still shipped to the two Australian islands — Tasmania and Norfolk Island. Moreover, a few shiploads were sent sporadically in the 1840s to ports in eastern Australia, and from 1850 to 1868 nearly 10,000 male convicts were sent to the isolated colony of Western Australia. Thus, nearly a generation elapsed between the decision of 1840 which seemed to herald the end of the convict ships and the arrival in 1868 of the last convicts at Fremantle on the western coast. Nevertheless, the great majority of the 162,000 convicts who reached Australia came before 1840, and that year marks the end of a long epoch in which the Crown selected most migrants to Australia, clothed them for the voyage, paid their fares, and prevented them from returning to Britain if their first impressions of Sydney or Hobart or the faraway sheep runs were distasteful. The decline of the convict influx therefore posed a dilemma: how could Australia attract migrants across the globe?

2

Australia's distance from Europe dictated its immigration policy in the transition era from convict to free labour. Australia could not compete with the English-speaking lands of North America for a share of the stream of emigrants from Europe in the generation after the Napoleonic Wars. Australia was too far away; the fare out was three or four times as high as the fare to North America; and moreover during the long voyage to Australia a working man was compulsorily unemployed. Most British working men or tradesmen who decided to emigrate to the new world therefore selected North America. On the other hand if they were offered a free passage to Australia on condition that they worked for so many years at a guaranteed wage for the Australian sheepowner or company which advanced his fare, they would probably choose Australia. But few working men were offered a free passage to Australia by private employers, because the employers knew from sour experience that they could not retain their free labourers once they reached Australia. The colony of Western Australia had tried that idea in 1829, and within a short time its landowners had lost the services of most English labourers whose fares they had paid.

While Australia could attract few working men it could attract men of capital, because it offered them two advantages over North America. It offered them free land until the late 1820s and it offered them convict labourers. So long as Australia granted free land to migrants who arrived with capital, it had some attraction to the wealthier strata of British society, but that was a relatively small strata and of course composed largely of people who had no incentive to emigrate. Even to those people — sons of merchants or landowners or professional men — Australia was hardly attractive if they were given a large estate but not enough hands to work it.

The problem of attracting working people to Australia was crucial. A way of paying their fares had to be devised. Britain could not be expected to help; if it decided to pay the fares of tens of thousands of paupers to the new world, it would get more value for its money by paying their fare to North America. The finance then had to come from Australia. In the limited range of taxes from which the Australian government could finance migration, import duties collected at Australian ports was the most promising, but that revenue helped finance the administering of the country. From existing taxes the governors in the Australian colonies had no spare funds for subsidising migration. They could of course impose new taxes. By taxing those Australian employers who used convicts as labourers, they might raise £20,000 a year with which to pay the fares of free emigrants from Britain; but rumours of such a tax aroused intense opposition in Australia. There remained the largest and most obvious untapped source of revenue: the vast sweep of Australian land which the Crown owned.

3

Edward Gibbon Wakefield was one man who pondered the problem of attracting migrants to Australia. He had much time to gnaw at the problem, because from 1827 to 1830 he was kept in Newgate prison in London. He also had an emotional incentive to think about Australia, to imagine the life of its people and the economic problems of the country, because he had perhaps been lucky to avoid being exiled there. He was an eloquent, personable, and apparently amorous fellow who had discarded some of the tenents of his Quaker ancestry. He had been a minor diplomat at the British embassies in Turin and then Paris, until, at the age of thirty, he abducted a schoolgirl heiress named Ellen Turner, married her at Gretna Green, and took her to France before the crime was discovered.

In prison in 1829 Wakefield wrote eleven long anonymous letters to the *Morning Chronicle*, a London daily, and the letters aroused such interest that they were republished at the close of the year as a thin book entitled *A Letter From Sydney, the Principal Town of Australasia*. In the book Wakefield masqueraded as a landowner who gained an insight into the problems of the colony while running an estate of 20,000 acres near Sydney. Wakefield in fact had not visited Australia but his diagnosis of its social ailments was sharp. He indignantly deplored the lack of women of marriageable age, affirming that in New South Wales 'open, naked, broad-day, prostitution is as common as in Otaheite'.* He deplored that drunkenness was

---

* Tahiti.

making common people brutal, that the corrupted slang of English thieves was becoming the accepted language of the colony. Convict labour, he argued, was a form of slavery which debased and made brutal the men of property who employed and disciplined and punished the convicts. Australian children were depraved by the adults about them, or by the sight of bloody punishments in a land where, in Wakefield's vivid mind, 'human beings are continually hanged in rows, as cattle are slaughtered in the French abbatoirs'. It did not surprise Wakefield that robbery and murder were widespread and property and life were unsafe.

Wakefield's diagnosis of Australia's economic ills was also alert. He described the acute shortage of labour. Most capitalists needed more convict labourers and servants than were available. The alternative was to recruit free migrants from Britain by advancing their shipping-fare. Once the free migrants reached Australia, however, they would use any trick to evade their contract of employment in order to become landholders, or to work for another employer at higher wages; free migrants could elope as easily as an heiress. Here then was a country with rich soil and great scope for employment but a scarcity of labourers. And on the other side of the world, outside the walls of Newgate prison, was a country with thousands of paupers who virtually starved for want of work.

For these social and economic ills Wakefield had a common solution. It was not original, but was simple, comprehensive and persuasive. He suggested that Australian land should not be given away to settlers but instead sold at a relatively high price. The revenue from the sale of land would then finance the ship fare from Britain of poor emigrants, in particular married couples. When they reached Australia they would usually have to work as labourers for a time before they saved enough to buy the dear land, and so a supply of free labourers would be assured. With an assured supply of servants in Australia, respectable and rich English people would be encouraged to emigrate, and those free emigrants would lift the moral tone of a corrupt society. Moreover, if the price of land in Australia was made artificially high, most settlers would no longer afford to buy big estates. Settlement therefore would be centred into a few populous regions instead of straggling far inland. And, he argued, 'that CONCENTRATION would produce what never did and never can exist without it — CIVILIZATION'.

This blueprint ultimately gave Wakefield immortality in Australia and New Zealand. After his death he was acclaimed by a shelf of books as one of the most influential men in the history of the two lands, a man whose fluent pen in a faraway prison caused revolutionary changes. One may suggest, however, that it was not the power of one man's ideas but the power of Australia's geographical isolation that was so influential, for Wakefield's ideas were only accepted when they conformed to geographical reality. His idea that the spread of settlement in Australia should be halted by increasing the price of new land was never effectively carried out, even though the colonial office in London was as anxious as Wakefield to check the march of settlement along the Australian coastline and inland. Wakefield's policy of selling grazing land at a high price would have checked the wool industry. That industry was too valuable to be checked and moreover was supported by a strong lobby in both Australia and England. On the other hand Wakefield's ideas that the Crown should sell Australian land at a relatively high price and use the revenue to subsidise emigration from Britain were ultimately adopted, with vital results for Australia. Although that policy was popularised by Wakefield's pen, one suspects that even if Wakefield had been illiterate or had died in the abducted one's arms, the same policy would have been adopted. It was the only effective answer and the obvious answer to the problem of how to build a free bridge on which poor emigrants could cross from one side of the world, where they were unwanted, to the other side where they could be employed. Significantly, only Australia and New Zealand — the two countries of the new world that were most distant from Europe — adopt-

154

ed part of Wakefield's theory; and they only adopted that part of his theory which answered the main problem created by their isolation from the old world: the problem of attracting migrants.

The Crown began to push up the price of land in Australia. Whereas in the 1820s it gave away land or sold it for a small sum, in 1831 it ceased to grant free land to new settlers. No Crown land was to be sold for less than 5s. an acre, and so new land in Australia roughly equalled the price of new land in North America. At that stage Australia's land policy was orthodox, not unique. Then in 1836 the new colony of South Australia was founded by private colonisers, disciples of Wakefield, who banned the importing of convicts and therefore had to rely on free labour; as the only way to attract that labour was to subsidise the fares of emigrants from England, they insisted that Crown land should be sold in their new colony for 12s. an acre and that the proceeds should pay the fares of poor migrants. Two years later, in 1838, the colonial office in London made another far-reaching decision. Knowing that the practice of assigning convicts to the service of pastoralists and private employers in eastern Australia would soon cease and that a stronger inflow of free migrants was necessary, it lifted the minimum price of land in eastern Australia from 5s. to 12s. an acre. Then in 1842 the minimum price at which Crown land could be sold throughout Australia was raised to 20s. The policy of dear land had come to stay.

The policy seemed likely to incite fierce resentment amongst the landed interests in the older Australian colonies. Much of the resentment, however, was hollow. Farmers and pastoralists who already owned land near Sydney and Hobart could not genuinely complain at the soaring price at which Crown land was sold because it indirectly raised the market price of their own land. Likewise sheepowners who grazed their flocks on Crown land — and most Australian sheep nibbled grass belonging to Queen Victoria — were not hurt by the rising price of land. For a ridiculously low fee of £10 a year, they could still run their sheep over areas exceeding 100,000 acres. Most of the great sheepowners in the country continued to pay virtually nothing for the land they used, and so they personally contributed nothing to the funds from which the fares of British migrants were paid. At first most of the land which the Crown sold at slowly rising prices consisted either of town blocks or agricultural land near the coast. But by the 1860s hundreds of pastoralists were being forced to pay huge sums to the Crown for the freehold of their land in order to retain their sheep runs.

Once Australia began to sell land instead of giving it away, it had a purse from which to pay migrants' fares. Whereas barely 7000 free people had migrated to Australia before 1830, the flow of free migrants quickened as money from land sales was siphoned to the owners of migrant ships from the year 1832. A decade later, in 1842, a law passed by Britain's parliament apportioned half of the Australian land revenue for encouraging immigration. By then more people were sailing to Australia in migrant ships than in convict ships, and by the late 1840s the total of free people who had migrated to Australia exceeded the total of convicts who had come since the start of colonisation. Many migrants paid their own fares but most came because most or all of their fare was paid for them.

News that Australia was a mint of gold sped the flow of unsubsidised migrants. Australia had 400,000 people at the end of 1850, a few months before the rush for gold began, and that number trebled to 1,200,000 in the next dozen years. But even in those golden years the fares of nearly half the migrants were subsidised. While gold built an escalator across that ocean, tens of thousands of people would not have stepped on that escalator unless they had been presented with a free ticket or a bargain fare.

4

Not only were fares subsidised on the passage to Australia but the conditions in the ships were carefully regulated too. The dangers and hardships as well as the expense of the long sea voyage were tempered. From the 1820s the British parliament had begun to pass Passenger Acts which regulated the conditions in British-owned emigrant ships. On the short voyage to North America these new laws seem to have been laxly enforced, but on the voyage to Australia these laws were much more rigidly enforced. The length of the voyage to Australia called for careful supervision. Above all, once governments began to select migrants for Australia and to subsidise their fares, they tended to become responsible for their well-being during the voyage.

Only a handful of wealthy emigrants travelled in cabins. They had privacy, their cabins were not stifling on hot evenings in the tropics and they dined in style at the captain's table. In return for these privileges, they paid three times as much as the average passenger paid for the voyage. Another group of intermediate passengers was berthed below the main deck, and their cabins or enclosed cubicles had a little less space and privacy. But at least nine of every ten migrants who came to Australia in its first hundred years travelled in the steerage. Most never forgot the congestion and the monotony of their three or four or five months at sea, or the idleness of the only long holiday they had in their lives.

The steerage passengers slept between decks, in effect a long low room traversing almost the length of the ship. This space was divided, for the sake of morality, into three large compartments on most migrant ships from the 1840s onwards. In the after part of the ship lived the single women with a strong matron to discipline them. A large bulkhead or wall separated them from the married couples and children in the centre of the ship. The single men were forward, behind another bulkhead. Within each of the three areas the floor space was divided into berths, generally six feet by six feet, and four people slept in each berth. One berth was separated from another by a partition of wood which, being only one foot high on most ships, gave no privacy unless everyone was asleep. The partition was merely a board that served as a fence. Thus each area between-decks was a huge dormitory, with four people to each bunk or berth, and in many ships there was a second tier of berths only three feet above the lower berths. The migrants dressed and undressed in full view of one another. Their quarrels were public. Their whisperings had an audience only two feet away. The rule that all passengers had to be in bed at 10 o'clock each night seems a petty piece of discipline, but in those long chattering, sweating, snoring dormitories it was probably sensible.

Many steerage passengers wanted more privacy. One of the bold planners of privacy was Lieutenant Lean, emigration officer at the port of London in the late 1840s. He insisted that many ships carrying emigrants to Australia should have partitions rising two feet high between each berth. He also thought there was less chance of married couples becoming intermixed beneath a pile of blankets if each berth was cut in half by a long board; and in 1852 this segregation was enforced by the Passengers' Act. It is doubtful if shipowners applauded Lieutenant Lean's practical morality. The merit of a passenger ship with few partitions and fittings between decks was that, at Sydney or Melbourne, the rectangular series of boards could be ripped away, and the ship could carry back to London bales of wool or casks of tallow on the very deck where the emigrants had slept. For thousands of emigrants their first sensual link with their new land was the greasy smell of wool and tallow as they first descended to their sleeping quarters in a British harbour.

Passengers' Acts, by the 1840s, allowed each migrant a specified amount of food for each week of the voyage. Each man or woman was given $10\frac{1}{2}$ pounds of bulky food, of which five pounds were oatmeal and the remainder rice, flour, bread or ship's biscuits. They also were allowed the weekly luxury of half a pound of sugar, two ounces of tea, and half a pound of molasses to spread on their bread, or gruel. Children under fourteen received half rations; if they were overgrown they suffered, or ate their parents' food. However, on most Australian migrant ships of the 1840s passengers got more than this official dietary scale and also had meat at midday dinner. By 1855 the diet of most migrants had become more balanced with less oatmeal and flour and more meat. The weekly ration also had more variety, and included 2 pounds of potatoes, $1\frac{1}{2}$ pounds of peas, $\frac{1}{2}$ pound of raisins, 6 ounces of both suet and limejuice, 4 ounces of butter, one gill of vinegar, and a pinch of salt, pepper and mustard. That was probably a luxurious diet to poor passengers from Ireland or the Scottish highlands.

Steerage passengers formed themselves into messes of about ten people, and shortly before each meal the head of each mess went to the cook's galley to receive the allowance of cooked food for the members of his mess. The head of the mess carried the gruel or the baked bread or meat stews and tea back to the mess, apportioned it to the members, who ate as they sat on the deckboards. When the meal was over, the fussier passengers washed their plates and quart pot and cutlery, putting them away clean for the next meal. The sole duty of the ship was to supply and cook the food; she provided no dining tables, seats, cutlery, or plates.

Australian emigrants were considered to be pampered compared to steerage passengers who went to the United States in the 1840s. Frederick Marshall, who kept a Plymouth boarding house where emigrants lodged for fourpence a night while waiting to board their ships, had travelled in migrant ships to both Sydney and New York in the 1840s. On the Atlantic crossing passengers had to cook their own food and he recalled that the galley held only six people and that hundreds were waiting to cook their meal. Marshall appeared before a House of Commons committee on the Passengers' Act in 1851 and was asked how all the American migrants managed to cook their meals in such a cramped galley. 'By incessant cooking and fighting from six in the morning till six at night,' he said.

An emigrant ship to Australia in the middle of the last

century was not a floating palace but she was closer to a welfare state than any nation or state on land during that era. As most migrants were so anxious to economise that they would have embarked in any tub, no matter how unseaworthy, and would have carried aboard inadequate provisions, the British parliament and emigration officials had to protect them with regulations that were slowly spun into an intricate web. The Passenger Act of 1855, for instance, restricted the number of passengers according to the ship's registered tonnage, the space and ventilation in the lower passenger deck, and the space available on the upper deck for the passengers' exercise. The passenger decks had to be at least six feet high from deckboards to ceiling and could be fitted with no more than two tiers of berths. A ship had to carry a specified number of water closets and lifeboats, a hospital with medicines and surgical instruments, and a surgeon if more than fifty passengers were on board. She could not carry, as cargo, either horses or cattle, guano, gunpowder, or green hides.

A careful inspection of the ship before it sailed, and heavy penalties for captains who infringed the Act, could of course enforce most of the rules; but no law could prevent a surgeon from being incompetent, could prevent typhus from spreading in the crowded 'tweendecks, could prevent fresh meat or water from fouling, could kill weevils in the flour, convert a grubby cook into a Parisian chef or change a bullying ship's master into a sensible servant. Living conditions differed much from ship to ship and year to year, and even in the same ship passengers who lived in the same conditions and ate the same food and were seasick and homesick for the same number of weeks could leave the ship at the voyage's end — some with complaints and protests, others with praise. It is difficult to agree that the picture of mid-century emigrant ships is veiled in black, except possibly in the first years of the gold rushes. There were some tragic voyages — 165 of the 800 passengers on the *Ticonderoga* died from typhus and scarlet fever in 1852 — and many voyages were miserable. But by the standards of the age the great emigration to Australia was reasonably humane and efficient. A House of Commons committee concluded in 1851, after questioning many witnesses familiar with British shipping, that emigrant ships to Australia were 'comparatively free from the evils and abuses which are charged upon the American passage'. Its dictum was probably true.

The long voyage to their new land was the one experience that knit together the majority of Australians in the nineteenth century. Scores of cabin passengers, people of some education, wrote down their impressions of the voyage; but they were always only a minority of those who crossed the globe. Usually they travelled comfortably, dined well, and were treated with dignity.

John B. Davies, a young Englishman, was in the ruck of passengers who migrated but he was more literate than most and left behind his handwritten memories. 'In common with many others in my station, I got dissatisfied with my prospects at home and determined to try my fortune in Australia,' he wrote. He left home for Liverpool in midwinter and took aboard the ship his own store of jams and hams and potatoes to spice the monotony of the ship's menu. On Christmas Eve, 1857, his ship *Sultana* was towed by a steam tug down the Mersey to the open sea. He heard the wind whistle through the rigging and saw the evening sun faintly piercing a bank of cloud in the west, and the land that was receding seemed suddenly dear to many who had been so anxious to leave it.

At sea early on Christmas morning he awoke with feelings of nausea, wanted to vomit, and stumbled on deck. In the darkness he could see several hundred passengers lying or standing on the tilting deck, all seasick on their first night at sea. For nearly a fortnight he could barely keep down his food and lived on bottled porter and wine and arrowroot, luxuries which the ship certainly didn't supply. His sickness went away but his inability to digest the ship's biscuits that appeared at most meals, left him hungry. He also had at times those fears common to most adult emigrants, fear that a contagious disease would spread in the cramped spaces of the ship, fear that the ship would be swallowed by the sea or hit a rocky coast.

As the ship approached the tropics the seas were calmer and the days warmer. Cold England and the first days of seasickness belonged to another world. When they crossed the Equator Davies was amused to see an old pilot peer through his glass and announce gravely that he could see the line of the Equator, and passengers eagerly asked for his glass so that they too could see the line that cut the world in half. On Sundays there was divine service for the emigrants and on weekdays experienced colonists lectured on the land that still lay far ahead. Many in the audience swayed between optimism and nostalgia.

Far to the south a young man died and 'the burial at sea was one of the most solemn sights I ever witnessed'. The ship rolled in the half gale so that the preacher had to be supported as he stood reading the burial service and the great crowd of passengers could not stand without holding on to part of the ship. 'I know,' wrote Davies, 'I felt a cold shudder as the poor fellow glided off the board on which he was placed into the great Deep. Although I know it matters but little where our bodies lie, I should wish to lie somewhere . . .'

Albatrosses chased in the wake of the ship and, about six hundred miles south of the Cape of Good Hope, flocks of Cape pigeons flew overhead. The sight of birds was strangely reassuring to those who had never before gone to sea. On some days in the high latitudes the westerlies blew so hard that the ship went along at fifteen knots with masts almost bare except for the close reefed topsail, and Davies loved to stand on deck in overcoat and cravat and watch the great waves roll in the same direction as the ship, and sometimes the ship perched on the crest of a mountain of water or cowered in the valley as if about to be swallowed.

John Davies, travelling in a big clipper ship, was possibly more fortunate than some who crossed the Southern Ocean in fierce storms or weaker ships. Night in a storm in that ocean must have been a nightmare to emigrants

162

who didn't trust the ship or the captain. One traveller of winter 1852 had the skilled pen to describe a storm and the kind of mind that could imagine its danger: 'one day we had a hurricane that never ceased for a minute, so that when it grew dark we all fairly turned into our berths to avoid being knocked and battered to pieces against the ship and each other, and there we all lay wide awake, listening to the various effects — such as roars, howls, hisses, gushes, creaks, clanks, shrieks, flaps and flanks, rumbles and falls, and sudden shocks, with the steady, monotonous, vibrating drone of the mighty wind holding on through all, without intermission. This lasted in all its force through the night, till from sheer exhaustion by attending to it I dropped off to sleep. Some time between twelve and two I awoke with a start, caused by a loud and violent booming blow, followed by a rush of water, which came dashing down the main hatchway, and flooding all the 'tween decks, every cabin inclusive.' As the ship lurched, all the water rushed to the other side of the ship. As the ship righted herself the water rushed back like a cataract, carrying pots, tins, kegs, cabin furniture and everything movable.

Conditions on a long voyage could never be luxurious or uniformly pleasant in the middle of the nineteenth century. But the voyage to Australia was made less forbidding by the slow reform of migrant ships and by the increasing speed of ships. The first fleet had dawdled out to Australia in convoy in about 250 days, an unusually slow passage, but by 1816–20 the average passage was only 140 to 150 days. By 1849 the average passage out had fallen to about 120 days, or four months from port to port; and with the coming of the American clippers in the 1850s the average passage continued to fall. Most ships had ceased to call at several ports for fresh water and supplies on the passage out, and they thus saved the unnecessary detours from the quickest route and the inevitable delays in port. The design of ships was slowly improving. The blunt ends of ships were being sharpened. The bottoms of ships were being sheathed with copper, and that prevented a crust of barnacles and wreaths of seaweed from fouling the ship and retarding her speed through the water.

Quicker passages and improved living conditions in ships were valuable aids to migration. But the passage to Australia remained long and expensive in contrast to the passage to the haven of migration, North America. The subsidising of migrants' fares still remained the vital solution to Australia's problem of distance.

5

Australia gained enormously by using land revenue to subsidise migration. The gain, however, had its penalty. Of all the countries in the new world to which Europeans in midcentury were flocking, the two where new land was dearest were Australia and New Zealand, the two countries most distant from Europe. There a settler who wanted to farm could not buy new land for less than £1 an acre. If instead he migrated to North America he could buy new land for 1s.9d. in Nova Scotia, for 4s. or 5s. an acre in many other parts of eastern Canada and in most of the U.S.A. And if he went to the U.S.A. after the Homestead Act of 1862 he paid the trifling sum of about 3d. an acre for a farm of 160 acres — on condition that he ploughed the land or lived on it for five years. North America was a bargain basement for land buyers. In contrast, by the 1860s, most Australian farmers were paying at least eighty times as much as U.S.A. farmers for new land, and Australian farmland was probably less rather than more productive of a comfortable living.

The astonishing difference in the price of land in Australia and North America seems to have been forgotten. The effects of dear land on Australia are unplumbed. One can speculate, not pontificate, on those effects. While dear land financed the coming of migrants, it probaby deterred those British emigrants who hoped to be farmers. An Englishman who possessed a little capital and the hope of ploughing his own soil was foolish to migrate to Australia in preference to North America.

Dear land cursed farmers. One of Australia's tragedies in the second half of the nineteenth century was the failure of tens of thousands of farmers and their families to make a living from small farms after slaving for years; and that was a poignant theme for Henry Lawson, Joseph Furphy, Miles Franklin, and many of the country's most gifted writers. Many poor farmers paid so dearly for their land that their farms were hopelessly small from the start or hopelessly mortgaged after the failure of a few crops.

When the sheepowners could no longer graze their flocks over wide stretches of grassland for the rental of a peppercorn, and had to buy their land or lose it, they too paid out huge sums at land sales. Dear land chained pastoralists as well as farmers to the money lenders. One reason why city streets were dominated by ornate banking chambers and why upcountry villages in Australia had three competing banks when similar-sized villages in England or the U.S.A. had none was the need of rural industries to borrow heavily to buy or retain their land. A few banks had wide power in the small economy, and much of their influence and activity came from the call to finance purchases of Crown land at inflated prices. In a similar way the Australian governments would play an unusually energetic role in economic and social affairs because, by selling land at high prices, they had a revenue which in many years exceeded their income from all other forms of taxation. Not only was their income within their own territory enhanced but their ability to raise large loans on the London market was enhanced because British lenders were more trustful of governments which possessed, in their kingdoms of unsold land, a ready source from which their interest could be paid.

A divorce was impending for the partners in the fertile marriage of land revenue and subsidised migration. Revenue from the auctioning of land soared from the 1860s as more farmers and sheepowners bought the freehold to land, but less and less of the revenue was handed to shipowners who freighted out migrants. One partner in the marriage, Land, remained rich, but it paid very little alimony to the other partner, Migration.

The courts which granted the divorce were the new parliaments of the Australian colonies. The old method of ruling Australia from distant London had slowly been modified until by 1856 all except one of the Australian colonies governed themselves through their own elected parliaments. The new parliaments now had control of the money raised by selling Australian land. Moreover the new parliaments were elected not only by rich merchants and sheepowners and professional men and shopkeepers but increasingly by miners, labourers, farmhands, dray-drivers, and men who owned little or no property. Many of these wage-earners resented the practice whereby much of the land revenue was used to pay the fares of new immigrants who, on landing in Australia, competed with them for jobs and depressed the level of wages. They particularly resented the arrival of subsidised immigrants in months when jobs were scarce in Australia. They preferred that the revenue from land auctions should be spent on roads and railways and schools. Alternatively, if the land revenue could defray most of the expenses of government, then the taxes they paid on the imported spirits they drank and the imported tobacco they smoked need not be so high. Thus, those Australian working men who had heard of Wakefield — by the 1850s he was living in New Zealand and a mental wreck — were entitled to consider him a puritanical busybody whose theories would lower their wages and increase the price of their pleasures.

Spurred by popular pressure, and by periodic shortages of money, most colonies allotted only a fraction of their land funds to assisting the passage of British and Irish migrants, Victoria ceasing in 1873 to allot even that fraction. Only the young colony of Queensland, which originally held few people in a vast area of warm or tropical terrain, persisted in subsidising migrants from Britain in the sixty years from 1860. Of the money spent in that era by Australian colonies in assisting emigrants from the British Isles, half was spent by Queensland.

In the sixty years 1860–1919, a total of 606,000 migrants were assisted financially to make the voyage to Australia, the average subsidy to each migrant being £14 14s. which was the largest part of the fare. But that army of assisted migrants was barely one tenth of the number whose fares could have been paid if the Australian colonies had clung to the 1842 formula that half of the land revenue should be spent on immigration.

The decisions of Australian wage-earners and democratic parliaments to subsidise migration less freely was perhaps one of the crucial decisions in Australia history. As most people who intended migrating from the British Isles dismissed the idea of migrating to Australia because of the length of the voyage and the expense of the fare, the subsidised or free fare was a vital bribe if Australia was to attract a larger share of migrants. Consequently the decision of Australian parliaments to use the bribe sparingly, even though funds to finance the bribe were available, prevented Australia's population from growing so rapidly. Indeed it is likely that Australia in the era 1860–1920 could have supported a population which was 50 per cent or 100 per cent higher than the number which it did in fact support. Though the standard of living of the larger population might have been slightly lower and the unemployment higher, most of the new jobs that would have been needed to support the higher population would have been created by the demand of the new migrants for food, clothing, firewood, houses, and civil and social amenities. Obviously, if Australia in 1920 had 10 million instead of 5.5 million people, then the nation today would have been very different.

One might suggest that the decision to neglect the vital task of subsidising migration, to half-raise the drawbridge across the moat, may go far to explain the curious way in which the societies of Australia and the United States of America diverged in the second half of the nineteenth century. In the U.S.A. trade unions remained relatively weak, and one reason for their weakness was probably the ease with which Europeans crossed the Atlantic and jostled for jobs; it was difficult to organize a strike for higher pay, if the jobs which the strikers vacated were quickly filled by men who had no work. On the other hand workmen in Australia, a less industrialized country, organized many trade unions and won much success with union activity. Even when Australian working men were not organized into unions, their bargaining position was often strengthened by a scarcity of labour; there was usually no flood of new workless migrants to take the places of men who had gone on strike. Moreover, in Australia, the trade unions were the effective organizers of a political party, the Australian Labor Party, which helped to make Australia more a welfare state and more a collective economy than the U.S.A. These changes in Australia would have been more difficult, and perhaps even unattainable, if much of the revenue from land had continued to pay the fares of migrants from the British Isles.

6

The value of subsidised migration was not simply in the working men it brought to Australia. Its value was also in the women it enticed to a man's land. One of Australia's sharpest social problems, and one of the problems which Edward Gibbon Wakefield lamented, was the scarcity of women of marriageable or elopable age. So long as Australia primarily served as a gaol for the British Isles, far more men than women came to the land. Of the convicts who sailed to the main Australian colony, New South Wales, men outnumbered women by more than five to one.

Australia's distance from Europe prolonged the dearth of women. A working man with a young family was reluctant to pay the fares of the whole family to Australia when he could travel more cheaply over the Atlantic to New York or Quebec; but for a single man the high cost of a berth to Melbourne or Sydney was less forbidding. Of those hundreds of thousands of migrants who paid for their own tickets to Australia in the nineteenth century, males outnumbered females by nearly two to one. In contrast, amongst the subsidised migrants, females were nearly as numerous as men. That balance of the sexes was the result of a deliberate policy of selection. One of the main aims of subsidised migration was to relieve the scarcity of marriageable women in Australia, and one of its main results was to lift the birth-rate in Australia.

Male dominance declined slowly. The year 1831 was the last in which males outnumbered females by more than three to one. By 1850 Australia had only 143 males to every 100 females, though the disparity was more marked in the adult population. By 1900 Australia had only 110 males for every 100 females. The year 1916 was the first year in Australia's history in which females were as numerous as males, but they were in equal numbers only because so many Australian men were fighting in Europe.

The dearth of women persisted for so long that it must have flavoured society in countless ways. In the years when it was most marked, the material standard of living was unusually high because most men only had to support themselves instead of a wife and children. Much of that higher standard of personal spending went into alcohol, and the incidence of drunkness in Australia until late in the nineteenth century was high. In a society dominated by men, a different set of values reigned. As Russel Ward observed in his book, *The Australian Legend*, the tradition of mateship — the collectivist idea that men should be loyal to the men with whom they lived and worked — had its roots in the time when Australia was a man's land, and that tradition was strongest in the outer rural regions where women were rare and the daily life of men was monotonous and lonely. The idea of mateship flavoured Australian democracy. Ambition and the desire to raise oneself beyond one's station were considered to be vices by a majority or an influential minority of Australian men. And it may be significant that from about 1900, when the Labor Party became politically strong — a

169

party that drew much of its philosophy from the mateship era and area — the emphasis on education in Australia lagged behind the nation's ability to pay for improved schools and universities. In the equalitarian bushman's society of the 19th century, education was often seen as a form of snobbery and a way of social advancement which broke up the cameraderie of working men.

Australia's emergence in the nineteenth century as one of the most sports-crazy nations of the world was not just an effect of a kind climate (most newcomers did not think the climate was favourable to sport), nor did it come necessarily from a high standard of living or from ample space in which to play sports. The United States had all these advantages and yet Australia seems to have become immersed in sports earlier and more intensely than the United States. Love of sport was more a male preference and was more to be expected in a society dominated by men, indeed by young men. Similarly, leisure was essential for the development of a love of sport. By the mid-nineteenth century thousands of Australian working men, in their quest for improved conditions, were giving a higher priority to shorter working hours and longer leisure than to higher wages. That priority was possibly a reflection of the importance of unmarried men in trade unions and industries — men whose income was adequate to support themselves, men who were under no pressure from a wife to earn more so that the family could live more comfortably. Certainly the success of these demands for more leisure came in considerable degree from the workers' bargaining position which was fortified by isolation from Europe and the consequent, weaker, flow of European emigrants.

Many of the characteristics of Australia's population and life were shaped by the simple fact that Australia was so far from Europe. Even that curious custom, so common at dances or social evenings in many parts of Australia, whereby women gather at one end of the room and men gather at the opposite end of the room, seems to have had its origins in the era when women were scarce. If Edward

Gibbon Wakefield could attend those country dances he would be puzzled. He had helped to popularize the art of abducting women to the other end of the world, but the formula for abducting women to the opposite end of the dance floor was not so easy to find.

PART TWO
THE TAMING OF DISTANCE

When the industrial revolution and the power of steam
were reshaping commerce in western Europe and North
America, and railways and steamships and telegraphs
were ceasing to be miracles, Australia still relied on the
strength of winds and animals to carry virtually all its
goods. Then, in the first years of the gold rushes, Australia got the instruments that could defy distance. In the
early 1850s it built the first railways and first telegraphs
and sent the first paddle steamer up the Murray River.
The repeal of the old Navigation Acts removed the
strait-jacket hindering ships coming from the outside
world. The first steamships entered the route from Britain
to Australia and Boston clippers sailed regularly to
Australian ports, opening the 'Great Circle' route and
snipping weeks from the previous record passages. At the
same time the four main Australian colonies received
self-government and the right to regulate and run communications in their own territory.

Innovations which had come slowly over many years in
the northern hemisphere were telescoped into a few years
in Australia. The long era in which distance was a tyrant
seemed to be fading away.

8   Gold Clippers

All ships that visited Australian ports until the last day of
1849 were controlled by a mesh of laws as complex as
the criminal code. The Navigation Acts had begun with
England's attempt in 1651 to overthrow the maritime
supremacy of The Netherlands, and during the following
two centuries they grew so complicated that by the 1840s
many British and Australian shipowners could not
understand them. And yet the very aim of those laws was
to ensure that their ships won the largest possible share of
the world's carrying trade.

The Navigation Acts guarded every Australian port
like a submerged minefield. British ships could easily
weave through the minefield but foreign ships came at
their own risk. Migrants and cargoes coming from British
ports to Australia could only come in ships which were
owned by a British citizen, manned mainly by British
sailors, and originally built in a shipyard of the British
Empire. Australian wool and whale oil exported to British
possessions could only go in British ships. Coastal commerce between all Australian ports was the monopoly of
the British flag. All that remained for foreign ships was
freight between Australia and foreign ports, and even that
was often diverted to British ships by an ingenious law.
Chinese tea, for example, could only come to Australia in
Chinese or alternatively British ships. As no Chinese
junks made long deep-sea voyages, the tea trade passed to
British ships.

Australian colonists sometimes cursed the Navigation

Acts. When they were short of tea or rice, a foreign ship could arrive with a cargo, arrange to unload it, and suddenly be ordered out of port with the cargo still unloaded. In Western Australia in 1842 or 1843 the colonists at Perth were short of rice, then a staple part of diet. An American ship called, heard of the scarcity of rice, and put to sea. At either Calcutta or another British port her master loaded a cargo of rice and returned to Western Australia, expecting to earn a high profit from his enterprise in ending the famine. At the Customs House, however, he was told he couldn't land the rice; American ships were prevented by the Navigation Act from carrying anything but American produce to Australia. The American master was now in a dilemma. The only ports that would want rice within two thousand miles of Perth were all in Australia, and yet he was not allowed to land his rice at any Australian port. His only answer was to sell the cargo at a loss to a British vessel in the harbour. Even then the rice could not be landed. Instead it was carried more than two thousand miles around the coast to Sydney where it earned probably a mere fraction of the price it would have earned at Fremantle. The loss to the American ship was severe. The loss to the hungry people whom the Navigation Act was supposed to serve was more severe.

Foreign ships which legally carried passengers or goods from their own land to Australia were invariably penalized when they sought a cargo for their homeward voyage. In the 1840s German sailing ships brought thousands of migrants from Bremen and Hamburg to South Australia. If those ships had been permitted to carry copper or wool back to Europe their round voyage would have been so profitable that they could have cut migrant's fares and so stimulated migration from Germany to South Australia. In fact the very wharves where they landed their passengers were stacked with bags of copper ore, awaiting shipment to Europe. But German ships could not take the copper. The best markets in the world for copper ore were the Welsh smelters in Swansea

and only British ships could carry Australian copper to
Wales. Thus German emigrant ships sailed away without
cargo, and South Australian mines suffered. Likewise,
sugar from plantations in the French colony of Bourbon,
in the north Indian Ocean, could come to Sydney in
French ships but the ships had to return home in ballast.

One strange effect of the Navigation Act was that
Australian shipowners could not salvage foreign ships
which had been wrecked on Australia's coast. Wrecks
were usually auctioned, and Australians who bought
them sometimes managed to refloat them. But having
bought a foreign ship they could not sail her into any
Australian port. When the fine French whaler *Bourbon*
was dismasted near the Tasmanian coast, she was bought
at auction by Benjamin Boyd, an Australian freebooter
and whaleman. As the Navigation Acts prevented Boyd
from repairing the ship in Sydney and sending her to sea
as an Australian whaler, and as the nearest market for
unregistered vessels was in Indo-China or the Arabian
port of Muscat, Boyd towed the ship to his own port of
Boyd Town and used her as a coal hulk. Insofar as the
law led to the scrapping of useful ships, it probably led to
the building of slightly more ships in Australian shipyards.

The imperial parliament repealed the Navigation Acts
in 1849. They had probably tended to increase Australia's
isolation and to increase the cost of that isolation. For
Australia the shattering of the mesh of shipping regulations came at a fortunate time. Within two years the
discovery of rich gold in Australia called for a fleet of fast
ships to bring out migrants and cargoes from Europe, and
the finest ships were American-built clippers which under
the old laws would have virtually been debarred from
Australian ports.

2

The first news of Australia's goldfields had reached
London late in 1851. Early in the following year each mail

from Australia blew like a bellows on popular excitement. Shipowners' offices in London and Liverpool were crowded with impetuous emigrants, and scores of ships were hastily diverted to the Australian run and booked out weeks before they were ready to sail. In 1852, 86,000 people left the United Kingdom for Australian ports, and the record was not broken for another sixty-one years. Migration in 1853 and 1854 was not as large but was still larger than in any year for almost sixty years. Most of the early gold migrants, unlike the majority of migrants before the gold rushes, paid their own fares. Seemingly frightened that they might arrive when the treasure hunt was almost over, they clamoured for swift passages and their money quietly under-wrote the most brilliant era in the history of sailing ships.

Shipowners sought a quicker route to Australia, and a new route was provided by an Englishman who had never seen Australia or the seas leading to it. John Towson was a watchmaker who made those chronometers with which navigators reckoned their longitude at sea. He also devised an effective method of taking a photograph on a glass plate, but his most useful invention was not an instrument but a simple idea. He believed that the world was round and that seamen should recognize that truth.

Towson thought it was time that navigators ceased to rely on Mercator charts of the world in plotting their courses. The Mercator map, originally devised for seamen in 1569 by the Rhineland geographer Gerardus Mercator, converted the world from a globe to a rectangle. It thus distorted areas and distances, and the distortion grew with distance from the equator. On the Mercator map, for example, Australia seemed much smaller than Greenland when in reality it covered three and a half times the area. On a Mercator map it was also clear — deceptively clear — that the shortest distance between two ports on the same latitude was to follow the line of latitude. Thus the shortest route from Cape Town in South Africa to Melbourne appeared to follow the 38th parallel of latitude; and as mariners could easily pinpoint their latitude (or distance from the equator) they had no trouble in following such a course with a compass. In fact, the shortest distance between the two ports was a curved line that went as far south as 66 degrees of latitude, or almost to the Antarctic Circle. If the earth was round — and the mariners of Liverpool did not deny it — then the shortest distance between two points was the arc of a great circle.

Mariners of the sixteenth century knew the attraction of sailing along a Great Circle route. They couldn't follow such a route, however, until they had a chronometer which enabled them to determine their longitude at sea and thereby also enabled them to make the frequent changes of course necessary to follow roughly the curve of a circle. The first delicate chronometers were not developed and proved until the 1760s, and for long they were luxuries. Now Towson made inexpensive chronometers, so the heart of his plan was simply that navigators should carry them and use them. In the late 1840s, with hundreds of emigrant ships crossing the north Atlantic each year, he suggested that the quickest route from England to New York or Boston was to sail along the arc of a Great Circle. The British Admiralty published his tables and sailing directions to guide mariners in 1849, the year of the great exodus to California.

A year later Towson became scientific examiner of masters and mates in Liverpool, and his simple idea was well known on the docks when that port became briefly the centre of the booming passenger traffic to the Australian gold ports. Indeed there was more scope for his idea on the sea route to Australia. From the south Atlantic to the southern coast of Australia was a vast stretch of ocean with no protruding necks of land to prevent ships from trying a shorter route. The winds along that Great Circle were more favourable than in any other part of the globe. Above all, the area was in high latitudes, where the distortions of the old Mercator charts were most acute, and thus the advantages of the Great Circle course were strongest. Between the Cape of Good Hope and Mel-

179

bourne a ship that forsook the traditional route along a latitude of about 40 degrees and instead curved far to the south could save over a thousand miles. The name of Towson, the watch-maker, is not to be found in histories of Australia, but for a decade his route was more important to Australia than the Suez Canal was to prove in its first decade.

Many ships that sailed from Liverpool and London with emigrants for the goldfields in the early 1850s had hungry owners and bold masters who tried the Great Circle route when they reached the south Atlantic Ocean, far to the west of the Cape of Good Hope. As the true Great Circle would have carried them across the frozen continent of Antarctica on their way to Melbourne and Sydney, most ships' masters adopted 'composite sailing' — a compromise between the Mercator route and the Great Circle route. Nevertheless they sailed farther south than any emigrant ship had ever intentionally sailed, and some went a thousand miles south of the old sea lane. In mid-summer they sailed perilously close to dazzling icebergs, and they rode mountainous seas in the roaring fifties. Some ships vanished somewhere in the cold wastes of the Great Circle, and some ships reached Melbourne in record times that at first were doubted by those who had crossed the world in the fast ships of a decade previously.

On the new sea route far to the south the racing ships found large islands that were marked on no chart; and so popular was the route that at least four ships discovered the same island before other ships leaving Liverpool could be warned. Masters and crew must have been stunned, out in the Indian Ocean and several thousand miles from inhabited land, to hear the lookout suddenly shout his warning from the masthead. The shock lingered, for they realized that their ship could have easily been wrecked in the mists so common in that latitude or could have run aground while scudding through the darkness.

Heard Island, with its snow-capped mountain, in latitude 53 south was found by a British sealing ship in 1833, and forgotten for another twenty years until Cap-

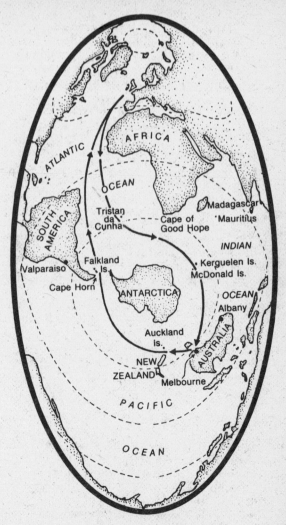

The Great Circle Route, 1850s.

tain Heard of the *Oriental* found it again while sailing between Boston and Melbourne. A few months later, on 3 January 1854, the nearby McDonald Islands were discovered by Captain McDonald in the *Samarang*. He reported his discovery when he reached Melbourne, but the news was slow to reach England and slower to reach those ships' masters on whose knowledge and alertness hinged the lives of thousands of passengers. Later that year the large sailing ship *Earl* of *Eglinton* (1274 tons register) left the Scottish port of Greenoch on her maiden voyage, carrying nearly 400 migrants but carrying no knowledge of the uncharted island lying on her course. It was the eve of summer when the ship reached the Indian Ocean and her master, James S. Hutton, thought he could follow the Great Circle without undue danger of meeting the icebergs that then drifted north. But it was not an iceberg that endangered his ship. Two hours after the formal beginning of summer, at 2 a.m. on 1 December 1854, he was astonished to see land ahead in a place where his charts pointed to a vast ocean. At once he called all hands on deck, and ordered them to take in the studding-sails. He steered the ship off course just in time to avoid disaster, and she passed close to the north-west point of the large island. When day broke, the passengers came on deck and gaped at the foaming coast and the snowy hills, brilliantly white in the sun, perhaps the first land they saw after leaving Scotland — and almost the last. Later that day the captain wrote that he had risked the lives of '415 souls, with a valuable cargo, and the most expensive ship of her tonnage built in our country'. He vowed never again to sail the Great Circle in high latitudes.

The erroneous charts which the *Earl of Eglinton* followed when she almost ran into McDonald Island were drawn by Matthew Fontaine Maury, but for every ship's master that cursed Maury a score revered him. While the Englishman John Towson probably did much more than the Virginian Matthew Maury to persuade navigators to try the Great Circle route to Australia, the 'Wind and Current Charts' which the ships carried were drawn and constantly corrected by Maury. He harvested the experiences of many ships on the same voyage at varying seasons of the year, and onto his charts and sailing directions he grafted sea currents and prevailing winds and variations of the compass needle. Navigators who had sailed the arc of a Great Circle between the South Atlantic and Australia corresponded with him, sending him abstract logs of their voyages; and in the observatory at Washington he collated them, publicised them, and gave them the force of holy writ. Maury's charts sped hundreds of ships on the new route to and from Australia. 'Every ship that navigates the high seas with these charts and blank abstract logs on board,' wrote Maury in 1855 in the preface to his celebrated book *The Physical Geography of the Sea*, 'may henceforth be regarded as a floating observatory or a temple of science.'

Around the new route to Australia sailed those graceful temples of science, the American clipper ships, liberated by the repeal of the Navigation Acts at the start of 1850. The age of steamships had arrived but no steamship in the world then could equal the speeds of the American clippers in the lonely latitudes of the Southern Ocean. The American clipper was the consummation of centuries of shipbuilding, the most glamorous ship that ever went with the wind. She had her swift glory on the eve of the dethronement of sailing ships as the sea's speedsters, and perhaps her finest achievements were on the Australian run.

Clipper ships became the darlings of shiplovers, but the lovers often disagreed on what were the distinctive marks of a clipper. At least they agreed that speed was an essential mark, and in fact the word *clipper* came from an American phrase — 'to move at a fast clip'. The first clippers were built at Baltimore in Maryland, fast schooners that were popularly known as clippers in the decade after the War of 1812. Baltimore clippers were low and fast, their slender hulls had fine lines and curves, and their tall masts carried a wide spread of sail. In the phrases of H.I. Chapelle, naval architect and historian,

Baltimore clippers had 'raking masts' which tilted from the perpendicular, a very raking stem, and a rakish appearance that indicated speed. That description suggests they were a kind of ocean playboy, and in a sense they were.

It seems that the clipper ship evolved to meet a new demand for speed on the ocean trade routes. Hitherto shipowners had had no marked incentive for speedy passages, but the growth of emigration from Europe to the New World and the spread of international commerce produced a few cargoes and a large group of wealthier travellers who wanted speed and could pay for it. The increasing habit of tea-drinking in Britain and the United States helped to create faster ships, because the first cargoes of the new-season teas from China earned higher prices in Europe and, moreover, tea was a light cargo that enabled ships to make more speed than if they were carrying lumber or the normal, heavier items of commerce. Similarly, in the 1840s the competition from new steamships on the short Atlantic crossing from Europe to the United States and Canada challenged shipbuilders to design sailing ships that carried emigrants quickly.

The gold rushes in California and Australia probably offered the highest rewards for fast sailing ships. Tens of thousands of men were eager for a quick sea passage to the new goldfields. Furthermore, the demand for luxuries, food, and equipment in the rich gold camps could not be met by local farms and factories and warehouses. As prices of a thousand scarce commodities from cigars and Scotch whiskey to tents and English boots inflated suddenly, there were fortunes waiting for the first New York or London merchants who quickly shipped the scarce goods to the new market. Never before had European communities far from Europe suddenly demanded a mountain of goods, and perhaps never before in world commerce had such rewards awaited shipowners with the fastest ships.

Australia more than California stimulated the building of fast clippers. While Australia could only be reached by sea, there was in contrast an overland route to California. Moreover, steamers following the coast and taking on coal at South American ports could compete with sailing ships on the sea route around Cape Horn to California; other steamships opened a shorter route to the Isthmus of Panama, which passengers crossed by riverboat and mule (or railway after 1855), and then boarded another steamer for San Francisco. In contrast the long sea route from Europe to Australia so lacked coaling stations that only a few ships, carrying both engine and sail, tried to compete with sailing ships in the 1850s. The clipper was useful on the California route but indispensable on the Australian route. For in essence the clipper ship flourished in the brief era when steamers were still slow and still had to be suckled at a line of coastal coaling stations. The clipper thus served the purpose which the fast, long-distance steamship was soon to serve.

The most famous clippers were built on the eastern seaboard of North America, and the most famous designer was Donald McKay who was born in Nova Scotia in 1810 and opened his own shipyard in East Boston at the age of thirty-five. His shipyard flourished for only ten years — from 1845 to 1855, the triumphant decade of the clipper ship — and it was on the booming emigrant runs to California and Australia that his clippers won fame.

McKay's clippers astonished the nautical world by clipping weeks off the previous record passages to and from Australia. Racing before fierce westerlies in the vast ocean between the tip of South Africa and the tip of South America, they sometimes covered more than 400 sea miles in a day. And if they had been able to maintain that pace — and of course fickle winds prevented them — they would have gone from Liverpool to Melbourne in thirty days, the same time which fast passenger steamers made on the Australian route until recent years.

No British-built sailing ship ever recorded 400 nautical miles in a day — a day from noon to noon being the accepted measure of speed in the era of sail. However, a small fleet of American clippers claimed such records in the 1850s. Two of Donald McKay's clippers, the *James Baines* and the *Lightning*, and the graceful Maine clipper *Red Jacket* each claimed two runs of more than 400 nautical miles in a day. At least another nine American clippers each boasted of one day in which they covered that astonishing distance, and they included the McKay clipper *Champion of the Seas* which claimed on 12 December 1854 to have travelled 465 miles while running east to Australia in latitude 50 degrees south, near Kerguelen Island. These 400-mile runs were all made in the 1850s and most of them were made in the years 1854–55–56. All were made by American clippers; all were made with westerly winds and most were made in the cold seas and high latitudes of the Australian route.

To stand in the rigging or even on the poop deck of a fully rigged ship racing in the Roaring Forties must have been sobering to anyone new to the sea. In the frequent storms the spars seemed to howl like deep organ pipes. The wind blew out the cordage on the bare mizzen mast like a lassoo. It scythed crests of waves into sheets of spray. Dr William Scoresby, travelling to Australia in a fully rigged ship, described such a storm nine days before his ship reached Melbourne in April 1856. The west wind made waves of enormous height, higher than any waves he had seen in the northern hemisphere, and from two other quarters cross waves rolled ceaselessly into the main line of waves to create tumultuous, undisciplined crests and peaks. Each wave was a breaker, and the spread of foam was so wide that he could hardly find a square yard of sea that was free of foam, and the spray was so thick and high that even when the sun slanted through the clouds the passengers on deck could only see objects one third of a mile ahead of the ship.

The danger was high for a ship scudding in a storm at the speed necessary to cover 300 miles, let alone 400 miles, a day. Ropes linking helm and rudder could snap, or a sudden shift of wind or a careless turn of the wheel could veer the ship side on to the full power of wind and sea; and in a few minutes the ship would be overwhelmed by the broadside of waves and wind. Old Dr Scoresby watched, with alternate feelings of awe and scientific detachment, the four men keeping the ship's wheel in active play, the captain standing a few paces away, now and then calling orders to the helmsmen as crashing blows from the sea deflected the ship slightly from its course. Scoresby wrote that if he were a painter there was no scene — since his Arctic voyages of more than thirty years previously — that he would so wish to place on canvas as the poop deck with the tensed men at the wheel and the haze of spray beyond.

3

Alert maritime historians who knew the hazards facing a racing sailing ship on the Australian passage doubted whether the clippers really covered the distances in the times they claimed. Their suspicions were sharpened by the curious fact that all the records were made in the 1850s. Captain J.S. Learmont suggested that the records may have been fabricated by the Yankee sea captains who wished to publicize the speed of their ships in order to win passengers and cargoes for their runs between Liverpool and Melbourne. It was certainly true that shipowners on the Australian run in the 1850s often boasted of speed. Thus the English newspaper *Trewman's Exeter Flying Post* on the last day of September 1858 announced that the White Star clipper-ship *Shalimar* would sail from Liverpool to Melbourne 'punctually at Noon' on 20 October; no ship sailing to Australia before 1851 advertised an exact hour of departure, and even those ships that announced the day of their departure rarely honoured their promise. The *Shalimar* of course publicized the luxuries supplied to saloon passengers — the piano, library, free bedding and linen, and the milch cow carried on board — but above all it emphasized speed. The ship, said the advertisement, had sailed 'the extraordinary distance of 420 miles in one day, a feat never equalled by the fastest steamers afloat'.

While the few clippers that had covered 400 sea miles in a day naturally boasted of it, they more frequently advertised the number of days they had spent on the entire passage to or from Australia. Thus, the *Shalimar* claimed that on her first voyage from Liverpool to Australia she took a mere 67 days to reach Cape Northumberland. (As that cape was 300 miles from Melbourne, and as ships in adverse winds sometimes spent four days in sailing from Cape Northumberland to Melbourne, the *Shalimar's* owners were perhaps elastic with their facts.) A study of shipping advertisements, especially in newspapers in Melbourne, where competition for the scarce passengers and cargoes for the homeward journey was more intense than in Liverpool, reveals that clippers gave more emphasis to the time of their swiftest voyages than to the speed of their record days. This was to be expected. Potential passengers of the clippers were rarely interested in how far their ship could sail on one charmed day; they were more interested in how far the ship could sail in 60 or 80 days. Hence one may suggest that owners and masters of clippers did not have such a strong incentive to claim that their ships had covered 400 or more miles in a single day.

Some critics of the clippers' records doubted the honesty or skill of captains in measuring a day's run. Captain Learmont plotted the course of the *Champion of the Seas* during the week in which she claimed her world record day of 465 nautical miles and he skilfully showed that the run was probably much exaggerated. On the other hand the log of the rival clipper *Sovereign of the Seas* in the National Archives at Washington showed that she almost certainly did travel 410 miles on 18 March 1853 and that the clipper *James Baines*, whose log is also preserved, had a swift day's run in May 1856 that was only six miles short of the magical 400.

Another doubter of the American clippers, the celebrated Australian seaman Alan Villiers, pointed out that those voyages in which runs of 400 miles were claimed were, surprisingly, not record passages. But on the long voyage to Australia a run of 400 miles is the equivalent of

188

only 60 yards in a mile race run on foot; part of the route having favourable winds (or downhill in a foot race), part of the route having adverse winds (or uphill in a foot race), and part of the route passing through tropic calms (or a sandy stretch in a foot race). A mile-runner may sprint the fastest 60 yards but lose the race. Likewise a clipper may sail the fastest day's run but not the fastest voyage. Even if the American clippers did not make their record sprint during a record passage, and even if some exaggerated the distance they had covered in a day, they still succeeded in capturing virtually all records for the sea route between Australia and England in the 1850s.

One final criticism came from sailors who had served their time in the later iron clippers and had rounded Cape Horn or rushed along with gales in the Roaring Forties. They found it difficult to believe that earlier wooden clippers could have made their recorded runs and survived to report them. But whereas iron clippers were designed not only to sail quickly but to carry large cargoes, the wooden American clippers were designed primarily for speed. Whereas the latter day iron sailing ships shook and shuddered each time their full bows smacked down on a wave, the bows of the older wooden clippers were sharp and overhanging and concave rather than full so that they cut through the top of the waves. And while the bottom of an iron ship quickly fouled, gathering barnacles and seaweed so that there was more resistance to the smooth gliding of the hull through the water, the bottom of a wooden clipper was sheathed with copper which remained relatively clean and smooth.

A few defenders of the clipper records argued that their performances in the 1850s must have been aided by years of unusually strong winds — winds that have apparently vanished from the globe. This argument is not as quaint as it seems. The 1850s, so far as we know, were not the Windy Fifties but they were unusual. And but for those unusual forces, the brilliant design of the American clippers might not have led to those swift passages in the 1850s.

The great age of the clipper was spurred by the profits of Californian and Australian commerce. Clippers could sail rapidly because they carried live or light cargoes and were not heavily laden with deadweight cargoes. They could also sail rapidly because — during the 1850s but in no other decade — they fully exploited the new Great Circle route in the southern hemisphere with its strong westerly drift that often added three knots to their speed and with its winds that were more favourable than those of any sailing route in the world. For a time the clippers were so profitable that they carried, in contrast to earlier and later ships, a large crew which could quickly alter sails to capture the advantage or lessen the dangers of every change of wind and sea. Shipowners allowed their captains to risk damage to sails, spars, and gear in their mania for speed. Clipper captains themselves had an incentive to speed, for often they shared in the higher profits that followed a fast voyage. The captains of fast ships in the 1850s had the glamour of film stars, and it was speed which gave them their glamour.

A legend arose that captains of clippers had such a craving for speed that when their ships were running before a high wind with an abnormally large spread of canvas they had to padlock the sails; otherwise the mates or sailors, terrified that the ships might founder, would have been tempted to take in sail and lessen the risk and thereby the speed. If 'padlocking the halyards' was actually practised, then a change of wind in the night could have dismasted the ship while the captain was fumbling for the key. There is no evidence that padlocks were carried but the existence of the myth reflects the part played by reckless, driving captains in the heyday of clippers.

Speeds achieved by American clippers in the 1850s, speeds probably never again achieved by sailing ships, came from the design of the clippers, the kind of cargoes they carried, their bold captains and big crews, the new short-lived Great Circle route, the charts of Matthew Fontaine Maury, and above all the unusual economic incentive for speedy passages. Today, some Americans are proud that their shipbuilders built the fastest of all sailing ships and some Britons are resentful that their shipbuilders, often world's leaders, did not produce faster ships. Hence the controversy is sharpened by national rivalry. The simplest and safest answer is that Americans designed and built the fastest ships during that flash of time when conditions favoured fast wind-borne voyages more than ever before or after. On the other hand the British, learning from and even surpassing North American shipbuilders, created their finest sailing ships just after the most favourable sailing environment was smudged by coal smoke.

The rapid dashes of the clippers were, to Australians, less important than their unprecedented times for the entire voyage out from England. The Black Ball Line of Liverpool bought American clippers and despatched them to Australia from 1852, and at once they shattered all the old definitions of a fast voyage. When the clipper *Marco Polo* reached Port Phillip Heads in 1852, and her master bragged to the Melbourne officials who boarded her that he had made the passage from Liverpool in 74 days, they must have thought him a liar. If so, they had to believe him when they saw the dates on the Liverpool newspapers he produced; they were less than eleven weeks old. Sceptics were also convinced by the testimonies of the passengers. They said the ship had sped in foul weather with acres of sail aloft, as if the master was mad.

The master was James Nicol Forbes, young and red-headed and brash, the most notorious of all the clipper captains. His slogan was 'Hell or Melbourne' and some said the ship passed through Hell before it reached Melbourne. Whereas the traditional ship used to bob on waves like a cork and whereas its decks usually were relatively dry even in turbulent seas, the clipper's decks remained wave-swept and awash in strong seas. To the nine hundred passengers on *Marco Polo*, men and women who had mostly never been to sea before, it must have been frightening or enthralling to see the water swirling

191

across her long maindeck in the high latitudes.

'Bully' Forbes drove his ship to Australia in 74 days but he also made the homeward voyage to Liverpool by way of Cape Horn in 76 days, a more remarkable performance because the homeward route was over a thousand miles longer. He left Liverpool in mid-summer and returned in mid-winter, being away for less than six months, and it must have been hard for his Liverpool cronies to believe that he had been to the other end of the world and back.

The first voyage of the *Marco Polo* to Australia is said to have begun the fortunes of James Baines of Liverpool and his Black Ball Line. He bought clipper after clipper from McKay's shipyard in Boston, and on the run to Australia his *Lightning* and *Champion of the Seas* and *James Baines* and other big clippers sometimes made voyages of less than seventy days. In 1854 the *James Baines* (2275 tons) made the run in a record 63 days — or exactly nine weeks from the day she disembarked her Liverpool pilot in the Irish Sea until the day she took on the pilot at Port Phillip Heads. In contrast most ships which sailed that year from Britain to Australia took more than 100 days, and the slowest, the *Druid*, spent 259 days (or eight and a half months) in sailing from London to Launceston.

The Black Ball Line was the most spectacular shipping firm that feasted on the emigrant traffic to Australia in the 1850s, but it had challengers. One was the White Star Line, and in Liverpool and Melbourne its swallow-tailed pennant with a white star on a red field became as familiar as the rival white flag with the simple back ball. Its flagship *White Star* (2360 tons register), the biggest clipper ever built in Wright's yard in New Brunswick, once ran nearly 3300 miles in ten days as she neared Australia. At least two of the White Star fleet, *Shalimar* and *Red Jacket*, laid claim to 400 miles in a day; in contrast their sister ship *Lord Raglan* in 1863 made what contemporary bethel preachers and port journalists were accustomed to call 'an eternal voyage', being last seen sailing south of the equator.

Both the White Star and Black Ball lines had Liverpool

as home port and used big North American clippers on the Australian route, but their two main London rivals employed mostly the smaller frigates built in the Blackwall Yard in London. Whereas Liverpool ruled the emigrant trade London ruled the cargo trade, and so London ships usually had less incentive for a swift passage. Messrs Green's Blackwall Line of Packets made a few fast voyages from London to Australia and the London firm with the apt name of Money Wigram & Sons had splendid ships of medium size that sometimes outsailed the American clippers. In 1858, Money Wigram advertised in Melbourne newspapers that their ship *Norfolk* had made its last five passages in an average of only 68¾ days; and it is doubtful if any sailing ship on that long, unpredictable route was ever so predictable and so consistently fast.

The fast ships of the 1850s, the *Champions of the Seas* and the *Sovereigns of the Seas*, were the spell-binders, the makers of legend and breakers of records. People boasted in their cups they had sailed on such ships or visited them or seen them in port, and on the walls of bush huts they pinned prints of ships in full sail which they had snipped from illustrated magazines. But most people had come to Australia in plain, unreverenced ships, and the shortening of the voyage of the average ship was a feat often overlooked at the time. According to Lieutenant Maury, the chart maker, the voyage of the average ship fell from about eighteen weeks to fourteen weeks between 1850 and 1855. Though he definitely exaggerated the fall in the human desire to stress the worth of his Great Circle charts, weeks were saved in the average voyage, and those weeks were prized by emigrants, shipowners, importers, politicians and by all Australian who depended on goods, comforts, and news from Britain.

Most clippers saw no land all the way from the Irish Sea to the coastline near Melbourne. On their long sweep down the Atlantic they usually skirted the coast of South America, where earlier ships had often called for water or supplies, and in the Southern Ocean the most southerly point of the Great Circle was usually the latitude of 51 degrees south; they had begun to haul up towards Australia before they reached the mist-shrouded islands of McDonald and Kerguelen. Invariably they steered for Cape Otway, a mountainous promontory only sixty miles south-west of Port Phillip Heads. The white circular lighthouse on Cape Otway — or its light which flashed every minute of the night — was the first Australian sight that hundreds of thousands of migrants saw. With virtually no land from Lands End to Cape Otway to endanger their chosen route the clipper captains could try for maximum speed in mist or darkness or stormy seas.

The most dangerous part of the voyage was the last 120 miles when ships reached an unfamiliar coast that had unknown currents and uncharted reefs and few lighthouses or beacons. If their bearings were astray and they veered to the south they approached King Island instead of Cape Otway; and in fact nineteen ships were wrecked off King Island in thirty years. Another long list of ships avoided the wild western coast of King Island only to go ashore at the narrow channel at Port Phillip Heads, the entrance to Melbourne. A fierce ebb tide raced daily through the entrance and the sandy hummocks along the coast concealed the Heads from some points at sea, and on the *Lightning's* first voyage to Australia her commander Anthony Enright had to wait near the Heads for day to break and then climb aloft to scan the coast for the opening. From the masthead he could not see the narrow channel, concealed by low sand dunes at the Heads, but he did see the humpy hill of Arthur's Seat, and that landmark enabled him to deduce from his charts the exact site of the entrance to Melbourne.

It was on the Victorian coast that Captain 'Bully' Forbes resolved his old dilemma 'Hell or Melbourne'. In 1855 the Black Ball Line entrusted him with the maiden voyage of the clipper *Schomberg* (2284 tons register). One of the largest ships to join the Australian trade, she also was perhaps the strongest clipper afloat. On Boxing Day 1855 her maiden voyage was almost over and she was sailing slowly along the coast towards Cape Otway. The sea was calm and the moon was rising across the water and passengers below were doubly celebrating the holiday and the first sight of the long-awaited land. Captain Forbes was playing cards in the saloon and out of luck when he was told about 9.15 p.m. that land was visible three miles ahead. He was outwardly a calm, bluff fellow, accustomed to ignoring warnings that had a trace of timidity. The card game went on. Half an hour passed before Forbes went on deck. Then he saw breakers only half a mile ahead and ordered that the ship change course. The big ship was slow to obey, was taken by a current, and wedged on a sand-topped reef. As the ship's bow now faced the open sea he kept her sails on for an hour or so in the hope that the breeze would push her clear from the reef. On 'Bully' Forbes' last day as a Black Ball Line captain the winds refused to obey the man whose orders were always obeyed.

A small coastal steamer passed Moonlight Head and saw the ship and rescued all passengers and crew. 'The *Schomberg* was quickly pounded to pieces by the surf, and the ship which had cost £43,000 and the cargo worth much more were eventually sold at auction for a total of £447 18s.

In Melbourne a public meeting of passengers denounced the conduct of Forbes. Other passengers went to the waterfront courthouse at Williamstown and charged Forbes with not giving them the water and food which the Passengers' Acts allowed them; but the charges were dismissed. The Crown charged Forbes with neglect of duty as captain on that moonlit night near Cape Otway; but his certificate was not suspended. He argued successfully that the reef which the clipper struck was not on the charts. It could have been argued, however, that if the clipper had not struck the reef it would have gone on to strike the coast of Australia, a coast that was certainly on the charts.

Some ships made astonishing return passages to England in the 1850s. Invariably selecting the Cape Horn route for the return voyage, they commenced their arc of a Great Circle from the day they sailed through Port Phillip Heads. Most sailed through Banks Strait on the north east tip of Tasmania and drove south of New Zealand to the fierce winds of the forties and fifties, where they raced like seabirds. Sometimes they reached the cold seas near Cape Horn less than four weeks after leaving Melbourne. Although the homeward voyage was usually much slower than the outward voyage, the clipper *Lightning* in 1854 sailed back to Liverpool in a mere 63 days. That record at first must have been hard to accept, for it equalled the fastest outward voyage to Melbourne in the 1850s.

Of the hazards of that route, Cape Horn with its mountainous seas and gliding icebergs was still most feared. But the greatest hazard, in the 1860s at least, were the Auckland Islands, in latitude 50, south-west of New Zealand. The islands were bleak, deserted, and sheeted with mist for part of the year. Sensible captains did not intentionally sail near them, and many survivors of ships wrecked there died from starvation or waited months to be rescued. Three ships ran into the islands in the opening five months of 1864, and those sailors and passengers who got ashore were still there that Christmas. The three ships by then were long overdue at their destination, and it was assumed that ships and passengers had all perished. In March 1865, however, a passing ship rescued four survivors from one wreck. Two months later three survivors from another wrecked ship were rescued. Two months later six castaways from the first of the wrecks were found; they had been in the Auckland Islands for eighteen months and, unknown to them, two ships had been wrecked in that time and two other passing ships had called and taken on board the survivors.

On charts the Auckland Islands seemed like pimples in the vast sea that stretched from New Zealand to Antarctica. It seemed as if a thousand ships sailing abreast could cross that sea without touching the islands. Less than a year after the three lots of castaways had been rescued, the American ship *General Grant*, sailing from Melbourne

Port Adelaide in the 1840s.   (State Archives of S.A.)

Geelong in the 1850s.   (Baillieu Library, Univ. of Melb.)

Bullock wagons and drays were seen everywhere from Queensland's ranges to Melbourne's town hall in mid-19th century.

(State Library of Tas.)

Mail coaches leaving Hobart.

(State Library of Tas.)

A Tasmanian punt, on the track to Zeehan silverfield, c. 1890.

Port Adelaide, 1870s: a tall sailing ship by a stone wool store once symbolised Australian ports.

to London with wool and gold, crashed one night into rocks beneath the high cliffs of one of the islands. Only ten of the 83 people on board survived the wreck and the spray-damp shore and these survivors were not found for a year and a half. Fewer lives were lost on the cold run to Cape Horn than on the outward voyage to Australia, but only because ships leaving Australia carried fewer passengers.

4

Journey's end for most ships in the 1850s was Melbourne, and the port was incapable of handling the fleet that suddenly made it Australia's busiest port. In the month of May 1853, ships arrived from Liverpool and Boston and ports in the northern hemisphere at an average of more than two a day. Counting the small ships that crept in from Australian and New Zealand ports the average was seven a day. On most days in 1853 a tide-waiter or water policeman could have counted more than 300 ocean ships in Melbourne — but the count would have taken all day because the ships were packed along the winding river and riding at anchor ten abreast in Hobson's Bay.

The 2000-ton clippers arriving in the 1850s dwarfed the ships that had traded with Melbourne in the decade before gold. Whereas small ships drawing only 9 feet of water could squeeze up the muddy river to the wharves flanking Melbourne's main streets, the big clippers and frigates had to remain in the bay. In the peak year of immigration, the bay lacked even a jetty, and large ships had to unload their cargo onto lighters and their passengers onto boats, paying dearly to land them on a bleak beach or carry them eight miles upstream to Melbourne. Ships which had ignorantly contracted to land their passengers in Melbourne, instead of Port Phillip Bay, quickly mended their error on subsequent voyages out; to move their passengers and luggage from the bay anchorage to Melbourne itself could cost them a sum equal to one tenth of the passengers' steerage fares from England, a journey of some 13,000 miles. When late in 1854 Australia's first railway linked Melbourne and the bay, thus offering an alternative route to the winding river, the shores of the bay still had only one pier and it could not berth large ships.

For long Australia's main ports had been Sydney and Hobart, natural harbours with safe entrances and sheltered anchorages and deep water along the shore. In contrast Melbourne and Adelaide, two of the three busiest Australian ports in the 1850s, had dangerous approaches and their wharves could only be reached along shallow rivers. Adelaide had a deeper river than Melbourne but the anchorage for larger ships was the open sea, and westerlies buffeted them. 'This is a most unsafe port for a large vessel,' wrote John F. Fawcett, master of the Liverpool ship *Harriet Humble*.

He had reached Adelaide in December 1853 but as his ship drew sixteen feet of water he was warned by the harbour pilot not to sail up the river until the tide was favourable. The ship lay nine days in the exposed gulf, was finally towed up the river by the port's only steam-tug, and even at high tide it cleared the bar at the river mouth with only a few inches to spare. At the wharves at low tide the water was only ten feet deep, and so most ships sank in the mud twice daily. They were so jammed against one another at the wharves that at low tide they often capsized, leaning on adjacent vessels. Fawcett was perturbed to see, in an ebb tide, the bowsprit of one ship settle down upon the stern of the adjacent ship; and as the tide raced out, the weight of the resting bowsprit hoisted the ship three feet until he heard the sound of breaking timber. He also saw with concern a row of hotels opposite the wharves, and eleven of his eighteen sailors went ashore one night and did not come back. He issued descriptions of the deserters and offered rewards for their return. None returned and he had to pay the enormous sum of £40 each to new sailors to sail the ship to Chile in South America for a cargo of copper ore.

Hundreds of seamen secretly deserted their ships in Melbourne and Sydney in the 1850s, willingly abandoning their back pay for the lure of the goldfields. Desertion in Melbourne was more like an organized invasion; it was unlikely that a British port anywhere in the world had witnessed the deserting of ships on such a massive scale. In the first week of 1852 only three of the 35 foreign ships anchored in the bay at Melbourne had full crews, and shipping was so crippled by the mass desertions that the Victorian government had to pass a harsh law, punishing those who obstructed persons in search of deserting seamen with a maximum penalty of two years' imprisonment. Migrants coming up the bay saw, where the gold fleet lay at anchor, a bare network of masts and spars like the interlocked scaffolding of a vast builder's site; hardly a sail was seen. On 11 September 1852 one new English emigrant jotted in his diary: 'Hobson's Bay. Who would have expected to see so many ships? Could not help feeling a momentary alarm, lest all the gold should have been picked up. But the ships looked all empty, deserted, as we passed. In one there seemed to be nobody but the captain, who was leaning disconsolately over the side. Others showed no sign of life at all. On this deck perhaps a boy, or that a dog, but generally no moving thing at all. Felt that if the gold had been picked up ever so extensively, at least it had not been carried away.'

Sea captains who were determined to sail their ships out of this prison of a port inveigled or kidnapped or bribed new crews. Sailors who had smuggled themselves ashore after dark were smuggled back unconscious after dark. Owners of hotels and waterfront boarding houses were rewarded for each drugged or drunken sailor they rowed out to anchored ships. Professional crimps and runners earned a rich living by shanghai-ing sailors. Melbourne's Chamber of Commerce estimated in 1852 that three of every four sailors recruited in Melbourne were induced or traduced on board by crimps or lodging-house keepers.

Ships which were returning to London or Liverpool might gather a new crew but rarely a return cargo. Australia had always lacked return cargoes for Europe-bound ships. Whereas ships sailing to Australia carried migrants and a huge range of manufactured goods and raw materials, they rarely had more than a handful of passengers for the return passage and they had much difficulty in finding any cargo. Australia's traditional exports of wool and whale oil commanded a high price for each ton weight, but they weighed only few thousand tons. It was only in the five years before the gold rushes that much backloading awaited ships returning to England. Ships then could not only take wool but also an even larger tonnage of copper ore from the new South Australian mines; moreover the wool was only available after the shearing season whereas copper cargoes were available all the year. At the same time the price of sheep in the 1840s was so mean that millions of sheep were boiled down and the melted fat was poured into casks and shipped to England as tallow for the soap and candle factories. For a few years ships leaving Australia for Britain had a good chance of gathering a profitable cargo, but the rough balance of inward and outward freights was suddenly upset in 1851 by gold.

Australia's traditional scarcity of cargoes for homeward bound ships became worse than ever. Hillocks of copper ore no longer shaded Adelaide's wharves; many copper mines were idle while their men rushed to new goldfields, and those mines that were active now smelted most of their copper ore in Australia and exported small piles of rich copper ingots instead of big piles of poor copper ore. Wool prices being higher, and miners being gluttons for lamb and mutton, few pastoralists now boiled down surplus sheep, so the casks of tallow that had filled the bottoms of so many vessels in the 1840s were rarely available. What remained for the vast fleet to carry home to England? There was gold, the dominant export, but all the gold dug in Australia in the 1850s weighed less than a thousand tons. If all the gold won in ten years had been stored in banks and then taken to the wharves it would have provided a good cargo for only two big clippers, and they could still have filled more than half their hold with bales of wool. Even wool could fill only a fraction of the space in most ships. The clipper *Sardinian*, sailing from Geelong in December 1858 with wool for the London sales, carried 4100 bales or 1,200,000 pounds — not a record cargo — and a mere 25 such ships could have carried Australia's entire annual wool clip and still have held space for other merchandise.

Most ships leaving Australia in the 1850s were lightly laden or carried ballast that earned them nothing. Even a fast ship had to be in port at the right season of the year, had to have a resourceful agent, and above all needed luck in order to win a profitable cargo for the voyage back to Europe. When Money Wigram's swift packet ship *Kent* advertised for cargo in Melbourne in 1858 she eventually scavenged the following:

535 bales of wool
9 bales of sheep skins
21 bags of bones
3094 cattle horns
98,000 ounces of gold
89 casks of pelts and hides
4881 ingots of copper
12 butts, 27 casks of sperm oil
and miscellaneous packages and junk.

It was a most impressive cargo; few ships that year carried away more; the ship's agents and captain must have been exultant. And yet my estimate of the space occupied by this miscellaneous cargo suggests that the ship was barely half full.

The heavy flow of goods and people from the north Atlantic ports to the gold ports on the other side of Cape Horn and Cape of Good Hope, and the scarcity of cargoes and passengers going in the opposite direction, created problems for the owners and masters of ships. San Francisco was the first of the gold ports, and her ships were the first to face that problem. They found a partial answer to the scarcity of outward cargoes by crossing the Pacific to

China. About 150 ships a year were needed in the early 1850s to carry China tea to Europe and the United States and Australia, and the tea trade was in fact one of the most profitable of all the long-distance trades. Tea ships were usually fast and seaworthy, and many of the Boston clippers which had carried gold seekers around Cape Horn to California were ideal for the tea trade. Thus, after unloading in San Francisco, they sailed 6000 miles across the Pacific to the tea ports in southern China, took on hundreds of cases of tea, and sailed around the Cape of Good Hope to ports in the north Atlantic. England's repeal of its old Navigation Acts in 1849 was most opportune, for American ships were now permitted for the first time to join in the leading part of the tea trade — the carrying of tea from China to Britain. Other ships from San Francisco, unfit for the tea trade, began to drum up another freight in China, a human freight. They began to carry large numbers of Chinese to California about four years after the gold rush had begun, and by 1860 California had some 35,000 Chinese, most of whom had come from the southern tea ports.

When Melbourne became a second San Francisco and was packed with ships that lacked a cargo for the long homeward passage to Britain, some ships went to China to find a cargo. Even before the gold rushes, when Australia's population was small, a score of ships carried in cargoes of green and black China teas. The average Australian even then drank more tea than the average person in any country outside China. When the gold rushes increased Australia's population, Australia became the fourth largest tea importer in the world. In the early 1850s the fleet of ships sailing from Australia to fetch China tea was swollen by fast clippers which carried migrants from England to Melbourne, sailed in ballast to China, and took on a cargo of tea for the long passage home to England. In the tea season of 1853–4, when the glut of shipping in Australian ports was most acute, so many ships arrived in China in search of a cargo of tea that for perhaps the first time there were not enough tea cargoes available. It is possibly significant that large-scale Chinese migration to the Australian goldfields began in that season; presumably some ships, unable to get a cargo of Canton tea, had contrived to arrange the only alternative freight which was profitable — Cantonese passengers. By June 1854 about 2000 Chinese were on the Victorian goldfields; fifteen months later there were said to be 17,000; and soon more Chinese were in Victoria than California.

In Melbourne many merchants and shipowners entered into the traffic. As Sir Charles Hotham, the Victorian governor, complained in June 1855: 'They send their ships to Hong Kong, or other ports in China, and receive a living cargo with as little scruple as they would ship bales of dry goods.' The profits of these private sponsors of Chinese migration came not only from the glut of ships in Australian ports but also from the winds. Ships which sailed from Australia to China during the period of six or seven months ending about October could make fast time for the five thousand miles, because the monsoons were favourable. Moreover, if they left China on the return passage between November and March, when the monsoons blew from the opposite direction, they could also make good time. Significantly, migration from China, in the opinion of a Melbourne merchant named Kong Meng, was mainly in those few months when the winds were fair. That too coincided with the time of the year when Chinese labourers were neither planting nor harvesting crops and therefore had perhaps more freedom to emigrate.

On the Victorian goldfields hostility to the Chinese diggers became so fierce that the government in 1855 severely restricted the number of Chinese passengers which each ship could land. It also imposed a tax of £10 on the Chinese who landed. In terms of modern currency the tax seems mild but it was as much as the fare which nearly all the Chinese had paid to travel to Australia. Sea captains evaded the tax by landing their Chinese passengers at the sleepy South Australian port of Robe, about a hundred miles west of the Victorian border, and the Chinese walked unchallenged across the unguarded border to the nearest goldfields. In April and May of 1857 sixteen ships from China sailed into the bay at Robe, all presumably having left China with the favourable monsoon. Other Australian colonies set up barriers against the peaceful Chinese invasion, but only after thousands of Chinese had entered their own territories.

The passenger traffic between China and Australia in the 1850s seems to have been cultivated by many independent shipowners rather than by a few firms operating the same ships on a regular run. As many ships which carried Chinese to Australia probably made only the one voyage, and therefore did not worry if the conditions in their ships earned them a bad reputation, the traffic was specially prone to abuses. The intervention of the British parliament in 1855 removed some of the abuses. A ship carrying Chinese emigrants now had to be seaworthy — a useful reform. It had to carry a surgeon and an interpreter. It was compelled by law to give daily to each passenger three quarts of water for drinking and washing, two pounds of firewood as fuel for his cooking, and an allowance of rice, tea, salted vegetables or pickles, and salted meat or fish. Any Chinese passenger who was able to read the law would have been heartened to learn that his ship had to carry a set of amputating instruments and bleeding lancets, two pieces of cloth for bandages, and forty different medicines ranging from rhubarb powder and ringworm ointment to a panacea named Jeremie's opiate.

It was not surprising that some Chinese should have crossed to the new goldfields on both sides of the Pacific. What is surprising is the size of the emigration of Chinese to lands that were much farther away than any other lands to which Chinese had previously migrated. The orthodox explanation is that China had poverty and that across the Pacific was rich gold; hence the movement of Chinese. The part played by shipowners in encouraging the Chinese traffic has long been known but has been seen as an example of the avarice of European entrepreneurs rather than as an essential cause of the large-scale emigration. One may suggest that but for the importance of the tea trade in attracting ships to China and but for the unparalleled scarcity of cargoes in the Indian and Pacific oceans in the 1850s, the exodus of Chinese might possibly have been too slight to cause concern in the gold countries to which they went. After all, China did not have its own fleet of ships capable of sailing long distances. It depended on foreign ships that came to trade. Those foreign ships came in such numbers and made such efforts to attract Chinese passengers in Canton and Hong Kong in the 1850s because they were desperate for profitable freight in the cargo crisis created by the new gold rushes.

The fact that most ships in the enormous fleet reaching the Australian coast in the 1850s faced the prospect of returning to Europe without a cargo or passengers had odd consequences. By fostering a Chinese invasion, it sharpened Australia's prejudice against immigration from Asia and hastened the adoption of the creed of White Australia. It not only affected the immigration of Chinese men but also the emigration of Australian horses; for ships which lacked a cargo in Australia and hoped to find one in India were willing to carry horses to India at cheap rates, and thus they stimulated the shipments of thousands of Australian-bred horses as remounts for the Indian Army. Australian coal mines along the Pacific coast gained even more than the horse breeders. As scores of ships were willing to carry cargoes of Australian coal at cheap rates to foreign ports because they had no other cargo to carry, Australian coal competed strongly in markets along the distant shoreline of the Indian and Pacific oceans. Australian coal was thus in a favourable position to compete as an export just when the age of steam was reaching that corner of the globe.

9 Black Cloud

While the Boston clippers were making their glamorous runs on the Great Circle route, they were challenged by steamships. In the struggle between steam and sail, the potential advantages of steamships were already clear. They could travel quickly on routes where unfavourable winds retarded sailing ships. In the doldrums near the Equator or on hazy days off the Australian coast a steamship could make a good day's run when a sailing ship was becalmed. The ability of steamships to reverse their engines or to turn quickly made them quicker and safer in coastal rivers or cramped harbours.

The winds, however, ruled the main sea routes long after the launching of the first steamships. A steamship had travelled on an inland waterway in Scotland in 1788, the year Australia was first settled. A steamship had first run profitably on a commercial route in 1807. Built by Robert Fulton in a New York yard and driven by an English engine, it steamed up the Hudson River from New York to the inland town of Albany, 132 miles away, in less than two days. Tiny wooden steamships multiplied on rivers and lakes and coastal waters on both sides of the north Atlantic, but did not venture far out to sea. Engineers had to find a track through a maze of technical problems before steam could drive a ship on long voyages.

Steamships at first used so much coal to generate a small amount of steam that on longer voyages they had to fill their holds, and the decks as well, with coal. They thus had no room for cargo. Steamships on the ocean at first filled their boilers with salt water, and such was the corrosion that they had to halt every four or five days while the boilers were cleaned. The early ships being paddle steamers, they had trouble with the wooden paddles that churned the water. The paddles were broken by storms or daily wear. When a ship had consumed much of her own cargo of coal she became lighter, stood higher in the water, and so the paddle floats or blades were too high to churn efficiently through the water. When the ship hoisted her sails because she had to economise with fuel, the paddles dragged in the water, impeding her speed. The solving of many of these formidable problems enabled the paddle steamer *Sirius* to cross the north Atlantic solely under steam power in 1837, and many paddle steamers began to carry wealthy passengers or packages between England and the United States. As late as 1862, when paddle steamers seemed outmoded, the *Scotia* won the blue riband of the Atlantic by paddling between Queenstown, Ireland, and New York in the record time of eight days and three hours.

Australia was slow to use steamships even in its coastal waters and estuaries. The busiest Australian cities were too far apart and the volume of traffic available was too small to attract many of those pioneer paddle steamers that were such gluttons for coal. In 1831 a tiny steam ferry was built in Sydney with an imported engine and ran on the sheltered waters around the harbour, but sailing ships continued to dominate the trade between Australian ports. At the end of 1850, a few months before the start of the gold rushes, Australian ports owned 27 small steamships and ten times as many sailing ships of comparable size. While New York harbour at that time was smoking with steamships which regularly crossed the Atlantic, Sydney had never seen a steamship which had come across the world with more than token assistance from steam.

The invention of the screw propeller as a substitute for the wooden paddle was meanwhile transforming steamships in the northern hemisphere. The iron propeller, unlike the paddle, was uniformly immersed in water and gave the ship more drive. Being submerged in the water, the propeller was less likely to be damaged in a storm. Being less cumbersome, it could be lifted more easily from the water when the steamship stopped her engines and hoisted her sails. The efficiency of the screw propeller saved fuel, and so a screw steamer could either make a longer voyage under steam or allot more space to the carrying of cargo instead of coal for her own furnaces. In turn the screw steamer vibrated so much that the wooden hulls were easily damaged, thus hastening the transition from wooden to iron ships; an iron ship could carry much more cargo or coal than a wooden ship of the same size. On no region of the world, predicted Charles Dickens' magazine *Household Words* on 22 October 1853, would the screw steamer have such powerful effects as on Australia and its overseas commerce. 'The Australians can no more get on without the potent aid of the screw, than they can do without cradles, dampers, wide-awakes, Guernsey shirts, and patent revolvers. The screw will bring them within a fifty-five days' run of home.' The prophecy was right. The one weakness was that it took so long to be right.

The steamer *Great Britain* entered the Australian run in 1852, and if any ship could defeat the new Yankee clippers she was the one. One of the largest ships in the world and the first to be both built of iron and fitted with a screw propeller, she sailed from Liverpool with 630 passengers and a crew of 137 — an enormous crew by the standards of that day, for she had to carry a full crew of sailors who went aloft as well as a full crew of engineers and firemen who stayed below. She reached Melbourne in just over eighty days, and large crowds of onlookers came to gape at her, paying 2s.6d. for the privilege of walking her decks. The big ship remained on the the England-Australia run for nearly a quarter century and her commander, Captain John Gray, was feted like a film star whenever his ship reached Melbourne, being presented with countless testimonials and illuminated addresses by emigrants who had sailed in her. But his ship was famous more for reliability and longevity than for speed. Eventually she became a plain sailing ship, then a coal hulk in the Falkland Islands and her last day of fame was in the First World War when she supplied coal to the British squadron that went out to defeat the German von Spee in the south Altantic.

The *Great Britain* and the early steamers rarely made the fast passages to Australia they were expected to make, and occasionally a clipper leaving port at the same time as a steamship would win a race across the world by thirty or more days. Steamships seemed to be accident-prone. They would run out of coal in the middle of the ocean or the coal in the bunkers would catch fire. Iron steamships often sprang a leak where the iron plates on the hull were joined; or through the poor design of the hull they became uncontrollable when steaming into a strong wind and sea. They were unable to use the stormy but quick 'Great Circle' route between Africa and Australia.

Navigators found that their compass in an iron ship — and most steamships by the 1850s were iron — behaved erratically. The magnetism of the iron in the ship affected the needle in the compass. Moreover an iron ship only had to sail from the northern to the southern hemisphere for her compass to deviate. On 1 March 1855 the *Iron Age* was sailing east along the Australian coast towards Melbourne, and at noon on that day the captain's observations of longitude and latitude showed that his ship was about a hundred miles from land. He continued to steer east by the compass but the compass was really pointing to the north. Seeing lights near midnight he assumed they were the lights of passing ships; in fact they were lights on the shore, and guided by his compass the captain cheerfully sailed his ship onto the shore.

Only the previous year Dr William Scoresby, an Arctic whaleman and explorer who had become a clergyman and scientist, angered Liverpool shipowners by insisting that the known methods of correcting the compasses in an iron ship were unreliable. Liverpool shipowners replied that the preacher was bringing iron ships into disrepute by his alarmist talk. Scoresby was so determined to find a way of correcting the compasses in iron ships that at the age of 65 he embarked for Melbourne in a new iron steamer, the *Royal Charter*. Each day throughout the voyage, and even in the wild swell of the Southern Ocean, the frail thin old clergyman climbed aloft to the mizzen-mast head to take readings from his own compass, which he believed was out of the reach of the ship's magnetic influence and therefore capable of correcting the compass on deck by which the ship was steered. He proved his point but lost his health.

The *Royal Charter*, in which Scoresby sailed, illustrated the promise and problems of the big iron auxiliary steamships. Leaving Liverpool on her maiden voyage to Australia in January 1856, she lost a month by calling at Plymouth for repairs. Using both steam and a large area of canvas she then raced to Melbourne in 59 days, the first steamship to take the record for the passage from the clippers. She became a regular steamship on the Australian run but her triumphs alternated with mishaps. On a return passage from Melbourne to Liverpool in 1858 her decks were often awash and so the main hatchway had to be covered, confining passengers below in the gloom until they were a fortnight past Cape Horn. Her passage was slow, and she ran low in food and exhausted all her coal before she crossed the Equator. Favourable winds fortunately drove her home to Liverpool in the slow time of just under a hundred days, but passengers were so outspoken about the passage that the owners paid back part of the fare. A year later, as if to show her worth, the *Royal Charter* sailed from Melbourne via Cape Horn to the Irish port of Cork in the astonishing time of 58 days — several days shorter than the fastest passage by a sailing ship. Landing a few passengers at Cork she sailed up the channel to the pilot ground near Liverpool, was driven aground by a change of wind, and 383 of her passengers and crew were drowned.

The route between Europe and Australia exposed all the weaknesses in the finest steamships of the age. Their fares and charges were so dear that they captured only a fraction of the passenger and cargo traffic in the 1850s. They relied so much on the winds that they were usually only a trifle faster over a long voyage than the latest clipper ships and were just as inconsistent. The winds between the Cape of Good Hope and Cape Horn were ideal for sails, while the long gap between coaling ports in that zone limited the use of steam power. On no important trade route in the world were steamships in the 1860s so ineffectual in capturing traffic from pure sailing ships.

2

Sailing ships still had the marked advantage of paying nothing for the power that moved them. None of their cargo space was occupied by engine room and coal bunkers. They were cheaper to construct and, on the Australian route, cheaper to operate than steamships. It was true that steamships were slowly becoming more competitive, but one of the steamships' vital technical advances was shared also by sailing ships. In the many shipyards which still built sailing vessels, iron was replacing timber as the main material.

The use of iron helped sailing ships to resist the challenge of steam. An iron sailing ship was cheaper to build than a wooden sailing ship. The framework or skeleton of an iron ship was less bulky, freeing more space for the carrying of cargo. An iron clipper, unlike a wooden clipper, was relatively watertight. Though the iron bottoms of ships became fouled and encrusted, thus increasing the resistance of the water and thereby slowing the speed of the ship, the iron bottom could be periodically scraped clean in a dock.

Iron clippers in the 1860s became the sturdy workhorses of the Europe-Australia route. They were not designed for record passages, nor did they make them, but they were cheap carriers of all kinds of cargo. The rows of Glasgow-built iron clippers which could be seen in Melbourne or Sydney no longer drew crowds of fascinated spectators to the harbour on Sundays, and yet their captains and sailors were probably worthier of hero worship than the crews of any other kind of ship which ever traded with Australia. For the iron clippers were not as buoyant as wooden ships, they did not ride the waves so neatly, and in the wild seas which so often ran between the Cape of Good Hope and Cape Horn they were battered and deluged. Any reader of Australian newspapers in the 1860s would have observed, if he read the long column of daily shipping news, that the so-called 'iron clipper ships' were usually pummelled on the last leg of the passage to Australia. The maiden voyage of the iron clipper *Melpomene*, built at Port Glasgow for the Australian trade, was typical of the ordeal which iron sailing ships faced in the Southern Ocean in winter. Running before the wind in August 1869, she was overtaken by a huge wave which smashed the wheel and broke every spoke. Huge waves washed away the binnacle and compass and hencoops. Several times the sea ran so high that the maindeck was filled with water and the new cabins were flooded, and the men who were exposed at the wheel to the seas breaking on deck were lucky to remain aboard. Even though iron clippers avoided the old Great Circle route of the 1850s, preferring instead the slightly fairer weather of the zone of latitude from 40° to 45° south, they could not evade punishment.

Once the emigration to the Californian and Australian goldfields had waned and shipyards had ceased to build fast passenger clippers, sound prophets would have sworn that the era of sailing ship records had ended. But steamships on the long trade routes were so slow and costly that at the close of the 1860s several British shipowners put in orders for new, fast sailing ships in the belief that they could even compete profitably with steamships in those cargo trades where speed was deemed essential. In short, steamships had not only failed to capture most of the humdrum cargoes on the Australian route but were not yet the clear victors in carrying valuable goods that demanded swift transit.

The new clippers were a compromise between the Yankee-type wooden passenger clippers of the 1850s and the iron, Scottish cargo clippers of the 1860s. Most were built on the composite principle with iron frame and iron deck-beams and an outer sheath of teak. Their lower masts and yards were iron, their upper masts and yards were timber, and the main rigging was made from galvanized wire. *Thermopylae* and *Cutty Sark* were the most famous of the new breed of sailing ships.

The *Thermopylae* had been launched in Scotland for the Aberdeen firm of George Thompson Junior & Co. in 1868. Registered as 947 tons, her carrying capacity was about 1600 tons, and in London she loaded a cargo of 923 iron rails, 30 tanks of malt, 265 cases of bottled beer, 25 cases of jujubes and pastilles, and thousands of other crates, cases and firkins for Melbourne. She was towed down the Thames and steered by a pilot along the English Channel to Start Point, a headland near Plymouth, where the pilot disembarked at 3 p.m. on 8 November 1868. The Melbourne importers and merchants for whom cargo had been consigned in the *Thermopylae* knew she would make a relatively fast passage, knew roughly the date when she was expected to sail from London, and accordingly expected her in Melbourne at about the end of January 1869.

On Thursday 7 January 1869, weeks before the *Thermopylae* could conceivably be expected in Melbourne, a small Australian coastal steamer was sailing east near Cape Otway, which was the Australian landfall for most sailing ships from England. The master of the coastal steamer observed in the distance a sailing ship flying the Thompson flag, and from the beautiful silhouette of the ship he deduced she must be the new *Thermopylae*, though in the haze of that summer morning he could not be certain. As there was no wind and as the sailing ship was still, the little steamer soon left her far behind. When she steamed into Melbourne and reported that she had sighted the *Thermopylae* near Cape Otway, the news was scarcely believed. Shipping men in Melbourne at first thought it

213

was impossible for a sailing ship to have made such a rapid passage. Moreover, the lighthouse keeper at Cape Otway, who daily telegraphed to Melbourne the names of ships which passed his light, had not confirmed the information given by the steamship captain. The puzzle was answered when the *Thermopylae* appeared off Port Phillip Heads, the entrance to Melbourne, on the Saturday morning. Despite some contrary weather, she had sailed from England to Australia in 61 days and 11 hours — measured from the time she left the English pilot until the time when she met the Australian pilot. No sailing ship had ever made such a swift passage from Europe to Australia. Of the hundreds of passages made by mail steamers on the same route, it is doubtful if more than half a dozen had been faster. As if to prove that her maiden voyage was not a fluke the *Thermopylae* clipped about a day from her own record in 1871, though that new record was not quite valid because she had parted with her pilot — and therefore officially commenced her voyage — at the southernmost point of England or some eighty miles beyond her starting point on her maiden voyage.

Crowds swarmed to see the *Thermopylae* at Port Melbourne at the end of her maiden passage in 1869, and many merchants and shippers wagered the price of a new hat that, when she continued her voyage to China and took in a cargo of tea, she would beat the whole fleet of China tea-clippers. From Melbourne she sailed up the Pacific Coast to Newcastle in five days, though she had to beat to windward all the way. The freight she collected in Newcastle to carry to China seems not to have been mentioned by the sea lovers who have written about this ship, for she carried black coal, the fuel of the enemy, and virtually a contraband cargo in the eyes of those who loved sailing ships. With her cargo of coal she sailed to Shanghai in 28 days, another record. She loaded tea at Foochow and sailed back to England in 91 days, a record for a homeward passage in the face of the south-west monsoon, though a record which lasted less than a fortnight. Thus she completed probably the most brilliant round-world voyage ever made by a sailing ship.

Ominously she made her maiden voyage in the last year in which sailing ships had a chance of reaching England first with the new season's teas. *Thermopylae* and her new rival, the *Cutty Sark*, carried China tea for a few more seasons in competition with steamships, then turned to the Australian wool trade. The opening of the Suez Canal, in effect a steamship canal, was driving sailing ships from the tea trade. At the same time the popularity of the Suez Canal reflected the quick advance in the power and endurance of steamships.

3

The narrow isthmus of Suez, a strip of desert separating the Mediterranean Sea from the Indian Ocean, offered an alternative way to Australia. The Suez or Overland Route had been started in 1837 by an English sea captain, Thomas Waghorn, as a short cut between England and its Indian possessions and an alternative to the traditional Indian route around the Cape of Good Hope. On Waghorn's route steamships carried passengers from England to Egypt, where they went up the Nile to Cairo, crossed the desert by caravan to Suez, and so boarded another steamship for the last stage of the passage to India. Eventually the Peninsular & Oriental Steam Navigation Company ran steamships from both ends of the route across Egypt, carrying mails and wealthy passengers between England and India in barely half the time taken by ships on the long ocean route.

As a seaway to Australia the Suez route was possibly no shorter than the 'Great Circle' route favoured by sailing ships but it was shorter than the steamer route out past the Cape of Good Hope and at least a thousand miles shorter than the normal route back to England by way of Cape Horn. The Suez route therefore seemed likely to be faster for urgent mails and for passengers who valued time. In addition the telegraph lines were slowly following that route from Europe towards Asia Minor and Asia; the farther the telegraph advanced towards Australia, the more recent were the European cables and news which ships could collect at ports en route to Australia; the more ports on that route which had a telegraphic station, the easier it was to summon another ship to carry the mail when the mail steamer broke down. A stronger advantage of the Suez route were the railways which linked the English Channel to the Mediterranean. They enabled British passengers and mails to save days on the journey to Australia by taking the train to Marseilles or ultimately to the Italian port of Brindisi, where they could board the steamer for Egypt. Above all, the coaling ports for steamships on the Suez route were more regularly spaced than on the traditional route to and from Australia. Thus ships could rely on steam for more of their passage and therefore make faster times.

With the aid of a heavy subsidy from the Imperial government, Australia was linked to the Suez route in 1852. Once in every two months a steamer left Australia for Ceylon, where passengers and mails were transferred to the regular P. & O. ships sailing between Asia and Suez. Four years later the high annual subsidy of £185,000 gave Australia a direct steam link with Suez. Even with the subsidies and the revenue from the inflated fares on the route, the various shipping companies failed to keep to their timetables or make satisfactory profits. It was probably the most expensive and most farcical mail service in the world. Ships broke down and arrived months late. Shipowners lost fortunes, not only in the expense of running their ships but also in the penalties they had to pay the British government whenever they arrived late with the mails.

The European mail usually reached Australia more quickly on the Suez route than on rival routes by 1860, but much of the speed came from the railway trains which carried the mail as far as Marseilles. The continuing weakness of the Suez route was that winds were mild or unfavourable in that long part of the passage spent in the

216

tropics, and marine engines were still so inefficient that ships depended much on the wind. The route could not be fast and reliable until the marine engines became more efficient in burning coal and raising steam. It could not be cheap until the cutting of a long canal through the isthmus of Suez allowed ships to go the whole way from Australia to England.

It was simply a route for aristocrats. They paid high fares to travel that way from Australia because they avoided the miserable homeward passage past Cape Horn, because they saw the sights at the tropical ports of call, and because the route was sometimes a few weeks faster. From Sydney the Suez mail steamers went to Melbourne, took on most of their passengers and occasionally some gold, called at the sleepy port of Albany in Western Australia for coal, and loaded more coal at Galle in Ceylon and at Aden. The end of the steamships' route was Suez where passengers went ashore at a landing place lit by flaming torches and spent a few hours in a warm stone hotel. If they made the journey before 1858 they had to send their baggage across the hot stony isthmus by camel team while they followed in a procession of box carts drawn by mules until they reached the advancing terminus of the Cairo railway. Once the railway linked the port of Suez on the Red Sea and the port of Alexandria on the Mediterranean, the transition from ship to ship was comfortable and made in less than a day.

The vision of the French diplomat Ferdinand de Lesseps for a canal across the isthmus was at last achieved at the end of 1869. How narrow the canal was can be easily understood by those who have seen the hulk of the small iron-clad warship *Cerberus*, which still stands as a rusting breakwater on a beach near Melbourne. On her maiden voyage she passed through the canal; and as the canal had been opened barely one year she may have been the first ship to use the canal on a voyage to Australia. 'No vessel of such broad beam, 45 ft. at top and 43 ft. at bottom, had previously been through the canal,' noted the *Nautical Magazine*, 'but by careful navigation Lieut. Panter suc-

ceeded in taking her through, touching only three times.'
Steamships unaided by sails were at first barely adequate
on that route to Australia, and the *Cerberus* had to take on
coal at eight ports and carry much coal on her deck during
the longer gaps between ports.

While the Suez Canal quickly transformed trade
between Europe and East Asia, its effect on Australia was
slow and undramatic. During the first dozen years in
which the canal was opened, only a dribble of ships used
the canal to go to Australia. The fast passenger steamers
still went to Australia past the Cape of Good Hope,
though for the return passage they preferred the Suez
Canal, that route being smoother and quicker than either
the old homeward route with the westerlies past Cape
Horn or the route against the westerlies past the Cape of
Good Hope. Australia's more valuable exports, gold and
wool, which could afford the high charges of fast steamers, went increasingly to market through the canal. In
May 1882 for example the big Australian pastoral house
of Goldsbrough Mort sent wool to London in seven
steamers, six of which went through Suez. As steamships
became more powerful Australian traffic through Suez
grew. But even on the eve of the First World War it was
much less important, for both passengers and cargo, than
the route past the southern tip of Africa.

The inability of the canal to capture more Australian
traffic partly reflected the fact that sailing ships even in
the 1880s were still the main carriers of cargoes to and
from Australia, and they were debarred from the Suez
route by unfriendly winds and by the cost of being towed
all the way through the canal. Even for steamships the
mileage which the canal saved had to be paid for. The
company which owned the canal exacted high fees from
ships which passed through. A generation after the canal
was opened, big mail steamers paid about 10 per cent of
the total cost of their Australian voyage for the privilege of
passing through the canal. So high were canal dues that
they influenced the design of steamships. Ships using the
canal were charged in part according to their breadth

across the upper deck, and English shipbuilders retaliated in the 1890s by constructing ships which had the normal breadth below the waterline but sides which curved inwards to form a narrow deck. Known as 'turret ships', their only defect was that they could be topheavy and unstable when carrying a full cargo. The *Clan Ranald* was one turret ship on the Australian route. She sailed from Adelaide in January 1909 with a cargo of grain and flour for Europe. On her first day out a strong wind made her list to starboard and that night she keeled over, drowning forty men.

The ability of steamships to make reasonable times on seas where adverse winds foiled sailing ships provided Australia with three new passenger and mail routes to Europe between the 1850s and the 1870s. The most popular of the new routes followed the southern coast of Australia, zigzagged to Ceylon and Aden, and passed through the Suez Canal and the Mediterranean. A variation of the Suez route went from Singapore through the Indonesian archipelago, along the southern coast of New Guinea, through Torres Strait, and down the east coast of Queensland as far as the city of Brisbane. That was the shortest route from Europe to the string of new ports which had arisen on Queensland's Pacific coast. Successful gold miners from Cooktown, and rich cattle men from the plains beyond Townsville, used that route to travel home in style to Europe in the monthly steamers of the British India Steam Navigation Company, and it was an important passenger and mail route so long as the Queensland government subsidised the ships. Perhaps the strongest reason why the colony of Queensland took steps to annex the south-eastern part of New Guinea in 1883 was its proximity to this new sealane from Queensland to Suez.

A third new route from Australia to Europe went across America. The narrow isthmus of Panama had the same importance for that trans-Pacific route as the isthmus of Suez had for the other routes. During the Californian gold rushes a short railway had been laid across the isthmus of

Panama, and from the Pacific railway terminus small steamships took passengers to California and from the Caribbean railway terminus another fleet of steamships took passengers to New York and Boston. Commodore Vanderbilt was one American steamship owner who fostered that short route to California, and he made so much money that he was able 'to visit Europe in a steam-yacht of greater tonnage and more superb appointment than the steam-yacht of any European Sovereign'. The *Illustrated News* of London, in noting Vanderbilt's display of wealth, predicted in 1853 that a steamship company proposing to use the Panama route to link England and Australia would become as rich. Not until 1866, however, did regular mail steamers run between Australia and Panama and they ceased to run in their third year.

The railway linking New York and San Francisco was completed in 1869, and San Francisco became the obvious terminus for any steamship company intending to link Australia and America. For New Zealand, now rich with its own gold, the San Francisco route promised to be the quickest to Europe. For Sydney — but not for Melbourne — it promised to be as fast as the Suez route. With heavy government subsidy steamships began to ply between Sydney and San Francisco, usually calling for coal and passengers and mails at New Zealand, Fiji, and Honolulu. Passengers using the Pacific route had the advantage of a fast train service from the west to the east coast of the United States and the advantage of fast and frequent steamships between New York and Liverpool. According to publicity handouts of the Pacific Mail Steamship Company, which operated the steamships from Sydney, the route had another asset. 'A trip across the United States, even when hurriedly made, has a good educating effect upon the traveller, particularly if all he knows of the world happens to be what he has picked up in the colonies.' Australian travellers were assured that, if they spent two days in Chicago watching pigs being sliced into bacon or ships being filled from the wheat silos, they would learn much from the 'enterprise, originality, shrewdness, and common sense of the Americans'. Many Australians were enlightened by the squeal of Chicago pigs on their way to Europe, but until the opening of the Panama Canal in 1914 few Australian cargoes went to Europe by way of North America.

By the year 1880 steamships had transformed the commerce of most countries of the world but their effect on Australia's isolation was not so spectacular. Steamships dominated the coastal trade between Melbourne and Sydney and other Australian ports, where the short distances between coaling points suited them. On the other hand most passengers and cargoes travelling between Australia and Europe still went in sailing ships. The achievement of steamships was their speeding of the passage of first class passengers, mails, urgent packages, and precious metals. In the span of a quarter of a century — from the early 1850s to the late 1870s — the average passage of mails between London and Australia had been halved from about 90 days to about 45 days. The average time taken by first class mails to travel from London to Melbourne in 1879 was 44 days, and the saved time had come from fast steamships and the Suez Canal and the trains which raced the mail from the English Channel to the southern Italian port of Brindisi. On the main competing route through New York and San Francisco, the average time taken by mails between London and Sydney was only 46 days. Henceforth improvements in the speedy transit of mail and wealthy passengers were to come slowly until the era of long-distance aircraft.

4

The glamour of the steamship as a fast carrier of messages between Australia and Europe was suddenly clouded in 1872. The quickest way of carrying news between Australia and the outside world had always been by sea. The coastal pilot who boarded incoming ships at the entrance to Australian harbours had usually been the first man in Australia to hear the latest news from Europe and America. The main job of Australian newsmen had always been the boarding of incoming ships and the collecting of the latest English newspapers. In October 1872, however, the submarine cable replaced incoming steamers as the fastest carrier of news. In Australian cities, telegraph offices replaced the waterfront as the receiving centre for world news.

Telegraph lines from Europe had steadily snaked across land and sea until by the mid 1860s they had covered more than half the distance to the main Australian ports. Ships sailing to Australia could collect in either San Francisco or Ceylon the latest news and advices which had been cabled through from London. Slowly the cable was continued from Asia across the Indonesian archipelago to the isolated northern Australian port of Darwin, where a long line of telegraph poles stretched two thousand miles across the continent from north to south.

Out in the centre of Australia stood a line of small stone fortresses where lonely telegraph operators lived more than a hundred miles or more from the nearest neighbour. Relaying the messages by code on to the next repeating station, they heard Europe's latest news before it was heard in Sydney or Melbourne. Often they saw no new face, except the face of a nomadic Aboriginal, for months on end. From time to time the slender thread of wire was broken by lightning or by Aboriginals who wanted wire to fashion into fish hooks; and repairers from the two telegraph stations nearest the break would ride horses along the line of poles until they came to the point where the wire was broken. Even on these repairing expeditions the parties of men converging from opposite stations rarely met unless the break was equi-distant.

The anonymous telegraphists who eavesdropped on every cable passing between London and Australia were themselves occasionally thrust into the headlines of newspapers. In February 1874 some of the telegraph men at the Barrow Creek office, out in the nowhere 1200 miles from Adelaide, were attacked by Aboriginals and wounded. The news of the attack was transmitted south to the next telegraph office, and so from office to office until it reached Adelaide. A doctor was hastily summoned to the Adelaide telegraph office, and medical advice was transmitted back to Barrow Creek. One of the telegraph men was dead, and another was dying, and so the wife of the dying man was hurried to the Adelaide office where, according to a journalist of the day, she heard 'the exhortations by wire of her husband — distant 1200 miles, the wire at his very bed side — each bidding an eternal adieu to the other by the click of the instrument'.

At first the cost of sending a message by telegraph from Australia to England was so dear that only about fifteen short messages were sent each way daily. A message of 20 words cost £10 — equal to five weeks' wages for a working man — but slowly the charges were reduced and after two decades newspapers could send message of the same length for £2 instead of £10. Each morning the Australian daily newspapers would print a few short messages in the following manner:

Direct Telegrams from Europe
[By Submarine Telegraph]

London, June 16.
The Czarewitch and Czarina of Russia have arrived in London.

Berlin, June 16.
The Emperor William is improving in health.

A few short items on the London price of wheat or copper or wool or money sometimes expanded the budget of overseas news.

If marine insects chanced to cut the underwater cable between Australia and Java or if Aboriginals had souvenired a strip of wire in central Australia the cabled news would cease. Even if the cable were operating, the news would often take several days to pass from England to Australia in the early years; but by the late 1880s the news was occasionally relayed across the world in less than two hours. On 10 September 1889, when thousands of Australians were anxious to know whether an Australian oarsman would win the world sculling championship on the River Thames, the result of the race was cabled from London to Brisbane in one hour and eighteen minutes. Much of the European news which the fortnightly mail steamers carried to Australia was now stale long before the ship left Europe.

The quick transfer of news across the world was not a dramatic development whose effects were as obvious as the opening of a new mining region or the building of a grid of railways or a fleet of faster ships; and for that reason its influence on Australia has been quite forgotten. Nevertheless the telegraph affected such a variety of commercial and social activities that its collective influence must have been powerful.

Australia received most of its migrants and capital and manufactured goods and shipping services from Britain, and in return exported most of its wool and minerals to Britain. Australia's economic life was dovetailed to Britain's. The efficient flow of people and goods and money between the two isolated countries depended on a swift and reliable flow of news. The effect of a dislocated news service is evident in the comment of a Sydney merchant, Henry Mort, in October 1858: 'We are now two months without news from England . . . you can imagine how inert and inactive everything is both politically and commercially.' In contrast, when commercial news could be wired across the world in 24 or 48 hours, the two linked economies could be dovetailed more efficiently. Tens of thousands of merchants, farmers, mine-owners, pastoralists, bankers and shipowners who had to anticipate the needs of customers on the other side of the world were more likely, if they had the latest news, to direct their own activities more profitably. After 1872, owners of overseas ships in Australian waters could send a telegram to the master of the ship advising him where to proceed in order to find a cargo for the return voyage, export cargoes in Australian ports still being scarce. English merchants who supplied the Australian market with iron rails or fencing wire or clothes or luxury goods could supply orders more quickly in times of scarcity. British exporters who had often flooded the Australian market with boots or foodstuffs or mirrors, because they had to gamble — in the absence of recent and reliable news — on the exact needs of a market across the world, could now supply goods in more realistic quantities; the telegraph made gluts or scarcities less frequent in Australia. In the era before the telegraph, many South Australian copper mines could be vigorously producing copper because the most recent news from London indicated that the world price of copper was high, when in fact the price of copper in London was so unfavourable that their mine was working at a loss. In many avenues of trade money was lost or opportunities to make money were lost simply because, in the era before the telegraph, businessmen or producers had to base their activities and make decisions on the strength of information which often was so stale that it was misleading. Australia's prosperity and its rate of growth in the nineteenth century partly depended on the degree of skill with which its people pursued financial profit in every form of business, and that skill in turn depended on an accurate knowledge of the price of the commodity on which each individual hoped to make his profit. For Australia the international telegraph perhaps served the same useful function that a long-range weather-forecast would have served for farmers.

In no branch of business was the telgraph so vital as in international investment. British investors were more likely to finance the building of Australian railways and reservoirs, the developing of Australian mines and pastoral houses, and they were more likely to lend money to Australian banks and governments, once the telegraph gave them a swift newsline to the distant country in which they were risking their savings. This was true certainly for investment in gold and base metal shares. Once the telegraph linked London and Melbourne, and charges for each telegram became cheaper, British speculators began to gamble heavily in Australian mining shares for the first time. Share prices have to fluctuate continually if they are to lure the speculator who invests in the hope of a quick change in the market value of his shares; and the price of Australian gold shares on the London market did not oscillate frequently enough to lure speculators until the telegraph wires carried swift and regular news from mines to share market. In the 1890s London replaced Melbourne as the great investing centre for Australian mines, and London money helped to revive Australia's output of gold to even higher peaks than in the golden 1850s. The lonely telegraph-operators in central Australia who each night tapped out the prices of shares and the latest news from the new mines were maintaining a line on which the life of scores of Australian mining towns depended.

10   A Magician's Act

When the first steam train ran in Australia, the puffs of smoke were like the opening of a magician's act. In a land where settlers had wandered far from the coast and navigable rivers were few — and often un-navigable — steam locomotives seemed likely to transform the country. Unlike steamships, they had quickly reached a useful pitch of efficiency. Whereas some steamships had to go 5000 miles between coaling ports, no locomotives in Australia in the nineteenth century had to go more than 500 miles from their base. Steamships had to compete with fast wind-driven ships, but inland railways only had to compete with slow bullocks and horses. A steamship could only take on fuel at port, but a locomotive could take on fuel anywhere along the line; in many parts of Australia it could raise steam by burning firewood cut only a few steps from the track. When a journalist on the *Sydney Morning Herald* on 11 February 1846 foresaw the railway 'diffusing its blessings over the whole community . . . like the atmospheric air and the beams of sun', he was not abusing poetic license.

There was one flaw in that optimism. A steamship could run on the sea but a locomotive could only run on iron tracks, and in Australia a thirty mile railway could cost as much as ten steamships. The promoters of Australia's first railway slowly learned that piece of arithmetic. They had formed a company to build a railway fourteen miles from Sydney to the small inland town of Parramatta, and had airy hopes of then extending two lines over the mountains to the sheep country around Bathurst and Goulburn. Although the government guaranteed to pay shareholders of the Sydney Railway Company 5 per cent annual interest while the railway was still being built and to continue the payment if the line made no profits, few investors bought shares. In the hope of arousing support, the company prematurely dug the first sod of earth for the railway on 3 July 1850 in the presence of ten thousand spectators who stood in the rain in a desolate paddock. Even then the company was so poor that it had to charge gentlemen shareholders 10s. and their ladies 5s. to join in the ceremony. By then some of the shareholders began to agree with the private opinion of the colony's surveyor general, Major Mitchell: 'I cannot hope much from a railroad speculation in a country where the population is far below a million . . . It is all flash-in-the-pan work in this land of humbug.'

It became even more a land of humbug early in 1851. Just when the company's contractor began to construct the earthworks for the railway, rich gold was found only 140 miles from his earthworks. His navvies deserted him and the remnant demanded high wages. The work dawdled along. The company spent nearly all of its meagre £25,000, or less than one twentieth of the money that was eventually needed, and then had to turn to the government for aid. To speed the work the government imported hundreds of railway navvies from England, and indirectly paid their wages by lending money to the company.

The sight of the advancing earthworks and the army of pick and shovel men and the portable two-storeyed hotel of wood and hessian that trailed them along the line inspired more businessmen to invest in the railway company. But the State still provided most of the money. Just before the line was completed, it finally bought out the Sydney company and also the company that was struggling to build a line from the port of Newcastle to East Maitland. 'The two railways,' wrote one historian, 'had earned the dubious honour of being the first to be nationalised in the

(*Illustrated London News*, 1850)

Between decks in an emigrant ship, c. 1850.

Destination of most gold emigrants was Melbourne; the railway and pier were built at the peak of the 1850s rush

(Holtermann Collection: Mitchell Lib.)

Gulgong goldfield, west of Sydney, in the 1870s. The absence of women outside the shops points to one social effect of distance.

(Holtermann Collection: Mitchell Lib.)

Ballarat, gold city of late 1880s.

Donkey team at Broken Hill, silver city of 1890s.

Kalgoorlie gold rush, 1895. Transport from the coast was so dear that the 'Golden West Bakery and Bed Rooms' charged as much as fine coastal hotels.

British Empire.'

Despite their long start on any rivals, they had missed the honour of being the first working railways in the land. When the first train left the Sydney suburb of Redfern for Parramatta on 26 September 1855, to the salute of 21 guns and to a band tune entitled the 'New South Wales railway waltz', Melbourne's first railway was already a year old. It ran 2½ miles from Flinders Street, Melbourne, to the deep water at Port Melbourne and snatched some of the cargo and most of the passenger traffic which had previously had to go in small ships to get from the bay to the city. Although the project cost the Melbourne and Hobson's Bay Railway Company a small fortune it was Australia's first profitable railway.

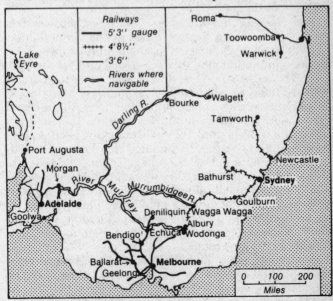

Inland Transport in South-eastern Australia, 1880.

It was also the only successful private railway for many years. Promoters of other private railways in Victoria soon wished they had never seen a locomotive. One band of promoters had decided in 1852 that a railway spanning the 39 miles between the two main ports of Melbourne and Geelong would pay 35 or 40 per cent a year in dividends. As Geelong was the closest port to most goldfields, its sea traffic with Melbourne was heavy; the railway company's solicitor vowed in his enthusiasm that the sealane was so congested that the little steamships could hardly make a trip without colliding. Many Geelong men even envisaged overseas ships unloading their cargo at Geelong, and part of the cargo going by bullock dray to the goldfields and the remainder going to Melbourne along the swift railway. They predicted that the railway would quickly vanquish coastal steamships on the same route.

The Geelong and Melbourne Railway Company employed more than a thousand men in 1853 in building a railway from the outskirts of Melbourne to Geelong. Running out of money, they scrounged and borrowed in England and Australia and after four years their trains were running roughly parallel to the bay. Mistaken in thinking a railway could compete with ships for general cargo, they earned no profit. If, however, they had not planned a railway until 1855, when the first hectic rushes by gold diggers across Victoria had slowed and the goldfields at the back of Geelong had gained a large and relatively settled population, they would probably have spent all their money on a railway from Geelong to the nearest goldfields, thus acquiring a profitable railway and making Geelong the port for a huge area of Victoria. They had made their error and in 1859 were glad to sell their railway to the government.

Australia's other long-distance railway had already been sold to the Victorian government. Its promoters had originally argued in 1852 that a line from Melbourne to the Mount Alexander goldfield near Bendigo would drive the cavalcade of loaded bullock drays from the rough, hilly road. They raised £130,000 of capital in Victoria, but needing at least a million their emissary went to

London to find it. In London he didn't even try. He was told that the Victorian Act incorporating his railway company stipulated that the shares were only transferable in Victoria, and so there was no point in Englishmen buying shares. If the telegraph had then linked London and Melbourne, he could have cabled a request that parliament quickly repeal this trivial and yet all-important clause. As it was, negotiations drifted in the ocean of silence isolating the two countries. The company grew tired of the problem of raising money on the other side of the world and sold its few miles of earthworks to the government.

South Australia, the other colony which built railways before 1860, repeated the pattern. Before the gold rushes four companies had each planned to build a short railway running paralled to one of Australia's busiest roads — from Adelaide to its port. One of the companies even shipped a cargo of rails to Adelaide. Its enthusiasm sagged in 1850. While the South Australian government guaranteed that the railway company would earn an 8 per cent dividend for the first seven years, it also prescribed the fares and freights which the railway could charge; and the company estimated that it would earn no more than 10 per cent in a year. Railway promoters demanded high rewards for their risks, but the government's terms were too restrictive. Thus the government built its own railways with borrowed English money. By 1860 Australia's railways, except for a short suburban network in Melbourne, were owned and worked by governments. Unlike the railways of the United States, Great Britain, and many European countries, all but a few Australian railways were to be built by the Crown.

Why did private companies fail to profit from railways when they were given the land for the lines and a government guarantee against financial loss? Most historians say that private companies failed because their leaders were inept, because they were unlucky enough to begin when the cost and turnover of labour was soaring in the excitement of the first gold rushes, and because local investors wisely decided they could make more money from mercantile speculations than from railway shares.

But there was a forgotten, more vital, reason for the failure of the railway companies. They were promoted in the years 1848–54 when Australia had only two routes that clearly merited railways; one was from Melbourne to its port and the other from Adelaide to its port, and together these suburban routes totalled only nine miles. Even the Melbourne railway had trouble in competing for cargoes against the small ships and lighters that snaked up the narrow river from the deep-sea port to Melbourne. It was saved by heavy passenger traffic.

To succeed in Australia in the 1850s a railway had to link two large towns or two closely-settled districts. As land transport was so dear in the pastoral age and as the inland was sparsely settled, the only large towns or populous regions were on the coast or rivers. Therefore they were already linked by steamships or schooners, and cargoes could be moved more cheaply by ships than by railways. Thus the railway from Geelong to Melbourne was a hazardous investment because its rates were cut by steamers, and the early New South Wales railways to Parramatta and Maitland were hazardous because river-boats could compete with them.

The sound path for railways was to go inland, where no waterway could compete. But in the early 1850s Australia had no inland pastoral town or farming area that was important enough to justify a railway to the coast. Even if, by an excess of imagination, the leading Australian pastoral towns of Bathurst and Goulburn with their huddle of a few thousand people could be called large, the same ripe imagination could not lightly plan railways from Sydney to these towns because they were on the other side of steep mountains and nearly 150 miles away. A prosperous sheep district in each year of the 1850s did not yield a large tonnage of wool. Much later the sheep population soared in inland districts and town populations grew and small farmers settled here and there, so improving the economics of a railway running to a distant pastoral district. The first railways built from a port to serve simply a pastoral area reached Echuca (V.) in 1864, Toowoomba (Q.) in 1867, and Goulburn (N.S.W.) in 1869. By then railways to some pastoral areas were at last justified.

Rich goldfields in the interior were the only other places which could conceivably merit a long railway in the 1850s. The Melbourne company which boldly surveyed a railway to Mount Alexander goldfield in 1852 understood that simple fact. At that time, however, it was still risky to plan a railway to a goldfield, for gold diggings were rising and falling like waves on the sea. For all the company knew it might, after gargantuan labours, push its railway to Mount Alexander just in time to see thousands of tents being dismantled and the population scampering away to the latest gold rush. The sluggish support for that company perhaps reflected the risk it ran. Nevertheless, once the Mount Alexander and adjacent goldfields had acquired a reasonably permanent population, the risk diminished. If the company had persevered, it would have made handsome profits.

2

Railways advanced at snail's pace after the initial flurry and promise of the early 1850s, and useful railway construction to inland towns only began towards the close of that decade. Not until State railways were advancing inland towards the gold towns of Ballarat and Bendigo, which were reached in 1862, did the railway age in Australia effectively begin. And those first inland railways were pioneer rather than pioneering railways, because they headed for the largest gold towns which by then had a permanent population and an assured traffic. Governments had digested the lessons the private companies painfully taught them in the 1850s. Moreover, they began to build railways at a time when railways were economically more justified. And they had the financial strength to borrow the necessary money in London at favourable rates of interest.

The first railways were built on the massive scale. An Englishman accustomed to the long tunnels, high embankments, stone viaducts and overhead road bridges of railways in his own land would have been impressed if he had travelled inland from Sydney or Melbourne. Victoria's two trunks lines ran from Geelong to Ballarat and Melbourne to Bendigo and both had double tracks and gentle curves, high bluestone houses for stationmasters, and arched, stone bridges over lonely stretches of the line in order to save farmers' and hawkers' carts from colliding with trains at level crossings. They were the most expensive country railways ever built in Australia, and £8,000,000 was spent on them in the belief that they would carry heavy traffic; they did, but four trains each way on a busy day did not justify double tracks.

Andrew Clarke, Victoria's surveyor-general, had insisted that the country between Port Phillip Bay and the goldfields was too rough and wild for the lightly built, cheap railways that crossed the North American plains. He explained that the country was far rougher than early surveyors had imagined, that the summit of Mount Buninyong which perched above Ballarat had been estimated by early surveyors to be about 1500 feet above sea level whereas the mere base of the mountain was that high. A military engineer, he insisted that the railways in such terrain should be as strong as a fort; but a later generation of engineers argued that light American lines could have easily crossed the Victorian ranges. His staff insisted in the soundest English manner that locomotives and wagons place nearly all their weight between the two rails, because if a train's carriages and wagons were too wide the train was in danger of toppling over; consequently when it was later proved that rolling stock could safely be made wider, some of the long bridges and tunnels on the trunk lines were too narrow to admit them. Ironically, Victoria had gone to heavy expense to build its railways on the wide Irish gauge, believing that its trains would thus be as capacious and safe as possible. In the light of

later engineering beliefs, Victoria could have saved
millions by making the railway track narrower and the
rolling stock wider.

Travellers going outback on the Great Southern railway from Sydney to Goulburn saw engineering works as
impressive as any on a Victorian line, though they would
have seen that the railway stations and locomotive round-
houses were less majestic and that their train had to wait
at a wayside station for the train coming the other way to
pass. The danger of sudden floods in eastern New South
Wales led to high bridges of brick and stone and tubular
iron, and the traveller who carried the *Australian Handbook*
to guide him would have learned that the bridge spanning
the river at Menangle was 1900 feet long and 'scarcely
surpassed by any similar work in the United Kingdom'
and that the Gibraltar tunnel was just as long.

The most arduous of the early railways crossed the
Blue Mountains from Sydney to Bathurst. After leaving
the plains near Sydney the easiest route the surveyors
could find up the mountains was in the shape of a zigzag,
the train climbing up a steep pinch to a level resting place,
then going backwards up the next steep slope to another
level resting place, and then going forward again. Once
on the mountain ridges it went west for sixty miles, the
engine smoke on crisp days floating across the blue misty
gorges. At a height of 3600 feet above the sea, the track cut
through a long tunnel and then edged itself down another
zigzag and across white, stone viaducts to the Lithgow
valley. The cliffs there were so steep that surveyors had to
be lowered on ropes to peg the site for the railway and the
navvies had to carry the construction plant on their backs
to many of the blasting sites. The railway was so slow to
span the 130 miles from Parramatta to Bathurst that the
horse-drawn mail coaches completely ruled the inland
plains until 1876.

The era of expensive railways had ended by the 1870s.
In eastern Australia most trunk lines had already crossed
the dividing range to the inland plains where there were
few rivers to cross and no mountains to tunnel into or to

flank with long viaducts and embankments. The march of the railways across the hot plains, and the swing to narrow or light railways, drastically cut the cost of making each mile of railway.

The main lines probed inland with many halts and starts. They were like snakes that hibernated for a few winters and then suddenly came to life and coiled forward another thirty or sixty miles, as more money was voted by parliament. When the snake began to stir, towns and villages were shaken as if a gold rush had hit them. A thousand or more railway navvies suddenly appeared, carrying their swags overland or coming by train to pitch their tents along the survey pegs of the new line. A railway contractor arrived and set up his engineering shop with engine and lathes and forges, and built his store with its issue of picks and shovels and blasting powder. Hundreds of farmers came with horses and drays to carry rock or earth or sleepers or fencing posts, and along the advancing line were fleeting towns of canvas and bark with grog shops and general stores and horse stables — towns so makeshift that five years later travellers who went down the new railway could see no sign except a few broken stone chimneys or tent poles that a town had ever existed. For many country towns around Australia their heyday was that brief time when they were the end of the railway, and horse or bullock teams carried supplies to all the settlements beyond and returned to the congested railway yards with wool or wheat or minerals. Then the arrival of railway gangs to extend the line to the next town provided the final flutter that preceded their drop as commercial centres.

It was hard to find many enthusiasts who thought Australia's early railways were run as efficiently as England's. Australia was weaker in technical skills; meddling by politicians in the daily running of railways may not always have fostered efficiency; and some senior railway engineers had unusual ideas. The manager of the South Australian railways apparently believed that the faster the train the higher the safety. He proudly illustrated his idea when the governor of the colony decided to visit Port Adelaide in April 1865. With such an important party of officials in the vice-regal carriages the manager himself drove the engine. When he reached a section of track that was being repaired, he made light of the fact that the rails were insecurely fastened to the sleepers. He was busily proving that there was safety in speed when the train left the track.

Two years later an English visitor, Sir Charles Dilke, had a similar experience which he thought was not exceptional. He was travelling on one of Australia's busiest railways between the gold towns of Castlemaine and Bendigo: 'On a level part of the line between the two great towns, my train dashed through some closed gates, happily without hurt. The Melbourne *Argus* of the next day said that the crash had been the result of the signal-man taking the fancy that the trains should wait on him, not he upon the trains, so he had "closed the gates, hoisted the danger signal, and adjourned to a neighbouring store to drink." On my return from Echuca, I could not find that he had been dismissed.' Dilke himself had apparently absorbed, during his short stay in Australia, the easy-going attitude of the railways, for one would also expect him to have condemned the locomotive driver who had dashed past a danger signal.

It was universal to complain about passengers' trains but a lot of complaints probably were made more to attack governments than their railways. It was commonly said that trains were slow, that they were contemptuous of timetables and comfort. On country lines the doors of many dog-box carriages were locked for long stretches in order to save passengers from boarding a train at a small siding and alighting a few sidings farther on without paying their fares; the locked doors annoyed passengers as well as fare-dodgers. When corridor or saloon carriages with their own water closet appeared on a few lines from the 1870s, they also fostered complaints. They were dusty, the lamps were not lit at night, they were stifling in the heat, or there was no leg room, or the noise of a shearer's accordion filled the carriage.

One of the fiercest critics was a Victorian journalist named The Vagabond, and when he went on a special train from Melbourne to the Kyneton races about 1877 he saw much that annoyed him: 'There were the usual disorder and insolence of officials to which travellers on Victorian lines are accustomed. Gentlemen, starving as it were on a few hundreds a year and gold-laced caps, walked about doing nothing. Two large saloon carriages were filled with bookmakers, reeking of oaths, tobacco smoke, and odds . . . The saloon carriages are an improvement on the close compartments, but the seats want arranging differently, as at present you cannot move your legs without getting them mixed up with your neighbour's.' And yet trains were far cheaper and more comfortable than the horse-drawn coaches they were superseding. Once a railway reached a country town the proportion of the population who went to the capital city for a visit multiplied; and on most country lines passengers provided at least a third and often half of the revenue.

At times trains went at speeds that silenced the critics. When the Duke of Edinburgh, visiting Bendigo in 1867, decided to go to the horse races at Ballarat, there was no direct line between the two cities, so he had to go in his special train by way of Melbourne and Geelong. He made the journey of nearly 200 miles in four hours and eight minutes travelling time, and then returned to Melbourne after the last race at a speed of nearly fifty miles an hour — probably the fastest speed hitherto reached on Australian sea or land. The fast special train rushing through the night, the glare of its coalfire flashing on passing trees, was to be a hero of many inland dramas. It took armed policemen to Glenrowan in Victoria in 1880 to capture the bushranger Ned Kelly; it took members of cabinets in a political crisis to governors' country residences for urgent conferences; it carried provisions and medicines to towns far inland that had been marooned by a flooding river and later carried tanks of water to the same towns in drought and it carried rescue equipment to mines where men were trapped. Curiously, the most famous of all Australian exploring expeditions ended in a steam train. In 1861 the only survivor of the Burke and Wills expedition, the first to cross the continent from south to north, returned from Central Australia in the company of his rescuers, and the journey which had begun from Melbourne with a string of camels ended in the same city after a fifty mile dash by railway.

3

While steam locomotives were still anchored relatively close to the coast in their first quarter century in Australia, steam boats pushed far inland. Australia had only one river system holding navigable water far from the coast — the Murray River and its main tributaries, the Darling and Murrumbidgee. A small steam boat could enter the river system on the southern coast, not far from Adelaide, and steam more than two thousand miles to western New South Wales. It was a narrow and shallow system of rivers in comparison with the Mississippi in the United States, but in a continent where rivers were so scarce it was precious.

The first paddle steamers went up the Murray River from South Australia in 1853, just four decades after one of Robert Fulton's vessels had opened the incomparably larger and more glamorous Mississippi trade. Burning wood cut on the river banks, the steamers were cheaper carriers than bullock teams; often they could carry goods 1700 miles up the river to points near the goldfields of north-eastern Victoria at a cheaper cost than bullock teams could carry them from Melbourne, a journey only one tenth as long. Moreover, the river was navigable in the winter months when the roads to the goldfields were quagmires. Paddle steamers were even more useful to the sheep districts lying farther inland, and soon the main cargoes on the rivers were bales of wool going down and station supplies coming up.

The owners of the paddle steamers, at first mostly

South Australians, had to overcome many obstacles. The river mouth was dangerous. The Murray channel meandered like a drunken sailor for nearly two thousand miles, usually taking three miles to cover one mile measured in a straight line. The river was very often too shallow for even shallow-draught vessels to proceed, and often too narrow to prevent overhanging trees from smashing the steamboat funnels. In ordinary seasons it was only navigable for seven months, from June through to December, and on the long Darling tributary some steamers were marooned in baked mud for more than a year waiting for the river to arrive. When eventually telegraph lines linked the main river ports, the daily telegrams reporting the depth of water at various points along the rivers were read by townsmen as anxiously as if they were reading the latest cables from a battlefield. Another impediment to navigation was the hidden, changing shoals and the piles of driftwood which accumulated at bends of the river. When the government of South Australia sent a 'snag steamer' 1300 miles up the river in 1859 to clear away logs and debris from a point known as Hennessey's, it hauled about 800 tons of timber from the river in the space of a quarter mile.

More than four thousand miles of the Murray and Darling and tributary rivers were navigable during much of the year. The river touched long stretches of three colonies. The most southerly river port was Goolwa, where labourers sweating on wharves or slipways could hear the roar of the Southern Ocean. The most northerly ports, Bourke and Walgett, lay out on the hot plains near the Queensland border where virtually no rain fell for most of the year. There were also flourishing river ports as far east as Albury, Wagga Wagga, and Gundagai, all of which lay on the main roads from Melbourne to Sydney. New South Wales gained most from the river system, and in the 1860s and 1870s more than one third of the wool grown in New South Wales went to market in the holds of paddle steamers or piled high in the barges they towed. They usually carried wool more than a thousand miles for

£4 or £5 a ton, whereas a bullock or horse team charged that much to carry wool less than a hundred miles. Even allowing for the meanderings of the river, the saving was high.

Although most of the main river ports were more than a thousand miles upstream from the ocean, they were not far from the coast. The river traffic was therefore vulnerable to the railways that were slowly penetrating inland. The first long railway to tap the river far upstream went 156 miles from Melbourne via the Bendigo goldfield to the river port of Echuca. In 1865 it began to attract much river traffic that had previously gone down to the mouth in South Australia, and in the 1870s an average of four ships weekly reached Echuca, berthed at a wharf that was nearly one fifth of a mile in length, and unloaded wool or redgum timber onto railway trains about to leave for Melbourne. Echuca became the main depot and emporium on the entire river system, a toy New Orleans, but its lifeline was as much the railway as the river, and the time was coming when other railways would tap the river. In the 1870s railways reached three more inland river ports and in the 1880s many more. Three colonies had each built rival railways to the riverbanks in their eagerness to capture the trade, and the river steamers became a minor shuttle service feeding the nearest railway lines. The thrashing of the side paddles was rarely heard on long reaches of the river, and grass sprouted in cracks in the wharf-planking of deserted ports.

Railway charges were dearer than river charges but railways still captured most of the cargoes. Trains were quicker and more reliable than the paddle steamers; and for wool — which provided the main downstream cargoes on the river system — speedy transit was worth money. Just as merchants preferred to send their wool from Australia to London on the faster steamships rather than the slower, and cheaper, sailing ships, so wool growers far inland found it profitable to use the fast railway instead of the slower, cheaper, paddle steamers. The tragedy for the river ports was that they were in wool districts which were

241

dry and sparsely settled. They could not provide enough foodstuffs, or minerals, timber or other low-value commodities which, demanding cheap freights rather than speed, were ideal for water transport. If the river captains, in seeking an additional cause of their latter-day idleness, had probed back far enough, they would have also been entitled to blame Nature for designing a river system which meandered interminably, never penetrated far enough from the coastline, and was thus within pouncing distance of the railways.

11   Railway Boom

Australia had nearly 4000 miles of railway in the year 1881. The most distant railway station in north Queensland was more than two thousand miles around the coast from the most distant railway station in South Australia or Tasmania. That did not mean, however, that a traveller could board a train at Townsville in the tropics and travel swiftly for 2500 miles around the coast to South Australia. In that vast distance were at least fourteen distinct public railway systems, each running from a port to inland towns. Between each railway system was a gap that varied from half a mile to hundreds of miles.

The government of South Australia had five railway systems; one was a complex system of railway tracks running north of the city of Adelaide, and four were short railways running a few miles inland from isolated ports. The government of Victoria had two unconnected railway systems, both radiating from the city of Melbourne but cut off at their closest point by blocks of city buildings. Thus a rail waggon of hay could not travel from western to eastern Victoria. New South Wales had two distinct railway systems, one pushing inland from Sydney and the other from the sooty coal port of Newcastle. Queensland's government ran five railway systems, all running west from the scattered ports of Brisbane, Maryborough, Bundaberg, Rockhampton, and Townsville. Tasmania's short railways were isolated from the mainland railways by ocean, but for all practical purposes they were no more isolated than many other railway systems.

If Queen Victoria had decided to tour Australia and — deaf to her advisers — had taken her own royal green carriages, her train would have had to run on dirt roads through the bush or go by steamship in order to get from the last railway station in one system to the nearest station in the next rail system. And when the royal train reached a new railway line the driver would have found that his wheels fitted neatly on the track in New South Wales, but that elsewhere his wheels were either too wide or too narrow.

Some of the busiest railway systems were linked together in the 1880s, and the variation of railway gauges began to annoy many military officers and a few politicians and railway engineers. Anger at the muddle increased as more of the isolated railways were linked, and when at last in the mid 1920s passengers could travel by train half way around the continent from North Queensland to Western Australia they found themselves forced to change trains (usually in the hours of darkness) at five stations, simply because the railway line suddenly became wider or narrower. In the Second World War these barriers to the quick passage of supplies and troops became costlier than ever.

Critics of the break of gauge raised sufficient heat to melt every railway in the land. Lord Kitchener, the soldier, observed in 1910 that the broken railway network seemed 'more favorable to an enemy invading Australia than to the defence of the country'. The secretary of the Commonwealth Railway Commissioners, pleading for a uniform railway gauge in May 1920, was no more caustic than a score of other critics when he informed the federal parliament: 'The railways seem to have been built without thought of the future. They were built without regard to neighbouring States. They were built to serve the purpose of the day.' Professor W. C. Kernot, Melbourne's first professor of engineering, called it 'the most lamentable engineering disaster in Australia'. Historians agreed, affirming that the men who created different railway gauges had no foresight. One may suggest, however, that these critics lacked hindsight.

The blame for the break was invariably laid on two engineers. Wentworth Shields was a young Irishman who planned Sydney's first railway, and he rejected the advice of the Imperial Government that all Australian railways should be built on the English gauge of 4 feet 8½ inches — a gauge which had reputedly arisen in Roman time when chariot wheels were that far apart. Shields preferred the Irish gauge of 5 feet 3 inches, and so the Sydney to Parramatta railway was planned on that broader gauge. Victoria and South Australia began to build their first railways in the early 1850s and also decided to use the Irish gauge. Unfortunately, Shields had by then resigned, with his railway still uncompleted, and his successor persuaded the New South Wales parliament to sanction the English gauge. It was then probably too late for the neighbouring colonies to alter their plans and their orders for rolling stock, and they went on to complete the first ten miles of what eventually became the largest network of Irish gauge in the world.

On the surface it seemed a silly misunderstanding. To modern engineers the Irish and English gauge are similar but in the 1850s many engineers genuinely believed one gauge had advantages over the other. Even so, they knew a common gauge would be wise if the Australian railway systems eventually met. In Great Britain a maze of railways had been built on different gauges — some on the mammoth seven feet gauge — and by 1846 England's parliament had seen the folly of building railways that could never effectively join into a unified network. England in fact warned Australia of the dangers of a divided railway gauge.

It is more relevant to examine, not the chance quarrel of two engineers that led to the first of many breaks of gauges in Australia, but why later engineers and politicians refused to repair the rift in the years when the cost of converting the few miles of railway to a standard gauge was still inexpensive. The answer seems simple. It paid Great Britain to standardise the width of its railway tracks because — being an integrated industrial economy — its raw materials and manufactures had to flow across the country between thousands of towns and cities. It was vital that London or Birmingham or Manchester should be able to send trains to any part of the country, and therefore a common gauge was essential. In contrast, Australia's geography and the type of its economy did not demand a uniform railway gauge in the nineteenth century.

The settled part of Australia — the eastern area that held all the early railways — was shaped like a huge kidney with sea on one side and dry sparsely-settled plains on the other. As nearly every large town was on the coast, and as the sea distance between each town was rarely longer than the distance by land, goods and passengers passing between the main towns went more cheaply by sea. Hence, for a long time, there was little call for a railway linking Sydney and Melbourne and Adelaide, the three biggest cities. The main purpose of the railways was not to link the ports but to link each inland area with the nearest port, and accordingly Australia in 1880 had many isolated railway systems, each linking a port and its hinterland. This disintegrated pattern also fitted the peculiar flow of Australian commerce. The main task of Australian railways was to carry overseas imports from the sea coast to the inland towns and Australia's exports from the inland to the sea coast. Australia did not have a unified economy with a heavy exchange of goods between each region. It had, instead, many isolated economies, each with a main port and a hinterland. The railways reflected that fact.

Politicians of the 1850s were realistic in accepting — occasionally with indignant complaints — the break of gauges which clashing engineers had given them. They were also realistic in refusing to spend large sums later in converting English gauge to Irish or the Irish to English. They knew that when eventually a New South Wales railway track met a broader Victorian railway track, there would not be much inconvenience, because most cargoes could travel more cheaply by sea than railway between Sydney and Melbourne. Moreover, by that time, railways might be outmoded as a form of transport, or a new device might enable a loaded train to pass from one gauge to another.

Many politicians, businessmen, and even railway engineers, thought the confusion over differing gauges was so trivial that ten years after the first break was made they went on to plan another. The narrow 3 feet 6 inch gauge was becoming popular from Norway to India. It seemed ideal for a new country where money for building railways was scarce and where traffic was light. A train on a narrower gauge could turn more sharply just as a small car can turn more sharply than a heavy truck. In rugged mountains the narrower railway could curve sharply to follow the contours of the hills, thus saving the excavation of tunnels and deep cuttings and the placing of long embankments or high bridges across gullies. A narrow railway was far cheaper to build in rough country, and so any government with a bare treasury was inclined to favour that guage even though it resulted in slow travelling.

In 1864 Queensland chose the narrow gauge for its first railway, which cheaply curved over the high mountains to the Darling Downs and Toowoomba and Warwick. Visitors from Victoria who toured Australia's first narrow railway marvelled at the ability of the train to round a curve with a radius of only five chains, whereas Victorian trains screeched and squealed in taking a curve with a much wider radius. 'The passengers,' wrote a touring newspaper editor, 'were astonished to find that the train ran round curves bending like a snake without any strain, without noise, and without any oscillation.' Trains on narrower lines were inclined to dawdle, but for Queensland or any colony with a vast territory and small funds the savings of a narrow gauge seemed inviting; even on the wide plains where these savings were often slight, Queensland adopted the narrow track. Tasmania built its first railway on the English gauge and its second on the narrow gauge in the 1870s and then, like Western Australia, built all narrow railways.

Three of the six governments had swung to narrow railways, and even one of the Irish-gauge colonies caught the world-wide craze for narrow railways. South Australia decided in 1870, a year of frugality, that a narrow railway was much cheaper to build on the plains as well as the mountains, and it built a series of short narrow lines into its wheatlands from Port Wakefield and Port Pirie and its northern ports. Thus South Australia had two railway systems, one on the Irish and the other on the narrow gauge, and in time the narrow had the longer mileage. The narrow gauge, the latecomer to Australia, came to dominate four of the six colonies; and by 1890 the mileage of narrow track was nearly as long as the united mileage of Irish and English gauges in Australia. Whereas the early preference for the English or Irish gauge had been the result of a muddle, the later preference for narrow gauge was a deliberate decision.

2

If the men who broke the railway gauges were really as blind and foolish as they are said to have been, then the day when railway tracks of varying gauge converged should have made plain their folly. Railways with conflicting gauges met together for the first time about the year 1880 at the small town of Hamley Bridge, some forty miles north of Adelaide. It was not a head-on clash, and it made so little inconvenience that historians have not observed that the event took place.

In 1883 the break of gauge had its severest test, for Australia's two largest cities, Melbourne and Sydney, were at last linked by a long railway that changed from English to Irish gauge at the border of the two colonies. A glance at the history of that railway is illuminating. The two railways had not raced inland to meet one another at the border, because the steamship service between the two cities was so cheap that a competing railway could only hope to capture first class passengers, mails, and urgent packages. The two railways approached one another more as enemies than as allies.

Sydney had the stronger incentive to forge a rail link with Melbourne because it would speed the passage of the Sydney-bound mails which came via Suez to Melbourne, and yet its railway stretched slowly towards the Victorian border more in order to attract the wool and commerce of that region. Likewise the railway from Melbourne went north-east towards Sydney more in order to serve the goldfields near Beechworth and the north-eastern sheep pastures and to attract trade from a corner of New South Wales. The line from Melbourne — one of the first to use steel rails instead of the fragile iron rails — eventually stretched 187 miles to the small town of Wodonga, near the New South Wales border, but had to halt there in 1873 because it could not leave Victorian territory. Sydney then extended its railway slowly from the wool town of Goulburn down to Albury, which it reached in February 1881. And, surprisingly, the two lines did not meet; instead they glared at each other on opposite sides of the border, the whistle of the Sydney locomotive clearly heard in the Victorian railway yards. If there had been prospect of a fast flow of commerce by railway between the two big cities, they could have been joined as soon as the Sydney railway reached the border. But another two years and four months elapsed before the English and Irish railways met together on opposite sides of the same railway platform.

Though Melbourne and Sydney were bitter rivals and their railways were competing for the traffic of the same region along the border, the rail link between the cities called for a celebration. Down the railway from Sydney came the governor and premier and officialdom in their special trains, and up the broader railway from Melbourne came three special trains carrying the rival governor and premier and officialdom; and on the winter afternoon of 14 June 1883 the governors emerged from their trains at the Albury platform, shook hands, and were escorted to the lofty locomotive shed where a banquet was spread for 1016 guests. On the wall of the shed, illuminated by tinted electric globes, hung the small hand-barrow into which in 1850 the first sod of earth had been shovelled at the start of the Sydney to Parramatta railway. The wheelbarrow was more symbolic than the rows of speechmakers realized; for it had opened the very railway that led to the first break of gauge. Along the dinner tables in the locomotive shed was a more obvious sign of the misunderstanding. The Melbourne guests wore morning dress, the Sydney guests wore evening dress.

The change of gauge which halted trains at the border of Victoria and New South Wales became such a barrier to the free flow of rail traffic sixty years later that it was easy to imagine that the barrier was always infuriating. But passengers going between the two cities found the changing of trains was not a hardship. Men who were accustomed to travelling long distances in horse-drawn coaches liked to leave a train to stretch their legs. As trains had no dining cars passengers had to leave the train to buy a meal; at the border, moreover, their luggage had to be checked by customs officials, so that some delay was inevitable even if they did not want a pie and tea. Even the carrying of their personal luggage from the Victorian to the New South Wales train at Albury was not annoying, because most train passengers were wealthy enough to hire a porter. The break of gauge lost its pleasures much later, when the customs inspection was abolished, when dining cars were coupled to passenger trains, the luggage porters' carts dwindled, the long train trip became a fast overnight journey in which Albury was reached late in the evening or early in the morning, and when we all had become lazier.

Nor was the trans-shipment of goods from one waggon to another at rail-break towns a severe impediment in the 1880s. Manual labourers then worked longer and harder for less pay, and so the cost of trans-shipping goods was not high. The volume of freight was not enough to create a bottle-neck in the busiest months. The ease and cheapness with which goods could be trans-shipped was illustrated simply in Sydney and Melbourne as late as 1890. No railway ran to Sydney's main overseas wharves at Circular Quay, and therefore wool or copper coming by steam train from upcountry had to be transferred to horse waggons at Sydney railway station and carted to the wharf. Similarly in Victoria the main railway system had no link with the main piers at Port Melbourne where overseas ships berthed. These transport gaps in the two biggest cities were worse than breaks of gauge; there the gauges did not break because they did not even join.

The 600-mile railway from Sydney to Melbourne soon cut the trip to 18 hours, or less than half of the time of the competing passage by coastal steamer. Most wealthier travellers who had previously gone in steamships now went by train, changing trains at Wodonga on the way down and at Albury on the way back, so spreading the refreshment room and portering gains equally amongst the rival railway stations of the border. Nevertheless the fares and freight rates on the railway were much dearer than on the steamships and the through traffic on the line was small. In its fourth year rail traffic coming into Victoria from Albury, and the New South Wales stations beyond, yielded the Victorian railways just over 1 per cent of its revenue; most of that revenue came from passengers and an average of only £4 a day came from goods and livestock. Even if there had been no break of gauge, intercolonial railways in Australia would have still been powerless to compete with the fast coastal steamers for most cargoes.

In 1889, when Australia's most expensive bridge belatedly crossed the wide Hawkesbury estuary between Sydney and Newcastle, the four largest Australian cities were linked together by 1800 miles of railway running roughly parallel to the coast in three distinct gauges from Adelaide to Brisbane. Whereas the linking of the bustling cities of the United States by railway created one huge common market that invigorated the nation's commerce, the same link in Australia in the years 1883–9 had scant effect. Most of the thriving Australian cities were ports, and were already linked by the cheaper seaway. And most Australian inland areas produced only wool or minerals or farm products for export overseas, and needed a railway only to the nearest port. The building of railways to the interior, rather than railways which linked coastal cities, was the goal and main achievement of Australian governments, and those radial traffic routes had no broken gauges. That simple fact made the break of gauge a mild nuisance rather than a barrier for two generations.

3

Australia had its first wild boom in railways in the 1880s. British rolling mills knew of the boom because they received a pile of orders for iron and steel rails. Sailing ships knew of the boom because thousands of lengths of rail seemed to be waiting on the waterfront whenever they returned to the Thames. At poky wooden shanties on the Queensland plains publicans who had served only shearers and drovers now slapped the backs of railway navvies arriving to brawl and drink on Saturday nights. Struggling farmers along the eastern dividing range had sudden windfalls when a long strip of their land was bought for a line to some bleak town, the local politician having persuaded parliament that the town would become the Chicago of the Antipodes as soon as a railway arrived.

Railways were built to country racecourses that had hillbilly races twice a year, and were built to distant mining and pastoral towns. They dissected the wheatlands in neat parallel rows, and pushed — with auctioneers and land sharks in the guard's van — to outer suburbs of the coastal cities. Two railways by 1890 stretched more than 500 miles from a capital city, one ending at Bourke (New South Wales) and the other at William Creek (South Australia) just west of Lake Eyre. From the coast of northern Australia the first trains went inland from Darwin and Normanton, returning with bricks of gold in

252

the van and sweating men in the locomotive. The first long railway was built inland from the coast of Western Australia, its dusty carriages usually empty. 'National Development' was the slogan and British money lenders were willing to pay for it.

The six colonial governments which owned railways were excited and worried by the spread of lines. In Victoria and New South Wales the steam monster threatened to swallow its masters. There the railway departments had become big businesses even by contemporary English and American standards. The New South Wales government railways for example employed nearly 12,000 men in 1890. Command of these complex businesses rested with a minister of railways who held office only while his ministry held power, who usually didn't know how a railway operated when he took office, and who was answerable, at his peril, to the requests and complaints of a hundred or so members of parliament. Politicians decided which lines should be built and what fares should be charged. They often chose the site of railway stations and the men who manned them. Ministers of railways were plagued in their offices and at their front doors by seekers of jobs, contracts, travel concessions, and new upcountry railways. 'A Minister of Railways,' it was said in 1883 by James B. Patterson, a farmer who was Victoria's nineteenth minister of railways, 'must look under his bed each night to see if an applicant for a place is not concealed there.' As the railway ministers were often replaced suddenly, some of the job seekers doubtless found themselves under the wrong bed.

In the 1880s the governments which ran the four largest railway systems in Australia handed over the detailed running of their railways to independent commissioners whom they usually imported from British railway companies at high salaries. In the cause of efficiency the politicians of Victoria, New South Wales, South Australia, and Queensland thus clipped their own power of controlling the largest single enterprise in their own colony; and they did this at the very time when Britain was strongly affirm-

253

ing that a cabinet minister himself should be personally responsible for the success and failure of the department he ruled. When Victoria boldly challenged this principle in 1883 it shaped the modern semi-independent government corporation that now rules so much of Australia's economic and social life.

For the first time Australia had railways kings, officials of power rather than personal wealth, who went on tour in luxurious trains and said yea and nay in ornate offices and controlled thousands of employees and hundreds of locomotives. The first chairman of commissioners of Victoria's railways was Richard Speight, and virtually the only powers denied him were the power to say which new lines should be built and which trains should run on Sunday. He came from the Midland Railway in England in 1884, a stout, bald, bearded little man who was as generous as Father Christmas. They were boom years in Australia and money was plentiful and Speight enjoyed spending it. The sack of this cheerful man was full of toys for the politicians on whom depended his continuity of office and the funds for his new railways. One politician asked for a railway siding near his farm, another a foot-bridge over the railway near his city house, and others requested free railway passes for their friends and children. Speight obliged. Bendigo politicians demanded a daily express train from Melbourne, and although Speight's advisers informed him that it would run at an enormous loss he put on the express. He spent £4000 on a railway station at a country racecourse, and it was only used once, for a Presbyterian picnic. When politicians complained that some of their electors had been dismissed from their jobs in the railways — for drinking claret they broached from a freight train or for some other misdemeanour — he often reinstated the dismissed men. When he bought land for new railways or stations he was courteous and compulsively kind; in western Victoria he paid £287 an acre for land worth £30. 'Just think of it,' said Mr Justice Williams, 'it almost makes one's hair stand on end to think of such a price being paid.'

Speight had plenty of time to think of it. When depression followed the boom he was urged to retrench and be frugal, but there was no meanness in him. He was suspended from office and his regime was denounced by David Syme in issue after issue of the *Age* newspaper. He had received £5250 compensation when he decided to resign his office but spent all that and £3000 more in suing David Syme for libel. Awarded a mere £100 damages he appealed for a new hearing. The new hearing ran for 86 days and ended in September 1894 with the award to Speight of one farthing damages. He hardly knew what a farthing was.

Some day a biogaphy of Speight may be written, and it may be found that he was the strange mixture of philanthropist and efficiency expert. He was unlucky enough to run Australia's biggest business in fat years, when the whole country spent extravagantly, and so the efficiency he often did introduce into the daily running of the trains was overshadowed in the end by the memory of his laxity and largesse. One suspects that his rule was at least as sound as when parliament ruled the railways, and fortunately E. M. G. Eddy in New South Wales and John Matheson in Queensland were already displaying the value of independent control of the railways when Speight was being hounded to his ruin.

Government railways in Australia were often extravagant in prosperous years, and in bad years their revenue was inadequate to pay the bondholders in London; of course the various governments had to meet the loss. Nevertheless the prevailing idea that Australian railways were always unprofitable because of the great distances and the sparseness of population seems wrong. If one remembers that government railways aimed for low fares and low freight rates instead of high profits, they were surprisingly profitable. In the three years 1897–1900 Australia's railways earned $3\frac{1}{4}$ per cent on the money that had been invested in them — nearly the same as the railway companies of Britain earned. And yet those were not very prosperous years in Australia and thousands of miles of new outback railways had not yet won the full benefit from the population they had settled along the tracks.

After the damnation of Speight some said that companies should run the railways. It is impossible to tell whether that would have been beneficial. Private railways had failed in Australia in the 1850s, and had little success in the 1870s in Tasmania where the first two railways were private. Company railways had another chance in the tail years of the nineteenth century, often on routes which seemed too risky for the governments to venture, and some of these railways were highly successful.

In Western Australia in the 1880s private promoters began to build two of the longest railways so far planned in Australia. Each costing nearly £3/4 million they pushed into deserted or sparsely settled scrubland and collected, as reward from the government, blocks of land on each side of the line totalling millions of acres. The Great Southern Railway ran 243 miles inland from the coaling port of Albany to Beverley, a cluster of redbrick houses far in the bush. When rich gold was found at Coolgardie the railway — though far from goldfields — suddenly became busy and was bought by the government in 1897. The other land-grant railway, the Midlands, so often ran out of money that it was nine years in the building. Those who travelled that line from the back of Perth to the back of Geraldton could see why moneylenders had been so cautious; the line ran from nowhere to nowhere with virtually nothing in between. Half the rail track in Western Australia was owned privately when in the mid 1890s the colony suddenly boomed as one of the world's great gold producers.

The richest territory for railway promoters was New South Wales, and only jealousy gave them their start. New South Wales had so much territory, and much of it was so far from the main port of Sydney, that railways from Victoria and South Australia tapped away much of the inland trade. But those railways did not cross the border into New South Wales, and New South Wales itself refused to extend them across its border and thereby encourage the diversion of its own trade to rival colonies. Railway promoters therefore stepped in. In 1876 a company opened 45 miles of railway across the plains from the terminus of the Victorian railway at the river port of Echuca to the New South Wales town of Deniliquin, and in carrying up manufactures and foodstuffs and bringing back wool and livestock it paid good dividends until the government railway arrived from Sydney to fight for the traffic.

Another three hundred miles to the north-west, out where hot ranges shimmered in the heat and the skeletons of thousands of sheep littered the empty waterholes in drought years, Australia's most profitable railway appeared in the late 1880s. It too was built by private promoters. A small silver field had arisen in New South Wales only a few miles from the border, and as the nearest port was in South Australia that government boldly began to build a line from Port Pirie to the border. There remained a gap of eighteen miles to Silverton, and to fill the gap a small company known as the Silverton Tramway Company was formed by J.S. Reid, a journalist who had written and printed his own newspapers at new gold rushes in north Queensland before coming south to set up his press at the river port of Wilcannia and then at the silver field. The company built its short line from the S.A. railway terminus at the border fence and the first train steamed in to Silverton just when the silver mines began to appear frail. Fortunately one of the world's richer silver fields, Broken Hill, was rising across the plains to the east, and the railway was rushed through, developing the shape of a dog's hind leg through its unexpected extension. The 36 miles of narrow railway from the border to Broken Hill became as rich as a silver mine, paying 30 per cent dividends in poor years and 50 per cent in good years. Success made J. S. Reid bold, and using his skill as a publicist he went on to launch other railways to new mining fields. His tramway from Broken Hill to Tarrawingee was soon useless. His Emu Bay Railway, commenced in the forests of

Western Tasmania in 1897, still runs but paid no dividend until 1965. His hundred-mile railway to Chillagoe, a copper-silver field in north Queensland, was less successful. Of the eleven main railways built by companies between 1873 and 1903 only five were sound investments: Silverton and Deniliquin in New South Wales, Mount Lyell and Mount Bischoff in Tasmania, and the Great Southern in Western Australia. Even so, the five were amongst the most useful railways in Australia.

Governments continued to build most Australian railways, borrowing the money from London. Between 1875 and 1891 the miles of railway in Australia jumped from 1600 to more than 10,000. In the following depression and drought less of the public purse was allotted to railway builders, but the money available went farther because most new railways were being built across plains where construction costs were cheaper and most new railways, moreover, had a narrow gauge. By 1921 the length of railways in Australia was 26,000 miles, close to the peak mileage. The busiest decade of railway building had come last, and in the orgy of tracklaying about the time of the First World War the first trains on many lines were met at stations by automobiles, their new challengers in overland transport.

In 1920 the long era of tracklaying was ending. Australia had a longer mileage of railways than the United Kingdom and a longer mileage than any countries except the United States and Canada, France and Germany, and Russia and India. In proportion to population, Australia had put down a longer stretch of railway than any country in the world. But most areas of the continent still had no railways.

4

Americans came to believe that the railways that crossed their continent in the nineteenth century were one of the forces moulding them into a powerful nation. They could point to new States which railways had settled, and in their sagas of the wild west the railway promoters and tracklayers and locomotives with their cumbersome cowcatchers were symbols of civilization. In contrast a locomotive appears only for a paragraph or page in most histories of Australia. One can't put a finger on a map of Australia and point, as Americans can point, to a vast territory which railways had tamed. Gold diggers and sheepmen opened so much of Australia; and as their cakes of gold and bales of wool were valuable enough to stand the long journey to the coast in animal-drawn carts these industries prospered long before a railway went inland. It was therefore easy to imagine that, because gold mines and sheep runs had prospered without a railway, they could continue to prosper without a railway. Nor could Australians point to rich regions which, like the Pacific and Atlantic seaboards of the United States or Canada, were utterly isolated from each other until railways joined them. Whereas, in the age before railways, the coastal ships cheaply linked each Australian colony, an American who wanted to send goods from the east to the west of his own land had to send them in a ship around Cape Horn, or more than half way around the world. Finally, the most important American railways thrust into new areas at a time when world prices of wheat and minerals and those primary commodities which the new areas produced were high, so that the new railways seemed to bring quick prosperity; in contrast Australia's first vigorous era of railways spanned the 1870s to the 1890s when prices of most inland commodities were falling, so that the railway did not falsely pose as a dramatic carrier of prosperity to most parts of Australia. And yet it seems that Australia's infant economy got as much strength and drive from its railways as the United States' big economy got, in proportion, from its network of railways.

In Australia the efficiency of steam trains over the horse teams they replaced was measured in 1898 by the Sydney statistician, Timothy Coghlan. To carry one ton of goods 100 miles in New South Wales by horse team cost £5 and to carry them the same distance by railway cost 18s.5d., or less than one fifth as much. That saving amounted to a huge sum each year for all the merchants, pastoralists, mine-owners, wheat farmers, and manufacturers who sent their goods along railways and for all the consumers who bought those goods. One could go further and say that down the railways went thousands of train loads of goods that would not have been produced if there had been no railways, and that up the railway went thousands of people to settle areas in which they would not have made a living but for railways. The advantage of a steam train was not simply cheapness. In the wet season the trains kept on running in many districts where teamsters were marooned in mud for months.

Wool gained less from the railway than any other inland product. The carrying in of fencing wire and groceries and supplies and the carrying out of wool could cost the more isolated sheep stations one eighth of their annual revenue but the railway cut that cost. In struggling outback sheep runs where the profit was low the cut was vital. Moreover, in droughts, a pastoralist near a railway often saved his flock from death by sending them down the railway to the fertile coastlands or by bringing up hay and fodder until the drought broke. When the bullock dray was his only carrier, his sheep or cattle remained in parched paddocks to die.

Wheat depended more than wool on cheap cartage to market. In the first years of the 1880s a ton of greasy wool was usually worth over £90 and a ton of wheat about £9, and in earlier decades wool was even more valuable than wheat. Therefore a wheat farmer, receiving so little for each ton of wheat, could not afford to spend much on the carting of his wheat to market. Thus the early Australian wheatfields were on coastal plains. Even there, expensive transport by dray could quickly break a wheat farmer, and at times coastal Californian and coastal Chilean farmers could land their wheat in Melbourne and Sydney more cheaply than a farmer who ploughed and reaped only thirty miles inland from Australian ports.

(ANARE photo: A Campbell-Drury)

Heard Island, an uncharted hazard for ships sailing the Great Circle route to Australia in the early 1850s.

Rev. Dr W. Scoresby, who sailed to Australia in 1856 to study erratic compasses in iron ships.

Rose, probably the first iron steamer on the Australian coast, 1841.

A giant of the England-Australia route in 1881, *Rome* had compound engines and one of the first refrigerated compartments.

(State Library of W.A.)
Albany (W.A.), sleepy coaling port on the Suez Route, c. 1900.

Port Adelaide c. 1880. Steamships were then common but still obscured by the trellis of masts and yards.

(State Archives of S.A.)

South Australia had two tongues of sea that protruded towards its best wheatlands, and from ports on those two gulfs short railways ran inland, so that the region had the cheap transport that made it Australia's granary from the 1850s to the end of the 1870s. When Victoria laid its railways across the dividing range to the northern and north-western plains, its wheatlands moved from the coast to the superior soil and climate of those plains. Long railways eventually opened the inland wheatbelts of New South Wales and Western Australia and southern Queensland. Once the railways enabled wheat to be grown far from the coast, Australia became a great supplier of wheat to European markets.

Most of the country's farming areas — not only wheat and dairying, but the irrigated plains that yielded fresh fruit and dried fruit — would either not have existed or not prospered so much without steam engines. One of Australia's three main political parties, the farmers' Country Party, would probably not exist but for the impact of steam engines. If it has a coat of arms a black steam locomotive rather than a sheaf of wheat or a pound of butter should be the centrepiece.

Australia mined rich gold and copper long before it had railways, but every railway that tapped an inland mining field prolonged its life. The main expense of mining was the wages paid to miners and millmen and smeltermen, and far inland the railways so cheapened the cost of living that a miner could often buy more goods with £2 a week than he could buy for £3 a week in the days of bullock teams. Thus companies which had only to pay £2 a week could work lodes that were previously unpayable. Railways also carried coke and coal and mining timber cheaply to inland mining and smelting centres, and they carried the minerals cheaply to the coast. Without railways nearly all the Western Australian goldfields found in the 1890s would have been abandoned after several decades. Such enticing fields as Mount Lyell, in the switchback mountains of western Tasmania, or Mount Isa in the hot ranges 600 miles from the nearest deepwater Queensland port, could never have yielded base metals before the age of railways. Broken Hill, lying nearly 300 miles from a port, could for a few years loot its richest silver without a railway, but it could not have produced a ton of zinc from one of the most famous of all zinc deposits nor utilised more than a fraction of the poorer silver and lead ores buried deeper. Traffic to Broken Hill in only the fourth year of the railway yielded the South Australian government 44 per cent of the entire revenue of its railways; but that was a small price that the mines had to pay for the wealth the cheap ore trains made possible. At the end of the century, when mines again briefly outstripped pastures as Australia's great export earners, much of the wealth was coming from new fields in inaccessible country where railways were vital.

Critics, old or recent, saw the huge debt each colony ran up for the sake of its railways, but were inclined to overlook the way locomotives were changing the land. The fuel they burned stimulated coal mines. The timber sleepers on which they ran spurred timber mills. The carriages and goods waggons, and even many of the locomotives from the 1870s, were made in Australian foundries and engineering shops, giving work to thousands. The railways' demand for thousands of tons of rails fostered a native iron industry, and the building of new lines gave work to a rugged, nomadic army of navvies.

Railways seemed to favour the big capital cities on the coast, rather than their smaller rival towns and cities. That became a frequent complaint against the State-owned railways. In their first forty years they were viewed as a political octopus which was trained by capital cities in the art of strangling lesser rivals. 'With one clear exception,' wrote one historian, 'railway systems were built on radial lines with different gauges and differential freight rates, so that the bulk of commerce was drained to each capital.' One hesitates, however, to carry the popular parable of the obedient octopus too far. Of the six capital cities, only Melbourne was favoured unduly by a railway system that drew in commerce like the arms of an octopus. In every other colony before 1890 nearly all the railways to inland districts radiated from the nearest safe port, irrespective of whether it was a capital city or a sleepy harbour. Nor is it easy to find any evidence that because railways were built on different gauges the flow of traffic to capital cities increased in the nineteenth century. On the contrary, if the break of gauge had any effect before 1890, it was to push Broken Hill's rich traffic to the small port of Port Pirie rather than to Adelaide, the capital city.

There remains the argument that Sydney or Melbourne or the other capital cities had such control over the government railways in the last century that they could manipulate freight rates to help their own warehouses and factories capture inland commerce. Until each railway system has been studied, the strength of the argument is uncertain. Certainly Melbourne seems to have manipulated freight rates in its own interests early in the twentieth century. Melbourne manufacturers could rail their goods through Ballarat to the pastoral town of Hamilton for a smaller sum than their Ballarat competitors, who were seventy miles closer to Hamilton. Farmers near Camperdown in western Victoria paid more to rail goods to the port of Warrnambool than to rail them twice as far to the port of Melbourne. Scores of such anomalies helped Melbourne merchants and manufacturers weaken their competitors in Victorian ports and inland towns.

Even if companies had owned the railways in Australia, the railways would still have funnelled commerce into the rising coastal cities at the expense of their inland rivals. The simple fact that railways carried goods so cheaply worked to the advantage of the capital cities. This is illustrated by glancing at the breweries which flourished in the 1860s and 1870s in hundreds of inland towns and which have long since closed. So long as bullock teams were the main carters between the ports and the interior, the carrying of goods was so expensive that an inland brewery had no competition from the breweries in coastal cities. Once a railway arrived, however, the barrels of

beer from city breweries could be sent cheaply to the
inland towns. Thus a city brewery which had a large
market and therefore the economies of large-scale production could afford to send cheap beer long distances by
railway to compete with inland breweries.

There was one disadvantage from the widening net of
railways. The governments which built them incurred big
debts in London. Though they borrowed the capital to
build railways in the form of long-term loans, they still
had to pay interest each year to the lenders. By June 1920
the Australian governments had spend £236 million of
loan money in constructing and equipping their railways,
or more than half of the public loans they had raised in
Britain since they first became clients of the London
money market. Whenever Australia suffered from depres-
sions, the payment of the fixed rate of interest on these
loans was a burden. Moreover, in bad years the colony's
voters, themselves short of money, pressed the governments for freight concessions on the railways. Railways
came to dominate the budgets of governments, often perhaps at the expense of education or social services. In the
minds of many Australians the railway was the sacred
and only symbol of progress.

12   A Hollow Triumph

Artists who sketched each new Australian mail steamer for the illustrated weeklies were accustomed, as late as 1880, to draw a white spread of sail. The sail was authentic but also a trifle romantic. New steamers depended far more on their hidden, compound engines than on the sails so conspicuous in the engravings.

In the 1850s a few steamers had tried the compound or dual expansion engine in which the same steam was used twice over, first to drive one piston and then another. On the west coast of South America, where coal was dear, the new engines halved the consumption of coal in some of the Pacific Steam Navigation Company's ships. Ten ships of England's P. & O. Company had compound engines by 1866. That was also the memorable year in which Alfred Holt sent one of his Blue Funnel Line steamers from Liverpool to Mauritius by way of the Cape of Good Hope, a passage of 8500 miles made without calling at one port for coal. Though she must have burned an enormous tonnage of coal she spectacularly proved the merit of compound engines.

Between England and Australia the scarcity of coaling ports favoured the compound engine. The triple expansion engine, devised by the Scottish engineer A. C. Kirk, was even more favourable. It passed the steam through three cylinders instead of the two in a compound engine. It wrung more power from each ton of coal.

In Scotland in 1880 the new triple expansion engines were installed in the *Aberdeen*, a new ship of 4000 tons deadweight. It was a reflection of the progress made by steam engines that the Scottish firm which, in 1868, had commissioned the magnificent sailing ship *Thermopylae* for the Australian trade should, only twelve years later, have commissioned for the same trade a ship which operated solely under steam and depended entirely on cargo for her profit. It was also remarkable that George Thompson & Co.'s Aberdeen Line, whose *Thermopylae* had had probably the most brilliant maiden voyage of any sailing ship, should cap that success twelve years later with one of the most successful maiden voyages ever made by a steamship. The *Aberdeen* sailed from England in 1881, called at Cape Town for coal, and reached her Australian destination after only 42 days' steaming. That would have been a fast passage for a mail steamer, but for a simple cargo steamer which had to carry much cargo in order to make a profit the passage was outstanding, heralding the era of the cargo steamer on long-distance sealanes. In the following two decades many steel steamships, whose engines used the same steam three or even four times over, entered the Australian trades. The same engines inaugurated a new era of speed in the north Atlantic, where big British and German passenger liners made speeds of twenty knots and more.

The geared steam turbine was another radical advance. Charles Algernon Parsons, an Anglo-Irish aristocrat, patented a steam turbine in 1884, and ten years later took out a new patent in which steam rotated a turbine that in turn rotated the shaft of a ship's propeller. Compared to the old method in which steam drove a piston in a cylinder, his steam turbine used less fuel, generated more speed, contained fewer working parts and so was less prone to break down. The first ship driven by a steam turbine was the tiny *Turbinia*, which steamed at the astounding speed of $34^{1}/_{2}$ knots, the fastest ship in the world. In the first decade of the twentieth century Britain adopted Parsons' steam turbine in its new warships, in a few cargo ships, and in passenger ships such as the huge *Mauretania* which snatched the north Atlantic riband from the German liners with their old piston engines. By the late 1920s steam turbines generated about one sixth of the power used by the world's steamships, and part of their efficiency came from the ingenuity of a young Melbourne engineer, A. G. M. Michell, whose device known as a thrust-bearing cushioned the tremendous, dislocating pressure which the spinning turbine exerted on the propeller shafts.

2

Mail steamers running to Australia became bigger but their times on the Suez route were no longer clipped dramatically in each successive decade. The average mail steamer took just over five weeks to steam from London to Adelaide on the eve of World War I, or about two weeks faster than the average passage a generation earlier. However, mail steamers ran more frequently and carried a much larger share of the passengers and high-value cargoes; since the 1880s British mail steamers using Suez had changed from a monthly to a weekly service, and moreover they ceased to tranship their passengers and cargoes at Ceylon but provided a through service from Australia to London.

The mail service was pepped up by the efficiency of new marine engines, the swelling volume of trade, and the rivalry of European nations for colonies and commerce and prestige. France had a sleepy colony with valuable nickel mines at New Caledonia, in the Pacific Ocean to the east of Queensland, so in 1883 the French shipping line 'Messageries Maritimes de France' opened a monthly steam service to the south Pacific with the bait of a generous subsidy from the French Government. The French mail steamers sailed from Marseilles through Suez, and coaled at Aden and at Mahé (in the Seychelles Islands, east of Madagascar), before steaming south-west to Australia. They called at four Australian ports before crossing to New Caledonia.

German steamers followed the French and outpaced

them. In 1886, two years after Germany had annexed its share of New Guinea, the North German Lloyd Line (Norddeutscher Lloyd) began a monthly steamship service from Bremerhaven to Sydney, and later the service was fortnightly and offered fierce competition to the British mail steamers. From Sydney the German line had a connecting mail service to German New Guinea, China, and Japan, where it linked with another Norddeutscher Lloyd service from Japan to Bremerhaven. In many ports in the last years of the nineteenth century the swift German mail steamers with all-German crews were the first sign of rising German economic power, but in many Australian ports they were welcomed as competitors for British mail steamers. In 1897 Norddeutscher Lloyd carried nearly 5 per cent of Australia's overseas trade. Australian workingmen praised the German mail steamers because they refused to employ cheap coloured labour in the stokeholds and because they treated their crews humanely. Tourists and businessmen praised them because in the Australian summer, when the passenger trade hit its peak, some of the fastest German ships were diverted annually to Australia from the north Atlantic run, where the passenger trade invariably waned in the northern hemisphere's winter. As the Norddeutscher Lloyd had the world's fastest steamers, capable of averaging 23½ knots, and as its ships held the blue riband of the north Atlantic from 1897 to 1909, some magnificent high-funnelled German ships visited Australia annually.

There was one Australian port which complained of the Germans' efficiency. The beautiful harbour of Albany in the south-west corner of Australia had been the coaling port since the 1850s for nearly all European mail steamers, whether they came through Suez or past South Africa. But in 1898 the Norddeutscher Lloyd ship *Prinz Regent* was persuaded to coal at Fremantle, a booming gold port more than three hundred miles around the coast. British and French mail steamers soon copied her. Henceforth Fremantle become the first or last port of call in Australia for ships travelling to Europe through Suez.

The swift mail steamers of 1900 were, in design, about half way between the early steamships and the modern ocean liner. No longer carrying sail, their masts were shorter and had been reduced from four to two. A large superstructure of cabins and staterooms rose above their maindecks, whereas the steamships of 1860 had an open deck with only a small roundhouse or structure near the stern. The steamships of 1900 were steered from a high bridge in midship instead of from the relatively low position towards the stern. Three or four tall funnels puffed out black smoke, and the dark wisps on the horizon betrayed their presence long before they came into sight.

On the Australia-Europe route the distance between coaling ports still hindered the speed of mail steamers. A big Australian mail steamer of 1905 burned about 4600 tons of coal on the outward voyage and averaged fifteen knots, but to make an additional five knots she would have had to burn almost double the coal. Apart from the high cost of the additional coal, the restricting of the space for general cargo would have drastically cut the profits of a faster voyage. Therefore, despite the subsidies of Australian, British, French and German governments, the mail steamers on the Australian route were much slower than on the north Atlantic. Moreover, most businessmen seemed satisfied with the slower Australian mails. They used the cheap telegraph more than ever before to communicate with Europe, and merely sent letters to confirm their telegrams. In one sense the mail steamer, as a fast courier, was becoming less vital just when it was becoming reliable and fast.

3

One triumph of the fast steamers was to carry frozen mutton and beef, chilled butter and fruit, cheaply and efficiently from Australia to Britain. Refrigerated ships raised the standard of living in millions of European homes and provided a new source of wealth to thousands of Australian farmers and pastoralists. Few innovations in the nineteenth century did more to improve health in one part of the world and to relieve waste in another.

Australia, New Zealand, South America, and other regions of the New World produced far more meat than their people could eat. In many years in Australia far more lambs and calves were born than the pastures could support, but distance isolated that abundance of fresh meat from the markets of Europe. It did not pay to ship surplus sheep and cattle in deckpens to London and Liverpool for slaughter. It was impractical to slaughter the animals in Australia and ship the meat; it would rot on the voyage home. It was possible to ship millions of tins of preserved meat or meat-extract from Australian meat preserving works, but the tinned meat was not tasty enough to tempt many customers in European shops. So in many years millions of Australian sheep were boiled down for their tallow, which was shipped to England for the making of soap. A Birmingham labourer could at least wash his hands cheaply whenever he dined from a flap of dear English mutton.

Theoretically it was possible to chill Australian mutton, encase it in blocks of water ice, and send it by ship through the tropics to England. In the 1850s some American ports had actually developed an export trade in ice to restaurants and hotels in Australian cities that were rich with gold. On 14 October 1858, for example, the sailing ship *Alma* reached Melbourne from Boston, U.S.A., with a cargo of lumber, lobsters, four cases of pain-killer, and 531 tons of ice that had been cut from Boston ponds. Though the ship had been at sea more than one hundred days and had passed through the tropics, most of the ice was still ice when it was hustled to city saloons. In the Victorian port of Geelong the newspaper owner, an ingenious Scot named James Harrison, had already designed and operated one of the first artificial ice works in the world. Thus, Australia had a source of ice if it wished to ship chilled or frozen meat to Europe. The main defect was that ice was bulky and a lot of ice was needed to preserve a little meat. It would have cost more to send the ice than the meat to England. The problem was to find a cheaper way of shipping fresh foods across the world.

From the 1850s many men invented machines for preserving food. New World pastoralists with surplus livestock applauded them; colonial governments offered them rewards. By the 1870s inventors were on the verge of mechanical success at the very time when long-distance steamships, by installing compound engines and by compressing coal bunkers, were promising them commercial success. In 1877 in Sydney the experiments of a little French engineer, Eugene Nicolle, backed untiringly by a Sydney merchant, Thomas Mort, seemed successful; and sheepowners donated £22,000 to send a trial cargo of frozen beef to England. An ammonia refrigerating machine was installed in the ship *Northam*, and 170 tons of beef froze on shore for months while engineers in the ship fiddled with the machine and the untameable ammonia. Eventually the ship sailed with the machine but no meat. Australia lost its chance to ship the first frozen foods successfully across the world. A year later the steamship *Paraquay* reached Marseilles with 80 tons of frozen mutton from the Argentine.

Two young Scotsmen launched the Australian trade in frozen meat. Andrew McIlwraith and Malcolm McEacharn formed a small shipping firm in 1875. They were interested in Australia as a field of business because McIlwraith's elder brother Thomas was a leading politician and owner of sheep and cattle in Queensland. As politician and pastoralist Thomas McIlwraith could see the immense value of frozen meat exports for his colony and for himself. As shipowners who began chartering ships to carry migrants to Queensland, McIlwraith and McEacharn could see the value of frozen meat as a return cargo for their ships.

Andrew McIlwraith had been visiting Australia on shipping business just when the Sydney promoter, Thomas Mort, was preparing to send his shipment of frozen meat to England. The two men had apparently met in a train crossing the Blue Mountains, and McIlwraith was invited to inspect the ship *Northam* which was being fitted in Sydney with refrigerating engine and chamber. McIlwraith decided that the equipment occupied so much space that the cargo would be uneconomical. He came to a similar conclusion when he later inspected the ship which had carried the first successful refrigerated cargo from the Argentine to France. More than perhaps any other man who had tried to promote the shipment of refrigerated meat, he realised that the cargoes had to be profitable for the shipowner or the trade would never succeed.

In Scotland he approached Bell and Coleman, inventors of a process which chilled rather than refrigerated meat. They argued that their chilled-air process had successfully preserved meat on the passage from North America to Europe and would suffice for the longer and hotter passage from Australia. McIlwraith was not so sure. In a shipbuilding yard he set up a Bell-Coleman machine and a cold chamber, and kept carcasses of meat at a temperature of about 35 degrees Fahrenheit. In less than a month the meat began to rot. Obviously a colder temperature was necessary to preserve meat on the long passage from Australia, so he tested more meat by keeping the temperature at about 15 degrees. The experiment succeeded. McIlwraith & McEacharn chartered a new Glasgow steamer *Strathleven*, of 2400 tons gross measurement, and in the after part of the hold they installed a cool chamber and a Bell-Coleman machine driven by a 50 horse power engine which burned only three tons of coal a day. The *Strathleven* carried emigrants to Australia, and in Sydney she loaded wool and copper and tin and prepared to load the meat and butter which McEacharn had carefully selected.

The cool chamber in the ship was no larger than a schoolroom, being 27 feet by 27 feet with a 6'6" ceiling, and it was soon loaded with quarters of beef and sheep carcasses and two tons of butter in small kegs. With about 28 tons of frozen food packed away and the refrigerating machine blowing chilled air into the chamber, the *Strathleven* steamed from Sydney on 29 November 1879. In

Melbourne she berthed at the Williamstown railway pier and news reporters walked the icy floorboards of the cold chamber and satisfied themselves that the meat was stiff and cold. A banquet in the ship convinced them that the meat was still sweet and sound. The 76-year-old refrigerating engineer watched the stowing of the last carcasses, sealed the doors, and the *Strathleven* steamed for the Suez Canal and London. News of the ship's progress and the state of her frozen cargo was anxiously awaited. On the 57th day out from Melbourne she reached London, and a banquet on board revealed that the meat and butter were palatable.

The shipment was conversation in London for months and those who had eaten some of the frozen meat were probably objects of curiosity at dinner parties and social events. The shipment was more successful than the earlier cargo from the Argentine to France, for the meat commanded a higher price and had come more than twice as far. McIlwraith & McEacharn, as shipowners, moreover were able to compute the costs of the shipment much more accurately than if exporters or a committee of pastoralists had hired the cargo space and installed the refrigerating plant. A larger frozen cargo would have to be carried to make a profit but they now sensed that profit was possible. They chartered a German steamer and took away another consignment of Australian refrigerated meat, again losing money.

McIlwraith & McEacharn did not gain from the huge trade they had pioneered. They moved their business from Scotland to Australia, concentrating on the Australian coastal trade, and their small steamships with red funnels and black tops made a lot of money carrying men and supplies to the West Australian gold rushes. McEacharn became more famous than McIlwraith, and his life story reflected the tragedies and triumphs of shipping. He could not remember his own father, a sea captain from Scotland's Western Isles who had been drowned when his ship was wrecked off King Island after completing the Great Circle course to Australia during the gold rushes. His family had little money, he himself became a shipping clerk in London, and then at the age of 23 joined Andrew McIlwraith in chartering and running ships. He travelled in the *Strathleven* on her vital voyage, then returned to settle in Australia. He married a Bendigo gold millionaire's daughter, made a fortune from coastal shipping and from Queensland pastures which had been enhanced by the demand for frozen meat, and at the age of forty-eight he was a knight and already three times Mayor of Melbourne.

Many fast mail steamers installed refrigerating machines and cold chambers in their holds in the 1880s and carried frozen meat from Australian or New Zealand ports to London. Freezing works and cool stores arose in Australian ports. As the trade increased and machinery became more efficient, ships charged less to carry frozen foods to Europe. Improved breeds of sheep and cattle on Australian pastures increased the trade. Ten years after the *Strathleven* sailed, New South Wales still earned more by exporting cases of tinned meat than carcasses of frozen meat, but by the last years of the century frozen exports were becoming a valuable source of Australian wealth.

Whereas in the Australian gold rushes firkins of salted British butter stood behind the counters in canvas diggers' stores, fifty years later Australia was supplying England with fresh butter and thousands of Australian farmers were making a living by producing butter for export. Whereas in the gold rushes Australia was importing barrels of dried apples from the northern hemisphere, fifty years later it was sending back fresh apples in the cool compartments of mail steamers. In 1910 Australia was earning one ninth of its export income by shipping frozen or chilled foodstuffs.

Most of the praise for the creation of this new international trade has been given to the inventors of mechanical refrigeration plants. Much of the praise, however, should go to the men who devised or provided cheap steampower for land and sea. If Australia had lacked long inland railways its export of frozen foods would have been much smaller. Similarly, fast predictable steamships with adequate cargo space were vital for the carriage of frozen foods. They made swifter passages than sailing ships by the 1880s, and so their refrigeration plants needed less coal and the meat they carried was also less likely to deteriorate. Above all, the heavy sums invested in their plants — and in the space they occupied — were repaid more quickly, for new steamships could complete two round voyages to Australia in the time usually taken by a sailing ship to complete one.

A few sailing ships did carry frozen foods across the globe. The *Dunedin* carried 5000 carcasses of frozen mutton and lamb from New Zealand to London in 1882, and though sparks from the steam refrigeration plant in the ship several times set fire to the sails and though the passage took 98 days, only one carcass of meat had to be discarded in England. It is doubtful whether the shipment was profitable to the shipowner. More important, the shipment was only possible because of recent changes in technology; she was an iron vessel and therefore reasonably fireproof, and the amount of coal burned in her steam refrigeration engine would have probably been prohibitive on a 98-day passage but for improvements in the efficiency of stationary steam engines.

4

The power of the new marine engines enabled steamships to overcome one of the main impediments on the Australian route: the lack of coaling ports in the stretch of 4800 sea miles between South Africa and Albany or the 3000 sea miles between Colombo and Albany. There was still another grave impediment to cargo steamships: the lack of return cargoes in Australian ports. While steamships in the 1880s had no trouble in finding profitable cargoes of manufactured goods to carry from Britain to Australia, their trouble in picking up profitable return cargoes often deterred them from making the round voyage to Australia.

The scarcity of cargoes for ships leaving Australian ports was probably as important as some of the more dramatic events which affected the pace at which Australia's population and standard of living grew. It was perhaps as important as a fall in the birth rate or the opening of a new region for sheep; and moreover it lasted for just over a century. The expense of shipping people or goods across the world was high enough without this additional burden. Overseas ships which sailed from Australia without a paying cargo still had to pay their crews; in fact desertions were frequent in Australian ports and ships often had to pay twice as much for a crew when sailing from Australia than when sailing from England. The empty ship still depreciated, still had to be insured against wreck, and she usually had to buy a hundred tons of barren rock to carry as ballast. It was almost as costly for the owner of a ship to send her across the world without cargo as with a full cargo. Ships on the Australian run usually resembled a factory that was idle for half the year. They had to earn most of their profit on the outward passage to Australia; and so passengers' fares and freight rates — inevitably high because of the length of the sea route — became higher than they would otherwise have been. Australians had to pay slightly more for imported English rails and hats and machinery, for American kerosene and tobacco, for Scandinavian timber, and for the big list of necessities and luxuries they imported across the world. Australia's long scarcity of export cargoes thus increased the cost of her own imports.

The shortage of cargoes was ended about the late 1890s by changes in Australia's commerce. The tonnage of imports was checked by drought in Australia and by the depression that followed the bank crashes of 1893. At the same time Australia was increasing its exports of the bulkier commodities — wheat, base metals, frozen meat, butter and fruit, timber and coal — partly as a result of the extension of the railways to the interior. These commodities did not yet rival the old giants, wool and gold, which together continued to provide more than half of

Australia's export income. In tonnage, however, these newer bulkier exports were formidable, and in the early 1900s they were filling ten or twelve times as much space in ships as that filled together by the richer items, wool and gold. They thus transformed and boosted Australia's overseas shipping.

Unfortunately, Australian shipping statistics are rare or primitive throughout the nineteenth century; but a roundabout calculation of the cargoes leaving Australia in 1881 and again in 1906 for ports other than nearby New Zealand suggests that they multiplied from about 1 million to 4 million short tons. In the same period the tonnage of incoming cargoes undoubtedly increased less dramatically. In 1881 nearly every ship which visited Australia brought cargo but many which sailed away merely carried broken rock as ballast because they could scavenge no cargo in Australian ports. In 1906 the position was reversed, and 31 per cent of the shipping that reached Australia came without cargo, but only 3 per cent sailed from Australia without cargo. The old scarcity of export cargoes in Australian ports had swung to the other extreme. No doubt many sea captains who could remember the years when they had to beg for a little cargo to carry away now strutted into exporters' offices and helped themselves to cigar and whisky and tried to dictate their own terms. Though some of the new cargoes were only available for outward-bound ships in summer, and other bulky cargoes offered little profit to steamships, Australia had become a more attractive goal for steamships. The prospect of profitable cargoes — both inward and outward — hastened the victory of steam on the Australia -Europe route.

5

Sailing ships had ruled the sealanes to Australia long after they had been dethroned from most other sealanes in the globe. It was not until about the late 1890s that the tonnage of sailing ships leaving Australia was passed for the first time by steamships. A decade later, in 1906, using the same measure, sailing ships were outnumbered three to one and had become the beggars of the ports, waiting for months at anchor while steamships filled themselves with the cream of cargoes. Few sailing ships were now being built in foreign shipyards, and the existing fleet was ageing and inclined to run to shabbiness. Every year many sailing ships were wrecked at sea or sold to salvage merchants, and losses were not replaced. Nevertheless many ships, losing their old freights to steamships in the northern hemisphere, came to Australia in ballast in the certainty that they could eventually gather a cargo. By 1906, French, German, Italian, Norwegian, and United States' sailing ships were common in Australian ports at a time when the British sailing fleet was waning.

The Indian Summer of the sailing ship was both heroic and miserable. Owners were making such slight profits that when their ships reached an Australian port they usually dismissed most of the crew rather than pay them while the ship was idle. Rather than pay wharf dues while waiting her turn to load, the ship rode at anchor in the bay, her master going ashore daily in a rowing boat. At sea she saved money by carrying fewer men than a ship of the same size had carried a generation previously; a reduced crew was made possible by the waning emphasis on speed and by modifying the lay-out of some of the sails and yards.

In deep-sea sailing ships the life of sailors was usually harder and the pay poorer than in the steamships. The dark ill-ventilated forecastles, in which the ordinary sailors were cooped, hastened the spread of tuberculosis. The iron windjammers tended to sweat, and the men's bedding could remain damp for weeks. In high seas in high latitudes sailors were drenched, had nowhere to dry their clothes, and many caught rheumatism. Men in sailing ships often had digestive troubles because the master had provisioned his ship with food of poor quality and a cook of poorer quality in order to save money. It was a dying, gasping industry, and the owners and masters had to be mean to survive.

In the Australian ports frequented by sailing ships, a band of boarding-house keepers preyed on the seamen. When a sailing ship came into port and, as was the custom, seemed likely to wait several months before she could load her coal or timber, the keepers of boarding houses went on board to recruit lodgers. They usually handed sailors a visiting card, similar to the card used by one Newcastle boarding house in 1905:

J. O'SULLIVAN & BRIDGES

Boarding-masters.

Gentlemen sailors attended to.

Aucher Frere's pianos, pills and salts for use of

boarders.

They took ashore the men who wanted board and kept them in food and pills and music so long as their money lasted. They supplied masters of ships about to sail with their crew, usually receiving a fee of £1 for each sailor they provided. One Newcastle boarding-house keeper named Andrew Wafer alone supplied 400 men annually from his lodging house to departing ships.

A sailing ship usually signed on her new crew a day or two before she was ready to sail from Newcastle. The master gave each man an advance on his first month's wages, usually about £3 10s.; if he paid cash, he ran the risk that the sailor might be missing when the ship was ready to sail so instead he paid a promissory note. As the promissory note could only be redeemed some three days after the ship sailed, and was only redeemable if the sailor had sailed with the ship, the tradesman who cashed the promissory notes for the sailors had every incentive to see that their man sailed with the ship. Sailors usually cashed their advance notes with boarding-house keepers or publicans or those waterfront clothing stores known as

'Johnny Allsorts', paying 15 or 20 per cent interest for the privilege. Whoever cashed the notes made certain that the sailors joined the ship. Often he had to pay a waterman to row drunken sailors out to a ship which lay in the harbour, ready to sail.

A sailor who deserted his ship forfeited all his wages and could spend three months in gaol if captured and convicted. On the other hand a sailor who remained with his ship received no further pay until the voyage was over or his contract had expired. If he squandered his advance note in a Newcastle hotel before the ship sailed and was carried to the ship with few sea-clothes, he paid dearly for new clothes when the ship reached stormy seas near Cape Horn. Once a week the master of the ship sent round an apprentice who announced that the captain's sea chest was open, and the captain would sell seaboots and oilskins and tobacco to needy sailors at inflated 'sea prices', docking the amount from their pay. Nevertheless, many old sailors preferred that life and many new sailors were keen to try that life in the belief that it was a romantic adventure.

The sailing ships were able to hold out against steamships by carrying those cargoes which could not afford high freight rates and which did not demand speedy transit. Wheat was one of those cargoes. Each summer at the turn of the century several hundred sailing ships were waiting at the wheat ports for the first long wheat trains to roll down from the interior. The most popular destination of the wheat fleet was the Cornish port of Falmouth. That port was open to sailing ships in all weather, was the English port nearest Lands End, and in the age before wireless telegraphy many ships called there to ascertain the European port to which their wheat was to be delivered. As steamships had grasped most of the wheat traffic by 1910, sailing ships in Australia concentrated almost exclusively on the thriving export trade in hardwood logs and black coal. They were the two commodities on which the shipping profits were so slender that steamships shunned them.

Western Australia's timber ports were magnets for sailing ships at the end of the century. Cheap sea transport helped the hardwoods from West Australian forests to win an export market in every corner of the world, and transport changes even provided their market. Most of the heavy logs and planks of undressed jarrah became harbour wharves or became railway sleepers on new lines in Uruguay, Portuguese East Africa, Natal, India, China or New Zealand. Another market for West Australian hardwoods was Britain where city streets that were scoured by heavy-wheeled horse traffic were being paved with cheap blocks of hardwood.

Australia's busiest timber port was Bunbury (W.A.) and in 1905 its wharf lumpers and ships' crews handled as big a tonnage in timber as the whole of Australia handled in wool. Sailing ships that had been driven by steamers from every fast and profitable trade now sailed in ballast to Bunbury from all ports of the world, knowing that there they could take on a cargo that at least gave them a little profit; and they were prepared to spend months waiting in the harbour for a berth and then spend perhaps another two months at the wharf while their crew working at token rates loaded the timber. At times thirty or more sailing ships converted Bunbury's bay into a bare lattice of masts and yards. In the Sailors' Home or on the waterfront one could hear the floating babble of Finnish and Russian, Italian and German, Yankee, and sometimes English voices; but the most common ship was Norwegian and when old King Oscar of Norway had his birthdays half the port was gay with flags and bunting. Jarrah timber was so heavy that any ship which filled its hold could not put out to sea but some ships leaving port for Lourenco Marques or Rio were riding so low in the water that watchers on shore wondered if they would ever reach their ports; some didn't.

While sailing ships carried away increasing tonnages of hardwood from the south-west corner of Australia, more and more sailing ships carried coal from the port of Newcastle on the east coast. Newcastle was probably the busiest coal port south of the Equator. In the steep hills behind the town lay fine seams of steam coal that was mined cheaply, carried cheaply the few miles to the wharves, and shipped cheaply to ports on nearly every coastline of the Pacific Ocean. That vast region lacked accessible seams of black coal. With the increasing fleet of steamships in the Pacific and the use of steam power in locomotives and factories and gasworks, its need for coal soared. Newcastle was able to ship its coal cheaply to San Francisco and Valparaiso, to Singapore and Manila, because for decades ships bringing migrants and cargoes to Australia lacked a cargo to carry away and so called at Newcastle for the only abundant cargo Australia could offer. Even when, at the close of the century, export cargoes ceased to be scarce in Australian ports, Newcastle's coal was so cheap that it continued to expand its overseas markets. Moreover, as more steamships traded with Australia, they took away coal for their own boilers. Coal ranked only twelfth amongst those commodities that earned Australia its export income in 1910, but in the volume of cargoes which it supplied to departing ships it had long ranked first and was only now being challenged by wheat.

It was in shipping coal to South America that sailing ships were able to resist the invasion of steamships. Not much coal was mined on the entire Pacific coast of the American continent, and as the Panama Canal did not cut through the long barrier of land until 1914 any ships that came from the coal ports of Europe or the eastern seaboard of the United States had to round Cape Horn or pass through the adjacent Straits of Magellan. In contrast the Australian coal port of Newcastle was as close as any other major coal port to Chile and, above all, had booming winds to blow its ships across the Pacific.

Many of those four-masted, iron windjammers of 2000 tons which left Newcastle at the turn of the century never carried a passenger or mailbag or precious cargo in their whole sailing lives, never lured a crowd to the waterfront when their arrival was signalled outside a port, and yet on the Pacific crossing from Newcastle to Chile they ran their way into the chronicle of speed which is published in *Lloyd's Calendar* for all sailors to argue about. In 1896 two of these ships, *Lock Torridon* and *Wendur*, doubtless heavily laden with coal, made the 6200 mile passage to Valparaiso in Chile in the astonishing time of thirty days. Most sailing ships could make reasonable times while sailing with the westerlies across the South Pacific, and at the other end was the added prize of cargoes of nitrates which they carried cheaply from northern Chile around Cape Horn and up the Atlantic to fertiliser and explosives factories in Germany. Hundreds of sailing ships which could not secure nitrates sailed back to Newcastle for another cargo of coal. As they had no South American cargo for the return passage to Australia, and as they had to carry ballast in order to stabilise the ship, they carried Chilean rock and sand which they dumped on the north side of the harbour at Newcastle. There, on stretches of coastal flat, a Chilean plant with conspicuous yellow flower is still to be seen, a forget-me-not of the last route dominated by sailing ships in the southern hemisphere.

In the early 1900s most ships which cleared Australia for foreign destinations went to Britain and New Zealand but Chile ranked a clear third. Whereas most ships bound for British or New Zealand ports were steamships, nearly all ships bound for Chile were sailing ships. In some years more than two hundred sailing ships went from Australia to Chile, most carrying coal from Newcastle but some carrying wheat and flour. Even that precarious trade was being snatched from sailing ships in the years just before the First World War, and by 1913 half the coal being shipped from Australia to South America was in steamships. Then came the war, and the world's battered fleet of sailing ships declined more swiftly, being slow-moving targets for submarines and destroyers. Even if there had been no war, sailing ships would have lost the coal trade to South America. The opening of the Panama Canal gave steamships a short cut from the Atlantic to South America, and moreover oil and hydro-electricity ·were challenging coal as fuel in countries which lacked coal mines.

Today few Australians visit South America and only oddments of commerce pass between the two continents; and yet for most of Australia's history the links between the continents had been made powerful by the force of the westerly winds. For nearly a century the only trade route for ships returning to Europe from Australia had passed the southern tip of South America, and even after alternative homeward routes were opened that old route was almost invariably favoured by sailing ships. One can often see the commercial links between continents reflected in political or social events; William Lane's band of Australian socialists would probably not have thought of creating their New Australia settlement in Paraguay but for the commercial links and friendly winds linking Australia and South America. Nor would John Christian Watson, the native of Chile who became the first Labor prime minister of Australia, probably have come to Australia but for the shipping which strongly linked the two regions.

After the First World War most sailing ships, deprived of coal to carry away, congregated at wheat ports in south-eastern Australia. In the year 1924-5 only 51 sailing ships called at Australian ports, and they represented just 1 per cent of the tonnage of overseas shipping in Australia; only thirty years previously sailing ships had provided half the tonnage. Once their wheat was loaded the sailing ships went to Europe by way of Cape Horn, and as they could attract no cargo in Europe they usually returned to Australia in ballast, if they returned at all. Perhaps the last sailing ship to carry Australian grain sailed away from the long jetty at Port Victoria in South Australia in 1949.

The westerly winds that circled the globe in the high latitudes of the south blew the spray from high waves in the Roaring Forties but they no longer ruled Australia's commerce and the life of her people. They continued to circle, their power unharnessed in an age of engines, doomed to wander alone in the purgatory of the oceans.

Sixty years went by from the early 1850s when steamships first challenged sailing ships on the ocean routes radiating from Australia until the era when the victory of steamships was overwhelming. The spacing of the land masses between Europe and Australia, and the direction of the winds and currents, favoured sailing ships much more than coal-burning ships. Thus the effect of steamships was subtle and indirect rather than sweeping. Steamships sliced the time taken to travel between the two countries, they encouraged more wealthy Australian and English visitors to cross the world, but they probably did not greatly stimulate immigration, except perhaps from southern Europe.

Once many steamships began to use the Suez Canal in voyaging to Australia, they called at Italian and Mediterranean ports where they sometimes signed on local sailors. Some of those sailors deserted ship in Australian ports, liked the country, sent home for relatives, and set in motion the chain of migration which multiplied in the manner of a chain letter. Perhaps more important, steamers using the Suez Canal cut one fifth of the distance from the traditional route between Italy and Australia. They made communication between the Mediterranean and Australia far more frequent and cheaper; one may suspect that the southern European migration to Australia between 1890 and the Second World War, and perhaps later, would not have been so strong but for the Suez route which so many steamships adopted.

Steamships did not substantially cut the cost of carrying goods across the world between the 1850s and 1914. The cost of shipping a ton of wheat or wool or manufactured goods between Europe and Australia fell, but it would probably have fallen nearly as much even if sailing ships had remained the main carriers; the increasing volume of trade between the two continents did more than any shipping innovation to lower costs. It certainly was true that the average ocean steamship in 1914 was twice as fast as the average sailing ship in 1854, and speed saved much money for many commodities. And it was true that steamships were less liable to be wrecked, and so the cost of insuring cargoes which went in steamships was lower. But nearly every Australian export, with the probable exception of frozen foods, would still have crossed the world in heavy volume even if there had been no steamships to carry them. The triumph of steamships, so long awaited, was slightly hollow.

In the years from 1920 to 1960 ships were more successful in easing Australia's isolation. The cost of crossing the ocean was pared down by the increasing size of the average ship, the shift from coal to oil or diesel fuel, the adoption of bulk carriers for many cargoes ranging from sugar to oil, the cheaper tolls charged by the Suez Canal, and the more frequent use of the Panama Canal which saved 3500 miles between Sydney and New York. On the other hand some of these gains were possibly lost by bedlam on the Australian waterfront and the cartel or conference of foreign shipowners which regulated most of Australia's overseas traffic. While shipping charges increased between the early 1920s and the early 1960s they generally did not increase as rapidly as the prices which Australia got for its wool, wheat, metals, and main exports. Similarly, over the same time, the sea freight added a relatively smaller surcharge to the landed cost of overseas manufactures imported to Australia; much of that saving, however, was lost because Australia increasingly protected its own industries by fixing heavy duties on most imported manufactures.

Despite the invasion of American clippers, iron clippers, fully-rigged steamships, compound-engine steamships, oil burning ships and motor ships, Australia still paid heavily for its isolation from the world beyond. Of all the innovations in transport in the last two centuries, the changes in shipping were less dramatic than those in land and air transport. They were less revolutionary because shipping, it seems in retrospect, was highly advanced when Australia was first settled; sailing ships harnessed the wind, which was then the strongest and cheapest motive power of all. Ships therefore did not make such dramatic gains by adopting steam and oil and those new sources of power which transformed all other ways of transport.

13   The Horseless Age

Timeless types of transport flourished in Australia at the start of the twentieth century. While railways were like a web in the south-east corner of the continent, elsewhere were vast gaps where no rails would ever be laid. Many places on the coast and innumerable points in the interior were hundreds of miles from the nearest railway. Many adult Australians had never seen a railway. In 1900 one could travel along half the coastline of the continent, from Geraldton (W.A.) to Cooktown (Q.) and find only two short railway lines in the intervening country.

Where no railway existed horses were the normal carriers, but there were still hundreds of bullock teams hauling timber from forests or wool from dry plains, and many strings of mules or packhorses which carried supplies on their backs to remote goldfields in the mountains. As late as the 1930s some sheep stations in the dry Kimberley district of Western Australia employed teams of thirty or forty donkeys to carry wool to port and supplies to the station. Their donkeys, allowed to run wild when motor lorries arrived, now number so many that they are vermin.

The carrier which dominated the largest area in Australia at the turn of the century was neither the railway nor horse nor bullock-team. Camels were the main carriers in more than half of the continent. They dominated those areas which were too dry for teams of horses or bullocks and too sparsely settled to attract railways. The tonnage they carried each year was small, their freight consisting of such items as fencing wire, foodstuffs and hardware, bore casing for wells, bales of wool and bags of gold-bearing or copper ores. Camel owners charged so much for carrying goods that only valuable and essential items could pay the charges.

At many railheads far from the coast — at Broken Hill (N.S.W.), Marree (S.A.), Mildura (V.), at Coolgardie and Peak Hill and Marble Bar in Western Australia, at Cloncurry and Chillagoe in Queensland — strings of pack camels met incoming trains and loaded supplies for towns farther inland. Many of those towns had mosques where the 'Afghan' camel drivers gathered. Mohammedanism, surprisingly, was the camel-man's asset. Their religion forbade them to drink alcohol and they were therefore entrusted with the carrying of beer and rum and gin to outback hotels whose owners or agents were wary of entrusting the same precious cargo to thirsty Australian teamsters. Most camel drivers came from Pakistan but for some forgotten reason they were invariably known in Australia as Afghans. They had first migrated to Australia with camels which had been engaged to explore the interior; and when gold diggers and pastoralists pushed farther into hot dry country in the 1890s the Afghans saw the advantage of camels as commercial carriers. Camels lived off the country, eating mulga, saltbush, and a variety of thorny or pod-bearing bushes. Unlike bullocks and horses, they could travel for several days without water; unlike bullocks and horses they could work for several years without a long spell; unlike horses they did not need to wear shoes; and unlike bullocks they could walk for weeks on stony ground without bruising their feet. These were formidable advantages.

Afghans specialised in pack camels. They mustered their hobbled camels each morning, assembling them into a long string by roping the nose of each camel with the tail of the camel in front, and loaded each camel with a quarter ton or more of goods. Most caravans travelled all day and did not usually halt until sundown; but in very hot weather some drivers rested in the day and travelled all night, the camels' soft pads making hardly a sound in the darkness. The disadvantages of pack camels, however, was that they had to be unloaded each evening and reloaded in the morning, a herculean and slow task for the drivers. Furthermore, pack camels did not fully utilise their strength. The alternative, on inland plains, was to make them pull a heavy-wheeled waggon. The waggon did not have to be unloaded each night, and on the plains a team of harnessed camels could pull double or treble the weight of goods which they could carry on their backs. On Western Australian goldfields at the turn of the century, teams of up to eighteen camels, each wearing collar and winkers and harness and side chains, pulled waggons with a strange swaying gait. They could pull a loaded waggon twenty miles or more a day on sandy plains.

Herbert Barker, a camel teamster, observed in his fine book *Camels and the Outback* that the wheels of waggons were so high and heavy that they made deep grooves in the sand like a system of railway lines. Once the grooves were formed they became so hard and smooth that a waggon following the tracks gained surprising momentum. Hence, if two camel waggons were converging from opposite directions, the lighter waggon temporarily left the grooves and allowed the heavy waggon to pass unimpeded. It was a bitter shock to the waggon drivers when motor lorries reached the outback and began to follow the camel-waggon ruts, for the motor lorries had a narrower gauge or wheel base than the camel waggons. They soon obliterated or corrugated the grooves, reducing the momentum of those camel waggons which still used the tracks.

And yet for a time the owners of camel or horse or bullock teams were confident they could defeat competition from the internal combustion engine. In dismissing the challenge of the new engine, they were rather like the majority of writers who still dismiss its influence on Australian history as negligible.

2

In Melbourne, on 11 March 1896, the president of the Victorian Institute of Engineers reviewed progress in the world of engineering and called his members' attention to one strange event. He reported that in Chicago a contraption had won a road race by attaining a speed of 16 miles an hour. Lest some of his audience should have been wondering what this monster of lightning speed actually was, he added: 'I refer to the Horseless Road Carriage, which is now beyond the experimental stage, and will soon be as useful in its own way as the bicycle.' Peering again into the future, he predicted that the new vehicles would not necessarily require more expensive roads because they 'will not destroy the macadam as much as do the feet of draught animals'.

The new engine came from a multitude of inventions and experiments in western Europe and North America. Its fuel was provided cheaply by the large petroleum industry, which had been launched in Pennsylvania in 1859 with the drilling of the first well to tap a hidden oilfield. The potential value of the internal-combustion engine was clear by the end of the century. Its distinction, as the phrase 'internal-combustion' suggests, was that the combustion occurred in the engine itself. A mixture of petrol and air was ignited, and the gas from the combustion directly drove the pistons of the engine. A steam engine, in contrast, had to be coupled to a power plant in which burning fuel heated a boiler of water, creating steam that in turn flowed to the engine where it drove pistons. Steam engines wasted much of the power imprisoned in the steam. They were also cumbersome on roads because the engine itself had to be accompanied by fire grates and boiler and a heavy weight of water. Much of the engine's power was spent in hauling the linked power plant. The combined weight of engine and power plant was such that a heavy road or track was necessary to bear the weight. For journeys overland a steam engine on iron or steel rails was much more efficient and faster than on a metalled road because it encountered less friction on the smooth rails. But that meant steam engines could usefully go overland only where a railway had been laid. As a method of transport they were expensive and inflexible. A few of those gargantuan steam engines known as 'traction engines' did travel on roads rather than rails. Their iron tyres did so much damage to the roadway that they were mainly exiled to rural districts where they moved from farm to farm, supplying power that threshed grain from straw, or cut straw into chaff.

As the internal-combustion engine did not have to be coupled to a heavy, inefficient power plant, it was lighter. It could use the same roads which horse vehicles used, and therefore had far more flexibility than a steam locomotive. It had more effective power than a steam engine because it did not have to waste power in hauling its own heavy power plant. And the petrol which it usually burned supplied 60 per cent more energy than coal for each pound in weight.

Motor cars at first had only a trifling advantage over a hansom cab. Petrol was expensive and not sold by many shops, whereas horse feed was sold by thousands of hay and corn stores or freely available on the side of roadways. Every town had its farrier and wheelwright for horse vehicles but few towns had men who could repair a motor car. Early cars had no windscreens and no hood and they raised far more dust than a dray, so motorists often looked like chimney sweeps after a long ride. The cars' rubber tyres were thin and often punctured by horseshoe nails which littered streets where horses far outnumbered cars. Moreover, until the birth of mass production in the motor industry, motor cars were expensive because they were produced in ones and twos by hundreds of little engineering shops. Thus the English firm which made the Wolseley sheep shearing machine, devised by an Australian pastoralist, F. Y. Wolseley, branched into the motor industry with relative ease. Even a few Australian engineering shops for a time made motor cars.

The arrival in Australia of the first Model T Fords in 1909 opened a period of cheaper cars and larger markets.

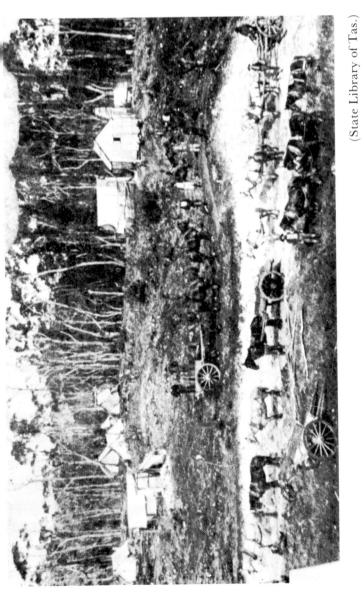

(State Library of Tas.)

Building a Tasmanian railway in the 1890s.

Trains were 'more comfortable than the horse-drawn coaches they were superseding': narrow-gauge Tasmanian railway, 1890s.

Night train, Mount Isa (Q.), 600 miles from the Pacific Coast.

'The anonymous telegraphists who eavesdropped on every confidential cable passing between London and Australia', c. 1890.

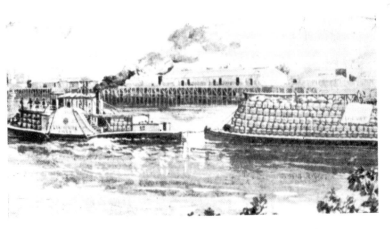

Carrying wool down the Murray, N.S.W., c. 1905.

Horse cabs swarmed in city streets in the 1870s: Swanston Street, Melbourne.

A new loquacious occupation emerged — car selling. Salesmen had to teach their customers how to start a car and how to steer before they had a chance of selling a car. Elderly farmers in particular were slow learners. They were accustomed to driving ploughs, which they always steered by pushing the lever in the opposite direction to that in which the plough was intended to go; they were slow to forget that knowledge. Driving their first car they would sometimes come to a bend in a road and instinctively turn the steering wheel in the wrong direction, thus running off the road. They were also so accustomed to driving or riding horses that they did not concentrate enough on steering. They knew a horse was never silly enough to run into a tree. They expected a Detroit car to be as sensible.

Australia owned just under 5000 motor vehicles in 1910, one year after the arrival of the first Model T Fords from the United States. The First World War checked imports of cars and trucks but in the 1920s motor cars became the rage. By 1930 Australia had nearly 600,000 motor cars and trucks — more than any European country except Britain and France and Germany. By 1963 Australia had 3,400,000 motor vehicles and an astronomical mileage of roads of medieval or modern standards.

Petrol engines replaced horses and bicycles as a means of private transport. They replaced horse waggons and vans in cities and on shorter routes. In remote areas where no railways had been built, motor lorries made long hauls on dusty roads once dominated by camels, mules, or horses. They competed with railways and coastal ships for passengers and cargoes. It was on the farms that the new engines were slowest to challenge horses. At the end of the Second World War only about 60,000 tractors worked in Australia though they quadrupled in the next fifteen years.

Even in the vigorous years of railway expansion, horses had been the most common and versatile means of transport. The population of horses was highest in 1918 and exceeded two and a half million, but thereafter the decline was rapid and today they number less than half a million. The eclipse of horses, however, was more than a sentimental event. It was part of a revolution in transport which affected all people, their habits, work, leisure, and standard of living.

So long as thousands of horses drew vehicles through city streets, mounds of manure lay on roadways and gutters and in the laneway stables; horses were as detrimental to public health as the exhaust fumes which replaced them as the distinctive scent of cities. So long as a city mainly used horses its backyard gardens were fertilised by manure and its kitchen windows swarmed with flies. Horses were tyrants and helped to keep alive — for better or worse — the cult of early rising, because tens of thousands of Australians had to wake early to muster horses, feed them, and harness them for the day's work. The spread of private motor cars partly changed the way in which cities spread. In the era when most people had depended on suburban railways and trams, Australian cities tended to develop the shape of a cart wheel, with compact settlement in the hub and with ribbons of settlement following the spokes of the wheel — the spokes representing the tramways and railways radiating from the city. In contrast motor cars, especially from the 1950s when they invaded most households, liberated their owners from public transport. The gaps between spokes radiating from cities filled more quickly. At the same time the thick ribbons of suburbia which had once followed railways and tramways were replaced by thin threads of commercial settlement — cafes and petrol stations and factories — which lined the highways miles beyond the residential suburbs.

The mobility provided by motor cars was converting suburbs from centres of social life into dormitories. Car keys became as important as door keys and most people slept in one part of a city, worked in another, spent their leisure and social life in other parts, and so turned suburbs into dormitories with television sets at one end and car ports at the other.

Australian cities, always prodigal in the manner in which they consumed land, had sprawled far from the wharves and city halls long before there were petrol fumes. But the proportion of Australia's people who lived in cities and large towns was much increased by internal-combustion engines. Motors were making farmlands more productive and at the same time driving people from the land. Tractors and mechanised farm machinery enabled one man to cultivate an area of land on which, in the era of horses, several farm labourers were necessary. After the Second World War rural population fell, and as a proportion of the workforce it fell rapidly. Fewer people lived on or near farms in many districts. As most rural people owned private motor cars and could travel much farther in a few hours than when they rode in a horse and buggy, they bypassed the small town and went instead to a larger regional town for their supplies and services. In most agricultural regions of Australia small towns were stagnant or declining at the expense of a few scattered large towns.

Most of the small agricultural towns of a few hundred people flourished so long as farms depended on the strength of horses and so long as inland transport was either slow or costly. But the new form of motive power reduced the population in their own neighbourhood and enabled manufacturers and tradesmen from rival and larger towns to capture much of their surviving business. In smaller towns, bakers and cordial makers had to compete with bread and cordials delivered cheaply by truck from the larger town where bigger factories had some of the savings of large-scale, mechanised production. Hotels lost the custom of commercial travellers who once had to stay overnight in the era when the daily train or horse-coach was the only way of leaving the towns. Retail stores had difficulty in competing with chain stores in the larger towns. The auctioneer, clergyman and banker moved to the larger town and motored occasionally to the smaller town when the need arose. Local farmers who, once depending on horses, had gone to the nearest farrier or wheelwright or waggon builder or saddle maker for their wants, now had mechanized equipment and usually went to the larger town to buy their cars and tractors and farm machinery, their drums of petrol and kerosene; and their repairs. While the large regional town was sucking trade from its outlying rivals, the fat coastal city continued to suck trade from all smaller towns.

The increasing use of machines in industry and transport led to more prosperity and leisure. How that leisure and prosperity were spent was influenced much by motor cars and aeroplanes. Before the First World War, few Australians could afford to spend a holiday outside their own State. Today most Australian adults have travelled outside their own State, usually by motor vehicles or aeroplanes. Tourism has become a major industry, planting holiday resorts along hundreds of miles of coastline. Holiday resorts at the turn of the century could only exist where cheap public transport existed, whether bay steamers or railway lines, and there were few points of coast or forest which were reached by those lines of transport; it was too costly to build a railway simply to serve a holiday resort, and so holiday resorts tended to flourish at a few scenic towns which railways happened to pass. Amongst the handful of popular holiday resorts at the turn of the century were the Blue Mountains (N.S.W.), Daylesford (V.), and Victor Harbor (S.A.), but transport routes probably forced more people to take holidays in the capital cities on the coast than in all the other towns of Australia added together. The growth of hundreds of new coastal resorts in Australia would have been impossible without motor cars. The rise of Surfers' Paradise in Queensland and other miniature Miamis — the first national as distinct from provincial holiday towns — would have been thwarted without the new transport.

The new engines altered the work of policemen and law courts, gave more work to doctors and hospitals and florists, influenced the design of houses and theatres and hotels, made the ancient practice of walking unfashionable, and made the art of flying feasible.

296

3

Aeroplanes emerged a decade or two after motor vehicles. They were made possible by the advancing knowledge of aerodynamics, by the light internal-combustion engine, and the power of petroleum fuels. When Orville and Wilbur Wright, American bicycle repairers, tested an aircraft that was heavier than air, the engine which they drove on their momentous kangaroo hop in 1903 was like the piston engines used in most motor cars. After another five years of risky experiments they developed an aircraft which they coaxed into staying aloft for more than two hours.

An Australian inventor, Lawrence Hargrave, had contributed much to the theory and technique of flight with his experimental box kites from the 1880s, but the first useful flights by engine-driven machines in Australia depended on European and North American experiments. In March 1910, at Diggers' Rest, near the old road from Melbourne to the goldfields, a European aeroplane soared a hundred feet into the air and covered a distance of two miles. The entire adventure was over in three and a half minutes. The pilot and owner of the plane was the celebrated United States, magician and escapologist, Harry Houdini, who was then displaying his tricks in a Melbourne theatre. It was fitting that a professional entertainer should make the first significant flight in Australia, for aeroplanes in their early years were popularly seen more as vehicles for stunts and dare-devilry than for transport. Even so, aeroplanes seemed to offer more hope of transforming distance in Australia than in the United States, for in Australia distances were as vast but railways and good roads were comparatively rare and seemed likely to remain rare.

The performance of aircraft was still erratic, and speeds were slow. A Frenchman, Maurice Guillaux, carried the first airmail for the Commonwealth of Australia's postal department in July 1914, but his flight was so interrupted by bad weather, air sickness, and the need to land frequently in country racecourses and pastures to take on fuel, that he spent nearly three days carrying the mail from Melbourne to Sydney. The daily express train was almost three times as quick. A month later in Europe the First World War began, and soon created a demand for efficient aircraft from which to observe gun positions and troop movements behind enemy lines. Technical advances which might have taken a decade or more were cramped into four years. Whereas the brothers Wright in 1903 flew with an engine which had a ratio of weight to horsepower of 15 to 1, some aircraft at the end of the war had a ratio of barely 2 to 1. The more that the crucial weight-horsepower ratio improved, the more an engine was capable of driving a plane on longer flights. Planes in 1919 had so much power in relation to their weight that they could carry fuel for long flights or alternatively carry half a dozen passengers or many bags of mail for short flights. In 1919 a band of young aviators trained for war were ready to show what aeroplanes, improved by war, could really do.

To cross the north Atlantic a plane had to fly almost 2000 miles without refuelling, even if it flew the shortest possible route — from Newfoundland to Ireland. An Australian airman, Harry Hawker, flying with K. M. Grieve, attempted that flight in May 1919 and half way across they landed in the sea and were rescued by a Danish ship. Harry Hawker's short life was to crystallize the transport changes of his generation; son of a blacksmith who worked with horses, Hawker worked for a motor firm in Melbourne, became an airman and record maker, and died in an air crash in England at the age of thirty-one.

One month after Hawker had failed to cross the Atlantic with the prevailing westerlies, two English airmen, Alcock and Brown, were successful, their flight of 2000 miles being the longest hitherto made. Eight years passed before the American Charles Lindbergh flew from New York to Europe, a flight of 3600 miles without refuelling. Another three years elapsed before a flight from Ireland to North America, against the prevailing winds, was successful. The airman was Charles Kingsford Smith, an Australian, and his three-engined, £3000 aircraft, *Southern Cross*, had already been the first to fly across the Pacific between North America and Australia and the first to fly across the Tasman Sea from Australia to New Zealand.

To fly from England to Australia was perilous, but at least it was feasible in primitive aeroplanes. While the situation of the land masses had prevented early steam-ships from linking Europe and Australia, the coaling ports being so far apart, the situation of the land masses made it relatively easy for aeroplanes to make the journey, landing grounds and petrol points being relatively close to one another. An aeroplane could leave England, hop the English Channel, fly over land virtually all the way through Europe and Asia to Singapore, then leap-frog along the Indonesian Archipelago to northern Australia.

That route from England to Australia was attempted by aeroplanes in 1919, after the Australian government had offered £10,000 to the first Australian airmen to cross the world in a British-made aircraft. In the race for the prize three planes crashed; and the winners, Ross and Keith Smith and their two mechanics, could have made an equally fast journey by booking berths in a new mail steamer. During their flight to Australia they spent far more time on the ground than in the air. Frequently they had to repair the plane or wait for bad weather to ease. At improvised runways where their aeroplane landed for fuel, they had to fill their tanks by hand from four-gallon tins of petrol and sometimes had to organize gangs to level the ground in order to take off. They carried no radio, they possessed only sketchy maps of many lands they flew over, and they had no forecasts of the weather that lay ahead. Sitting in an exposed cockpit they suffered from intense cold. The din of the engines drowned conversation, compelling them to communicate with one another by pencilling notes. They flew in low altitudes where the atmosphere and weather were most turbulent. Their cruising speed was 80 miles an hour, and if they flew at a speed of only 60 the engines stalled. The route they hazardously pioneered eventually became the main airway from Europe to Australia.

4

Years usually elapsed between the flights of the pathfinders and the opening of a regular air service. Early aeroplanes were like early steamers. On short routes they had enough space to carry a small paying load of mail or passengers in addition to their fuel; but where gaps between refuelling depots were long, they could only carry the crew and fuel and a few pounds of first class freight. Like early Australian mail steamers, early aeroplanes on long flights needed a government subsidy in order to maintain regular flights. A few air routes in Australia were subsidized in the 1920s, and one of the first commercial airlines was the tiny Queensland and Northern Territory Aerial Services (QANTAS), which carried mails from railheads in western Queensland to remote pastoral and mining towns. As aircraft became larger and safer and more powerful, airways promoters were able to fly them profitably between the larger towns and cities. As late as 1939, however, only a tiny fraction of Australians had ever flown, and those who had were entitled to swagger or to reminisce without interruption.

Planes regularly carried passengers and mail between Europe and Australia from the year 1931. But some of the importance of aircraft had been recently snatched away by the opening of a direct beam wireless which sent radiograms swiftly and cheaply between Australia and both sides of the Atlantic, by the opening of wireless telephone links between Australia and England, and by the radio set which, beginning to appear on thousands of mantelpieces, could pick up static and news rebroadcast from Daventry in England. Air travel between England and Australia in the early 1930s was expensive and not fast enough to lure many passengers away from the mail steamers. But the duration of the flight — with the coming of Donald Douglas's twin-engined DC3s — was soon clipped to one third of the time taken by mail steamers. In 1938 London businessmen could fly to Singapore and transfer there to a QANTAS flying boat, which landed them on Sydney Harbour only nine or ten days after they had left home.

The Second World War, like the previous war, heightened the efficiency of aircraft. The falling cost of air transport extended its uses. Australians became more accustomed to flying than the people of probably any other country, and were encouraged to fly by the safe record of Australian aviation. The ease with which businessmen and politicians could travel from Australia to foreign countries probably weakened the insularity which had marked the attitudes of so many Australian leaders in government and business in the half century before the Second World War. The ease with which foreign politicians and entertainers and artists could visit Australia probably dulled the sense of isolation and the apathy to the outside world which had characterised the average Australian. The ease with which foreign bombers, in time of war, could fly to Australia was probably the sharpest mental change.

Within Australia aircraft had more tangible effects in the two decades 1945–65. They fostered tourism, particularly to Tasmania and Queensland. They changed life in remote towns in northern Australia by carrying in fresh fruit and vegetables, medical supplies, newspapers, and all kinds of luxuries and necessities; when a vital machine broke down at the copper smelter at Mount Isa in 1954, three tons of new machinery flown from New York averted a long closure. Small aircraft were increasingly used to drop clouds of fertiliser or pesticide or seed on farmlands, to cast poisoned bait for dingoes and rabbits, to sight sharks near crowded beaches and to drop fodder to cattle which had been stranded and starved by sudden floods. Aircraft aided the making of maps and the finding of new mineral deposits. They carried more than one million letters a day within Australia. They carried beef from remote cattle runs to coastal freezing works, shell fish from Tasmania to mainland markets, and a wide variety of freight. Even with generous government subsidies, however, air traffic was too costly to have much share in carrying goods within Australia. On the basis of ton-miles, the comparison which most favoured air transport, aircraft probably carried only one thousandth of the goods carried in Australia in 1960. As freighters, aircraft were perhaps no more important than railways had been in Australia at that brief time in the 1850s when their total length of line was less than a hundred miles.

Each recent generation is inclined to think that its own achievements in transport are more momentous than the achievements of any earlier generation. Flight is the glamorous achievement of this generation and has affected Australia more than most countries, but its influence in Australia should be placed in humbler perspective. Were aircraft ever as miraculous as the first Australian mail steamers which were faster than any other form of passenger transport and carried the latest news as well? Did aircraft shape the lives of Australians more than the network of railways in the nineteenth century? Were aircraft in their first half century ever as miraculous as the international telegraph which conveyed messages and news faster in the 1870s than the latest aircraft can carry them? Answers to such questions should probably all be negative. Perhaps the greatest effect of aircraft was on the art of war, and Australia — except for a few small northern ports — escaped aerial attack in the Second World War.

5

Railways were first challenged by the new vehicles at the very time when they were gaining more of the appearance of a national system than a series of isolated networks. In 1917 the completion of a 1050 mile line across deserted plains from Port Augusta (S.A.) to Kalgoorlie (W.A.) linked the main Western Australian railways with those of the eastern States, and for the first time passengers and goods going between east and west no longer had to travel by ship. A long railway running along the Pacific coast from Brisbane to Cairns joined together the ports and isolated railway systems of North Queensland in the 1920s. Passengers with eight days to spare could then travel by train from Cairns to Perth, traversing nearly all the east and south coast of the continent. Their journey and often their sleep were interrupted, however, by the need to change trains at the break-of-gauge stations at the southern border of Queensland, the southern border of New South Wales, at the small towns of Terowie and Port Augusta in South Australia, and at Kalgoorlie in the hot interior of Western Australia. Many parcels or crates which made the same journey were battered in the frequent changes from train to train. The cost of transhipping was now exorbitant on rail tracks which suddenly widened or narrowed.

Railway tracks with different gauges had met since the 1880s, but these breaks in the flow of trade had only worried a few politicians and soldiers. They did not worry any major business group; if they had, there would have been more pressure to mend the breaks by converting existing railways to a uniform gauge. By 1920, however, the broken gauges annoyed merchants, farmers, manufacturers and all kinds of customers.

The economy was changing, and the change magnified the breaks in the gauges. With the creation of a federal government in 1901 and the abolition of those import duties which each individual state or colony had imposed on the produce of its neighbours, Australia became a common market. Sydney factories could sell cigars freely to Melbourne, and Melbourne factories could sell boots freely to Adelaide. Aided by the common market within Australia and the protective duties which the federal government imposed on foreign imports, manufacturing became stronger and passed the old primary industries as employers of labour. As most factories and more than a third of Australian customers lived in the four coastal

303

cities of Brisbane, Sydney, Melbourne and Adelaide, traffic between the cities soared. The traditional and cheapest way of sending goods between those cities was by coastal steamship, but the cheapness of sea freight was becoming less marked. Trains left Sydney for Melbourne every day, but ships sailed less frequently and less to schedule. For many manufactured goods the dearer railway was therefore preferable. Moreover, ships charged each cargo roughly according to the space it occupied while railways charged merely according to the weight of the cargo; space was not so decisive in railway waggons because cargoes could protrude well above the sides of the waggon. Accordingly many manufactured goods which were light and bulky — shoes for example — were more cheaply carried by railway. Thus the growth of Australian manufacturing, geared to a national market, gave much freight to interstate railways.

The most awkward break of gauge was at Albury, which lay between the two largest cities, Melbourne and Sydney. Just before the First World War the rail cargoes between the two cities began to increase. Shortage of shipping and maritime strikes became acute during the war, and from 1917 to 1920 the Victorian State railways had to import much of the coal for their locomotives overland instead of by sea. The additional cost of carrying that coal to Melbourne by railway rather than steamship was £358,000. A large slice of that cost was presumably added by the need to transfer every ton of coal from a New South Wales rail waggon to a Victorian waggon at the Albury goodsyards. Once the strike had ended, the coal trade reverted to coastal ships, but for perhaps the first time the public was strongly conscious of the disadvantages of broken gauges.

Only a fraction of the goods carried on Australian railways was affected by breaks of gauge, but those goods were multiplying and had to pay dearly for the break. Some of the more serious breaks were mended at heavy cost, and by 1962 a uniform gauge linked the three largest cities of Brisbane, Sydney and Melbourne. The value of a through, uniform-gauge railway between Sydney and Melbourne was proved in the first full year the line was opened. Goods traffic increased by more than 100 per cent in both directions.

The ability of some trunk railways to compete with coastal ships was impaired by the breaks of gauge. A more serious challenge to railways came from the motor industry. Each Australian state owned a long system of railways and usually operated them at a loss after paying interest to the British bondholders who had financed the railways. Motor competition increased these losses. But railways so dominated State budgets that, when railways made heavy losses, substantially less money was available for education and social services or roads. To protect their railways from steeper financial losses, governments began to suppress or regulate road competition. Simply by spending meagrely on the building of bitumen highways, a government could check much competition from road hauliers. In addition State governments taxed or controlled or prohibited motor hauliers and buses on routes which competed strongly with their railways. Similarly, State governments restricted road transport between States until that policy was declared unconstitutional in 1954 by the Privy Council of the United Kingdom, the court of appeal in Australia's hierarchy of courts.

Whereas the United States' railways were privately owned, were not favoured by governments, and were therefore more vulnerable to competition from automobiles, Australian railways were protected from competition. Moreover, in Australia throughout the 1940s, petrol was a rationed import, thus checking the increase in road hauliers. Nevertheless road transport continued to grow, and by the early 1960s was carrying more than three times the tonnage which railways were carrying, though the average road haul was shorter than the average rail haul. Even on a ton-mile basis, in which both tonnage and distance were reckoned together, road transport was more important. And yet railways were carrying more goods than ever before, and carrying them more efficiently as they changed from coal-fired to diesel locomotives.

6

In the United States in the nineteenth century the transport industry nourished a gallery of Vanderbilts and Morgans and Harrimans and other magnates, but the same industry in Australia nourished few 'magnates' by the humbler Australian definition of the word. In contrast to the United States, railways and telegraphs and street tramways in Australia were largely government property and shipping between Australia and the rest of the world was largely in the hands of foreign shipowners. That left coastal shipping as the only wing of Australian transport which allowed much wealth and power to fall into private hands. Although large coastal fleets belonged to two London companies, the Union Steamship Company of New Zealand and the Australasian United Steam Navigation Company, most coastal steamships were owned by Australian joint-stock companies. Those Australian shipowners — Howard Smith, Adelaide Steamship Company, McIlwraith McEacharn and a bracket of others — were as well known then as automobile makers are today. They ranked amongst the largest Australian public companies. Their leaders and biggest shareholders were wealthy and often powerful in politics.

Those shipowners who took to the new automobile and allowed themselves to be driven to their waterfront offices had little idea of the strength of the poison contained in their petrol tank. Their industry was booming. At the outbreak of the First World War, 174 steamships were busy in the coastal trade; they had accommodation for 16,000 passengers as well as space for a mountain of cargo, and they measured 340,000 gross tons or double their tonnage at the start of the century. The revenue earned annually by coastal ships was perhaps only one fifth of the revenue earned by Australian railways, but the profits of coastal shipping were handsome. Coastal shipowners had a tight organisation which fixed rates for passengers and cargoes, and controlled more than 90 per cent of coastal trade. Overseas mail steamers or cargo steamers which called at Australian ports gave them little competition even before 1921, when a Commonwealth law precluded overseas ships from the Australian coastal trade for a generation.

After the First World War coastal shipowners began to denounce the changing world. Wharf labourers and seamen often went on strike, the turn round of ships was slower, and sailing times were less predictable. Shipping firms themselves began to suffer from lack of that aggressive competition which their collusion over freight rates had virtually banished from the industry.

Coastal ships in the 1920s loosened their grip on passenger traffic and livestock, which had once given them from one third to one half of their income. Railway fares between the main cities were no longer so dear. The opening of trans-continental railways to Western Australia and North Queensland destroyed the coastal fleets' monopoly of carrying passengers to those regions. Aircraft later destroyed their monopoly of passenger traffic to the island of Tasmania and to remote north Australian ports. By 1938 the passenger accommodation on coastal ships was only 40 per cent of that available at the start of the First World War. The coastal passenger fleet still dwindled, and was eventually left with only the short Tasmanian passage.

Slowly coastal steamers lost the more valuable cargoes to railways and, in the late 1950s, to motor transport too. Fortunately the rise of bulk cargoes, which did not have to be carried so quickly and which used less waterfront labour, was some solace to shipowners. Before the First World War nearly all cargoes except coal had been shipped around the coast in bags or packages or crates, but by 1960 bulk cargoes predominated and were carried long distances. Coastal steamers carried iron ore from Yampi Sound in the north-west and Whyalla in the south to steelworks at Port Kembla and Newcastle on the east coast. They carried bulk sugar from the North Queens-

land sugar mills to refineries in the south-east; they hauled alumina long distances to aluminium smelters in the
south-east corner; they carried Borken Hill zinc concentrates from Port Pirie (S.A.) to the zinc refinery in Hobart. But the symbolic changes in the 1950s were the
decline of coal shipments, for long the heaviest coastal
cargo, and the compensating rise of oil shipments from
new Australian refineries to oil terminals around the
coast. With the increasing shipment of raw materials, the
coastal fleet had lost status but not importance.

The old shipping companies ceased to be giants in the
economy, or even ceased to exist. The Commonwealth
Government set up a shipping line to serve the coast and
Australia's largest public company, the Broken Hill Proprietary Company, carried much of its own iron ore, coke,
coal, and steel to and from its steelworks in its own ships,
many of which had been built in its own South Australian
shipyards. The two newcomers owned two thirds of coastal shipping in the early 1960s.

While coastal ships had suffered through the competition of oil-powered transport, they had gained by adopting the same motive power. The diesel engine, devised by
the German Rudolf Diesel at the end of the last century,
proved its value in submarines in the First World War,
and after the war it invaded merchant shipping. At the
same time, fuel oil — the residue left after gasoline had
been extracted from the crude oil — was available in huge
quantities for the furnaces of steamships. Though fuel oil
had to be imported to Australia, it could compete by the
1920s with coal from the Australian shipping companies'
own mines. Oil increasingly supplanted coal as the motive power of Australian ships. By the early 1960s the
coastal fleet got four fifths of its power from oil and motor
spirits, but even that innovation did not transform its
ability to compete with land and air transport.

7

Some of the diverse effects of motor vehicles, tractors,

aircraft, diesel locomotives, and diesel ships have been described. The internal-combustion engine and its ally, the oil industry, also had collective effects on Australia which are easy to overlook.

Australia in 1900 had produced nearly all its own sources of motive and industrial power. Its own coal mines yielded the fuel for steamships and railways, city factories and gasworks and electricity powerhouses, and also had a surplus for sale to visiting ships and foreign ports. Australian firewood cut by thousands of men fed most household stoves and fireplaces, the steam plants of mines, sawmills, butter factories, and the Murray River paddle steamers; as late as the year 1908–9, one of every ten tons of goods carried on State railways in Australia was firewood. Australian farms grew sufficient grass and hay and oats to feed several million horses, with often a surplus for export, though with the decline of horse transport that land could be used to support other crops or sheep. Other beasts of burden — bullocks and donkeys and camels — readily found their motive power growing on the side of the roads they travelled. The free wind provided power for sailing ships and for the windmills which raised water on farms and sheep stations. The power of water was harnessed a little for driving waterwheels at gold batteries and flour mills or for floating lumber down rivers. Australian sheep yielded tallow which was made into candles for illuminating houses and mines. Virtually the only fuel which Australia had to import was the illuminant, kerosene, a product of United States, oil refineries.

Australia lost its self-sufficiency with the move to oil products as the main fuel of transport and as a useful form of energy in steam plants. Producing virtually no crude oil, it had to buy its oil overseas. In the 1940s and 1950s, 7 to 10 per cent of the money which Australia spent annually on imported goods went into oil. Heavy imports of oil aggravated the periodic balance of payments crises and the recessions which followed. The oil deficiency was crucial from 1942 to 1945, war years during which the nearest Allied oilfields were in California and the Middle East.

Although Australia had been one of the world's most vigorous and versatile mining countries since the middle of the nineteenth century, and though rocks which seemed relatively favourable to oil lay near the five largest cities, Australia's search for oil was long financed on the smell of an oil rag. When the Commonwealth government in January 1920 offered the absurd prize of £10,000 for the discovery of petroleum oil, it seemed to reflect the idea that someone with a few hundred pounds to spare could find oil if only a monetary bait was dangled before him. In fact nearly £80 million was spent in seeking oil in Australia and New Guinea — and two thirds of it was spent by foreign oil companies — before the first payable oilfield was found at Moonie, near Brisbane, in 1961. More oil was found at Barrow Island (W.A.) in 1964 and large oil and gas fields in Bass Strait were glimpsed in 1966. The long drought was over.

The transport changes which demanded foreign oil simultaneously clipped the profitable export trade in Australian coal. After the First World War the coal output of Britain, Germany, U.S.A. and the great coal countries ceased to expand. Electric power stations were harnessing the energy in coal more efficiently or using fuel oil; ships burned less coal; and a fleet of oil tankers was chasing the international colliers from the sea. Australia's exports of coal also slumped, and the busy coal city of Newcastle would have slumbered but for the steelworks that arose on the banks of that wide river, which overseas ships were deserting. The declining importance of black coal was one reason why New South Wales' population in the 1950s grew at a slower rate than the population of its rival, Victoria, for the first time since the 1850s.

The transport changes had made Australia depend on foreign nations for its main vehicles as well as its fuel. In the First World War, when the internal-combustion engine was just beginning to affect the country, Australia had been making most of its own railway rolling stock and locomotives and had been expanding output of rails from local steelworks. Its shipbuilding industry, crushed by the transition from wooden sailing ships to iron steamships, was reviving. It produced all its own horses and beasts of burden and made nearly all its own waggons and carts and horse-coaches. However, it was unable to compete in the manufacture of motor vehicles, the expanding sector of transport. Australian factories, encouraged by high sea freights from North America and by Australian protective tariffs, made motor bodies and assembled vehicles from imported parts, but the annual import of motor vehicles and parts increased as the market for motor vehicles soared. In the year 1948-9 more than 17 per cent of the money with which Australia paid for imported goods went into oil products, motor vehicles and parts. That was also the year in which the American firm, General Motors, launched an Australian-built car, named the Holden, which soon captured the largest share of the Australian car market and reduced the need for vehicle imports. Success in making cars was not matched by success in making aircraft, except in the emergency of the Second World War.

Manufacture of motor cars, trucks, and tractors in Australia became a major industry. One person in every sixteen in the workforce made or distributed or serviced motor vehicles in 1960. The needs of automobile manufacturing created demands for Australian steel, glass, plastics, paints, and rubber. The rise of the Australian oil refineries in the 1950s created more work, and by-products of the refining process created new synthetic rubber, plastics, carbon black, and other industries. The first effect of oil-driven transport had been to make Australia pay heavily for imported fuel and vehicles. The slower effect was an enormous stimulus to Australian manufacturing.

Oil engines spurred foreign investment in Australia. Just as the spread of railways had once been the largest single avenue of foreign investment in Australia, so the oil engines spurred a new wave of foreign investment.

North Atlantic companies came to control all the main automobile and tractor factories in Australia, the main oil refineries, the petro-chemical industry, most of the petrol-selling companies, a line of roadside service stations. They invested the most money in the search for oil and reaped the rewards. Through transport changes key sectors of Australian industry belonged to overseas owners. Partly through transport changes North America began to challenge Britain's tradition as main investor in Australian industries. It is symbolic, though unintentionally so, that the brick walls on which militant sloganmakers usually painted the white message YANKS GO HOME were in the subways where American-financed motor traffic passed under the British-financed railway viaducts.

With new forms of transport, economic activity was less easily halted by industrial troubles. Coal mines had been the main seat of industrial trouble in Australia, but coal strikes became less disruptive when an alternative fuel was available for land and sea transport. The ability of wharf labourers' and seamen's trade unions to disrupt economic life when they had a grievance was weaker with the decline of those coastal ships that carried general cargo between Melbourne and Sydney and the main port. By the 1970s the employees in the new forms of transport were using their bargaining power; and strikes by transport drivers, air-traffic controllers and air crew were as dislocating as the strikes on coalfields had been.

The decline of hard physical labour may have been the sharpest change for those who worked in the transport industry in 1900 and lived to see the industry transformed. Firemen in a steamship or steam locomotive spent hours daily shovelling coal into the furnace, sailors in a sailing ship had to climb aloft and tug at wet heavy sails, camel and bullock teamsters walked beside their teams, and even horse drivers used physical strength if only to load or unload their drays. The fuel for transport was partly won by physical strength, the coal cut with a pick, firewood with an axe, though hay and chaff for

312

horses were cut by machine. Railways and roads were made with picks and shovels and wheelbarrows and stone-breaking hammers. The farrier and wheelwright could be picked by their arm muscles. At wharves and railway sidings, bags of wheat or baskets of coal often weighing more than 250 pounds were carried on the backs of men. Frozen carcasses, bags of ore, bales of wool, and crates and barrels and packages of imported goods were usually lifted at several stages of transit by sheer physical strength. Then sweat was replaced by boredom. Oil flowed from the ground, the petrol engine started with the switching of a key, oil ran into furnaces with the turn of a tap, and heavy loads were moved by travelling cranes, fork-lift trucks, conveyor belts and pipelines. Many of these effortless tasks in the age of oil were done in streets where once the main beasts of burden were English criminals.

14   Antipodes Adrift

Englishmen in the nineteenth century commonly called Australia and New Zealand 'the Antipodes'. Those lands were on the opposite side of the globe to England, and their people seemed to walk upside down, and had winter when England had summer and had night when England had day.

In geography England and her Antipodes were far apart, but the Antipodes developed the kind of community one would expect to find within a few miles of Lands End. Nearly all their people spoke English, conformed to British political and social customs, obeyed or disobeyed most of the laws which Britons obeyed, and were subjects of the British monarch. Most of the money which was invested in Australasia came from the British Isles and most of the new techniques, ideas, and machines came also from the British Isles. Poles apart in position, in commerce they behaved as if they were neighbours, and most of the exports from Australasia went to the British Isles and most of the goods imported into Australasia came from the British Isles. British merchant ships carried most of those goods and Britain's navy protected those ships and also the ports which they entered at both ends of the world. Australia and New Zealand depended so much on Britain, were in most senses imitations of Britain, that their geographical position near the end of Asia's tail and near the islands of Oceania seemed irrelevant.

Australia's closeness to Asia had not always been irrelevant. As we have observed, the wealth of Asia had

314

mesmerised western Europe in the eighteenth century, and it was during the search for new Asias that the east coast of Australia had been discovered. Britain's decision in the 1780s to settle the east coast had possibly been influenced by Australia's promise of furnishing a port of call on some of the trade routes to Asia and had been much influenced by Australia's promise, an empty promise, to supply naval stores for British ships in Asian waters. The Australian colonies, in their first four decades, were vitally affected by their relative proximity to Asia. Their supply line from Europe was made both stronger and cheaper by all those ships which detoured to Sydney on their way to Indian or Chinese ports. Many of Australia's early exports — sandalwood, pearl shell, sealskins, whale oil, and timber — were collected in Oceania and sold entirely or partly in Asia. Australia received much of its rice, meat, flour, rum and sugar, all of its tea, a variety of other foodstuffs and hardware, and many of its flocks and herds, from Asian ports. It is even conceivable that Australia in its first struggling years would have been abandoned by the British, or perhaps left to stagnate, but for the succour and stimulus which came from Asia. And when at last withdrawal from Australia was no longer necessary, and the governors in Sydney planted new settlements at scattered points of the Australian coast, most of those early settlements were inspired by Australia's proximity to Asian and Pacific trade routes.

In the middle years of the nineteenth century Australia's contacts with Asia were less vital but more conspicuous. Chinese were shipped to Australian goldfields, and in the late 1850s they formed about 4 per cent of the country's population, a figure not exceeded again. Later in the century, when the Chinese population in Australia waned, Malays and Japanese and Indians came, a few thousand of each race. While these peoples congregated mostly in the outback or isolated tropical ports, the Chinese at first favoured the south east where most Australians lived. The only Asians whom most Australians had seen in their own towns were Chinese, and most of the Australian racial legislation and suspicion was directed against Chinese.

Ease of communications had increased the inflow of Chinese to Australian goldfields; the migrant ships from Canton had been in part a by-product of the glut of shipping in Pacific ports during the gold rushes. Ease of communications also increased the inflow of indentured labourers from the New Hebrides and Solomon Islands to the neighbouring coast of Queensland, where new sugar plantations would not have paid without the work of cheap, acclimatized Pacific Islanders in the canefields.

By the 1880s most of the coloured men who had migrated to Australia from Oceania or Asia worked in the northern or tropical region. Forty per cent of Australia lies in the tropics, and there most of the camps and towns, meagre and scattered as they were, relied on coloured labour. More Chinese than Europeans dug for gold in the north; Chinese ran the market gardens near the towns and many of the shops; Chinese navvies built one of the few northern railways, which linked Port Darwin and Pine Creek goldfield; Pacific Islanders did the hard work in the sugar fields and the dangerous work in the pearling grounds; and Afghans and their strings of camels were about to dominate the carrying trade in many districts. Coloured races were essential to the early development of the vast area, partly because they were more acclimatised than Britons but more because they worked for low wages. As most resources in the north existed in isolated areas where the burden of distance was reflected in a high cost of living, they could only be utilised if wages were low. The fact that coloured races were essential pioneers in tropical Australia has long slipped from memory, but it is almost a wishful lapse of memory.

By the 1880s nearly all Australian colonies agreed that coloured labour was a curse. It was a curse not because the coloured labourers themselves suffered by living in apparent squalor and working for low wages in Australia; it was rather a curse because coloured labour might jeopardize Australian material and cultural standards. A miscellany of restrictions on the immigration of coloured labour to various colonies became in the early 1900s an outright ban. Australia isolated herself from Asia and Oceania with the policy known as White Australia.

That policy was only made possible by an anomaly of geography. There were six colonies in Australia, and all were governed from the south; even the three Australian colonies that contained the tropical north were governed from the temperate south, where stood their capital cities and most of their voters. The northern part of Australia needed coloured labour if it was to produce more wealth, and probably a majority of European settlers in the north wanted coloured labour, but they were outvoted by Australians of the south who neither wanted nor needed coloured labour. So Australia achieved racial unity; and the gains of that unity were obvious. The price of the unity was that many Asians later resented a nation which discriminated against Asians. A less obvious price of that unity was to retard the using of those few scattered resources in northern Australia which seemed capable of supporting many people at an Asian standard of living and few at an Australian standard of living.

Late in the nineteenth century many Australian politicians and writers forecast that Asia would some day become powerful and dangerous militarily. Perhaps the best known western forecaster of the rise of the east was Dr Charles H. Pearson, a former English don who had spent twenty years in education and politics in Australia. His book of 1893, *National Life and Character: a Forecast*, foresaw a gloomy future for the West and the probable triumph of yellow and black and brown over white races throughout the tropics. His gloom had many echoes in Australia. Here it was believed widely that some day hordes of Asians might descend from the north. This belief usually rested not on the idea that Asians would quickly absorb western science and technology, but on the simpler ideas that the invasion would take the guise of mass infiltration. When cartoonists sketched scenes of an

Asian phalanx landing on the Australian coast, the only caption they needed was 'The Yellow Peril'. Every Australian reader followed the message. At the same time it would be unwise to conclude that most Australians feared Asia's potential military power. If that fear existed, their immigration policy and their publicly expressed attitudes to Asians would probably have been conciliatory rather than provocative.

The wall against Asian migrants was not extended to Asian goods — Australia's commerce with Asia near the close of the nineteenth century was useful but not large. As nearly three quarters of Australia's trade — both outward and inward — was with the United Kingdom, the share remaining for Asia and the rest of the world was small. In the five years from 1887 to 1891, less than 9 per cent of Australia's imports came from Asia and the islands in the Asian trading network. Nearly half of the Asian import bill consisted of tea from China and Hong Kong, though in the next twenty years virtually all that tea trade was to pass to Ceylon and India. The other imports from the Asian trading network were bags and sacks from India, sugar from Java, and an assortment of tropical products. Of the money which Australia earned from exports in the same five years, only 5 per cent came from exporting goods to Asia, though in the early 1900s that percentage was to treble with heavy shipments of gold and silver to India and Ceylon. In Australia the coal proprietors and horse dealers and flour millers who sold their products in Asia had reason to be thankful that Asian ports were relatively close and that therefore freights were cheap. The shorter distance separating Asian and Australian ports, however, was faint compensation for the long distance separating Australia from her chief trading partner, the British Isles.

2

Some of the most revealing and important facets of Australian history came from events which did not happen. Australia has never been invaded since the British invasion of 1788 and the subsequent slow conquest. Australia has had no civil war and no war of independence. It has had a few serious racial disturbances but by the criteria of many countries they would not be classed as serious. When Douglas Pike wrote a short history of Australia and gave his book the sub-title, *The Quiet Continent*, there could not be much doubt, except perhaps in the minds of the literate penguins of Antarctica, which continent his book described.

It is easy to see why Australia was relatively free from racial or nationalist conflict compared to many other newly settled lands. As we have seen, the inflow of coloured labourers was checked by laws. The coloured population which inhabited Australia before the white conquest was relatively sparse, and made sparser by the diseases and guns which Englishmen carried. The conflict between Aboriginals and European invaders was costly for the Aboriginals but not for the invaders. At the same time conflicts in Australia between niggling European nationalities were rare and mild. While Canada had been a French colony and the Cape of Good Hope a Dutch colony before falling to British arms, eastern Australia was first settled by the British; and through the curious interplay of distance and trade routes described in chapter four, all the other attractive parts of the continent quickly passed to Britain in the first third of the nineteenth century. Later in the same century, when migration from Europe to the new world burst into an invasion, Australia was too far away to compete with North America for free migrants from Holland or Scandinavia or continental Europe. Moreover, when Australia subsidised immigration, it naturally preferred, being a British land, to pay the fares of British migrants. Virtually all the migrants assisted to Australia were British.

Perhaps the main reason why Australia's history was so peaceful was simply its geographical position. It was too remote from Europe to be affected seriously by the main European wars and disturbances of the nineteenth century — the Napoleonic Wars, the revolutions of the 1840s, the Crimean War, and the Franco-Prussian War. At the same time Australia was surrounded by sea, and therefore had no real frontier to any southern land. Most islands near Australia were either owned by Britain or by Western European powers whose military and economic strength was inferior to Britain's; thus Portugal held part of Timor, Spain held the Philippines, and Holland held most of the Indonesian archipelago and the western half of New Guinea. France, a stronger power, held New Caledonia, and in 1887 joined Britain in governing the New Hebrides, but French interests in Oceania were not imposing. Germany was the latecomer to Australia's sphere of interest but when it occupied a segment of New Guinea, New Britain and New Ireland in the mid 1880s it was the leading military power in continental Europe. The coming of the Germans was at first alarming to Australians who were accustomed to their country's isolation. The German flag worried Australia in the 1880s into strengthening its own meagre defences. It also hastened the federating of the six colonies, in 1901, into a Commonwealth with a common defence organization.

Australia's weakness, in the eyes of its leaders, was the chance that any European war in which Britain fought could extend to Australia. Thus in the 1850s and 1880s Australia had brief jitters about the danger of a Russian attack on its coast. Articulate Australians regarded Europe rather than Europe's possessions in Oceania as the potential source of any conflict. Fortunately, Europe was far away, and Britain's navy guarded the intervening sea lanes. Australia's position and Britain's navy continued to give most Australians a sense of security, even after Germany's entry to the Pacific.

One might have expected these physical conditions to produce strong isolationism in Australian minds. One might have expected most Australians to turn their backs on distant Europe and its rivalries. Indeed, late in the nineteenth century, an influential group of Australian nationalists wanted their country to drift away from

Britain. But most Australians still viewed Britain as 'home', devoured the long columns of English news and the latest telegrams from London which Australian newspapers printed, and regarded any insult to Britain by an unarmed Dervish or an armed Sheikh as almost an insult to themselves.

While Australians had to fight no war in defence of their own country they helped fight in some of Britain's wars in outposts of empire. In 1885 a field battery, an infantry battalion, and an ambulance corps left Sydney for the Red Sea but arrived too late to fight with Britain in the Sudan; in manpower that contingent was as big as the Australian force of May 1965 which left for South Vietnam. In 1900 the two main Australian colonies sent a naval force of 460 volunteers across the Pacific to swell the international contingent of 18,000 men who quelled the Boxer uprising in China. At the same time Australian troops were crossing the Indian Ocean to South Africa to fight the Boers; 16,000 Australians and as many horses served in the Boer War. That army was small but equalled 2 per cent of the men of military age then living in Australia.

A decade later the speed of the European armaments race increased, and Germany became a mighty naval power. Many Australians sensed that their own isolation was no longer a safeguard against disaster. Australia carried on most of its foreign trade with Britain; and a naval blockade by the Germans in the north Atlantic during a war would cut the vital supply lines. At the opposite end of the world German colonies were close to Australia. Rabaul and Madang and other German colonial ports could become coaling bases from which cruisers or armed merchantmen could attack Australian commerce and even bombard Australian ports. Australia had another vulnerable point as one of the largest producers of base-metals in the world, for most of the zinc concentrates and much of the copper and silver-lead went to Germany for the final stage of the treatment process. If war occurred, those Australian industries depending on special German skills would be dislocated.

In the five years preceding the outbreak of the 1914-18 war, Australia jettisoned its old policy of spending sparingly on defence. In the last year of peace it was probably spending more on defence, for each head of population, than all but three of the countries which were soon fighting in the war. In 1913-14, each Australian's share of the defence expenditure was higher than that of the average Italian, Belgian, Russian, Japanese, or North American. Australia had already become the first part of the British Empire to compel all fit males to undergo military training, though when war came it refused to compel them to fight overseas. Australia spent heavily on its own navy, which became an operating fleet in 1913.

When Germany and Britain began to fight in August 1914, Germany owned a string of islands across the Pacific. Its main strength in the Pacific was the fortress of Tsingtao on the north China coast and the German East Asiatic squadron under Admiral von Spee which had just left Tsingtao. So long as the Germans held Tsingtao and so long as their cruisers roamed the Pacific the European war was relatively close to Australia. Fortunately for Australia, Japan was one of Britain's allies. It had already proved its naval and military strength and surprised European military seers by defeating Russia in the war of 1904-5, thus becoming the first Asian country to defeat a major European nation in modern times. Now, in 1914, the Japanese attacked and eventually conquered the German fortified port of Tsingtao with its garrison of 13,000 troops and its strategic harbour. At the same time Japan captured the German islands north of the Equator, and Australia and New Zealand captured German New Guinea, Samoa, and Nauru.

If the German empire had created somewhere in the South Pacific a fortress and coaling base as strong as Tsingtao, or if Australia and New Zealand had been slower to capture the wireless stations and potential coaling bases in the South Pacific, von Spee's squadron might have menaced Australian shipping and ports for a few months. As it was, his squadron lacked coaling ports when it reached the south-west Pacific, and had to sail east towards the neutral ports of South America. On 1 November 1914, forty miles from the coast of Chile, von Spee met two British cruisers in the Battle of Coronel and destroyed them. He then rounded Cape Horn with his five large warships and three coal and supply ships. Luckily for Australia and New Zealand the old route past Cape Horn was waning fast; otherwise the Germans could have sunk with ease a score or more ships in a month by patrolling near Cape Horn. The German squadron then approached the British coaling base in the Falkland Islands in the South Atlantic, encountered a larger British fleet, and on 8 December 1914 lost six of her eight ships. The battle of the Falkland Islands was one of the main naval battles in the First World War, and for Australia and New Zealand the battle virtually marked the end of the Pacific as a theatre of war.

One month before the Battle of the Falkland Islands, a lone German raider was intercepted on the trade route between Australia and Suez. The *Emden* had escaped from Tsingtao before the Japanese attacked the port, and in two months she sank fifteen ships, bombarded Madras, and played havoc in Penang. She eventually steamed to the Cocos Island, a small coral atoll in tropical waters just south of the Equator. The island had recently become a vital link in Australia's communications with the outside world, for it was a telegraphic station on the line of cable between Australia and South Africa and a radio telegraph station transmitting messages to ships going between Australia and Colombo. A German cruiser making a surprise attack on Cocos Island could easily destroy the cable and radio stations and then prey on ships which passed close to the island on their passage from Australia to Suez and England.

The German warships south of the Equator in the first months of the war suffered from two unfortunate coincidences. Von Spee's squadron approached the Falkland Islands just when a British fleet was taking in coal there, and similarly the *Emden* steamed into sight of Cocos Island on the very morning when the largest convoy of ships ever to cross the Indian Ocean happened to be only fifty miles away. The convoy steaming from Albany (W.A.) to Colombo consisted of 38 troop and supply ships, carrying Australian and New Zealand troops for service in the Mediterranean, under the powerful escort of two Australian cruisers and one Japanese and one British cruiser. On the morning of 9 November 1914 the convoy received a radio message from Cocos Island that a strange ship was in sight. The Australian cruiser *Sydney* steamed over to investigate, found the stranger was the *Emden*, and sank her before the end of the same morning. Two more German raiders were to appear south of the Equator and jeopardize steamship routes in 1917, even approaching the eastern Australian coast, but otherwise the seat of the war was on the far side of the world.

Australia's remoteness from Europe and the western front in the First World War seems in theory to have been an advantage. However, it was too remote. Australia and New Zealand were impeded more than any other countries outside the region of actual warfare by the shortage of shipping. German submarines destroyed more than five thousand Allied and neutral ships, and ships became so scarce that Britain preferred to bring in her supplies from the nearest possible source, which was usually north or south America. The tonnage of ships visiting Australia more than halved between pre-war and the last full year of the war. The export of Australian wool and wheat and metals and many other primary commodities was frequently dislocated by scarcity of shipping, and Australia would have had an acute depression if Britain had not paid for commodities that were stockpiled in Australian warehouses and silos. One partial solution to the war-time shortage of shipping was the purchase by the Australian government of a fleet of 15 secondhand cargo vessels and the building of more ships in Australia, but Australia's international shipping line was disbanded during the shipping glut of the 1920s.

(State Archives of S.A.)

Royal Tar, about to leave Adelaide with settlers for 'New Australia', Paraguay, 1893.

(State Library of W.A.)

Western Australian timber ports were amongst the last havens for deep-sea sailing ships in the early 1900s.

Camels were more common than motor cars in most W.A. gold towns before 1912.

Charles Kingsford Smith's *Southern Cross* above the new federal capital, Canberra, *c.* 1930.

Arthur Butler, who in 1931 flew solo from England to Australia, refuelling at Tooraweenah, central N.S.W.

Emotional ties with Britain: Melbourne's stock exchange had just sung the hymn Old Hundredth on hearing that Boer War was won.

(*Australasian*, 7 June 1902)

Australia nevertheless was relatively prosperous in the war. There was no rationing of food or clothes. Imported goods were often scarce but that in turn stimulated the manufacture of those goods in Australia. Likewise Australia began, slowly at first, to smelt or refine those metallic concentrates which before the war had gone to German and Belgian industrial plants. The nation's economy was stronger and more self-reliant at the end of the war than at the beginning. Its main losses in the war had been in men, and those losses were heavy. In all 330,000 Australian soldiers went overseas to fight, and nearly 60,000 were killed in battle or died from wounds, a total which exceeded the United States's death roll during that war.

Australia's long distance from Europe was almost certainly more a disadvantage than an asset during the 1914–18 war. The best position for a country during that war was to be outside European theatres of war and yet near enough to enrich itself as a supply base. Canada and the United States held the ideal position and were stimulated immeasurably more than Australia by the demands of war. In the Second World War Australia was much closer to a vital theatre of war, the South-West Pacific, and although it was in greater danger of invasion, its economy gained immeasurably more stimulus from the demands of war.

Australia, however, gained something from its geographical position in the 1914–18 war. In the Peace Treaty it received, under mandate, German New Guinea and the equatorial island of Nauru — an island rich in the phosphates which Australian wheatlands needed as fertilizer. Australia was becoming a colonial power, and when in 1936 it formally acquired one half of the continent of Antarctica it became one of the world's great landowners, though most of its land inside and outside Australia was not an auctioneer's delight.

During the war Australia's relations with Britain had tightened. Australia still acted on most issues as if it were the Isle of Wight. There were only a few issues on which Britain and Australia diverged. At the Versailles Peace

Treaty of 1919 Australia and Britain disagreed on the Japanese proposal that people of all nations should be treated as equal; the Australian Prime Minister argued that such an axiom would throw open Australian ports to an inflow of Japanese. Nevertheless, disagreements were rare, and in the 1920s Australia showed no signs of drifting away from Britain. When Britain passed the Statute of Westminster in 1931 and conferred on Australia, Canada, New Zealand, and other British dominions the last remnants of autonomy, Australia did not bother to pass its own legislation confirming the Statute of Westminster until 1942. Australia was a self-governing country within the British Empire, but outsiders who judged Australia by her behaviour rather than by her constitutional status were entitled to think that she had no independence and was in fact a British colony.

3

If one can select any year which marks Australia's transition from its traditional role as echo and image of Britain and an outpost of Europe, the year which stands out is 1941. One can go further and select 7 December 1941, when Japanese planes bombed an American fleet at Pearl Harbour, Honolulu, 4000 miles to the north-east of Australian soil, or alternatively select 10 December — three days later — when the British battle cruisers *Prince of Wales* and *Repulse* were sunk off the Malayan coast. These two shocks marked for Australia the waning of an era in which history or tradition was dominant and the emergence of a new era when geography was probably as crucial as history. To use another analogy, they marked the end of a time when heredity ceased to be so powerful, when Australians ceased to have nearly all their emotional, commercial, military, financial and human ties with Britain. It marked the start of a new time when Australia's environment — her position on the tail of Asia and on the shores of the Pacific — again became more important.

Pearl Harbour and the chain reaction which followed that explosion reflected changes in the world's balance of economic and military power which had long been taking place but which had not been fully appreciated by Australia's leaders or, for that matter, leaders in many other countries. Those changes were the relative decline of Britain as a world power, and the rise of the United States of America and Japan. The emergence of two powerful nations on the shores of the Pacific, for long a backwater of world economic and military power, was vital to Australia, which itself bordered the Pacific. It ceased to be so far from the seat of trouble in war, and so far from the centre of investment, advanced technology, trading opportunities, and popular culture, in time of peace.

The shuffle in the relative importance of Britain and Japan and the United States of America was visible long before events of 1941–5 made it stand out. But in Australia the rise of Japan was perhaps viewed through the eyes which Gilbert and Sullivan had bequeathed to the British Empire or through the shoddy lens of a Japanese-made toy binocular. Japan was viewed with alarm but not with sufficient alarm to make the Australian government in the mid 1930s spend much money on defence, or even on defence production which, to an isolated country, would be vital in a highly mechanized war; the Labor Party, then in opposition, had isolationist strands which made it even less perturbed by the aggression of Japan. Likewise, in Australia the compensating advantage of the enormous economic power and enormous military potential of the United States of America did not seem relevant. America's belated entry into the First World War and her policy of isolationism between the wars did not encourage Australia to view her as a heavyweight in the Pacific's balance of power. Nor did most Australians fully realize the economic power of the United States, because its role in the Australian economy was small compared with that of Britain's, not only as a source of investment but also as a source of skills.

Australians' chief blindness to the changing world in

327

which they lived was blindness to what had happened to Britain. They did not quite realize that Britain had long ceased to have the world's most powerful industrial economy and that her navy no longer dwarfed that of any rival. Most did not notice the change in Britain's relative position as a world power, partly because they did not wish to notice it, partly because their main news came through British channels, and partly because few Australian leaders of policy or opinion had had much opportunity to travel overseas; when they did travel they saw more of Britain than any other land.

In Australia most of the older generation did not accept Britain's decline. Men who were aged fifty or sixty in the year 1940 usually retained many of the beliefs of their youth. They had spent their youth when Britain was perhaps the most powerful and dynamic nation in the world. They had been suckled by *Kim* and *Deeds that Won the Empire*. They had also accepted the late Victorian mythology which implied that God was on Britain's side, that the Empire was great because God had blessed it. The mythology lasted long after the Empire had ceased to be so great. Nor was the creed confined to the older generation which had breathed it firsthand. Schoolchildren in Australia got it secondhand, and one of the curious effects of Australia's education system was that, as late as the late 1940s, most of those who left secondary school or university probably carried away the idea that Britain was still the leading power.

One household article that had perhaps preserved the idea of the might of Britain and its empire was the map of the world. The splashes of deep red across the map seemed visual proof of Britain's power. The assumption that military and economic power could be neatly totted up in a few minutes on any diningroom table, either by adding the number of square miles or the number of people which an empire possessed, was widespread. Both those ventures in arithmetic seemed to support Britain's might. And yet it was also clear that the real might of the British Empire lay in the British Isles, mere flecks on the

328

maps of the world. Perhaps most Australians believed that Britain was still dominant simply because it was a comforting belief.

In December 1941, when Australians began to sense that they were plunged into a new environment, the spectacles they had carried out from Britain were obsolete. They needed spectacles that would correct short-sightedness. They had to see the environment they were in as clearly as the environment they had left across the world.

In the month Japan bombed Pearl Harbour and began its lightning advance on British Malaya and then the Dutch East Indies and New Guinea, Australia's most experienced soldiers were in the Middle East and its airmen in Britain. Britain did not willingly sanction their return to defend Australia's north. At the same time Britain's own ships and aircraft and armies in South-East Asia were unable to halt the Japanese advance. Australia had no alternative but to turn to the United States of America for aid. At that time it is doubtful if more than one member of Australia's federal cabinet had ever visited the country whose aid they invoked.

Without the intervention of American military strength in 1942 Australia would probably have been invaded or blockaded by Japan. Furthermore, in stemming and then repelling the Japanese thrust in New Guinea and the Solomons and nearby islands, America played the major part and suffered most of the casualties; and America's main partner in that sphere of war was Australia, not Britain. The role of the Americans was recognized and honoured but realization that Australia was no longer simply an outpost of Britain, that Australia flanked the Pacific and Indian Oceans rather than the English Channel, came slowly. While in the nineteenth century Australians had erected, by public subscription, many statues to General Gordon, the British general who lost a skirmish on the banks of the Nile, it was perhaps significant that they erected no statues, by public subscription, to General Douglas MacArthur, the American general of the forces which had won battles near the shores of Australia.

After the war the Western Powers slowly abdicated or retreated from their long rule over most of coastal Asia. The British Empire in Asia dissolved. India, Pakistan, Ceylon, Burma, Malaysia, and Singapore became independent and self-governing. France's colony in Indo-China was cut into new countries no longer ruled from Paris. The Hague ceased to rule the Indonesian Archipelago, and Washington ceased to govern the Philippines, and Australia slowly accepted the fact that eastern New Guinea would sooner or later become independent. The Allied Occupation forces withdrew from Japan, which again governed itself. And China changed from a weak nation into a strong nation.

Whereas Asia in 1941 was still in Europe's sphere of influence and had only one strong independent nation, one quarter of a century later it was both a theatre for northern hemisphere rivalries and even more a theatre in its own right with its own set of conflicting rivalries and ambitions. Moreover, it had more seeds of turbulence than Europe now had. The new Asian nations had a more vigorous nationalism and far more acute social and economic problems than the average European nation. Australia, after existing in secure isolation for more than a century, had drifted into a new orbit of dangers and opportunities.

The strongest effect of the resurgence of Asia was to make Australians dig up the bones of Edward Gibbon Wakefield, the apostle of assisted migration from Europe to Australia. His old formula of using Crown revenue to pay the fares of migrants across the world had been increasingly neglected in the latter years of the nineteenth century, when working men had enough political power to check the practice of paying out public moneys in order to bring to Australia men who competed with them for jobs. Australia had continued to pay the fares of some migrants in periods of relative prosperity, but except in the 1920s it was not a vigorous policy. It went in fits and starts. Australia's net gain from immigration from 1860 to 1945, from the close of the main gold rush inflow to the end of the Second World War, was only 1,400,000. It is hard to believe that Australia could not have absorbed far more migrants if it had set out vigorously to recruit them and pay their fares.

The delayed shock of the war in the Pacific closed the long era of sluggish immigration. Higher population became a first commandment of national security. 'The days of our isolation are over,' said Mr A.A. Calwell, the federal minister for immigration, in November 1946 when he inaugurated his bold scheme to subsidize immigration on a large scale. He had hoped to attract ten Britons for every continental migrant, but so anxious was Australia to increase its population quickly that it turned eventually from Britain to continental Europe for most of its migrants.

Australia's ability to attract migrants from the British Isles and from lands bordering the Baltic and Mediterranean and North Seas was improved by the United States of America's barriers against massive migration from Europe. Since the 1920s the United States had firmly restricted her immigration, thus following the same policy which Australia had long pursued by the simple method of spending less money on subsidizing immigration. When, after the Second World War, Australia reversed her policy and spent liberally on paying the fares of migrants, it received in some years more European migrants than the more attractive but half-closed ports of the United States.

In encouraging massive migration, Australians could foresee some sacrifices — perhaps a weakening of their social security, perhaps unemployment, and perhaps the importing of racial and national tensions from Europe. The main fears have so far been unfulfilled. The migration, on the contrary, was possibly the mainspring of one of the most dramatic spans of growth in Australia's history. The soaring population needed more houses, hospitals, schools, electricity, and used more cars, electrical equipment, food, and clothing, To provide these goods and services and equipment required much capital from overseas. One of the main reasons why so much overseas capital crossed to Australia in the period 1945-65 was because sustained immigration was multiplying the population; and, curiously, in the 1960s the strongest critic of the grip which those overseas investors had gained on so many Australian industries was the architect of post-war migration, A. A. Calwell. Like E.G. Wakefield more than a century previously he was perturbed by some of the tall trees which his creative vision had sown. There was one other irony. Many foreign investors preferred to invest in Australia rather than in other countries in the new world from the 1950s onwards because Australia had never been much affected by internal or external turbulence; and yet the tide of migrants which gave the main opportunities for foreign money to earn fine dividends in Australia, had been set in motion by Australia's fear that their land was no longer such a safe land in which people could work, play, and invest.

Since the end of the Second World War the population of Australia has grown from seven millions to almost fifteen million; about half of that increase has come from overseas migrants and the children to whom they gave birth in Australia. So many migrants were attracted that Australia's net gain through migration in the period 1947 to 1977 exceeded the net gain in all its previous history. Less than half of the new migrants came from the traditional source of migrants, the British Isles. By the census of 1971 the number of Australians who had been born in England equalled the number of Australians born in Italy, Greece, Yugoslavia, Germany, Holland and Malta all added together. And those Australians born in the remainder of Europe slightly outnumbered the Scots-born and Irish-born Australians. This emigration from continental Europe affected every facet of Australian life, from food and sport to work and religion. In the long term it also weakened Australia's links with Britain but it had little such effect in the short term. Many of the immigrants from continental Europe were so nervous of communism that their votes helped to keep in power the Australian politician Sir Robert Menzies, whose loyalty to Britain was most intense. Prime Minister from 1949 to 1966, he presided over the late-afternoon of British influence in this land. Then quickly was to come the twilight.

At the same time our contacts with east Asia proliferated in the Menzies era. Asian students, rarely seen at Australian schools and universities before the Second World War, numbered 12,000 by the mid 1960s. Restrictions on Asians migrating to Australia were reduced or eliminated; and the official census of 1971 revealed that 29,000 Australian residents had been born in India and another 23,000 had been born in China or Hong Kong. Today the people of Chinese origin living in Australia outnumber those who lived here during the gold rushes of the 1850s. In the late 1970s thousands of refugees from East Timor, Vietnam and other lands were allowed to settle here in numbers which would have been unimaginable only ten years previously. Meanwhile hundreds of Australian engineers, physicians, teachers and tradesmen were volunteering to offer their skills in eastern or southern Asia, for low salaries. Our television and newspapers increasingly focussed on parts of Asia. Our tourists went increasingly to Singapore, Bali, Delhi, Hong Kong and Tokyo; and in the late 1970s the Australians visiting China were exceeded only by the Japanese and the overseas Chinese. This did not mean that Australian tourists were turning their back on Europe and their own strong ancestral and cultural links: but clearly they were no longer turning their back on east Asia.

The strongest contact between Australia and east Asia was commerce. Japan bought our wool, metallic ores, coal, and foodstuffs in such quantities that by the mid 1960s it was overtaking Britain as our main customer. In the decade before the First World War, Japan had bought a mere 1 per cent of our exports compared to Britain's 67 per cent; and it seemed inconceivable that Britain could ever be supplanted by Japan. But the inconceivable happened in 1966. A decade later Japan was ten times more important than Britain as a buyer of our exports. In the year ending June 1974 Japan also passed Britain as a source of our imports. Japanese cars, cameras, wrist watches, calculators, transistor radios, and other precision goods were commonplace in our households, and Japan was now a narrow second to the United States as the main outside supplier of goods to Australia. Commerce between Australia and China had also grown rapidly, especially in wheat. In 1978 China was trading more with Australia than with any countries except Japan, Hong Kong and West Germany.

Our traditional obstacle of distance from our main trading partners had been dramatically eased in the 1960s and 1970s. Moreover an important part of that trade consisted of iron ore and bauxite shipped from those north-western and northern coasts which were closest to Japan. Those giant ships of more than 100,000 tons which sailed from Port Hedland and Dampier, the iron-ore ports of north-western Australia, represented an assault on distance. One mammoth bulk-carrier could now carry a cargo such as fifty of the largest clippers could not have carried in the 1850s.

Increasingly, in parliaments and newspapers and textbooks, was heard the statement that we were now a part of Asia. The statement became almost a catchcry. But it embodied only half the truth. Increasingly true of commerce, it was not true of culture and other facets of our life. Moreover it was not convincing as a statement of geography. The Australia of the atlas appears to be relatively close to Asia but the Australia where most people live is not close. Moreover most of Australia's commerce is with north-east Asia rather than the closer south-east Asia. Between the main cities and farmlands of Australia and their markets in China and Japan lies not only a barrier of sea but an equally formidable barrier of dry Australian land.

The long stretch of Australian coastline which faces

Asia is sparsely peopled. The north-western and northern coasts of Australia, and a coastal corridor running inland for some four hundred miles, hold only two towns with more than 25,000 people. One is the port of Darwin and the other is the inland mining town of Mount Isa, and they are more than a thousand miles apart by road. They are also remote from the 'Boomerang Coast' of the south-east, where eight of every ten Australians live. Thus the north Australian port of Darwin lies as far from Canberra, the Australian federal capital, as from the capital of the Philippines. Darwin is closer to Saigon than to the most southerly Australian city, Hobart. Darwin is also closer to Singapore than to Melbourne. These are distances by air: by the sea routes Darwin is even more remote from the main Australian cities. Its sea route to Sydney is longer than its sea route to southern China. The sea routes from the isolated ports of northern and north-western Australia are important, for no railways join those ports to the big cities on the opposite side of the Australian continent. It is a common comment to exclaim how close northern Australia is to Asia: it is not so often observed how far northern Australia lies from those regions where most Australians live.

4

An orator who was conscious of the close ties between Britain and Australia would have been ridiculed if, in the year 1938 when Australia celebrated the 150th anniversary of Botany Bay, he had publicly predicted that in the following quarter of a century most of those ties would be greatly weakened. And yet such a prediction would have been correct.

During that quarter of a century 1938–63, Britain ceased for the first time to supply Australia with a majority of its new immigrants; they now came more from continental Europe than the British Isles. Britain ceased for the first time to virtually monopolize the flow of capital to Australia, and in the early 1960s its share of the total overseas funds invested in Australia each year was not far ahead of the North American share. Britain ceased to be the main source of the technical innovations which Australia applied to transport and farms and factories. Britain ceased to be the nation on which Australia most relied for its military security.

Britain ceased to be the inspiration of our foreign policy. Britain ceased to dominate our cultural life; for American universities, films, books, comics, hit tunes, plays, television programmes, and American industrial design and architecture, influenced channels of leisure and entertainment and culture in which the incoming flow was once overwhelmingly British.

The symbols of British influence continued to vanish or become misty. As the material links grew weaker, the political and ideological links weakened. In 1965 an Australian battalion went to fight in Vietnam — the first time Australian soldiers had fought in a war in which Britain was not an ally. In the same year the last of a long line of British governors-general left Australia; and it seemed unlikely that any Briton — except perhaps an heir to the throne — would again become the ceremonial head of the Commonwealth of Australia. During the Whitlam government of 1972–75, new Australian honours and decorations and an Australian national anthem supplemented rather than supplanted the old English honours and anthem. When Britain joined the European common market in 1973, old trading ties and treaties were severed. When Papua New Guinea became an independent nation in 1975, that ended an imperial role which Australia had inherited from Britain. Meanwhile the old English ways of counting and measuring were being abandoned: the pound and the shilling were no more, and the pint and the mile were receding. The Church of England, which claimed the nominal allegiance of the largest group of Australians, changed its name to the Anglican Church of Australia, and for the first time the head of that church was a native of Australia and not the British Isles. Even the Queen became known as the Queen of Australia. The movement away from England had been quiet and undramatic. It is not yet observed in most of the history books which are read in Australian schools and colleges. The post mortem has not yet begun.

Much of our history had been shaped by the contradiction that we depended intimately and comprehensively on a country which was further away than almost any other in the world. Now the dependence had faded. The distance too had diminished.

15   The Shrinking Seas

It became a common complaint in the 1970s that the
prime ministers of Australia made too many visits overseas. Fifty years earlier nobody could possibly complain
that a prime minister or premier was making too many
visits overseas. Even one visit by a ruling politician
during his term of office was unusual, and those who did
go overseas had to be sure of the loyalty of their colleagues
at home because, by sailing for England, they ran the risk
of sailing into political exile. In the days of slow travel a
prime minister rarely visited Perth, let alone London.

Only a crisis or celebration attracted an Australian
prime minister to England, and once there he stayed until
his mission was completed. W.M.Hughes went overseas
in April 1918, during the First World War, and remained
away for sixteen months. In 1930, during the world depression, J.H.Scullin made a 'lightning' trip by sea to
England and was absent for fifteen weeks. A decade later,
in the Second World War, R.G.Menzies as prime minister actually flew to London to confer with Mr Churchill;
but the aircraft was slow and landed at many airfields
over many days. A revolution in communicating had
begun but it was not easy to predict how quickly, and how
far, Australia's isolation would be eased.

2

Even in 1955 the flow of news, people and cargoes to
Australia was slow. The glamorous aircraft was the

Super-Constellation; it had four propellors and its cruising speed was less than 300 miles an hour. It could carry 82 passengers but not many Australians could afford the fare and, even if they could, they preferred the luxury and safety of the slow ocean-liner. Nearly all migrants bound for Australia still came in the ocean liners, a long voyage which even with the aid of the Suez Canal averaged about four weeks.

Most of the international telegrams travelled here along the submarine cables built before the First World War, and the few international telephone calls depended on wireless and were expensive and not always audible. Even in the Australian cities the telephone was not very automatic, and all trunk calls had to be booked through the operator. No satellites were used for long-distance messages; no coaxial cables crossed the beds of the oceans. Television was soon to burst into living rooms, but radio was still king. The coronation of Queen Elizabeth II was heard on the radio by almost the entire nation in June 1953, and the flinging open of the great west door of the Abbey was heard more vividly in Australia than in England because people here magnified the sound with their imagination and nostalgia. And yet distance was diminishing. The first visit by a reigning sovereign in 1954 and the staging of the Olympic Games in Melbourne in 1956 were signs that Australia was no longer considered impossibly far away.

Between 1955 and 1980 we were drawn closer to the rest of the world. The black-and-white television arrived in 1956, a satellite was used experimentally for television between Australia and England in 1966, and the landing of men on the moon in 1969 was televised directly to Australia. The telephone was also becoming an effective international instrument. It had traditionally been a way of speaking over short distances within Australia, and an interstate telephone line did not reach Tasmania until 1936 and Darwin until 1941. As late as the year 1961–62 only sixteen international telephone calls were made to and from Australia in the average hour. The opening of the submarine coaxial cable between Australia and North America in 1963 multiplied the voice circuits, and more coaxial cables were laid. In 1976 Australians for the first time could directly dial people in other lands, and for each word transmitted the real cost was tiny in comparison with the cost of each word on the slow international telegraph of a century earlier. Thereafter, on Christmas Day the channels with Europe were crammed with the conversations of people, many of whom had immigrated to Australia believing that they would never again speak to friends and relatives at home.

Telephone and television, as ways of crossing the seas, had an immediacy, a vividness, which seemed to shrivel long distances. They enlarged the awareness of most of us. We were slowly awakening to the fact that the world was shrinking.

The flow of people across the globe was also transformed in the quarter century 1955–1980. Jet aircraft entered the long-distance routes to Australia at the end of the 1950s. Our politicans, state and federal, now travelled overseas so often that in some months the cabinet rooms were half-empty. Australia at last found a place in the itinerary of world leaders. In the 1960s the first prime minister of Britain visited Australia, and the first president of the United States and the first president of Italy. Pope Paul made a short visit in 1970. The Beatles and scores of pop stars noisily came and noisily went. Business and sporting visits were multiplied. People with skilled occupations found it possible and payable to spend the year in two hemispheres, and Australian shearers could be found at work in the Welsh hills each year and Austrian ski-instructors spent the European summer in the Australian winter.

Aircraft had passed ocean liners as the main form of travel to Australia by the mid 1960s. The airport replaced the wharf as the place of farewell and welcome, and the airport terminals suddenly bulged. Sydney and Melbourne were building new terminals and longer runways in the late 1960s, in readiness for the jumbo jets which arrived in 1971. Each jumbo jet carried nearly five times as many passengers as the largest aircraft of twenty years previously. They placed foreign travel for the first time within the pockets or the ambitions of the average Australian. They did more than anything to cheapen fares, and to drive the last of the regular passengers liners from the Europe-Australian routes. Today old passengers who insist on travelling to Europe by ship can wait nine months for a ship. Not since the eighteenth century have sea passages to England been so scarce.

The transport of goods had been cheapened but not transformed. At sea the mammoth carriers of minerals became common in the 1960s and container ships were often seen by the early 1970s. The floating sheep-pen with its tiers of crowded sheep bound for the Middle East was one of the waterfront sights of the late 1970s, and the biggest of these ships probably carried in one voyage far more sheep than had been carried to Australia by all the ships in all the years to 1850. Despite these changes, sea transport remained dear, prohibitively dear, for many commodities which did not lend themselves to bulk handling and shipping.

Distance has been visibly tamed in the last quarter century but it has not been conquered. Distance has been tamed more quickly on the map than in the mind. Those people brought up in a more isolated era — and they still hold nearly all the influential positions — believe much more than the young that the isolation persists. Even the young have perhaps not fully realized the impact of jet aircraft. One may suggest that when we travel by air, we are mentally still walking or still travelling on the firm earth or firm sea. Flying, for part of our mind or senses, is still a fantasy. It is too revolutionary an invention in human history to be absorbed fully. We have not yet become accustomed to it and, perhaps for some generations, will not.

We still live in one of the billabongs of the world, away from the mainstream. In 1982 the average journey from western Europe to Sydney took about 24 hours and was often as many as 36 hours to some capital cities if the normal timetable was followed. Most of the international journeys we make are long by the standards of other nations. In a world which is increasingly programmed by time, even a few hours can seem an eternity in an aircraft which is crowded and as confined as a bird-cage.

Australia will continue to be seen as isolated. All isolation is relative. To a traveller who has flown 13,000 miles to reach Australia, even an additional 500 miles from Sydney to Melbourne can seem an intolerable burden. The most important reason why Sydney in the years 1955–1980 was able to challenge Melbourne as the financial hub, and to become the base for so many of the American and Japanese companies in finance and banking, was simply its slight advantage in proximity to East Asia and North America and its possession of the main international airport. Sydney's advantage was a few ticks of the clock, but that was a big advantage.

Though isolation has been dramatically eased, some of our attitudes belong to a more isolated era; and we have not fully re-examined those attitudes in the light of the new geography. Many of the viewpoints which shape national policies were themselves moulded by the era of isolation. Many important issues in the next decade, however, will be influenced by the fact that the world is shrinking. The nuclear missile — even more than the jumbo jets and the satellites — has turned the isolated continents and islands into one world. Henceforth no place can be an island. The world no longer has a hideaway. There can no longer be a Botany Bay.

In a shrinking world we cannot be sure of the answers to questions which we once answered with some confidence. But the questions will not go away. We cannot be sure whether more and more 'boat people' will arrive; we cannot be sure whether we will have to accept them or be able to turn them back. We cannot be sure whether in our immigration policies we can continue to admit more Europeans than Asians. And will we accept more manufactured goods from east Asian factories? Will Japan and

China become even more vital as markets? Will our vital sealanes which pass through the Indonesian straits to those Asian markets remain always open? Will our foreign policy centre on alliances or on an equally precarious neutrality? Will all the new nations in our part of the world retain their independence? Will our schools turn more to the languages, culture and history of Asia? Will our method of quarantine for incoming plants and animals, a method based on long isolation, collapse in the era of fast travel, thus leading to rural disasters? Will this country one day be threatened by an outside power and will we, in a world of shorter distances, be able to defend ourselves? Many of these questions will ultimately be answered not only by public opinion and governments within this country but also by pressures from an encroaching world.

3

In the long human history of this land, the rise and fall of isolation has been a powerful influence. The Aboriginals themselves held this land during periods of both contact and isolation. In 1788 they were a small population, living in relative abundance, but internally divided, simple in their technology and unable to defend their land adequately. When suddenly their long isolation ended, under the influence of British and French navigators, they quickly lost their lands.

Our Australia resembles that of the Aboriginals. We are a small population holding a land rich in natural resources. We have been far less isolated than the Aboriginals of 1788; we know the outside world; and we are not likely to suffer the same fate. But we would be unwise to think that the easing of a long period of isolation was an event of no significance, or an event whose effects could be predicted or even controlled.

343

Notes

The following notes are far from comprehensive. Designed largely for the kind of reader who consults notes, they cover mainly those details and issues in which such readers are most likely to be interested. In addition, they give the source of all quotations.

Originally the notes were made about twice as long by the inclusion of recent writings whose evidence or interpretations I disagreed with; they included some of my own writings. In the end I deleted most of those notes, partly to keep the book to a reasonable size and cost, and partly because the main interpretations with which I disagreed are so widely held — and often unanimously held — that interested readers wishing to make up their own minds can easily find examples of them in standard histories of Australia.

ABBREVIATIONS

B.A. & H.	*Business Archives and History* (Sydney)
C.P.P.	*Commonwealth Parliamentary Papers*
C.Y.B.	*Official Year Book of the Commonwealth of Australia*
E.H.R.	*Economic History Review*, Second series
H.C.P.	*House of Commons Papers*
H.R.A.	*Historical Records of Australia:* in the following notes the series no. is always cited before the volume no.; thus a reference to 3, *VI*, 576–8 means series 3, volume *VI*, pages 576–8
H.S.	*Historical Studies: Australia and New Zealand* (Melbourne)
M.M.	*The Mariner's Mirror: the Journal of the Society for Nautical Research*
S.A.P.P.	*South Australian Parliamentary Papers*
T.H.R.A.	*Papers and Proceedings* of the Tasmanian Historical Research Association (Hobart)
V.P.P.	*Victorian Parliamentary Papers (Votes and Proceedings of the Legislative Council* to 1855–6, and of *Legislative Assembly* thereafter.)

In the notes the verbose titles of some parliamentary papers are slightly condensed.

Notes

1. SEARCH

What were the motives for the early voyages of discovery in the South Seas and why did those discoveries have so few initial effects? These questions seem to be answered by giving more attention than is usual to contemporary commerce — the problem of winds and navigation, the prevailing trade routes from Europe, the rewards and difficulties of trade, and the nature of European colonization at the time. What knowledge I have of these issues came in large part from reading many files of *The Mariner's Mirror*, mostly historical articles that had no relation to Australia or the Orient, and mostly articles which seemed at the time to be irrelevant to my quest. The collective and delayed effect of these articles was stimulating and informative, and I acknowledge my debt to that excellent journal as well as to individual contributors who are mentioned in subsequent notes.

PAGE

3 Bird flights: J. Dorst, *The Migration of Birds* (London, 1962, trans. by Constance Sherman) *passim*.

6 'Man's luck': Henrietta Drake-Brockman, *Voyage to Disaster: the life of Francisco Pelsaert* (Sydney, 1963) 48.

9 Increased British shipping on long routes: Ralph Davis, *The Rise of the English Shipping Industry* . . . (London, 1962) 41–2.

10 Wallis 'sights' the South land: H. Carrington ed., *The Discovery of Tahiti* . . . (Hakluyt Society, London, 1948) xxiv and 135.

11 Cook's statement to a Whitby friend: cited by G. Arnold Wood, *The Voyage of the Endeavour* (Melbourne. 1944 edn.) 115.

12 Opinions of Norfolk Island: J. C. Beaglehole ed., *Journals of Captain James Cook* (Hakluyt Society, Cambridge, 1961) *II*, 565–6, 868.

13 The value of the *Almanac*: R. A. Skelton, 'Captain James Cook as a Hydrographer', *M.M.* (1954) 111, 118.

14 'Mr Kendals Watch': Beaglehole ed., *II*, 692.

2. EXILE

18 Lucid versions of the traditional interpretation of why Australia was settled are Eris O'Brien, *The Foundation of Australia* (Sydney, 1950 edn.) and C. M. H. Clark, *A History of Australia* (Melbourne, 1962) *I*, ch. 4.

19 Lord Howe on the long voyage: cited by W. Oldham, 'The Administration of the System of Transportation of British Convicts, 1763–1793' (University of London thesis, 1933) 314.

19 Phillip's opinion: *H.R.A.*, 1, *I*, 51.

21 For the evidence, but not the inferences, I have drawn on the

declining British slave traffic: R. Coupland, *The British Anti-Slavery Movement* (London, 1933) 20–38.

22 Das Voltas Bay: O'Brien, 122–3; Oldham, 278–82.

23 K. M. Dallas, 'The First Settlement in Australia; considered in relation to sea-power in world politics,' *T.H.R.A.*, 1952. no. 3.

26 I have taken the liberty, in summarising Mr Dallas's theory, of eliminating some points which seem dubious, adding others which tend to strengthen the broad sweep of his theory, and rearranging the sequence. This seemed justifiable because his theory seemed to have more merit than was conceded by most critics. New points I added to support Botany Bay's commercial attractions were Britain's right under the Treaty of Paris of 1784 to navigate freely through the Dutch East Indies, and the dramatic expansion of the China tea trade from 1784: see Hoh Cheung and Lorna H. Mui, 'The Commutation Act and the Tea Trade in Britain, 1784–1793,', *E.H.R.*, Dec. 1963, *XVI*, 234–53). New points I added to support the strategic attractions of Botany Bay were France's control of Mauritius and the failure of Captain Cook's third voyage to find the avidly sought North-West Passage to the Pacific.

28 Discussions on Dallas's theory: M. Roe, 'Australia's Place in the "Swing to the East", 1788–1810', *H.S.*, May 1958, *VIII*, 212–13; five short articles in *T.H.R.A.*, 1952, no. 4.

The French: fine research by Alan Frost is in *Convicts and Empire* (Melbourne, 1980) esp. 116, 230.

29 Lord Sydney's statement: reprinted in V. Harlow and F. Madden, British *Colonial Developments 1774–1834: select documents* (Oxford, 1953) 435.

30 Dependence on Baltic flax and hemp: G. S. Graham, *British Policy and Canada 1774–1791* (London, 1930) 105–13.

Markets for flax and timber: the main market for the mast-timber, being a heavy bulky item, was to be the relatively close ports of India. On the other hand flax was light, and had a high value per ton, and so could easily afford the cost of transport to either India or Europe.

30 Political relations with Russia: M. S. Anderson, *Britain's Discovery of Russia 1553–1815* (London, 1958) 5, 143–6.

31 Committee discussions in August 1786: Minute Book BT5/4 (Public Record Office, London), 7, 8, 19.

32 Length of flax fibre: 'Norfolk island' in *Encyclopedia Britannica* (Dublin, 1792) *XIII*, 102–3.

32 'One of the most valuable presents': *A Voyage Round the World . . . Under the Command of J. F. G. de la Perouse* (London, 1799, tr. from French) *I, 130*.

33 R. G. Albion, 'The Timber Problem of the Royal Navy, 1652–1862' in *M.M.* (1952) 10–11.

34   Plan to use surplus labour for growing flax in Australia: *H.R.A.* 1, *I*, 13.

34   Voyage of first fleet: see C. Bateson, *The Convict Ships 1787–1868* (Glasgow, 1959) ch. 7.

35   'Prevent it being occupied':*H.R.A.* 1, *I*, 13.

36   Phillip to Nepean: *H.R.A.*, 1, *I*, 104.

37   Canvas output: *H.R.A.*, 1, *I*, 98, 186, 233, 428; D. Collins, *An Account of the English Colony in New South Wales* (first published London 1798–1802, but I used James Collier's edn., Christchurch, c. 1910) 289–90, 352.

37   On the marked differences betwen Baltic and New Zealand flax, see R. H. Kirby, *Vegetable Fibres* (New York, 1963) ch. 2, 12.

38   In the first edition of this book I argued that the British in 1786 selected Botany Bay for these reasons: the need for a new place for her convicts, the attractions of naval stores on Norfolk Island, and *possibly* as a half-way house for English ships in a time of increasing rivalry and trade potential in the Twin Oceans. In this edition I have retained all these reasons. My new interpretation, however, is now more complex. I now think the half-way house argument is reasonably proven, if seen as a long-term British aim. I have added, too, the strong fears of the French — the result largely of Frost's research. I have also added, in chapter one, another reason which, I think, influenced the British decision: the unduly false hopes centred on the climate and soil of Botany Bay. For an elaboration of that last point, see *A Land Half Won* (Melbourne, 1980) 10–12.

3.   ISOLATION

40   Ocean-land ratio in zones of latitude: J. Lyman, 'Ocean and Oceanography', *Encyclopaedia Britannica* (Chicago, 1962), *XVI*, 682.

41   'Green Hills': M. Maury, *The Physical Geography of the Sea* (London, 1856 edn.) 292.

41   Passage of *Otago:* C. H. Williams, 'Under Sail to New Zealand in 1870', *M.M.* (1954) 142–3.

42   Icebergs in 1854–5: 'Meteor' in *Nautical Magazine* (1892) 815.

44   *Glasgow Mercury:* cited in (Anon.) *Sea Sketches about Ships and Sailors* (Religious Tract Society, London, n.d. but c. 1863) 231–2.

45   Hunter's voyage: J. Hunter, *An Historical Journal of the Transactions at Port Jackson and Norfolk Island . . .* (London, 1793) esp. 93–101; *H.R.A.* 1, *I*, 141.

46   Famine: Collins, 28, 66, 69, 70–5; *H.R.A.* 1, *I*, 165–8, 173–5.

50 Scarcities after 1790: *H.R.A.* 1, *I*, 468, 528, 530, and 704 ('We are nearly destitute'); M. H. Ellis, *Lachlan Macquarie: his life, adventures, and times* (Sydney, 1958 edn.) 187, 199, 269.

51 Cape Town captured: *H.R.A.* 1, *I*, 649.

52 Hunter's complaint: *H.R.A.*, 1, *I*, 561.

53 Cape Town famine: L. C. F. Turner, 'The Cape of Good Hope and the Anglo-French Conflict, 1797–1806', *H.S.*, May 1961, *IX*, 370–1.

53 'I must observe': *H.R.A.*, 1, *I*, 444.

54 Tracks of first ships from Sydney to Java: Collins, 174; 197; Hunter, 214–66; *H.R.A.*, 1, *I*, 69, 443, 730.

57 Bligh in 1787 was to have collected two pots of N.Z. flax as well as the breadfruit plants: W. R. Dawson, ed., *The Banks Letters* (London, 1958) 826.

57 Bampton episode: *H.R.A.*, 1, *I*, 419–26, 469, 507, 530, 774, Collins, 219–20, 226–8, 230–1.

61 Flinders' misfortunes: *H.R.A.*, 1, *IV*, 381–2, 400ff; 1, *V*, 433–8.

62 Cripps' route: G.W. Earle, 'The Steam Route from Singapore to Sydney, via Torres Straits', *Nautical Magazine* (1853) 175.

62 Commerce with India, 1817; compiled from details in J.S. Cumpston, *Shipping Arrivals and Departures: Sydney, 1788–1825* (Canberra, 1963) 105, 107, 109.

63 'And though every possible measure': Collins, 357.

63 Wilson's complaint: *H.R.A.*, 1, *VII*, 502–3.

64 China convoy, 1804: *H.R.A.*, 1, *V*, 258, 325–6.

67 Russian ship *Neva*: Cumpston, 61.

68 Sydney as a maritime base: M. Roe, 'Charles Bishop, Pioneer of Pacific Commerce', *T.H.R.A.*, July 1962, *X*, 6–15; M. Roe, 'Australia's Place in the "Swing to the East", 1788–1810', *H.S.* (May 1958) 202–13; Cumpston, *passim*.

69 Convicts absconding from ports: *H.R.A.*, 3, *III*, 284, 341–2, 459–60, 530.

4. LIMPET PORTS

72 'A great Hulk': *H.R.A.*, 1, *XI*, 321–2.

73 Historians' assumption that Britain wanted the whole continent: examples are S.H. Roberts, *History of Australian Land Settlement* (Melbourne, 1924) 40; W. P. Morrell, *The Great Powers in the Pacific* (London, 1963) 11.

74 Discoveries at Preservation Island: W. R. Dawson, ed., *The Banks Letters* (London, 1958), 436, 437.

76 'Saved much time'; *H.R.A.*, 1, *IV*, 232.

76 Most ships using Bass Strait would come with the prevailing winds from the west but in summer, when the westerlies were

milder and the adverse monsoon dominated Torres Strait, ships bound from Sydney to India etc. would use it: e.g. *H.R.A.*, 1, *IV*, 250.

76   Baudin's expedition: J.B. Walker, *Early Tasmania* (Hobart, 1950 impr.) 9–26; H. M. Cooper, *French Exploration in South Australia . . .*' (Adelaide, 1952) *passim*.

78   Reasons for move from Port Phillip to Hobart; *H.R.A.*, 3, *I*, 29, 35–40, 211. For neglect of King Island, see *ibid.*, 47, 51, 227, 316.

82   Macquarie on need for port: *H.R.A.*, 1, *VII*, 582–3.

83   Trepang fleet at work: A. Searcy, *By Flood and Field* (Melbourne, 1911) 17, 45, 159, 162; *H.R.A.*, 3, *V*, 738, 743.

85   Motives behind Melville Is. fort: *H.R.A.*, 3, *V*, 737–55; H. R. C. Wright, 'The Anglo-Dutch Dispute in the East, 1814–1824', in *E.H.R.*, *III*, 229–39; and two works by N. Tarling, *Anglo-Dutch Rivalry in the Malay World 1780–1824* (Brisbane, 1962), and 'British Policy in the Malay Peninsula and Archipelago 1824–1871', *Journal of Malayan Branch of the Royal Asiatic Society*, *XXX*, 188–9. The latter article, while valuable on the political rivalries, has the common arguments that the Melville Is. fort was inspired by fear of French.

87   History of Raffles Bay: *H.R.A.*, 3, *V*, 737–824, and 3, *VI*, 643–845.

89   London's mistaken decision to abandon Raffles Bay: *H.R.A.*, 1, *XIII*, 793–7; 1, *XIV*, 410–11; 3, *VI*, 837.

90   Bathurst's letters: *H.R.A.*, 1, *XII*, 192–5, 218.

91   'The importance of King George's Sound': *H.R.A.*, 3, *VI*, 505.

93   Stirling's opinions of Swan River: *H.R.A.*, 1, *XII*, 777–80; 3, *VI*, 576–8, 585–6.

97   St Allouarn's claim: L. R. Marchant, 'The French Discovery and Settlement of New Zealand, 1769–1846', *H.S.* (May 1963) 516n.

5.   WHALEMEN

100   'From her account the whales . . .': cited in W. J. Dakin, *Whalemen Adventurers* (Sydney, 1934) 1.

102   My calculation that the whalers' cargoes in 1800–6 were worth at least £200,000 is based partly on prices cited in K. Brandt, *Whale Oil: an economic analysis* (Stanford, 1940) 210, 238.

102   Whalebone whale: E. J. Slijper, *Whales (New York, 1962, trans. from Dutch)* 259–67.

103   'We passed so many whales': cited in Dakin, 38.

103   Catches of 1818: Amy Rowntree, 'Early Growth of the Port of

Hobart Town', *T.H.R.A.*, Oct. 1954, *III*, 93.

104 Birch's ventures: *H.R.A.*, 3, *III*, 354–7, 458–63.

106 Bass Strait islands: *Ibid*, 461–2; M. C. I. Levy, 'G. A. Robinson and the Whaling-Sealing Fraternity', *T.H.R.A.*, Feb. 1957, *V*, 73–5.

106 Macquarie Is. seals: R. Carrick & Susan Ingham, 'Studies in the Southern Elephant Seal', C.S.I.R.O. *Wildlife Research*, *VII*, no. 2, Aug. 1962.

107 Walker and Jones: *H.R.A.*, 1, *XIV*, 135, 761.

109 Adventures of *Offley*, *Maid of Erin*, and *Fortitude:* H. O'May, *Whalers out of Van Diemen's Land* (Hobart, n.d., Govt. Printer) 42, 60, 66.

110 Cheap equipment of bay whalemen: R. M. Martin, *History of Austral-Asia* (London, 1836) 291–2.

113 T. A. Coghlan, *Labour and Industry in Australia* (Oxford, 1918) *I*, 509.

114 Whaling ships entering Sydney in 1840s: *Statistics of New South Wales 1837–1853* (Sydney, 1854) 31.

114 Temperance in American whalers: Select Committee on Navigation Laws, *H.C.P.*, 1847–8, Reports from Committees, *XIV* (part 2), Q. 1442; E.P. Hohman, *The American Whaleman* (New York, 1928) 136 ff.

115 Comparison of whaling and wool exports: G. Blainey, 'Technology in Australian History', *B.A. & H.*, Aug. 1964, *IV*, 120–2.

117 Tasmanian shipbuilding: R. M. Hartwell, *The Economic Development of Van Diemen's Land 1820–1850* (Melbourne, 1954) 156–60.

117 'Sudden death': O'May, 49.

6. LAND BARRIER

118 T. M. Perry, 'The Spread of Rural Settlement in New South Wales, 1788–1826', *H.S.*, May 1955, *VI*, 395.

120 Pittwater grain: evidence to Bigge enquiry, *H.R.A.*, 3, *III*, 220, 222, 246, 311.

121 Cost of carrying wheat: *H.R.A.*, 1, *XIV*, 139; E. Dunsdorfs, *The Australian Wheat-Growing Industry 1788–1948* (Melbourne, 1956) 64n.

121 Austin's ferry: Anne McKay, ed., *Journals of the Land Commissioners for Van Diemen's Land 1826–28* (Hobart, 1962) 109, 115.

123 Fodder ration for horses v. bullocks: *New South Wales Government Gazette* 11 Nov. 1851, p. 1855.

125 It is difficult to average accurately, in most decades of the 19th

century, export prices for wool and wheat on the common basis of so much a ton; the quality and therefore the price of wool varied so much from bale to bale. Nevertheless, the price ratio of wool to wheat was usually even higher than the price ratio of gold to silver.

126 Riley's Saxon sheep: Jill Ker, 'The Wool Industry in New South Wales, 1803–1830', *B.A. & H., II, 30.* For other expensive sheep imports, see *H.R.A.*, 1, *XIV*, 759–60.

128 Road gangs: *H.R.A.*, 1, *XIV*, 70.

129 Charles Darwin, *The Voyage of the Beagle* (Everyman edn., London, 1961) 416–26.

130 James Graham: letter of 12 July 1839, Graham Papers, Melbourne University Archives.

130 Expenses of N.S.W. sheep runs, 1841: cited in S. H. Roberts, *The Squatting Age in Australia 1835–1847* (Melbourne, 1964 edn.) 311–12. The author may not agree with the inferences I've drawn from his figures.

136 Sheep runs and urbanization: G. Blainey, 'Technology in Australian History', *B.A. & H., IV, 128–9.*

138 Distances and mineral discovery: G. Blainey, 'Gold and Governors', *H.S., IX, 344–5.*

139 Fastest passages to California: C. Bateson, *Gold Fleet for California: Forty-Niners from Australia and New Zealand* (Sydney, 1963) 15, 109.

142 Goldfields transport: Report of the Commissioners on the Internal Communication of the Colony, *V.P.P.*, 1854–5, *I*, p.v. Report of the Select Committee on Railways, *V.P.P.*, 1854–5, *III*, No. D 7, 7–8.

143 'They are horses': Report of Board Enquiring into Post Office Department, *V.P.P.*, 1855–6, *I*, No. A12, Q.1067.

7. THE ART OF ABDUCTION

153 E.G. Wakefield, *A Letter from Sydney and Other Writings* (Everyman edn., London, 1929). The passages I successively quote are on pp. 52, 50, 47.

154 One exception to the common exalting of Wakefield's influence is June Philipp's 'Wakefieldian Influence and New South Wales 1830–1832', *H.S., IX, 173–80.*

159 'By incessant cooking': Select Committee on the Passengers' Act, *H.C.P.*, 1851, Reports from Committees, *XIII*, Q.4002.

161 'Comparatively free from the evils': *Ibid.*, p. iii.

162 J.B. Davies' memories: Diary Ms., Melbourne University Archives.

163 'One day we had a hurricane': R. H. Horne, 'A Digger's Diary', *Household Words* (London, 3 Sept. 1853) 6.

164 Comparative prices of land: J. R. McCulloch, A *Dictionary . . . of Commerce* (London, 1856) 353–4. By contrasting the prices of land in various countries with the shipping fares out from Europe (p. 344) one sees the vital correlation between dear land and dear fares.

167 Migration statistics: F. K. Crowley, 'The British Contribution to the Australian Population: 1860–1919', *University Studies in History and Economics* (Perth, July 1954) 55–88.

169 Russel Ward, *The Australian Legend* (Melbourne, 1958) esp. 88 ff.

8. GOLD CLIPPERS

176 Rice cargo: Select Committee on Navigation Laws, *H.C.P.*, 1847–8, Committees, *XIV* (Part 1), Q. 1373. The wreck of the whaler *Bourbon* is mentioned in Q.1063–5.

176 German Ships in S.A.: *Ibid*, *XIV* (part 2), Appendix K, 954–5.

180 Composite sailing: W. Allingham, 'Great Circle Sailing', *Nautical Magazine* (1892) 25–9.

182 McDonald Island: correspondence in *Nautical Magazine* (1855) 219–21, 674–5.

183 H. I. Chapelle, 'The First Clipper', *M.M.* (1948) 26–33.

186 R. E. Scoresby-Jackson, *The Life of William Scoresby* (London, 1861) 372–9.

188 The controversy on clipper speeds ran in *The Mariner's Mirror*. See in particular the fascinating comments and replies by J. S. Learmont and A. Villiers in 1957 and by H. Daniel, R. M. Bousefield, and H. I. Chapelle in 1958. The crucial factor perhaps lacking in the controversy is the exceptional economic incentive for fast passages in the 1850s.

188 *Shalimar* advertisement: cited in note by M. R. Bouquet, *M.M.* (1959) 159–60.

193 M. F. Maury, *The Physical Geography of the Sea* (London, 1856 edn.) introduction, viii.

193 Route of clippers: evidence of A. Enright, Papers Relative to the Lighthouses on the Australian Coast, *V.P.P.*, 1856–7, *IV*, no 31, 75–6.

196 Auckland Islands: J. B. Cooper, *Victorian Commerce 1834–1934* (Melbourne, 1934) 88–9.

197 Melbourne's lack of jetties: C. Pasley, Report upon the various Plans for the Improvement of the Port of Melbourne, *V.P.P.*, 1854–5, *III*, no. C.50, p. 3.

198 'This is a most unsafe port': J. Fawcett, 'Voyage of the *Harriet Humble* from Liverpool to Australia . . .' *Nautical Magazine* (1855) 78.

198 'Hobson's Bay': R. H. Horne, 'A Digger's Diary', *Household*

Words (London, 3 Sept. 1853) 7.

201 Lack of export cargoes: Melbourne *Argus*, 6 Oct. 1858 for *Kent*, and 7 Dec. 1858 for *Sardinian*.

202 Growth of tea trade: D. R. MacGregor, 'Some Early British Tea Clippers', *M.M.* (1948), esp. 67, 72, 195, 282–3; J. K. Fairbank, *Trade and Diplomacy on the China Coast* (Harvard, 1953) *I*, 289–91; Sel. Com. on Navigation Laws, *H.C.P.* 1847–8, *XIV*, part 2, 133–4. Hotham's complaint: cited by Myra Willard, *History of the White Australia Policy* (Melbourne, 1923) 19.

203 Kong Meng's opinion: Select Committe on Chinese Immigration, *V.P.P.*, 1856–7, *IV*, No D.19.

204 Checking abuses in Chinese emigrant ships: J. R. McCulloch, *A Dictionary . . . of Commerce* (London, 1856), 966–7.

9. BLACK CLOUD

206 Problems of early steamships: D. J. Struik, *Yankee Science in the Making* (New York, 1962 edn.) 166–70; G. S. Graham, 'The Transition from Paddle-Wheel to Screw Propeller', *M.M.* (1958) 35–48; and R. Young, *The Southern World* (London, 1854) which describes (pp. 3–49) a journey to Australia by steamships in 1852.

208 *Great Britain's* voyages: J. A. Gurner, *Life's Panorama . . .* (Melbourne, 1930) 77–9; H. I. Chapelle, note in *M.M.* (1933) 341–2; *Argus*, Melbourne, 25 Aug. 1864, 24 Nov. 1869.

209 *Iron Age* wrecked: *Nautical Magazine* (1855) 392.

210 *Royal Charter*: R. E. Scoresby-Jackson, *The Life of William Scoresby* (London, 1861) ch. 16, 17; *Argus* 18 Oct. 1858.

212 Iron clippers: shipping column of *Argus*, 1868–9, esp. 20 Sept. 1869 for *Melpomene*.

213 *Thermopylae*: *Argus*, 9, 11, 13 and 25 Jan. 1869, 24 Nov. 1869, 4 Mar. 1871. My calculations of the time for her maiden voyage to Australia differ from the 60 days, 0 hours given by Basil Lubbock in *Lloyd's Calendar, 1940*, 513.

215 China tea: B. Lubbock, *The China Clippers* (Glasgow, 1946 edn.) 178–80, 267.

215 Via Suez: 'The Overland Route', series of 6 articles in *Argus*, 12–18 Oct. 1858; J. R. McCulloch, *A Dictionary . . . of Commerce*, 14–20; W. S. Lindsay, *History of Merchant Shipping and Ancient Commerce* (London, 1876) *IV*, 384–402.

217 *Nautical Magazine* (1871) 355.

218 Wool via Suez: *Argus* 5 June 1882.

218 Increased traffic through Suez; W. Woodruff and L. McGregor, pamphlet, *The Suez Canal and the Australian Economy* (Melbourne, 1957) 8–9.

218 High charges of Suez Canal: Royal Commission on Ocean Shipping Service, *C.P.P.* 1906, *III*, Q. 300, 1826, 2041; A. G. Course, *The Deep Sea Tramp* (London, 1960) 37–41, 83.

219 Annexation of New Guinea: Thomas McIlwraith, premier of Queensland, listed on 26 February 1883 the reasons why his government wanted to annex New Guinea. The first reason he gave was the increasing steamer traffic through Torres Strait. Most historians, not knowing where that steamer traffic was going, and not realizing that Torres Strait at the time seemed likely to become Queensland's main trade route to Europe, minimized or discarded this motive for the annexation.

220 *Illustrated News:* cited in *Nautical Magazine* (1853) 504.

220 'A Trip across the United States': *The Australian Handbook . . . for 1881* (London, 1881) 517.

221 Competition between steam and sail: G.S. Graham, 'The Ascendancy of the Sailing Ship 1850–85', *E.H.R.*, 1956, *IX*, 74 ff. One of the most valuable articles written on 19th century shipping in recent years, it challenged the common idea that steam quickly defeated sail. In discussing the sea routes to Australia, however, it goes too far with the contentions that in the 1860s and 1870s the fast clippers were as fast as the mail steamers (p. 82) and that 'the Australian trade remained throughout the 1880s almost exclusively sail' (p. 84). An examination of shipping news in Australian newspapers suggests these contentions are too sweeping.

221 Mail times, 1879: *Ibid.*, 512–3.

223 'The exhortations by wire': W. B. Wildey, *Australasia and the Oceanic Region* (Melbourne, 1876) 350.

223 Cost of Cables: Report on the Post Office and Telegraph Department for the Year 1872, *V.P.P.*, 1873, *III*, no. 13; Wildey, 56–7; *Australian Handbook . . . for 1890*, 551–2; *The Official Year Book of New South Wales 1905–6*, 202.

223 'Direct Telegrams': *Argus*, 19 June 1873.

224 'We are now two months': cited in A. Barnard, *Visions and Profits* (Melbourne, 1961) 116.

10. A MAGICIAN'S ACT

228 'The two railways': A. Birch, 'The Sydney Railway Company, 1848–1855', Royal Australian Historical Society's *Journal and Proceedings*, 1957, *XLIII*, 78–9. The quotation from Major Mitchell is cited on p.56.

229 Traffic returns of the Melbourne & Hobson's Bay Railway Co., published monthly in the *Argus*, indicate that most profit came from passengers rather than freight, Cf. G. Serle, *The Golden Age* (Melbourne, 1963) 236.

230 Optimism of Geelong's promoters: evidence of J. Harrison and G. King, Select Committee on the Geelong and Melbourne Railway Company's Bill, *B.P.P.*, 1852–3, *II*.

230 Mount Alexander railway's troubles: evidence of T. Oldham, Select Committee on Railways, *V.P.P.*, 1854–5, *III*, No. D 7, Q.390.

231 South Australian railways: D. H. Pike, *Paradise of Dissent* (London, 1957) 345–7.

234 Clarke's engineering credo: Report of Andrew Clarke on Railways, *V.P.P.*, 1856–7, *IV*, No. 33.

234 Bridges and tunnels too narrow: W. C. Kernot, 'Railway Gauge', *Proceedings of Victorian Institute of Engineers*, 1906, *VII*, 77–80; see also Lord Monkswell, *Railways, Their History and Organisation* London, 1928), 18, for the dictum that the 'loading gauge' is more important than the gauge of the track.

237 Port Adelaide crash: J. W. Bull, *Early Experiences of Life in South Australia . . .'* (Adelaide, 1884) 325–6.

237 Sir Charles W. Dilke, *Greater Britain* (London, 1869 edn.) 309.

238 The Vagabond's complaint: (Julian Thomas), *The Vagabond Papers*, Third series (Melbourne, 1877) 45.

240 Impediments to navigation: Report on Public Works, 1859, *S.A.P.P.*, 1860, *II*; W. B. Wildey, *Australasia and the Oceanic Region* (Melbourne, 1876) 26–8, 327–9.

241 River traffic: N. G. Butlin, *Investment in Australian Economic Development 1861–1900* (Cambridge, 1964) 305–14, 401–3; T. A. Coghlan, *The Wealth and Progress of New South Wales 1886–87* (Sydney 1887) 294–5, 326–7; Interstate Royal Commission on the River Murray, *V.P.P.*, 1902–3, *III, passim.;* series of 9 articles in Melbourne Argus, 19 Jan. to 11 March, 1876.

11.   RAILWAY BOOM

243 Much of the statistical information in this chapter comes from annual publications: *Official Year Book of the Commonwealth of Australia*, the year books of the various colonies, and *The Australian Handbook* published annually by Gordon and Gotch from 1870.

244 Critics of break of gauge: 'Railways of Australia: break of gauge problem', *C.P.P.*, 1920–1, *V*, 3, 6.

244 'The most lamentable': W. C. Kernot, 'Railway Gauge', *Proceedings of Victorian Institute of Engineers*, 1906, *VII*, 83.

245 Origin of first break of gauge: Kernot, 73–4; E. Harding, *Uniform Railway Gauge* (Melbourne, 1958) ch. 1, 2.

247 'The passengers were astonished': cited by W. B. Wildey, 358.

249 Rail link at Albury: *Argus*, 14 and 15 June, 1883.

251 Goods traffic through Albury: Report of Victorian Railways

Commissioners, year ending 30 June 1887, *V.P.P.*, 1887, *III*, No. 87, Appendix 15.

253   'A Minister of Railways': cited in R. L. Wettenhall, *Railway Management and Politics in Victoria 1856–1906* (Canberra, 1961) 22.

254   Commissioners and their significance: Wettenhall, 24–5.

255   Speight's reign: *The Great Libel Case: Speight v. 'The Age'* (Melbourne, 1894) — a verbatim report of addresses by counsel in the second trial.

255   Comparative profits of Australian and U.K. Railways: T. A. Coghlan, *The Seven Colonies of Australasia, 1901–2* (Sydney, 1902) 858, 860.

259   Savings of railways over horse teams: T. A. Coghlan, *The Wealth and Progress of New South Wales, 1897–8* (Sydney, 1899) 520.

260   Transport costs for remote sheep stations: N. G. Butlin, *Australian Domestic Product, Investment and Foreign Borrowing 1861–1938/39* (Cambridge, 1962) 72.

260   Relative price of wool and wheat: computed from T.A. Coghlan, *The Wealth and Progress of New South Wales 1897–8, 341, 590.*

262   'With one clear exception': I. D. McNaughtan, 'Colonial Liberalism, 1851–92' in G. Greenwood ed., *Australia: a social and political history* (Sydney, 1955) 109.

263   Manipulating freight rates: H. R. Meyer, *Government Regulation of Railway Rates* (New York, 1905) ch. 8; Royal Commission on Management of Railway Department, *V.P.P.*, 1902–3, *III*, No. 5, Q.3429, 3436–44.

12.   A HOLLOW TRIUMPH

266   Advance of marine engine: E. C. Smith, *A Short History of Naval and Marine Engineering* (Cambridge, 1937) 179–81, 238–46, 272 ff.; W. S. Lindsay, *History of Merchant Shipping and Ancient Commerce* (London, 1876) *IV*, 434–5.

267   British mail steamers more frequent: Royal Commission on Ocean Shipping Service, *C.P.P.*, 1906, *III*, Q.1454.

268   North German Lloyd:*ibid.*, Q.4899 ff.

268   Coaling at Fremantle: *ibid.*, Q.7274.

269   Popularity of telegraph: *ibid.*, Q.2147–9, 5791–2.

270   Ice in *Alma:*Melbourne *Argus*, 15 Oct. 1858.

271   *Northam* fiasco: A. Barnard, *Visions and Profits* (Melbourne, 1961) 204–6.

271   McIlwraith and refrigeration: interview in The *Australasian Pastoralists' Review*, 15 Nov. 1894, 444.

272   *Strathleven* venture: *Argus*, 3, 4, 6, and 8 Dec. 1879.

Notes

275 *Dunedin:* Sir Arthur Bryant, 'One Hundred Years under the Southern Cross (Shaw Savill Line)', *Bulletin* of the Business Archives Council of Australia, May 1958, 5–6.

277 My calculation of the tonnage (in weight, not measurement) of cargoes in 1881 and 1906 is based on official export returns. I converted these figures from super feet, pounds, etc. to a common unit. Unfortunately, in the absence of similar information, it seems impossible to compute tonnage of imports for the same years.

277 Ships in ballast, 1906: *C.Y.B.*, no. 1, 535. Unfortunately this vital information is only available from 1904.

278 My estimate that tonnage of steam first equals sail in Australian overseas trade c. late 1890s was reached thus: In 1904, the earliest for which figures exist (*ibid.*, 535), sail tonnage was 2.2 m. or 33% of total. Even if the sail tonnage was only slightly higher in 1898 — and it probably was higher — it would have just exceeded half of the total overseas shipping in that year. For total overseas shipping, see *C.Y.B.*, no. 14, 536.

279 O'Sullivan's visiting card: Royal Commission on the Navigation Bill, *C.P.P.*, 1906, *III*, Q.21,290.

280 Captain's sea chest: information from Commander F. W. Heriot, who sailed past Cape Horn pre-1914.

280 Steamers capturing wheat: E. Dunsdorfs, *The Australian Wheat-Growing Industry 1788–1948*, 172n..

281 King Oscar's birthday: *The Southern Times* (Bunbury) 24 Jan. 1905.

282 Coal exports: K. H. Burley ingeniously pointed out the link between Australia's lack of export tonnage and the rise of her coal exports in 'The Overseas Trade in New South Wales Coal and the British Shipping Industry, 1860–1914', *Economic Record*, Aug. 1960, 405. He similarly explained (p. 410) the decline of coal exports in the 1920s by suggesting that the space in departing ships was at last filled by other, more valuable exports. The explanation of decline seems to be refuted by figures in *C.Y.B.*, no. 1, 535.

283 *Lloyd's Calendar* (London, 1940) 515.

285 Chain migration from Italy: C. A. Price, *Southern Europeans in Australia* (Melbourne, 1963) *passim*; advertisements in *Australian Handbook*, 1898, indicate that Brindisi, Naples and Genoa were all ports of call for Australian mail steamers.

286 Shipping charges 1920–60: K. Trace, 'Australian Overseas Shipping 1900–60', University of Melbourne thesis, 1965, ch. 2, 4.

Notes

13. THE HORSELESS AGE

290   H. M. Barker, *Camels and the Outback* (Melbourne, 1964) 200.

291   'I refer to the Horseless Road Carriage': A. C. Mountain in *Proceedings of Victorian Institute of Engineers, II*, 7–8.

292   Wolseley car: S. B. Saul, 'The Motor Industry in Britain to 1914', *Business History*, Dec. 1962, *V*, 27–8.

297   Harry Houdini: I. F. McLaren, 'Australian Aviation: a bibliographical survey; *Victorian Historical Magazine*, Aug. 1958, *XXVIII*, 108–9.

299   Smith's flight: D. G. Anderson, *Australia's Contribution to International Civil Aviation* (pamphlet, Adelaide, 1960).

304   Increased rail traffic through Albury: Report of Victorian Railways Commissioners, year ended June 1920, *V.P.P.*, 1920, *I*, 23; Report on Commonwealth Railways, 1919–20, *C.P.P.*, 1920–1, *V*, 18.

305   Statistics of road and rail freight: R. R. Hirst, 'The Transport Industry', A. Hunter ed., *The Economics of Australian Industry* (Melbourne, 1963) 72.

307   Revenue of Australian coastal ships: Royal Commission on the Navigation Bill (*C.P.P.*, 1906, *III*, Q.26,009) suggested a revenue of about £2.1m. a year. This sum was just under 1/5th of the average annual gross revenue earned by government railways in 1900–4 (*C.Y.B.*, no. 1, 573).

308   Shipping's share of Australian freight traffic was 5% of total tonnage or 49% of ton-miles in 1959–60: R. R. Hirst, 72.

311   Workforce in motor industry: G. Maxcy, 'The Motor Industry' in *The Economics of Australian Industry*, 511.

312   In all but one year between 1913 and 1934, transport workers and miners (mainly coal miners) lost more hours through industrial disputes than all other workers in Australia added together: *C.Y.B.*, no. 28, 380.

14. ANTIPODES ADRIFT

317   C. H. Pearson's forecast: *National Life and Character* (London, 1894 edn.) 94.

318   Trade with Asia: computed from *C.Y.B.*, no. 1, 500, 505.

319   D. H. Pike, *Australia: the quiet continent* (Cambridge, 1962). This book, incidentally, is perhaps more alert to possible effects of distance than any other Australian history book.

322   Defence spending: *C.Y.B.*, no. 14, 927.

326   Statute of Westminster; J. C. Beaglehole, 'The British Commonwealth of Nations', *The New Cambridge Modern History* (Cambridge, 1964) *XII*, 541–6.

328 A minority of Australians was not blind to Australia's changed position in the mid 1930s. One example was W. Macmahon Ball's *Possible Peace* (Melbourne, 1936) which pointed to the Japanese threat and Australia's unwise faith in Britain's navy.

329 Of the members of the Australian war cabinet which made the decision to appeal to the U.S.A., only two — Mr Norman Makin and Dr H. V. Evatt — had ever visited the U.S.A., so far as I can determine. For information on this point I am grateful to two members of that cabinet, Messrs N. Makin and E. J. Holloway, and to Mr P. R. Heydon, now the secretary of the Commonwealth Department of Immigration. In supplying this information Mr Makin wrote: 'There was not a single thought about a change in loyalties or relationships with Great Britain'. Mr Holloway wrote too in the same vein.

331 For Mr A. A. Calwell's changing views and his swing from a belief in a high birthrate to a belief in high immigration, see his *How many Australians Tomorrow?* (Melbourne, 1945), and his statements in Commonwealth Parliamentary Debates, Vol. 184, pp. 4911 ff. and Vol. 189, p. 502.

332 Australia's net gain from immigration (excess of arrivals over departures) in the two periods 1860–1947 and 1947–77 was computed from *C.Y.B.*, no. 14, p. 142 and no. 38, p. 572, and from official statistics.

Index

Aboriginals, 3, 7, 87, 131, 222, 319, 343
Adelaide, 98, 133, 198
Agriculture; hindered by transport costs, 119–125;
  effects of dear land, 164–5; effects of railways, 261;
  wheat, 260–1, 280, 284
Air transport, 298–302, 326, 329, 338–42
Albany (King George Sound), 91–3, 217, 256, 268
Albury, 240, 249–251, 304
Antarctica, 325
Auckland Islands, 196

Baines, James, 192
Bampton, William, 57–60
Banking, 165
Banks, Sir Joseph, 11, 74
Barker, Herbert, cited, 290
Barns, William, 85–6
Bass, George, 75
Bass Strait, 60, 66, 105–6, 132;
  discovery of, 74–5;
  strategic value, 75–8, 81–2, 92
Bathurst, Earl, 90, 92
Bathurst (N.S.W.), 128, 232
Bayley, Captain, 110
Bengal, 55, 62–3
Birch, T. W., 103–5
Bligh, William, 56–7, 60
'Boomerang Coast', 145–6, 335
Botany Bay, 10–11, 22, 23, 26–28, 30, 34, 47, 342
Boyd, Benjamin, 111, 116, 177
Boyd Town, 111

Brindisi, 216, 221
Brisbane, 72
Britain: expansion, 8–10, 23–8, 84–5;
  fear of France, 76–8, 89–90, 92;
  relations with Australia, 98, 133, 224, 314, 320–1, 326, 335–7
  railways, 245–6; decline as a world power, 327–9, 330, 336
  see also, Settlement of Australia
  shipping, 9; convict transports, 18, 51; slave trade, 21; cargoes (tea) 26, 63–4, 184, 202, 215, (flax) 30–1, 38, (timber) 32–3, (whale products) 100–2, (wool), 158; whalers, 100, 114; emigrant ships, 158–64; effect of Navigation Acts, 173;
  clippers, 191–3
Broken Hill, 257, 262, 289, 308
Broken Hill Proprietary Co., 308
Brouwer, Hendrick, 5
Bullock-teams, 123–4, 129–30, 141–2, 239, 288
Bunbury (W.A.), 281

Calcutta, 16–17, 50, 5, 62, 105, 126
Calwell, A. A. 331–2
Camel-teams, 288–90
Canada, 23, 164, 319, 325; see also, North America
Canary Islands, 34, 50
Canton, 51–2, 64, 84, 205
Cape of Good Hope, 40–2, 218

Cape Horn, 10, 27, 45, 195–7, 210–11, 218, 280, 283
Cape Otway, 194–5, 213–4
Cape Town, 8, 11, 16, 35, 45–6, 49, 126, 266;
  as supply base for N.S.W. 51, 53
Carteret, Philip, 54
Ceylon, 28, 318
Chile, market for coal, 282–4
China, tea trade, 26, 63–4, 175, 184, 202–3, 205, 318;
  imports, 67–68, 84, 334;
  emigration, 203–05, 333
Clarke, Andrew, 234
Coal, 281–4, 304, 307, 310; *see also,* Mining: Shipping: steamships, problem of coal
Cobb and Co., 143
Cocos Islands, 323–4
Coghlan, Timothy, 113, 259
Collins, David, 63, 78, 80–1
Colonies, nature of in eighteenth century, 15–17
Commercial relations, with Asia, 52–3, 314–18, 330, 333–6;
  with Britain, 98, 133, 224–6, 314, 321, 326–30, 336–7;
  with India, 62–3 with South America, 282–4
Convicts, escapes by sea, 68–9,
  and economic development, 128–9, 148–9;
  see also, Transportation
Cook, Captain James, 8–14, 28, 56
Coolgardie, 256, 289
Copper, *see* Mining.

Dallas, K. M. 23–7
Darling, Governor Ralph, 90, 128
Darling River, 132, 239–40
Darwin, 86, 222, 252, 335, 339
Darwin, Charles, 128–9
Das Voltas Bay, 22–3, 28, 35
Davies, John B., 161–2
Defence, 319–332
de la Perouse, Jean, 32
de Lesseps, Ferdinand, 217
de Torres, Luis Vaez, 8, 56
Diego Garcia, 28
Dilke, Sir Charles, 237
Distance, summary of effects, viii–x, 173, 334–7, 341–3; and

eighteenth century trade, 4; and early settlement of N.S.W., 19–20, 42–3, 48, 51–2; and Northern Australia, 88–9, 334–5; and whaling, 117; and wool, 125–7, 130–1, 144; and population distribution, 136–7, 145–6; and mining, 137–8, 141, 144; and immigration, 147, 150–1, 154–5; and land prices, 164–5; and balance of sexes, 168–71; and isolationism, 319–21 and World War I, 324–6; and relations with Asia, 334–5; decreasing influence of, 286–7, 297, 301, 338–43

Djakarta, 11, 47, 54
Donkey-teams, 288
D'Urville, J. D. 89, 93

East India Company, 51, 63, 94
East Indies, 16, 53
Echuca, 241
Eden (Boyd Town), 111
Encounter Bay, 112
England, *see* Britain
Esperance (W.A.), 112

Falkland Islands, 323
Fawcett, J. F., 198
Fiji, 68, 220
Flax, on Norfolk Island, 12, 31–2, 36–7;
  importance to England, 29–31
Flinders, Matthew, 60–2, 75
Forbes, James Nicol, 191–2, 194–5
Fort Dundas (Melville Island), 86
France, 28–9, 320; shipping (cargoes) 32, (in Australian waters) 76–8, 89–90, (steamships) 267
Fremantle, 95, 268

Geelong, 133, 136
Germany, 320–5, 332; shipping, 176, 267–8
Gold, *see* Mining
Gold Coast, 20
Gold Rushes: California, 139–40
  Australia, 140–1; effects of, 114,

144–5, 156, 177–8, 184–5, 197–205; transport costs, 141–3; and railways, 233
Goulburn (N.S.W.), 232, 233
Graham, James, 129–30
Great Barrier Reef, 55–6, 58, 60–1, 62
Great Circle route, 12, 178–83, 190, 193, 194, 195–6, 209, 215
Guillaux, Maurice, 297–8

Hargrave, Lawrence, 297
Hargraves, Edward, 140
Hawker, Harry, 298
Heard Island, 180–2
Hepburn, John, 131
Hobart, 78, 81, 121, 133, 137; as a port, 67, 69, 102–3, 113–4, 116–7, 198
Holland, 26, 84–6, 320; shipping in Australian waters, 6–8
Hong Kong, 203, 205, 334
Horses, 122–3, 143, 205, 288, 293–4
Houdini, Harry, 297
Hunter, Governor John, 44–6, 47, 52, 74–5

Immigration, assisted, 150–69, 319, 331; effects of distance on, 147, 150–1, 154; conditions in ships, 156–64, 204; finance, 151–6, 164–8; effect of gold rushes, 177–8; Asian, 203–5, 289, 315–16; European, 285, 319, 330–2; restriction, 317–9, 333; post-war, 331–2, 339–41; value of 332.
India, 16, 51, 53, 57–9, 318, 332; shipping, 62–3, 74, 323
Indonesia, trepang fleet, 4, 83–9, market for English goods, 84, 86–7
Inland waterways, lack of, 119–22; river boats, 239–42
Isolationism, 319–21, 327

Japan, 322, 327, 329, 330, 333–4, 342, 343
Java 5, 6, 53, 54–5, 62, 84

Kangaroo Island, 106, 112

Kelly, James, 104–5
Kendall, Larcum, 14
King, Governor Philip Gidley, 76–8, 80–2
King Island, 77, 81, 82, 106, 194
Kingsford Smith, Charles, 299

Labor Party, 168, 169–70, 327
Labour organization, 168, 170, 312
Land policy, 150, 153–6, 164–5
Launceston, 82, 133
Lean, Lieutenant, 158
Learmont, Captain J. S., 187, 188
Leisure, 170–1, 296
Liverpool (Eng) 178, 179, 185, 193
Lockyer, Major, 91
Longitude, problem of, 5–6, 13–4, 178
Lord Howe Island, 43, 46

McDonald Islands, 182
McEacharn, Malcolm, 271–4, 306
McIlwraith, Andrew, 271–4, 306
McIlwraith, Thomas, 271
McKay, Donald, 185–6, 192
Macquarie, Governor Lachlan, 82, 120
Macquarie Harbour, 105
Macquarie Island, 106
Marseilles, 216
Marshall, Frederick, 159
Mauritius, 27, 61, 90
Maury, Matthew, 41, 182–3, 190, 193
Meat, export of 269–75, 341
Melbourne, 78–80, 98, 132, 133–6, 262–3, 191–2, 340, 342; as a port, 197–9
Melville Island, *see* Fort Dundas
Menzies, R. G., 333, 338
Mercator, Gerardus, 178
Mining, and pastoral industry, 137–41; and distance, 137, 141–5, 334, 341; copper, 138, 176–7, 200, 225; gold, 139–45, 200; silver lead, 138; coal, 205; effect of telegraph, 222–5; effect of railways, 260–4
Moluccas, 84
Mort, Thomas, 271

Motor Transport, 291–3, 305; effects of, 293–6, 310–12

Mount Isa, 261–2, 301, 335

Mount Lyell, 261

Murray River, 105, 239–41

Nauru, 322, 325

Navigation Acts, 30, 63, 66, 175–7, 183, 202

Netherlands, *see* Holland

New Caledonia, 12, 267

Newcastle (N.S.W.) 72, 279, 281–3

New Guinea, 54, 219, 268, 310, 320, 322, 325, 329, 336

New South Wales, problem of supplies, 43–53, 55, 58–60, 62, 65–6;
spread of settlement, 71–98, 118–20, 128–33;
railways, 227–9, 234–5, 243, 256–7;
see also Botany Bay; Norfolk Island; Settlement of Australia

New Zealand, 10, 12, 32, 34, 37, 98, 220, 324

Nicolle, Eugene, 271

Norfolk Island, 46–7, 64–5, 75; discovered by Cook, 12; flax on, 12, 32, 34–7; naval timber on, 12, 32–3, 37–8; a key to settlement of Australia, 32–4; as a gaol, 72–3, 150

North America, nature of colonies, 16; transportation to, 20; effects of War of Independence, 17, 20, 33
see also, Canada; United States

Northern Australia, visited by Indonesians, 83–8, strategic value, 82, 85; establishment of trading posts, 84–8; today, 335

Norway, shipping, 281

Oil, 309–13

Overseas Investment, 225–6, 264, 311–12, 332, 342

Panama route, 185, 219–20, 221, 283–4, 286

Parsons, C. A., 266

Passenger Acts, 158–61, 195

Pastoral Industry, *see* Meat; Tallow; Wool

Pearl Harbour, 326–7

Pearson, C. H., 317

Penang, 26, 323

Perry, T., cited, 118

Perth, (Swan River), 93–5, 176, 338

Phillip, Governor Arthur, 19, 35, 36, 43, 44, 45, 48

Population; balance of sexes, 168–71
distribution, and whaling, 116–7; and wool, 136, 144–5; and gold rushes, 145; 'Boomerang Coast' 145–6, 335; and railways, 232–3, 246; and motor transport, 294–6; and relations with Asia, 335

Port Davey, 105

Port Fairy, 112

Port Jackson, *see* Sydney

Portland, 112

Port Macquarie, 72

Port Phillip Bay, 78–81, 89, 194

Portugal, 4–5, 320

Preservation Island, 74

Queensland, 132, 166, 219, 243, 316

Queensland and Northern Territory Aerial Services, 300

Raffles Bay (Fort Wellington), 87–9, 93

Railways: role of governments, 228–9, 230–31, 253–6, 258, 264, 305;
investment in, 227–8, 230–2, 264;
problem of gauges, 234–5, 244–52, 262–3, 303–5;
criticism of, 236–8; effects, 241–2, 258–64, 293, 307;
revenue, 250–1, 255–6, 262;
boom of the 1880s, 252–5; commissioners, 253–5; in 1920s, 258;
and motor transport, 305–6

Private railways, 227–31, 256–8; reasons for failure, 231–3;
Sydney Railway Co., 227–9; Hobson's Bay Railway Co., 229;
Geelong and Melbourne Railways Co., 230; Silverton Tramway Co., 257;
Railway-lines, Albury, 249–50; Ballarat, 233, 234; Bathurst, 228, 235; Bendigo, 233, 234, 238; Bourke, 252; Cairns, 302; Chillagoe, 258; Deniliquin, 257; Echuca, 233, 241; Emu Bay 257–8; Geelong, 230, 232; Goulburn (N.S.W.), 228, 233, 235; Great Southern (W.A.), 256; Kalgoorlie, 302; Maitland, 227, 232; Melbourne–Sydney, 248–51; Midlands (W.A.), 256, Mount Alexander, 230–1, 233; Newcastle, 251; Normanton, 252; Parramatta, 227–9, 232, 245, 250; Port Melbourne, 229; Silverton, 257, 258; Tarrawingee, 257; Toowoomba, 233; Warwick, 247; William Creek, 252; Wodonga, 249
Reid, J. S., 257–8
Rio de Janeiro, 34, 50–1
River Transport, *see* Inland waterways
Roads, 120–1, 128–31
Roaring Forties, 5–6, 40–2, 46, 186–7, 284
Robe (S.A.), 203–4
Russia, 31, 67, 322

St. Helena, 11, 16–17, 22
Sandalwood, 59, 67–8
San Francisco, 139, 185, 201, 220–1
Scoresby, Dr William, 186–7, 209–10
Scurvy, 12, 14, 43, 45, 87–8
Sealing, 66, 71, 74, 80, 105–7
Sea Slug, *see* Trepang

Settlement of Australia: discovery, 3–7, 11; proximity to trade routes, 5–8, 23–7, 53, 62–8, 70, 73, 75, 90–1, 96–8, 314–15; value as a colony in 1770, 15–7; reasons for settlement, 18–34, 38–9, 73, 95, 315; *see also*, Botany Bay; New South Wales; Norfolk Island
Shark Bay, 90–91, 93
Shields, Wentworth, 245
Shipping; coastal, 207, 221, 232, 246, 251, 273–4, 304, 305, 306–8; shipbuilding, 117, 177, 207, 311; decline of passenger ships, 340–1;
effects of World War I, 324; *see also* Navigation Acts; Passenger Acts
hazards, ice, 10, 42, 45; islands, 180–2, 196–7; *see also* Longitude; problem of; Roaring Forties; Scurvy; Winds
imbalance of cargoes, 52, 101, 176–7, 199–205, 276–7, 282
routes, 5, 10, 23–6; Cape of Good Hope, 40–2, 218; to Asia; 53–6, 90; through Torres Strait; 55–62; to China, 63–8, 90; through Bass Strait, 75–7; *see also* Great Circle Route; Panama route; Suez Canal route
sailing ships, rise of clippers, 183–93; challenge of steam, 206, 213–15, 219; decline of, 278–80; cargoes, 281–6
speed records, 184–91, 195–6, 208, 210, 213–14, 266
steam ships, rise of, 44, 183–5, 206–21, 227, 265–7;
problem of coal, 185, 206–7, 269; mail steamers, 267–9; refrigerated ships; 269–75; effects of, 285–7;
Shipping Lines, Aberdeen, 266; Adelaide Steamship Co., 306; Australasian Union Steamship Co., 306; Black Ball, 191,

192-3, 195; Blackwall, 193; Blue Funnel, 265, Money Wigram and Sons, 193, 201; Norddeutscher Lloyd, 268; Pacific Steam Navigation Co., 265; Peninsular and Oriental Steam Navigation Co., 215, 216, 265, Samuel Enderby and Sons, 100; Union Steamship Company of New Zealand, 306; White Star, 192

Ships, *Aberdeen*, 265-6; *Alma*, 270; *Ann*, 101; *Argo*, 69; *Batavia*, 6, 48; *Beagle*, 129; *Bounty*, 57; *Bourbon*,177; *Bridgewater*, 61; *Britannia*, 52, 101; *Cato*, 61; *Cerebus*, 217-18; *Champion of the Seas*, 186, 188, 192, 193; *Chesterfield*, 58; *Clan Ranald*, 219; *Cumberland*, 61; *Cutty Sark*, 213, 215; *Cyclops*, 62; *Daedalus*, 37; *Dolphin*, 10; *Druid*, 192; *Dubuc*, 104; *Dunedin*, 275; *Earl of Eglington*, 182; *Emden*, 323-4; *Emilia*, 100; *Endeavour* 9, 13, 32, 56; *Endeavour* (India), 59; *Fancy*, 59; *Fortitude*, 109-110; *Frederick*, 69; *General Grant*, 196; *Geographe*, 77; *Golden Grove*, 36; *Great Britain*, 208-9; *Guardian*, 49; *Guiding Star*, 42; *Harriet Humble*, 198; *Henrietta Packet*, 105; *Hope*, 65; *Investigator*, 60; *Iron Age*, 209; *James Baines*, 186, 188, 192; *Kent*, 201; *Lady Emma*, 117; *Lady Juliana*, 36, 48-9; *L'Atheniene*, 65; *Lightning*, 186, 192, 194, 196; *Lock Torridon*, 283; *Lord Raglan*, 192; *Maid of Erin*, 109; *Marco Polo*, 191-2; *Mauretania*, 266; *Melpomene*, 212; *Naturaliste*, 77; *Nautilus*, 22; *Neva*, 67; *Norfolk*, 193; *Northam*, 271; *Offley*, 109; *Oriental*, 182; *Otago*, 41; *Pandora*, 57; *Paraguay*, 271; *Philadelphia*, 65; *Porpoise*, 61; *Prince of Wales*, 326; *Prinz Regent*, 268; *Red Jacket*, 186; *Repulse*, 326;' *Royal Charter*, 210;

Samarang, 182; *Sardinian*, 201; *Schomberg*, 194; *Scotia*, 207; *Semiramis*, 66; *Shah Hormuzear*, 58-9, *Shalimar*, 187-8, 192; *Sirius*, 35, 44-5, 46; *Sirius* (Paddle Steamer), 207; *Sophia*, 104, 105; *Sovereign of the Seas*, 188, 193; *Stedcomb*, 86, 87; *Strathleven*, 272-4; *Success*, 87, 93; *Sultana*, 161; *Supply*, 35, 38, 43, 47, 54; *Sydney*, 324; *Sydney Cove*, 74; *Thermopylae*, 213-15, 266; *Ticonderoga*, 160; *Turbinia*, 266; *Unity*, 69; *Waaksamheyd*, 54; *Wendur*, 283; *White Star*, 192; *Will and Ann*, 101; *Young Lachlan*, 69

Singapore, 84-5, 333

Smith, Keith and Ross, 299

South America, relations with Australia, 283-4

South Australia, settlement, 97-8, 112, 132, 155; railways, 231, 243

Spain, 8, 26, 320

Speight, Richard, 254-5

Steam ships, rise of, 44, 183-5, 206-21, 227, 265-7

Stirling, Captain James, 87, 93-4

Suez Canal route, 215-19, 267, 285, 286, 339

Sydney (Port Jackson), 35, 133, 137; as a port, 67-9, 100, 101, 103, 116-7, 198; supply base for Californian gold rushes, 139; airport, 340, 342

Sydney, Lord, 29, 31

Syme, David, 255

Tahiti, 9-10, 57, 96-7

Tallow, 200, 270

Tasmania, 132, 150, 335, 339; settlement of, 77-8, 80-2; water transport, 120-1

Telegraph, 215-6, 222-6, 240, 269, 302, 323

Telephone, 339-40

Television, 336, 339-40

Timber, 29-33, 37-8, 105, 280-2

Timor, 5, 333

Torres Strait, 11, 53-62, 76, 82-3, 87

Towson, John, 178–80, 182
Transportation, first fleet, 18–19, 34, 163; aim of, 20; search for suitable colony, 19–27; second fleet, 48–9; penitentiary settlements, 71–3; and economic development, 148–9; cessation, 150; *see* also Convicts
Treaty of London (1824), 86
Trepang, 4, 71, 83–9
Tsingtao, 322, 323

United States; inland waterways, 119; frontier settlement, 131–2; gold rushes, 139–40; land prices, 164; immigration, 147, 150, 157, 159, 202–3, 331; labour organization, 167–8; railways, 219–220, 251, 260, 305; rise as a world power, 327; relations with Australia, 329–30, 334; *see* also North America
shipping, 26; cargoes, (general) 65–6, (ice) 270, (tea) 184, 202; whalers, 103, 114–5; effect of Navigation Acts, 176, 183, 202; clippers, 183–91

Vancouver, George, 26, 37, 38
Vancouver Island, 26
Venus, transit of, 9
Victoria, settlement, 78–80, 92, 97–8, 112, 132; railways, 229–31, 234–5, 243, 263

Villiers, Alan, 188
Von Spee, Admiral, 322–3

Waghorn, Thomas, 215
Wakefield, E. G. 152–5, 168, 330
Wales, William, 12
Wallis, Captain Samuel, 10, 96
Ward, Russel, cited, 169
Watson, J. C., 284
West Africa, 21
Western Australia, settlement, 90–95, 112; railways, 256
Western Port, 92, 97
West Indies, 16, 20–21, 23, 57
Whaling, 26, 99–102, 102–115, 148–9; value of exports, 112–15; effects, 103, 115–17; decline, 114–5
Wheat, *see* Agriculture
Winds, 179, 189, 216–17; westerlies, 10, 40, 45, 284–5; monsoons 53, 203
see also Roaring Forties
Wireless, 300, 339
Wolseley, F. Y., 292
Wool, 115; early development, 124–133; effects (on commercial relations) 133, (on population distribution) 133–7, 144, (on mining) 137–40, (on immigration policy) 154; importance of convict labour, 149; and dear land, 165; and railways, 260; as cargo, 200–1
World War I, 298, 322–6
World War II, 301, 325, 326–7, 329–31